The Great Wells of Democracy

Also by Manning Marable

African and Caribbean Politics
Beyond Black and White
Black American Politics
Black Leadership
Black Liberation in Conservative America
Blackwater
The Crisis of Color and Democracy
editor, *Dispatches from the Ebony Tower*
coeditor with Leith Mullings, *Freedom*
How Capitalism Underdeveloped Black America
coeditor with Leith Mullings, *Let Nobody Turn Us Around*
Race, Reform and Rebellion
Speaking Truth to Power
W.E.B. DuBois—Black Radical Democrat

The Great Wells
of DEMOCRACY

The Meaning of Race in American Life

Manning Marable

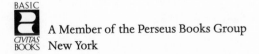
A Member of the Perseus Books Group
New York

Hardback edition first published in 2002 BasicCivitas Books, A Member of the Perseus Books Group

Paperback edition first published in 2003 by BasicCivitas

Books published by BasicCivitas are available at special discounts for bulk purchases in the United States by corporations, institutions, and other organizations. For more information, please contact the Special Markets Department at the Perseus Books Group, 11 Cambridge Center, Cambridge MA 02142, or call (617) 252-5298, (800) 255-1514 or e-mail j.mccrary@perseusbooks.com.

Design by Jane Raese

A CIP record for this book is available from the Library of Congress.
ISBN 0-465-04393-3 (hc); ISBN 0-465-04394-1 (pbk)

03 04 05 / 10 9 8 7 6 5 4 3 2 1

Contents

Preface

The goal of America is freedom. Abused and scorned though we may be, our destiny is tied up with America's destiny. . . . We will win our freedom because the sacred heritage of our nation and the eternal will of God are embodied in our echoing demands.

—Martin Luther King, Jr.
"Letter from Birmingham Jail," April 16, 1963

In the early evening of April 4, 1968, in Dayton, Ohio, I was in my father's Ford station wagon driving from my girlfriend's house, heading home. The car radio was on, and I was soulfully singing along with Otis Redding's "Dock of the Bay." I pulled into the closest gas station to my house to fill up the tank. The radio, which was still turned on, stopped playing rhythm and blues and announced an unconfirmed report that Dr. Martin Luther King, Jr., had been shot, less than an hour before, in

Memphis, Tennessee. By the time I had driven home, the radio news-caster had announced that Dr. King was dead. Stunned beyond compre-hension, I ran into the house and turned on the television to learn more about what had happened.

I stayed up during most of that terrible night, knowing that the dream of nonviolent democratic change in America had been irrevocably lost. What I would later call the Black Freedom Movement could not replace its most articulate spokesman. And for teenagers and college students like myself who opposed the war in Vietnam and favored the with-drawal of U.S. military forces, King had become a central figure in the struggle for world peace. I was at the time only seventeen years old, a high-school senior only seven weeks shy of graduation. During my last year in high school, I'd begun writing a newspaper column for the local, black-owned weekly newspaper called the *Dayton Express*. The editor permitted me to name my political commentary series with any title I felt was appropriate, and I decided to name the column "Youth Speaks Out." In the days immediately following King's assassination, I scoured the newspapers for information about what was happening.

Some rioting and the looting of several stores had already occurred in Dayton's Westside district, a predominantly African-American neighbor-hood. News reports on our local television stations said that similar ur-ban rebellions generated by the mass anger over King's assassination were erupting throughout the nation. I had no idea at the time how widespread the violence had become. Within seventy-two hours after King's murder, 110 cities experienced racial rebellions, with hundreds of millions of dollars' worth in property damage. Thirty-nine people had been killed, most of them African Americans. More than 75,000 National Guardsmen and federal troops were deployed to the country's largest ghettoes. Despite the violence, there were also impressive displays of in-terracial hope and solidarity. President Lyndon Johnson had declared Sunday, April 7, a national day of mourning, and all American flags were ordered to fly at half mast in honor of King's life and legacy.

My mother was a schoolteacher in the Dayton public school system and, ever since I was a child, had given me history books to read. At an early age she instilled in me a hunger for knowledge about history, especially that of Negro Americans. I had read W.E.B. Du Bois's *Souls of Black Folk* and Booker T. Washington's *Up from Slavery* when I was in junior high. Paul Laurence Dunbar's home in Dayton, Ohio, was only several blocks away from the first house we lived in when our family had moved to Dayton, and I had memorized by heart many of his verses. Black history was not something to be "studied" or "celebrated" during one month; it was something to be lived. The special knowledge from the histories and experiences of the African-American people gave me a sense of purpose and meaning, a context in which to understand the whirlwind of events then taking place in our country. I saw myself as an American, but blessed with a unique history of struggle and a sense of obligation to my race.

We attended St. Margaret's Episcopal Church, which had a predominantly black congregation. After mass the Sunday after the King assassination, my mother suggested that I travel to Atlanta to cover the funeral services for our local black newspaper. Homework and the household janitorial job I worked after school could wait for a few days. Black history was unfolding in Atlanta, and June Marable wanted her seventeen-year-old son to be a witness to it. My father consented with the decision and purchased a one-way airplane ticket to Atlanta, with the understanding that I should take the Greyhound bus back home from the South later that week. I'd never flown on a plane in my life, and when I arrived at Dayton's modest airport I was thrilled with the spirit of adventure and expectation. The flight arrived on Monday afternoon at Atlanta's Hartsfield airport, and Aunt Alice, my father's younger sister, who lived outside the city, and her daughter JoAnne picked me up. I was given a small transit map of the city, indicating what public bus routes I would need to take in order to locate Ebenezer Church.

I don't recall sleeping that next night, and well before 5 A.M. I stood alone on a rural country road, waiting for the early morning bus that took workers into the city. After reaching downtown, I followed the map carefully. The sun was just coming up, and the air was still crisp and cool as I first saw Ebenezer. I walked up to the front entrance; the door was locked, and I sat down to rest. I was the first person there to witness history that day.

By 7 A.M., about fifty people had arrived at the historic church. The Reverend Ralph David Abernathy arrived, and standing on the hood of an automobile, explained that the sanctuary could hold not more than 800 people, and that all of us would have to listen to the services outside. In the next two hours, thousands of people gathered, crushing me against the front door. Some of the dignitaries who arrived, such as Vice President Hubert Humphrey, entered the church from a side entrance. Most of the prominent civil-rights leaders in attendance who were King's closest comrades I would not have recognized, but other celebrities were easy to identify: Harry Belafonte, Lena Horne, Mahalia Jackson, comedian and activist Dick Gregory. For several minutes Republican presidential candidate Richard Nixon stood impatiently behind me, trying his best to push through the crowd. I could hear bitter complaints and expressions of disgust from those in the crowd that the "politicians" who had done nothing to advance the struggle that King had lived and died for were now exploiting his assassination and funeral for their own partisan advantage.

By the time the funeral service had concluded, it was already hot and muggy. An estimated 60,000 to 100,000 mourners surrounded the church. King's body was carried to a specially prepared hearse, a simple farm wagon hitched up to several mules, which symbolized the Southern Christian Leadership Conference's national "Poor People's Campaign" that had just been launched. Tens of thousands of us began the long march: past black folks' homes, where children and elderly African Americans stood weeping; past the shiny, domed Georgia capitol building, where the state's segregationist governor, Lester Maddox, had just protested the lowering of the flag in honor of King. In several hours, we arrived at the campuses of the Atlanta University complex, where we gathered in front of Morehouse College's Harkness Hall. President Benjamin Mays, one of King's intellectual mentors, read the eulogy, an unforgettable experience for those who heard his voice that day:

We have assembled here from every section of this great nation and from other parts of the world to give thanks to God that He

gave to America, at this moment in history, Martin Luther King, Jr.
. . . Truly God is no respecter of persons. How strange! God called
the grandson of a slave on his father's side, and said to him: "Martin Luther, speak to America about war and peace; about social
justice and racial discrimination; about its obligation to the poor;
and about nonviolence as a way of perfecting social change in a
world of brutality and war."

I wondered if Martin's death had been in vain. Would white Americans ever reach the level of human understanding where we could one
day "live in a nation" where Negroes "will not be judged by the color of
their skin but by the content of their character," as King had boldly asserted in his famous address at the 1963 March on Washington, D.C.?
How could we be satisfied "as long as the Negro is the victim of the un-
speakable horrors of police brutality?" King had asked. How could we
be satisfied "as long as the Negro's basic mobility is from a smaller
ghetto to a larger one?" How can we be satisfied "as long as a Negro in
Mississippi cannot vote and a Negro in New York believes he has nothing
for which to vote?" King told white America that compromise was impossible: "No, no, we are not satisfied, and we will not be satisfied until
justice rolls down like waters and righteousness like a mighty stream."
  King believed that this nation's flawed and often hypocritical democratic project could be reconstructed to be truly inclusive, reflecting the
rich diversity of humanity that makes up this nation. That hope resides
in our history, a shared experience of suffering and struggle, and forms
the foundations of the American story, our collective past. There would
never be racial peace without racial justice, and there could be no justice
without a common recognition of the deep, structural inequalities that
circumscribed the freedoms and opportunities for millions of American
citizens. Could we dare to envision another kind of democracy, based on
a new social contract between the people and the state, anchored in the
principles of human fairness and real equality under the law? Could a
democratic society be constructed with a public commitment to abolish
poverty and homelessness? The struggle to realize such hopes, these

"dreams deferred" in the words of our greatest poet, Langston Hughes, have represented the basis of our political challenge to America's white majority for nearly 400 years.

This book is my attempt to provoke a new conversation about the meaning of race in American life and history, largely from the unique vantage point of the African-American people. Although the book is grounded in academic research, I have attempted to write in an accessible style, appropriate for general readers. The primary audience for whom the book is designed are people who are largely unfamiliar with African-American history and the protracted struggles that generations of black folk have fought to be free. The vast majority of white Americans have, at best, a fragmentary understanding of the rich discourses about freedom and democracy crafted by African Americans over several centuries. To find a common future together, as a nation and as people, we must reconstruct our common past.

The Great Wells of Democracy is organized around three central themes or critical observations. First, that there have been essentially two major national narratives about the meaning and evolution of race and racism that have been constructed over time in the United States. One narrative, the story that is still largely taught in our schools and promulgated within the national media, within our major cultural institutions, and by our political and corporate elites, is that America has always been the world's finest example of "democracy"; that our Founding Fathers crafted a Constitution that preserved and guaranteed basic freedoms to all. This is the dominant national narrative, the story Americans like to celebrate and tell about themselves. The second, subaltern narrative, however, a strikingly different version of these same events, informs the view of the most marginalized and disadvantaged.

These two strikingly different stories about democracy, two warring ideals within the same national body, are recreated in the periodic conflicts that have erupted throughout our history. Can a reconciliation be forged that bridges the racial chasm of our history to create a new national consciousness, a new dedication to a democracy that has never truly existed, but one that could conceivably be made whole? Can the "goal" of the processes of American history be "freedom" for all? Is "our destiny tied up with America's destiny," or do we continue to exist in parallel racial universes, where we speak the same language, are theoretically governed by the same set of laws, but perceive reality in fundamentally different ways? The chapter on "structural racism" presents an alternative view of America's racial history that in my judgment more accurately describes our collective experiences than the standard version of history everybody knows. The American state was constructed first and foremost on a racial foundation; its major laws and its constitutional framework were originally designed to preserve the institution of slavery and to give permanent structural advantages to propertied classes through elitist devices, such as the Electoral College and the winner-take-all political system, that significantly restrict minority access to public decision making. In rewriting our common history to illustrate how race was deliberately used to restrict democratic processes over several centuries, we may begin to move toward a new understanding about how racial politics works to reinforce class hierarchies and inequality today.

The book's second section describes the dimensions of structural racism, especially in the post–civil rights era, the period of American history covering roughly the past twenty-five years. It examines the failures of our electoral political system, the criminal-justice system, our educational institutions, and our national leaders in advancing a meaningful dialogue about the continuing burden of racism in American life. This also includes a critique of the effects of class stratification within the African-American population, which has fostered the widespread illusion that equality has been achieved simply because Michael Jordan, Oprah Winfrey, and Michael Jackson are multimillionaires, or because Condoleezza Rice's desk is located next to the president's Oval Office.

I do not believe that the black American middle class, as a class, has the capacity or political agency by itself to transform the deep structures of racialized power in the United States. What we have historically identified as "whiteness" is being radically reconfigured to include broad sectors of the Asian-American, Latino, and even black American professional and managerial elites. "Affirmative-action" policies were successful in fostering greater racial and gender diversity with the existing social-class hierarchy, but they did little to transfer wealth to working-class and poor minorities and failed to create greater democratic access to the real centers of power for the broad majority of Americans, regardless of race. Consequently, it seems to me, the problem of racial inequality cannot be solved by pursuing the simplistic, liberal integrationist approach of "symbolic representation"—getting racial minorities, women, and other underrepresented groups into limited positions of authority within the government. Fundamental change within our system will largely have to occur not from the top down, but from the bottom up.

What are the new sources for democratic renewal and resistance? My third point is to illustrate the tremendous capacities for social change that are reflected in the activities of ordinary black Americans—including the hip-hop generation, prisoners and those impacted by the destructive effects of mass incarceration, activists in community-based organizations in disadvantaged neighborhoods, and people involved in faith-based institutions that are actively engaged in social-justice projects. I try to give examples of hopeful models of practical social change that may give shape to a new kind of freedom struggle that goes beyond the desegregation of lunch counters. Part of the rationale for a new conversation about race must inevitably include the issue of black reparations, compensation for centuries of structural racism—not just for enslavement and the transatlantic slave trade, but also for a century of Jim Crow legal segregation, urban ghettoization, and mass incarceration. Any nation that incarcerates 2 million of its own citizens behind bars, and disfranchises over 4 million for life cannot expect to have social peace unless fundamental changes occur. The contemporary issue of terrorism must also be viewed, in part, through the lens of race, if we are to negotiate new terms for what our democracy should become.

The great challenge of any democracy is to ensure that all of its citizens are "stakeholders" in a common project called civil society. Millions of racialized "Others" are today experiencing "civil death"—the destruction of their social, legal, and economic capacities to play a meaningful role in public life. We must find creative paths to reinvest in citizenship, to build civic capacities within the most disadvantaged sectors of our society. Combating civil death is the key toward revitalizing democracy for all of us.

Black political history has largely been constructed around two major paradigms of public activism—"state-based" and "race-based" reform movements. Liberal integrationists, on one hand, endeavored to increase opportunities for the upward mobility of black people by changing U.S. laws and pushing for reforms within the state and civil society. Reforms such as affirmative action were the result and greatly expanded the black middle class. "Race-based" politics, or the politics of black nationalism, emphasized the construction of strong black institutions, families, and communities and gave millions of African Americans a sense of cultural integrity and pride. Both strategies, however, represented in some respects by the tension between Martin Luther King, Jr., and Malcolm X a generation ago, were limited. "Integration" into a system of inequality did not make the system fundamentally more egalitarian or create a more vibrant civil society; racial separatism kept African Americans from the larger recognition that our dilemma could not be solved in isolation from the oppression and exploitation of others within our society. The first social theorist who really understood this was W.E.B. Du Bois. Through his work spanning nearly a century, Du Bois attempted to imagine a different kind of multiracial democracy, a society of access and opportunity where our unique voices and cultural gifts would not be lost in the process of desegregation.

In the post–civil rights era, the strategies of "state-based" integration and "race-based" separatism have reached a dead end; a creative synthesis must be constructed, informed by the ongoing protests and leadership of the truly disadvantaged. As suggested by Antonio Gramsci, the citadels of inequality in advanced capitalist societies will not be transformed through a confrontational "war of maneuver"; what is now required is a "war of position," a national debate about what constitutes a truly civil society and what policy measures we could implement to guarantee full access and democratic rights to citizens who have been marginalized and disadvantaged. The new civil-rights movement must reframe its strategy around combating civil death, pushing for meaningful, winnable reforms that increase the civic capacities of oppressed people, permitting them to assume greater roles in determining society's future. Successfully redefining the racial debate by bringing millions of disfranchised and marginalized citizens back into the public arena is the necessary first step toward a larger public debate about class inequality.

Many colleagues and friends have contributed to the development of this book. For nearly a year, I participated in a research project examining structural racism funded by the Aspen Institute and led by Keith Lawrence and Anne C. Kubisch. Staff members and researchers who contributed to the project included Andrea Anderson, Karen Fulbright-Anderson, Khatib Waheed, Stacey A. Sutton, and Ronald Hayduk. Many of the original concepts developed in the first section of this book were a product of collective conversations, largely organized around Keith's creative paradigms about the institutional dynamics of modern American racism. I owe a major debt of gratitude to the Aspen Institute for making it possible for me to rethink old assumptions and to critically re-examine the American experience from a different point of view. Several chapters here appeared in earlier versions in the academic publication I edit, *Souls: A Critical Journal of Black Politics, Culture and Society*, produced by the Institute for Research in African-American Studies at Columbia University and published by Taylor and Frances. The Reverend George Webber of the New York Theological Seminary provided the opportunity for me to regularly visit Sing Sing Prison and to gain a new perspective on the cruel nature of oppression and the limitations of our justice system.

Elizabeth Maguire, my editor, has been extraordinary as a friend and consultant during the two years that this manuscript evolved into a book. I appreciate the efforts of the staff of the Institute for Research in African-American Studies—Jennifer Jones, Sharon Harris, and Kecia Hayes—who carried too much of the burden in running our office to permit me to have the time to complete this manuscript. Graduate student Amy Kedron was invaluable as my chief research assistant and fact-checker as the final versions of the chapters were being prepared. Ms. Kedron's near-encyclopedic knowledge of hip-hop culture was invaluable as I learned to appreciate and better understand the art and imagination of young black people today. My greatest debt, however, is to my intellectual collaborator and soulmate, Leith Patricia Mullings, who patiently read different versions of the manuscript, gave me many great insights, and tried, sometimes without success, to steer me away from faulty concepts. Leith continues to set a standard of brilliant scholarship and political commitment that I endeavor to reach in my own work. She will always be, and remains, my "bright and morning star."

Manning Marable
August 26, 2002

Author's Note

Earlier versions of several chapters in this book were previously published in my quarterly publication *Souls: A Critical Journal of Black Politics, Culture, and Society:* "Race-ing Justice: The Political Cultures of Incarceration," vol. 2, no. 1 (Winter 2000), pp. 6–11; "Structural Racism and American Democracy: Historical and Theoretical Perspectives," vol. 3, no. 1 (Winter 2001), pp. 6–24; "Race, Class, and Academic Capitalism: The Future of Liberal Education," vol. 3, no. 2 (Spring 2001), pp. 6–14; "Transforming Ethnic Studies: Theorizing Multiculturalism, Diversity, and Power," vol. 3, no. 3 (Summer 2001), pp. 6–15; "9/11: Racism in the Time of Terror," vol. 4, no. 1 (Winter 2002). All *Souls* articles are copyrighted by Manning Marable.

Other earlier versions of chapters or sections in this book were published in: "Race, Class and the Future of Higher Education," *Transformations*, vol. 12, no. 2 (Spring 2001), pp. 29–48; "Blacks and Criminal Justice," in Joy James, ed., *States of Confinement* (New York: Palgrave, 2002); "On Race and History," in Curtis Stokes, Theresa Melendez, and Genice Rhodes-Reed, eds., *Race in 21st Century America* (East Lansing: Michigan State University, 2001); Race, Difference and Historical Imagination (Cambridge, Mass.: Episcopal Divinity School, 1998), 14 pp.; and "Forty Acres and a Mule: The Case for Black Reparations," *Jewish Currents*, vol. 56, no. 4 (July-August 2002), pp. 12–16.

Chapter 1

Introduction

What We Talk About When We Talk About Race

It is an historical fact that privileged groups seldom give up their privileges voluntarily. Individuals may see the moral light and voluntarily give up their unjust posture; but, as Reinhold Niebuhr has reminded us, groups tend to be more immoral than individuals.

—Martin Luther King, Jr.
"Letter from Birmingham Jail," April 16, 1963

When I was twelve years old, growing up in an African-American community in Dayton, Ohio, something happened at our church one Sunday afternoon that I've never forgotten. My family and I attended St. Margaret's Episcopal Church, which had a congregation that was almost completely black. Occasionally after mass, we'd go downstairs to the church basement and have Sunday dinner for the members of the congregation. On this particular afternoon, the church had organized a raffle. Each ticket cost fifty cents, and the first prize was a $100 U.S. savings bond.

My allowance at the time was about one dollar and fifty cents per week. I calculated that I could afford to buy one raffle ticket. Before dinner was served, everybody gathered for the drawing. Much to my amazement, I had purchased the winning ticket.

As I walked forward to receive my savings bond, church members and family friends stood up to applaud. One elderly, somewhat heavyset church lady with a beautiful broad smile hugged me and proudly pinched my cheeks. She exclaimed, "Son, this must be your lucky day!"

There are moments like that in everyone's life. Like when you're standing at a city crosswalk and, looking down, see a crumpled twenty-dollar bill on the pavement. The event is unexpected, something that is unusual. I don't know what happened to that savings bond; it's probably somewhere in my mom's basement back in Dayton. But that doesn't diminish how I felt that special day when I was twelve.

Four decades have passed since then. I usually speak about once or twice each week, and I travel more than 120 days every year. Because of deregulation and the new post-9/11 security regulations, air travel for most Americans is nothing less than a kind of torture: long lines, surly ticket agents, uncomfortable seats, terrible meals, and constant delays. Sometimes I can observe the corporate executives sitting up in first class. They're usually chilled out. They seem pampered, well fed, and on especially long flights, generally intoxicated. Then I realize the obvious. For them, almost every day is their lucky day. These are the material benefits of whiteness and upper-class privilege in twenty-first-century America.

Sociologists often use a concept called "life chances." These are things that are likely to happen to you simply because you are identified with a particular group. If you're black or Latino in a racist society, where whiteness is defined as the social norm, you are statistically far more likely to experience certain unfortunate and sometimes even life-threatening events—not based on your behavior, but merely because of your identification with an oppressed social category. The Marxist philosopher Louis Althusser once described this process as "overdetermination." You become a social actor in the real world not on the basis of any objective criteria, but by the stereotypes imposed on you externally by others. The boundaries of one's skin become the crude starting point for negotiating access to power and resources within a society constructed around racial hierarchies. And after a period of several centuries, a mountain of accumulated disadvantage has been erected, a vast monument to the pursuit of inequality and injustice that to most black Americans is the hallmark of our "democracy."

Sitting back into my uncomfortable coach middle seat, I looked again at the first-class section. I then recalled the plot of comedian Bill Murray's movie *Groundhog Day* (1993). In the film, Murray plays an obnoxious weatherman who becomes trapped in a small Pennsylvania town on February 2, Groundhog Day. Despite every effort, he finds that he can't escape. The day repeats itself over and over again. The real world is similar, I thought: People wake up to the same racial discrimination or white upper-class privilege day after day. Affluent whites usually experience a lucky day and, with some minor variations, enjoy that same day repeatedly. The structure of white privilege sets certain parameters of existence that guarantee a succession of lucky days.

Then I began to have second thoughts. Are the overweight white guys in the first-class section *personally* responsible for an entire race being placed permanently back in coach, figuratively speaking? I recalled that Connecticut senator and former Democratic vice presidential candidate Joe Lieberman had traveled south in 1964 to participate in the "Mississippi Freedom Summer," organizing and registering African-American voters. And after all, more than 3 million white people did vote for Jesse

Jackson in 1988. Some whites even endorsed Louis Farrakhan's 1995 "Million Man March."

But sympathy for the oppressed is not the same as having a shared or linked fate. We can only truly understand someone else's pain when we step outside the protected confines of our lives to take risks. The political culture of whiteness is conformity. Let's accept the way things are—because things aren't too bad. Power translates itself into "merit." Privileged access and opportunity create spaces for comfortable lives.

Conversely, the structural limitations and restrictions on black life have been continuous in this country. The effects can be seen in many realms, especially in the arts. Racism has produced aesthetically some of this country's most powerful music: for example, the blues. The politics behind this art form, simply put, are based on the harsh reality of having a "bad day" over and over again.

To take this example further, why were the blues produced by oppressed black sharecroppers in the Mississippi Delta, but not by the privileged families of George W. Bush and Dick Cheney? According to 2002 estimates, President Bush's personal assets are between $11.1 million and $21.6 million; Vice President Cheney's total assets are between $19.3 million and $81.8 million. Perhaps we might understand why Bush and Cheney don't sing the blues by reconsidering the real life chances of most African Americans who live under a system most of us call "democracy."

African Americans and Latinos constitute 25 percent of the U.S. population but represent nearly 60 percent of the 2 million Americans currently in prison. Statistically, blacks account for only 14 percent of all illegal drug users. Yet we make up over one-third of all drug arrests and 55 percent of all drug convictions. Are blacks just unlucky in the courts, or is something else at work here?

If it's bad luck, it must start before birth. White Americans in 1995 had an infant mortality rate of 6.3 deaths per 1,000 live births. The African-American infant mortality rate that same year was 15.1 deaths per 1,000 live births—a higher rate than in such places as Taiwan, Portugal, Cuba, Chile, or Bulgaria. Are black babies just unlucky, or are their deaths an inevitable consequence of inadequate health care, poor housing, and the destructive impacts of poverty, unemployment, and the extreme stresses of everyday life for pregnant black women?

The stresses are financial as well as emotional and physical. In several recent studies, major insurance companies were found to charge black homeowners significantly higher rates than whites to insure homes of identical value. Supermarket chains routinely charge higher prices for most groceries in minority urban neighborhoods than in predominantly white, upper-class suburbs. Are African-American consumers in the marketplace just unlucky, or is it the logical result of "equity inequity," the racial profiling of credit and capital investment in our communities? "Bad luck" clearly has nothing to do with the unequal outcomes that construct the normal conditions of our existence. If President George W. Bush and his buddies in the first-class seats who voted for him experienced what we see and feel in our daily lives—omnipresent racial inequality in the courts, in health care, education, employment, and many other areas—they might have invented the blues, too.

The two distinct sections of the airplane also symbolized for me the two strikingly different narratives that have evolved about the character of U.S. democracy and the nature of our social contract, the written and unwritten rules governing relations between the American people and their leaders that theoretically protects their collective interests. For most white Americans, especially those in the first-class seats, U.S. democracy is best represented by enduring values such as personal liberty, individualism, and the ownership of private property. For most of us African Americans and other marginalized minorities, the central goals of the Black Freedom Movement have always been equality—the eradication of all structural barriers to full citizenship and full participation in all aspects of public life and economic relations—and self-determination—the ability to decide, on our own terms, what our future as a community with a unique history and culture might be.

"Freedom" to white Americans principally has meant the absence of legal restrictions on individual activity and enterprise. By contrast, black Americans have always perceived "freedom" in collective terms, as something achievable by group action and capacity-building. "Equality" to African Americans has meant the elimination of all social deficits between blacks and whites—that is, the eradication of cultural and so-cial stereotypes and patterns of social isolation and group exclusion gen-erated by white structural racism over several centuries.

The airplane metaphor is somewhat useful in understanding the problems of race, gender, and class, but in other ways it is limited. The vast majority of the passengers in the coach section are also white, mid-dle-class males. Perhaps one-quarter of the passengers are women. There are several Asian Americans, one or two Latinos, and maybe three other African Americans sitting side by side in two separate rows. As part of the middle class, we have the means and the resources to fly to our destination in relative comfort. But the vast majority of the African-American population, and a significant number of women and other racialized minorities, never board the plane at all. Their physical and so-cial mobility is severely and deliberately restricted. During the era of Jim Crow segregation, the "white" and "colored" signs were the demarca-tion of society's racial fault line, and black "travelers" were restricted by the boundaries of color. Today, the segregationist signs have been taken down, but the ugly patterns of racialized inequality and white privilege persist in most respects. Through extraordinary efforts, those who never had access to the airplane fought and sacrificed to get some of us on board. Our tickets were purchased at an exorbitant price. Yet those of us fortunate enough to gain that access should recognize that the monop-oly of power that severely restricts the mobility of our own community is still in place.

Think for a moment about the individuals in the first-class section. Relative to nearly everybody else, they have a privileged lifestyle. They have set up trust funds for their children, and they take advantage of elit-ist policies such as "legacies" to guarantee that their descendants will have access to the best university education. They lobby vigorously for the elimination of the inheritance tax to preserve the accumulation of their wealth over several generations. For the most part, they control the national discourse about politics and public policy, and they largely de-termine the outcomes of national elections. But despite their privileges and power, they nevertheless do not own the plane. They are favored customers, privileged "frequent flyers," but not the owners. They don't control the airplane's schedule or the direction the flight is taking. In fact, those who own the airliner are rarely on it, because they have their own private jets. In the 1990s, 90 percent of the total income gain of the upper one-fifth of U.S. households went to the top 1 percent. As Kevin Phillips observed, "Attention should focus on the top one-tenth of 1 percent, because these are the raw capitalists and money-handlers, not the high-salaried doctors, lawyers and Cadillac dealers." About 250,000 Americans have annual incomes above $1 million. As Phillips noted, "The 30 largest U.S. family and individual fortunes in 1999 were roughly *ten times* as big as the 30 largest had been in 1982, an increase greater than any comparable period during the 19th century."

We are living in a period when the concentration of wealth and economic power is unprecedented in human history. Wal-Mart, which in 1979 had $1 billion in sales for an entire year, now sometimes generates that amount in a single day worldwide. In 2001, Wal-Mart netted $219.81 billion in revenue, outdistancing the second-largest corporation, Exxon-Mobil, which had 2001 revenues of $191.58 billion. General Motors, which held the top spot for fifteen years until 2000, had $177.26 billion in revenues. Enron, the nation's largest energy corporation, which filed for bankruptcy in December 2001, nevertheless reported 2001 earnings of $130.9 billion. For many of the hundreds of thousands of Americans, regardless of race, who lost all or part of their pensions and life savings from the Enron fiasco, it may be difficult to reconcile such vast inequalities generated by this concentration of wealth within a political system that still claims to be a democracy. The racialized inequality that African Americans have brutally experienced and deeply feel is only one important dimension to the larger problem of inequality that is structured across the entire American social order.

The profound differences between the two narratives about the meaning of the American project are often reflected in our conflicts over historical symbols. For example, several years ago, the New Orleans School Board announced the renaming of one of its oldest elementary schools. What was previously George Washington Elementary had become the Dr. Charles Drew Elementary School. The name change was initiated and enthusiastically supported by the school's students, teach-

ers, and parents. The school's African-American History Club had proposed the name to commemorate a famous black surgeon who had established research procedures for processing and storing blood plasma.
Drew had been the leading organizer of blood-bank programs during
World War II and was responsible for saving millions of lives.

When it became public knowledge that the first U.S. president had
been symbolically "dumped" in favor of a black man, many local whites
were outraged. But the white "Founding Fathers" aren't the only ones at
the center of the school-naming controversies in New Orleans. Over the
past 100 years, New Orleans public schools have been named for a series
of white racists, slaveholders, and former Confederate army officers. A
short list includes: John McDonogh, a wealthy Louisiana slaveholder
who freed many of his slaves only on the condition that they would return to Africa; Henry W. Allen, a sugarcane planter and Confederate
general; Confederate army commander Robert E. Lee; and Confederate
president Jefferson Davis. Some people who have supported racial name
changes have argued that the overwhelmingly black student population
of the New Orleans public school system should be presented with positive role models from their own history and culture. Certainly this is a
valid point. By cultivating greater awareness and appreciation among
African-American young people about their heritage, they may acquire
valuable lessons about black achievement against the odds.

But perhaps the greatest beneficiaries in the changing of public honorific names are white Americans. "Whiteness" imposes blinders that
shut off the full spectrum of social reality, the shared experiences of people from different racialized backgrounds in the making of a common
history. The symbolic act of naming makes a public statement about our
relationship to the past and about the principles and values that should
be preserved.

The larger political issue that lies just behind the debate over names is
far more disturbing. The United States, from its origins to the present,
has consistently lied to itself about what it actually is. We claimed to be a
"democracy" in the early nineteenth century, even while denying voting
rights to the majority of citizens. We claim "equal protection under the
law" while millions of black, brown, and poor people have been and

continue to be unjustly treated in our courts and prisons. Our economic system favors the privileged few, while allocating greater poverty and unemployment along the unequal boundaries of race.

There have always been Americans who have challenged the political hypocrisy of this nation. They have been black, brown, and white. In the 1960s, they were activists in civil rights, in the antiwar movement against U.S. involvement in Vietnam, in women's rights, and in the welfare-rights movement. In the nineteenth century, they were the abolitionists who fought to outlaw human bondage. They are the "Other America," those who dreamed of a truly democratic, pluralistic society. Their names—such as W.E.B. Du Bois, Cesar Chavez, Fannie Lou Hamer, Ida B. Wells-Barnett, Eugene V. Debs, William Lloyd Garrison, Joe Hill, and Paul Robeson—represent an alternative perspective on what America has been and what it could become. Our debate over history therefore is a debate about the future of the country itself.

I

"E Pluribus Unum": Out of many, one. Americans have been taught to believe that they have always been champions of religious, ethnic, and cultural pluralism. "Diversity" has become our multicultural mantra about America's past as well as its future. Offices of student life and student activities groups throughout the United States now fund thousands of celebrations promoting diversity, from the annual birthday events honoring Dr. Martin Luther King, Jr., to Cinco de Mayo, from programs for lesbian, gay, bisexual, and transgender awareness to those honoring the heritage of American Indians. Administrators in the private sector now routinely talk about "managing diversity," of creating workplace environments in which "difference" is not coded into institutional hierarchies. Yet there's a crucial difference between the recognition of "difference" and the acknowledgment that the reality of difference has produced unequal outcomes and divergent life chances for citizens within the same society. As Ron Wakabayashi, the executive director of the Los Angeles County Commission on Human Relations, has observed:

"Politicians like to say that diversity is our greatest strength. That is b.s. Diversity simply *is*. The core question is how do we extract its assets while minimizing its liabilities."

Instead of "celebrating diversity," we must theorize it, interrogate it, and actively seek the parallels and discontinuities in the histories of the people who over many centuries have come to call themselves "Americans." Instead of talking abstractly about race, we should be theorizing about the social processes of racialization, of how certain groups in U.S. society have been relegated to an oppressed status, by the weight of law, social policy, and economic exploitation. This process of subordination has never been exclusively or solely grounded in a simplistic black-white paradigm. Although slavery and Jim Crow segregation were decisive in framing the U.S. social hierarchy, with whiteness defined at the top and blackness at the bottom, people of African descent have never experienced racialization by themselves.

As ethnic studies scholars such as Gary Okihiro and Ronald Takaki have observed, the 1790 Naturalization Act defined citizenship only for immigrants who were "free white persons." Asian immigrants who were born outside the United States were largely excluded from citizenship until 1952. U.S. courts constantly redefined the rules determining who was "white" and who was not. For example, Armenians were originally classed as "Asians" and thus were nonwhite, but they legally became "whites" by a 1909 court decision. Syrians were "white" in court decisions in 1909 and 1910; they became "nonwhite" in 1913, and became "white" again in 1915. Asian Indians were legally white in 1910, but they were classified as nonwhite after 1923. Historians such as David Roediger and Noel Ignatiev have illustrated how a series of ethnic minorities, such as the Irish and Ashkenazi Jews, experienced fierce racialization and discrimination but over several generations managed to scale the hierarchy of whiteness.

What many white Americans still refuse to consider is that their numerical majority in the United States is rapidly eroding. By approximately 2016, the population category defined by the U.S. Census Bureau as "non-Hispanic whites" will peak in size, and then it will gradually decline. As Asian Americans, Caribbean people, Latin Americans, Arab

Americans, and other nationalities enter the national dialogue about democracy, we will inextricably move away from history's old honorific icons toward new names and symbols of political accomplishment. American democracy is still an unfinished project. Navigating within that new diversity will not be easy. One central reason is that oppression in the United States—or anywhere else, for that matter—has been constructed around interlocking systems of prejudice, power, and white heterosexual male privilege in which the vast majority of the population has been defined outside the acceptable boundaries of the mainstream.

There was, of course, the hierarchy of race: the social construction of whiteness as a category of privilege, the racial stereotyping of the vast majority of non-Europeans, the genocidal elimination of most American Indians, and the enslavement of people of African descent. But there was also a hierarchy of gender oppression or patriarchy: the beliefs of heterosexist male authority and domination, and female inferiority and subordination; the absence for centuries of voting rights and property rights for women; the deliberate uses of violence, such as rape, sexual harassment, and physical intimidation, to preserve patriarchal power.

The hierarchy of heterosexism and homophobia relied on beliefs and practices that reinforced heterosexual superiority and power and promoted institutional discrimination and subordination against lesbian, gay, bisexual, and transgendered people. It permitted the systematic use of violence of different types and degrees to intimidate and control people based on their sexual orientation. And there was the hierarchy of class: the unequal distribution of the bulk of all private property, productive resources, factories, banks, and financial institutions into the hands of a small minority of the population, with the great majority forced to live and exist only by its labor power; the development of an ideology of class privilege that masquerades by calling itself "merit"; and, increasingly, the monopolization and exploitation of global resources and transnational corporations to manufacture and preserve the privileges of class.

The key to properly understanding and theorizing what "racialization" has meant in our historical past and still means today was first conceptualized by legal scholar Cheryl Harris: "Whiteness as Property." To be white is not essentially a biological or genetically based, fixed social category; it is the social expression of power and privilege, the consequences of discriminatory policies in the past, and the practices of inequality that exist today. Thus we will never dismantle structural racism as a system unless we are also willing to address the transformation of the American social structure and the full democratization of our political and economic institutions.

The dynamics of socioeconomic and political marginalization and of social isolation and exclusion inevitably impact the behavior of any oppressed group. Oppressed people are constantly forced to define themselves, largely unthinkingly, by the crude boundaries of the formal, legal categories that have been imposed on them. Any people dwelling at the bottom of a social hierarchy will see themselves as the "Other," as individuals outside of society's social contract, as subordinated, marginalized, fixed minorities. Frequently, oppressed people have used these categories, and even terms of insult and stigmatization, such as "nigger" or "queer," as a site for resistance and counter-hegemonic struggle.

The difficulty inherent in this kind of oppositional politics is twofold. First, it tends to anchor individuals to narrowly defined, one-dimensional identities that are often the "inventions" of others. For example, how did African people become known as "black" or, in Spanish, "Negro"? Europeans launching the slave trade across the Atlantic 400 years ago created the terminology as a way of categorizing the people of an entire continent with tremendous variations in language, religion, ethnicity, kinship patterns, and cultural traditions. Blackness, or the state of being black, was completely artificial; no people in Africa prior to the transatlantic slave trade and European colonialism called themselves "black." Blackness only exists as a social construct in relation to something else. That "something else" became known as whiteness. Blackness as a category relegates other identities—ethnicity, sexual orientation, gender, class affiliation, religious traditions, kinship affiliations—to a secondary or even nonexistent status.

In other words, those who control or dominate hierarchies, whether by ownership of the means of production or by domination of the state, have a vested interest in manufacturing and reproducing categories of difference. An excellent recent example of this occurred in the United States in 1971, when the U.S. Census Bureau "invented" the category "Hispanic." The term was imposed on a population of 16 million people reflecting divergent and even contradictory nationalities, racialized ethnicities, cultural traditions, and political loyalties: black Panamanians of Jamaican or Trinidadian descent, who speak Spanish; Argentines of Italian or German descent; anti-Castro, white, upper-class Cubans in Miami's Dade County; impoverished Mexican-American farm workers in California's Central Valley; and black Dominican service and blue-collar workers in New York City's Washington Heights. Yet when states or hierarchies name the "Other," the act of naming creates its own materiality for the oppressed. Government resources, economic empowerment zones, and affirmative-action scholarships are in part determined by who is classified as Hispanic, and who is not. Identities may be situational, but when the power and resources of the state are used to categorize groups under a "one-size-fits-all" designation, the life chances of individuals who are defined within these categories are largely set and determined by others.

II

In post–civil rights era America, most white commentators on issues of race emphasize the necessity for all of us to become "color blind." That is, we should be "blind" to any imputed differences that tend to divide people by skin color or phenotype, by physical appearance, or by genetic background. The political version of this argument is that any special measures that created privileged classes based on racial categories are inherently unfair and discriminatory.

The color-blind thesis almost always is accompanied by an appeal to "forgive and forget." The logic of this argument goes as follows: Black Americans were certainly terribly oppressed during slavery and Jim Crow segregation. But no white Americans alive today owned slaves. There's been much social progress in recent years, thanks to the constructive cooperation between the races. It's time for us to move beyond ancient grievances and racial bitterness, toward taking greater personal responsibility for our own lives. All of us bear part of the blame for the burden of prejudice—that is, the minorities themselves are partly responsible for getting themselves into their current predicament.

With certain variations, this basic argument is repeated over and over again in the white media by white political leaders and institutions about the dynamics of race. Their thesis is that African Americans must stop being so "sensitive" and "defensive" about the problems of their people and communities. Whites have nothing to apologize for, and African Americans have little really to complain about.

In popular films and culture, the message is largely the same. At the beginning of *Die Hard with a Vengeance* (1995), a white actor, Bruce Willis, stands in Harlem, just off Amsterdam Avenue, wearing a huge sign that reads: "I Hate Niggers." A cluster of justifiably outraged young black men surrounds the undercover white cop. Yet the film, remarkably, portrays not the white cop, but the African-American males, as emotional, dangerous, unstable, and threatening. In the award-winning film *Pulp Fiction* (1994), a white criminal played by John Travolta "accidentally" blows off the head of a young black man when his gun discharges. Covered with blood and gore, the white killer and his black partner (Samuel L. Jackson) take refuge in the suburban home of a white criminal associate (Quentin Tarantino). The suburban mobster is outraged that this "dead nigger" has been dragged into his home. Yet to display that he could not really be a racist, the film then cuts away to show that this bigot is married to an African-American woman. The fact that he has a sexual relationship with a black woman is supposed to clear up any misunderstandings about his repeated stream of utterances about "dead niggers"!

The white corporate-oriented media loves to publicize stories about "black bigotry." Several years ago, for instance, when the Oakland, California, board of education suggested that African-American young people may learn best in an environment that validates the language they actually speak ("ebonics") in their neighborhoods and in daily interactions with friends, blacks everywhere were attacked for "rejecting" standard English, as if none of us speak it. When African-American students now demand black studies courses, or advocate campus housing emphasizing

Caribbean, African, and black American cultural traditions and identity, they are subjected to ridicule as proponents of "self-segregation."

We will never uproot racism by pretending that everyone shares an equal and common responsibility for society's patterns of discrimination and inequality. Black people were never "equal partners" in the construction of slavery, Jim Crow segregation, and ghettoization. We weren't individually or collectively consulted when our criminal-justice system imprisoned one-third of our young men, or when we continue to be burdened with twice the unemployment rate of whites. To be "color blind" in a virulently racist society is to be blind to the history and reality of oppression. To forget the past and to refuse to acknowledge the color-coded hierarchies that constitute our parallel racial universes is to evade any responsibility for racial peace in the future.

Perhaps the greatest lie in the arsenal of the "color-blind" proponents of racism is the assertion that black people can be understood only as part of the larger narrative of standard American history. That is to say that "black history" is somehow inferior to or at odds with "American history." To be part of the national project, culturally and ideologically, means that we must surrender and abandon those lessons we've learned in our struggles along the way.

While it is certainly true that black Americans are survivors of a very destructive historical process from slavery, Jim Crow segregation, and ghettoization, we know within ourselves that we have never stood silently by, succumbing to the forces of white oppression. Any understanding of black history illustrates that we have consistently fought to maintain a unique set of cultural values that have shaped and continue to define our core identities as a people. We have, in effect, always been not only the makers of "our" history but also central to the construction and evolution of the larger American experience.

What are the cultural reservoirs that create the psychological, emotional, and cultural foundation of the strength and vision that the adventure of blackness in American life has produced? Even in the shadows of slavery, we found our humanity in the gift of song. Our music tells us much about who we are, how we have worked, how we have loved, where we've been, and where we're going. From the blues of the Mississippi Delta, to the soaring sounds of bebop in Harlem in the 1940s, to the provocative rhythms of today's hip hop, black music reflects the pulse and sensibility of blackness.

Black history and culture reveal the gift of grace, the fluidity of motion and beauty that an oppressed people have claimed as their own. It is constantly recreated in many ways: from the artistry of dance to the spectacular athleticism of Michael Jordan. Grace is the ability to redefine the boundaries of possibility. We as a people were not supposed to survive the ordeal of oppression and Jim Crow segregation, yet our very existence speaks to the creative power of our collective imagination. That power is reflected in our language, the rhythm of gospel, and the power of black preachers on Sunday morning in our churches. That power is found in the creative energy of our poets and playwrights. The gift of grace can be heard in the writings of Toni Morrison, James Baldwin, Amiri Baraka, and Alice Walker.

The experience of work has always been the foundation of black strength and capacity-building throughout history. Slavery was the only moment in American history when people of African descent experienced full employment: Everybody worked. If financial gain was commensurate with hard work, African Americans would undoubtedly be among the wealthiest people on earth. Yet despite our economic marginalization, despite the historic pattern of receiving barely 60 cents for every dollar of wages that comparable white work commands, we nevertheless have found real meaning in the world of work. Black labor, more than any other, is responsible for establishing much of the foundations of the economic productivity of this country. Black working-class women and men have for generations been at the forefront of the trade-union movement and collective efforts to improve the quality of life and the conditions of work for all Americans.

And then there is the historical strength of family and community, kinship and neighbors within the black experience. An oppressed people cannot survive unless there is close cooperation and mutual support by and for each other. The reservoir of strength within the black family has been anchored in our recognition that kinship is collective, not nuclear, in structure.

Throughout black history, along with the strength of family there has been the strength of our faith. During slavery, a prayer was in many ways an act of resistance. When we sang "Steal Away to Jesus," our eyes looked to the North Star, to the faraway promised land of freedom. Today that faith still resounds as the cultural heart of black community life in thousands of towns and cities across the country. From the courage of Dr. Martin Luther King, Jr., to the contemporary activism of a Jesse Jackson or an Al Sharpton, black faith has been most powerful as a historical force when spirituality reinforces fundamental social change.

It is only through the telling of our stories about the destructive dynamics of racialization that many white Americans will be able finally to come to terms with the social costs of "whiteness," for themselves, their children, and for the larger society. No genuine dialogue about race is possible when millions of whites are taught to believe that blacks have been marginal to the construction of American society, or that the "race problem" has now been solved.

No meaningful dialogue can take place when some whites still think about race as a "zero-sum game," where any economic or political advances by racial minorities must come at their expense. I believe that the only way for us to move toward a nonracist society is for white Americans to acknowledge that the struggles and sacrifices that blacks have made to destroy structural racism in all of its forms throughout history have directly contributed to enriching and expanding the meaning of democracy not just for ourselves, but for everyone within our society. As Martin Luther King, Jr., observed in the "Letter from Birmingham Jail," the "real heroes" of American democracy are those who actively challenged the immorality and injustices of racial inequality:

> One day the South will recognize its real heroes. They will be the James Merediths, with the noble sense of purpose that enables them to face jeering, and hostile mobs, and with the agonizing loneliness that characterizes the life of the pioneer. They will be old, oppressed, battered Negro women, symbolized in a seventy-two-year-old woman in Montgomery, Alabama, who rose up with a sense of dignity and with her people decided not to ride segre-

gated buses, and who responded with ungrammatical profundity to one who inquired about her weariness: "My feets is tired, but my soul is at rest." They will be the young high school and college students, the young ministers of the gospel and a host of their elders, courageously and nonviolently sitting in at lunch counters and willingly going to jail for conscience' sake. One day the South will know that when these disinherited children of God sat down at lunch counters, they were in reality standing up for what is best in the American dream and for the most sacred values in our Judeo-Christian heritage, thereby bringing our nation back to those great wells of democracy which were dug deep by the founding fathers in their formulation of the Constitution and the Declaration of Independence.

The American Dilemma

PART ONE

The African Dilemma

Chapter 2

Structural Racism

A Short History

Before the pilgrims landed at Plymouth, we were here. Before the pen of Jefferson etched the majestic words of the Declaration of Independence across the pages of history, we were here.

—Martin Luther King, Jr.
"Letter from Birmingham Jail," April 16, 1963

I

In 1900, W.E.B. Du Bois, the great African-American scholar and co-founder of the NAACP, predicted that "the problem of the twentieth century is the problem of the color line—the relation of the darker to the lighter races of men in Asia and Africa, in America and the islands of the sea." In truth, the color line Du Bois described has been a prominent feature of American life since its origins in the seventeenth century. From the vantage point of people of color, and especially Americans of African descent, our collective histories and experiences of interaction with the white majority have been largely defined around a series of oppressive institutions and practices. Although laws regarding the treatment of racialized minorities have changed over the years, the deep structure of white prejudice, power, and privilege forming the undemocratic foundation of most human interactions has not fundamentally been altered. In order for American democracy finally to become a reality for all of our citizens, we must, first, understand historically how and why these deep structures of racial inequality came into being, and how they continue to be decisively expressed in the daily lives and life chances of racialized minorities and whites alike.

Millions of Americans still think and talk about race in terms of fixed biological or genetic categories. A strikingly different way to view the concept of "race" is as an unequal relationship between social groups based on the privileged access to power and resources by one group over another. Race is historically and socially constructed, created (and recreated) by how people are perceived and treated in the normal actions of everyday life. As such, "race" is never fixed. It is a dynamic, constantly changing relationship. Some groups defined as an "inferior race" within American society at a certain historical moment may successfully escape racialization and become part of the privileged majority, the "whites," at a later time. Other groups, especially those of African, Latino, American Indian, Pacific Islander, and Asian descent, have found the path for group socioeconomic mobility far more difficult to navigate. The unequal boundaries of color have been at times permanent barriers to economic, educational, and social advancement for millions of Americans living in what for them has been a deeply flawed, and often hypocritical, democracy.

The fundamental problem for the viability of American democracy, therefore, is that of "structural racism": whether the majority of American people, along with their leaders, political organizations, and institutions, have the capacity and vision to dismantle the complex institutional barriers that continue to severely curtail the democratic rights and socioeconomic opportunities of millions of their fellow citizens. To paraphrase Thomas Jefferson—the Founding Father of democracy: Does this nation possess the political courage to affirm these truths as self-evident, that all citizens regardless of race are born with certain inalienable rights, and that first among these is the right to be acknowledged as human beings? Can American democracy ever be more than an abstract ideal, when tens of millions of its citizens feel alienated and marginalized by what have become the "normal" and routine consequences of American racialization in daily life? I believe that a multicultural democracy can be achieved within American public life: a civil society that treats every citizen with fairness and respect, a political culture that encourages the broadest possible involvement and participation, by all racialized groups and social classes, in decision-making processes, and a criminal-justice system that does not routinely stigmatize entire classes of individuals solely on the basis of their physical appearance. The difficult political and moral challenge is to transform those lofty ideals into a democratic movement that has the capacity to transform the real structure of racial power in our society.

More than a half century ago, sociologist Gunnar Myrdal characterized structural racism inside the United States as "an American Dilemma." Although racism has been central to the construction of U.S. society, it has of course never been solely or even essentially an "American problem." Indeed, for several centuries, African-American leaders and the Black Freedom Movement took the view that racism as a system of structural inequality had to be critiqued globally, in a worldwide context, rather than as an exclusively American ordeal. The two central architects of African-American social and political thought, Frederick Douglass and Martin R. Delany, both in different ways incorporated international issues into their views on slavery and the emancipation of black people. During World War II, the NAACP board of directors issued a direct challenge to the administration of Franklin D. Roosevelt, declaring that the United States should be "utterly opposed . . . to any policy which means freedom for white people . . . and continued exploitation of colored peoples. . . . We ask that it be made clear that the United States will not in any fashion, direct or indirect, uphold continued exploitation of India, China, Abyssinia and other African areas, the West Indies, or of any other part of the world."

With the subsequent formation of the United Nations, a universal Declaration of Human Rights was adopted by its General Assembly in 1948. Fifteen years later, the United Nations General Assembly adopted a more extensive statement, the Declaration on the Elimination of All Forms of Racial Discrimination. To realize the objectives of the declaration, the International Convention on the Elimination of All Forms of Racial Discrimination was established in 1965. The convention defined racial discrimination as "any distinction, exclusion, restriction or preference based on race, colour, descent, or national or ethnic origin which has the purpose or effect of nullifying or impairing the recognition, enjoyment or exercise, on an equal footing, of human rights and fundamental freedoms in the political, economic, social, cultural or any other field of public life."

Yet this international definition of racial discrimination, seemingly comprehensive, was also restrictive in several important respects. The 1965 International Convention was not applied to member governments' policies of "distinctions, exclusions, restrictions, (and) preferences" between citizens and non-citizens in their own countries. Legal restrictions concerning the establishment of citizenship or naturalization were also excluded from the definition of racism, so long as specific nationalities were not treated differently from other groups under the law. Policies that in the United States have been termed "affirmative action," or frequently in Europe as "positive discrimination," are not defined as racism, so long as such corrective measures do not create a privileged status for certain racial groups. Moreover, this terminology did not address the social intolerance and discrimination of certain religious groups or faith-based institutions, which is a serious and growing problem throughout the world. And finally, the UN definition of racial discrimination does not adequately consider the problem of coerced or forced assimilation, the extermination of a population's cultural distinctiveness. In the United States and most European countries in recent years, extremist conservative political movements have arisen against new Third World immigrant populations, advocating discrimination against the speaking of certain languages (through "English Only" campaigns) or the harassment of non-Western cultures and religious traditions (such as those represented by Islam).

For various political reasons, the United States has largely remained apart from the general global discussion about racism. The American government refused to recognize the Declaration on the Elimination of All Forms of Racial Discrimination for many years. After all, the United States maintained a legal system of Jim Crow segregation for nearly a century and could not easily acknowledge the vast racial contradictions of its own history. Only under the administration of George Bush did the United States become a party to the convention, and even then only conditionally and with stipulations. There is also a strong tendency within the United States to perceive the world from the peculiar vantage point of the American experience. Thus, "race," something most Americans already think they know a good deal about, is rarely interrogated or understood comparatively or transnationally.

What can be learned from a global perspective on racism? Anthropologist Etienne Balibar has provided some useful insights along these lines. All social formations constructed around the idea of race are posited upon the concept of "frontiers," or "boundaries." A nation or a people only have integrity when there are boundaries separating them from the "Other." Sometimes these boundaries are literally that, geopolitical divisions that serve to separate neighboring populations. But more frequently, they are the constantly shifting divisions separating individuals from each other within a single society. "This is the double function of the notion of frontier," Balibar argued. "What theoretical racism calls 'race' or 'culture' (or both) is therefore a birthright of the nation, an historical backbone, a concentration of qualities that belong 'exclusively' to the nationals: it is in the race of 'its children' that the nation can contemplate its true identity at its purest. Consequently, it is to the race that the nation must cleave." In the American experience, the frontier was the physical boundary separating European settlers from potentially hostile American Indians. But it was also, in many ways, the barrier separating the slave shanties from the masters' mansions. Affiliation to the nation through citizenship was closely tied to one's position in the racial hierarchy. This concept helps us to understand why the vast majority of Asians born in Asia who emigrated to the United States were not legally allowed to become citizens until 1952. It explains why Native Americans, the only group truly indigenous to the continent, were excluded from citizenship until 1924. It also illustrates why the majority of African Americans, who had been formally extended the rights of citizenship in 1865, did not actually vote in a presidential election until 1968.

Frontiers between nations frequently change over time. Boundaries are disputed and redrawn as the result of wars or negotiations. Similarly, racial frontiers in a racist society, while appearing to be fixed, shift over time, as certain groups that at one point were defined as outside the race/nation are assimilated within it. Individuals within oppressed groups may, based on their phenotype or physical appearance, transgress the boundaries of race by "passing." Oppositional or social protest movements by those defined as subordinate may force the white majority to negotiate new rules, new boundaries that permit limited access and opportunity for nonwhites. Balibar's point here is that the national and racial identities and superstructures are so interwoven that an "obsessive imperative" is established that demands the "racialization of populations and social groups whose collective features will be designated stigmata of exteriority and impurity." Thus nonwhite or non-European Others must be invented, even where they do not exist. Or we could see racism as a type of social negation, where whites can only exist as "whites" when a group is relegated to the inferior status of being nonwhite. Without a racialized Other, "whites" cease to exist.

It would be a mistake, however, to think of racism primarily as a national phenomenon, or located within particular forms of nationalism. As Balibar pointed out, one of the characteristics of racism that gives it such longevity is its ability to transcend individual nation-states. In a kind of twisted way, racism has a universal quality as "supernationalism." "Since there is no way to *find* racial-national purity or to guarantee its source in the origins of the people, it must be *fabricated*," Balibar argued. The supernationalism of racism "tends to idealize certain timeless, or pseudotemporal, communities" such as "the West" or "civilized man." The state of being civilized allows white travelers to cross boundaries that separate Western nations by language, religious beliefs, culture, and ethnicity. The real frontiers therefore become interior, that is, "inseparable from the individuals." Thus, black people in a society built on white racism are those individuals who carry their essentialist frontiers or boundaries around with them wherever they go.

Racism always manifests itself among its proponents as an all-encompassing worldview, a way of interpreting and understanding phenomena. Balibar observed that "racism is a philosophy of history, or better yet a historiosophy, by which I mean a philosophy that *merges* with an interpretation of history, but makes history the consequence of a 'secret' hidden and revealed to men about their own nature and birth; a philosophy that *reveals the invisible cause* of the destiny of societies and peoples." The philosophy justifying racial hierarchy thus provides not only an explanation for the continuation of racial conflicts throughout the world but also a historically grounded method for thinking about the real differences in physical appearance that separate human beings from each other. In this mental universe, some people are simply "destined" to live in the netherworld of inferiority. Others can claim a "natural" superiority that is validated by the forces of history.

The entire logic of racism points toward the inevitability of conflict between racial groups and the ultimate inability to negotiate a long-term agreement with the racialized Other. Because the Other does not share our biological origins, values, and culture, it can never be trusted to fulfill its promises. Coercion is ultimately the only language it understands. More than twenty years ago, as a Fellow at the Aspen Institute, I became acquainted with General Edward Rowney, who would subsequently become the Reagan administration's chief arms negotiator with the Soviet Union. Both Rowney and I were participants in an Aspen Institute Seminar, and we traveled by shuttle bus together from our housing quarters to the seminar site daily. One day I asked Rowney about the prospects for peace, and he replied that meaningful negotiations with the Russian Communists were impossible. "The Russians," Rowney explained, never experienced the Renaissance, or took part in Western civilization or culture. I pressed the point, asking whether his real problem with Russia was its adherence to communism. Rowney snapped, "Communism has nothing to do with it!" He looked thoughtful for a moment and then said simply, "The *real* problem with Russians is that they are *Asiatics*." What Rowney was saying is that there was a distinctly racial foundation for the Cold War that transcended the conflict between capitalism and communism. This raises the interesting question of whether the Russians, having now overthrown communism, have become "white."

The Rowney story reveals not only a "civilizational" or even cultural deterministic foundation to the mentality of the Cold War but some important insights into the "logic" of racialized thinking. The forces of history, if not biology, have "fixed" the racialized Other, suspended through time and space. It is not the overt behavior of the racialized Other that the racist finds so objectionable. It is his or her very being. The reduction of social conflict can be achieved only through the forced subordination and perhaps even the physical elimination of the Other. It is this kind of thinking that has constructed what legal scholar Randall Kennedy has described as "America's paradigmatic racial pariah, the Negro. . . . Racist perceptions of blacks have given energy to policies and practices (such as racial exclusion in housing, impoverished schooling, and stingy social welfare programs) that have facilitated the growth of egregious, crime-spawning conditions that millions of Americans face in urban slums and rural backwaters across the nation." Thus, it is not the objective reality of difference between "races" that produces disparities and social inequality between groups; it is structural racism that reproduces "races."

II

The central difficulty in uprooting racism in America's consciousness, its identity of itself as a nation or a people, is that racism predates national identity. Decades before the American Revolution, enslaved African Americans and American Indians were specifically excluded from the social contract that linked individuals and classes to the state through sets of rights and responsibilities. What evolved was a uniquely American racial formation—a dynamic set of discourses and racialized stereotypes, hierarchies of dominant and subordinate behaviors in both public and private settings, organization of political institutions, and patterns of economic production and ownership to preserve white privilege and power. The reality of American structural racism, even more than the omnipresent factors of gender oppression and class location, set the rough parameters for group participation and individual mobility within the national society. Citizenship was defined in very practical terms by determining whether one belonged to the "racialized Other" group or not. Thus, "whiteness" became the gateway through which successive waves of European immigrants gained admission, access, and advancement into American civil and political society. As political scientist Robert Lieberman has observed:

> Racial division in any society is not a simple fact; it is a complex condition, deeply contextual and situated in a set of particular social relations. It is the product not merely of shades of skin pigmentation distributed among the population but of the belief that such differences matter and above all of structures that constitute regular patterns of social, economic and political understanding and behavior according to these shadings. Political institutions, one form that such structures can take, can thus reflect the racial basis of social distinctions in the society's power structure. The state, in short, may stand on a racial foundation.

Over several centuries, as America's political economy was constructed, there were several important stages in how the racialized

Other was socially controlled. From the outset, American Indians were subjected to a series of genocidal wars that ultimately marginalized them to specific reservations, a kind of territorial apartheid, to the point of near extermination. The first enslaved Africans arrived in British North America at Jamestown, Virginia, in August 1619. It is crucial to note that the Africans were not immediately placed into the permanent state of bondage. For several decades the general rules of indentured servitude, which governed the activities of many whites, were simply extended to black people. In less than a generation, however, the status and physical treatment of Africans became far more repressive. In 1642, Virginia prohibited by law any direct assistance or harboring of escaped slaves. Twenty years later, Virginia law was changed to assert that any children born of African women would follow their mother's legal status. In other words, the child of any slave woman was also enslaved for the duration of his or her natural life.

By the early eighteenth century, severe legal restrictions against African Americans were virtually uniform throughout the British colonies. In Connecticut, African Americans, regardless of whether they were slaves or free, were not permitted to be outdoors after 9:00 P.M. without a written pass. In 1740, the South Carolina slave code declared that all people of African descent in that colony, including mulattoes, would be legally defined as slaves in perpetuity. At least 650,000 Africans were transported against their will to what became the United States. Although the majority of them were sold for work in the southern colonies, there was virtually no aspect of American life that was not affected by chattel slavery. Even in the small colony of Rhode Island, local merchants sponsored more than 900 separate slave voyages across the Atlantic in the eighteenth century. Rhode Island–based ships and crews were responsible for transporting more than 100,000 West Africans to the Caribbean and North America.

The profits from the sale of human beings helped to establish the foundations of American capitalism. In 1791 Rhode Island slave trader John Brown, for example, established Providence Bank, which was the predecessor bank to today's Fleet Boston Financial Corporation. Aetna Life Insurance, founded in 1853, sold life-insurance policies to slave own-

ers who were concerned about protecting their investments. One 1856
Aetna policy, recently discovered by the South Carolina Historical Society, was purchased by one Thomas P. Allen, the owner of a twenty-four-
year-old slave woman named Sabrina. In the unlucky or unforeseen occurrence of Sabrina's death, Allen would receive the sum of $600 from
Aetna. Two of Chase Manhattan Bank's predecessor institutions, the
Merchants Bank and The Leather Manufacturers Bank, both of New
York, in 1852 advertised their services as underwriters for policies that
would protect slave owners from loss.

Many of America's oldest universities were founded on the profits of
slavery and the slave trade. An excellent example is provided by Yale University. According to the research of Antony Dugdale, J. J. Fueser, and J.
Celso de Castro Alves, three of the financial endowments that allowed
Yale to thrive in its first century depended directly upon slavery: Yale's
first endowed professorship, its first scholarship fund, and its first endowed library fund. The first endowed professorship was established by
slave trader Philip Livingston, whose father, Robert, had owned a one-
half interest in the *Margriet*, "a vessel that journeyed to Madagascar, Bar-
bados, and Virginia to trade in slaves, sugar and tobacco." When Robert
Livingston died in 1728, his son Philip inherited six of the twelve slaves
noted in his father's will. According to historian Cynthia A. Kierner,
"Philip Livingston was a leading importer of slaves from Jamaica and
Antigua during the 1730s. He was part owner of a number of vessels,
some of which were owned in partnership with his sons. . . . In August
1733, Philip's sloop *Katherine* brought in fifty blacks from Jamaica, an un-
usually large shipment from that source." Several years later, in 1738, Livingston expanded his entrepreneurship in slave trading to the Guinea
coast, "where two hundred slaves were purchased and consigned to his
son . . . and his partner in Jamaica." Yale's first scholarship was "funded
for up to fifty years with money earned from slave labor." Yale's esteemed early alumni included John C. Calhoun, South Carolina senator,
vice president, and foremost defender of America's "peculiar institution"
during the nation's first half century, and Judah P. Benjamin, the Confederate States of America's secretary of war and attorney general. In all,
nine of the ten men after whom individual colleges are named at Yale

University either owned slaves or actively defended the institution of slavery. Although a number of abolitionists attended Yale, there is no question that the university's great financial resources and academic prestige are directly linked to the history of enslavement of African people.

Slave labor was also largely responsible for the construction of many public buildings in the young democracy, especially in those states where African Americans were a major share of the labor force. Slave labor was used in the original construction of the White House and the U.S. Capitol building in Washington. The U.S. Department of the Treasury commissioned and supervised the construction of these buildings. More than two-thirds of the 650 workers employed on the projects were people of African descent. White workers received wages, while the slave owners were paid five dollars per month in compensation for the use of their slaves. Slave labor was even used to produce the Statue of Freedom, which was elevated to the apex of the Capitol dome in 1863.

The long-term human consequences to the black community from centuries of brutal experiences from the transatlantic and domestic slave trade were profound. Historians have long examined the destructive psychological and social costs of mass enslavement to the African-American family and community. About 1 percent of all slaves were sold apart from their immediate families or households in any given year. Families were routinely divided and sold apart after the death of their owners, or as a result of marriages or bankruptcies. Researchers W. Michael Byrd and Linda A. Clayton, both at Harvard's School of Public Health, have compiled a wealth of statistical evidence documenting the horrific costs of enslavement to black people. They have estimated that anywhere from 40 million to 100 million Africans were enslaved on the African continent, and that approximately 15 million to 25 million survivors arrived in the Americas and the Caribbean. Millions of deaths occurred in the infamous "Middle Passage" of slave ships shuttling their human cargoes across the Atlantic. The unsanitary quarters of these ships, and the brutal physical treatment, quickly spread diseases such as dysentery, worms, scurvy, malaria, diarrhea, yaws, small pox, and pneumonia. Usually about 15 to 20 percent of the enslaved Africans traveling across the Atlantic died en route. Once in the Americas, Byrd and Clayton observed, "The break-in period was one of increased risk for slaves, because of their exposure to new diseases and climatic conditions. The stress of being torn from home and familiar environments combined with the process of 'deculturation' (e.g., the colonial custom of forbidding the practice of indigenous religions, outlawing the use of African dialects, systematically dissolving the family structure, and prohibiting any formal education) compounded the health problems among Black Africans."

Few slaves had regular access to trained physicians, many lived in unsanitary conditions, and most field hands worked twelve- to fourteen-hour days. The great disparities we see today between whites and African Americans in measures of longevity and mortality were created by slavery. By the end of the nineteenth century, white Americans could expect to reach the age of fifty or more; African American males had a life expectancy of thirty to thirty-two years, and black women, thirty-four years. Historian Robert Fogel has suggested that "slave babies, probably disproportionately weighing less than 5.5 pounds at birth, were predisposed to diseases such as diarrhea, dysentery, whooping cough, respiratory diseases and worms." The lack of "nutritional supplementation for pregnant slaves" and oppressive working conditions were prime factors leading to extremely high fetal, infant, and childhood death rates. As anthropologist Leith Mullings frequently observes, while "race" is not a valid biological concept, "racism" has profoundly destructive biological consequences that can be objectively measured.

It was from this inherently contradictory position on race that America's master narrative on democracy was forged. The United States was formed with a republican form of government and a model of citizenship that appeared to be inclusive. It established a democratic political and legal framework that was based on a lively civil society, with safeguards for individual liberty guaranteed in the Bill of Rights. The national democratic narrative guaranteed that economic opportunity would be available to all, and that through individual initiative, sacrifice, and merit, all citizens could achieve a decent life. Yet interwoven within the national political culture was the reality of whiteness, a privileged racial category justified by negative racist stereotypes, passed down from generation to generation so as to become acceptable, normal, and part of the public common sense. America's legal establishment and public institutions rationalized and condoned this massive exploitation of black people. At the 1787 Constitutional Convention, the delegates agreed to count each slave as three-fifths of a person regarding each state's representation in the House of Representatives. Article IV, Section 2, of the Constitution also declared that persons "held to Service or Labour" in one state who fled successfully to another "shall be delivered up on claim of the party to whom such service or labour may be due." Historian Roger Wilkins has noted that the notorious three-fifths compromise "would prove sufficient to give the South undue influence in national affairs up until the Civil War. The compromise that was deemed necessary to create the nation also preserved for posterity a mathematical expression of the cruelty and inhumanity at the core of American culture." Over several centuries, white Americans successfully constructed their own distinct racial universe, a white supremacist worldview in which, as Wilkins argued, "white people's versions of the way things were *are* the way things are; that black people's versions of the way things were are discredited at the source and thus may be discounted without any attempt at analysis."

Perhaps the most unambiguous and decisive expression of this white supremacist perspective was the 1857 Supreme Court decision in *Dred Scott v. Sanford*. Scott, born as a slave in Virginia in 1795, had been taken by his master first to Illinois, a free state, and subsequently to the free territory of Wisconsin. Scott sued for his freedom, claiming that his enslaved status had been nullified by his residence in free territories. The Supreme Court, predictably, ruled against Scott, observing that African Americans were not citizens of the United States and therefore had no legal standing in the courts. Chief Justice Roger B. Taney's decision went significantly further than the narrow issues regarding Scott's legal status, however. Taney also asserted that Congress could not outlaw slavery in any state, therefore nullifying the 1820 Missouri Compromise. The memorable phrase "all men are created equal" written by Jefferson into the Declaration of Independence had absolutely nothing to do with black people, whether enslaved or legally free. The Founding Fathers "perfectly understood the meaning of the language they used and how it would be understood by others; and they knew that it would not in any part of the civilized world be supposed to embrace the Negro race, which, by common consent, had been excluded from civilized governments and the family of nations and doomed to slavery." Taney was convinced that people of African descent had for centuries "been regarded as beings of an inferior order and altogether unfit to associate with the white race, either in social or political relations; and so far inferior that they had no rights which the white man was bound to respect." Wilkins's commentary on Chief Justice Taney's ruling in the Dred Scott case is an eloquent summary of the American Dilemma: "It all adds up to a very complex strategy for removing blacks from the rank of humans. If you extinguish blacks' voices, you eliminate their ability to validate the realities of their lives. That leaves the field open for white fantasies to become truth."

The racist thesis presented in *Dred Scott v. Sanford* was reflected throughout the entire corpus of slave law enforced across the South. By law, slaves were not allowed to own property or to make contracts. They had no right to carry firearms and could not defend themselves if attacked by a white person. Slaves had to obtain the permission of their masters in order to marry. Slaves were unable to testify against whites in courts. Enslaved women could not technically be raped by their owners, because the law defined all slave women as chattel or property. In 1853, the Alabama state legislature passed a law that ordered one hundred lashes to be inflicted on any slave who had been taught to read and write. Maryland prohibited free blacks from selling wheat, tobacco, or corn without a license. Even in the northern states, where slavery had gradually disappeared as a viable economic institution, free African Americans faced severe restrictions on their legal rights and civil liberties. In many northern cities, throughout the nineteenth century blacks were prohibited from attending white schools, from staying in white-owned hotels, or from eating in white-owned restaurants. In Indiana, Pennsylvania, and several other northern states, free blacks were ineligible to vote in local and state elections. New York state did allow free

African Americans to vote, but restricted the size of the black electorate with property and literacy qualifications.

African-American leaders who emerged prior to the Civil War were under absolutely no illusions about the nature of the regime under which they lived. One of the most important black political manifestos in this early period was "David Walker's Appeal," printed originally in 1829. Born in 1785 in Wilmington, Ohio, Walker moved to Boston and quickly made a name for himself as a powerful opponent of slavery and white racism. In the uncompromising language that would later be echoed by Malcolm X, Walker challenged black people to confront "the inhuman system of slavery":

Will any of us leave our homes and go to Africa? I hope not.
. . . Let no man of us budge one step, and let slave-holders come to beat us from our country. America is more our country, than it is the whites'—we have enriched it with our blood and tears. The greatest riches—in all America have arisen from our blood and tears:—and will they drive us from our property and homes, which we have earned with our blood? . . . I will give here a very imperfect list of the cruelties inflicted on us by the enlightened Christians of America.—First, no trifling portion of them will beat us nearly to death, if they find us on our knees praying to God . . . if they find us with a book of any description in our hand, they will beat us nearly to death—they are so afraid we will learn to read, and enlighten our dark and benighted minds—They will not suffer us to meet together to worship the God who made us—they brand us with hot irons—they cram bolts of fire down our throats—they cut us as they do horses, bulls, or hogs—they crop our ears and sometimes cut off bits of our tongues—they chain and hand-cuff us, and while in that miserable and wretched condition, beat us with cow-hides and clubs. . . . They put on us fifty-sixes and chains, and make us work in that cruel situation, and in sickness, under lashes to support them and their families.—They keep us three or four hundred feet under ground working in their mines, night and day to dig up gold and silver to enrich them and

their children.—They keep us in the most death-like ignorance . . .
and call us, who are free men . . . their property!!!!

"David Walker's Appeal" is a significant historical document because
it is perhaps the first concise expression of several key concepts that
would characterize black American political discourse during the next
200 years. Walker's statement, first, articulates deep moral outrage that
people of African descent are defined outside of the human family. It lo-
cates the fundamental source of this outrage in stark economic terms:
Blacks are the private property of whites. The entire racial domain of
American Negro slavery was organized around that brutal reality.
Walker came close, in fact, to advancing a Marxian labor theory of
value, as he linked blacks' labor power exploitation to whites' capital accumulation. Second, Walker argued that while black Americans may be
of African descent, their future destiny was in the United States. He explicitly rejected the schemes of groups like the American Colonization
Society, which favored the return of free blacks to West Africa. Most important, however, "David Walker's Appeal" confidently declares that
"America is more our country, than it is the whites'." This bold claim was
based on two centuries of collective sweat equity: "The greatest riches—
in all America have arisen from our blood and tears." In today's language, Walker made a convincing case for black reparations, but on the
basis of being an American, not as an African who happened to live in
America. The "Appeal" implies a bold vision of American democracy
that is fully pluralistic rather than racially monochromatic.

The racial totalitarianism of American Negro slavery made it difficult
for blacks to initiate effective protests against the regime. In the South,
the majority of slaves engaged in what historians have termed "day-to-
day resistance"—the destruction of equipment, farm animals, and food
supplies, work slowdowns, and other forms of disruption short of violence. Some slaves successfully ran away from their owners' farms or
plantations for weeks or months, establishing "maroons," runaway slave
communities. Tens of thousands of slaves managed to escape to the
North, with many relocating to Canada. In several hundred cases, desperate slaves decided that their only course of action was outright rebel-

lion. We know today the names of the most famous race rebels: Gabriel Prosser, Denmark Vessey, Nat Turner. The political focus of northern blacks was to build broader support for the goal of complete abolition, to provide material support and protection to runaway slaves, and to fight for greater civil and political rights as Americans.

It was at this moment that two distinct, yet overlapping political approaches or strategies to the problematic of white domination and black oppression were advanced. In my collaborative research with anthropologist Leith Mullings, we have described these as "inclusion," or integration, versus "autonomy," or black nationalism. These two tendencies were personified by the great abolitionists Frederick Douglass and Martin R. Delany. Douglass, born a slave in Maryland in 1818, escaped from slavery at the age of twenty and quickly emerged as a major orator and leader of the antislavery crusade. Douglass's *Narrative of the Life of Frederick Douglass* (1845) was a powerful statement of human triumph and dignity over oppression. Delany, born six years before Douglass in Virginia, of Mandingo and Gullah descent, established himself as a physician, journalist, publisher, military officer, and politician. Delany's chief work, *The Condition, Elevation, Emigration, and Destiny of the Colored People of the United States, Politically Considered* (1852), over time has come to be identified as the premier theoretical statement for black nationalism. The general interpretation of the two men is that Douglass favored the complete cultural and social integration of black people into every institution of American life, whereas Delany sharply rejected the possibility of blacks being assimilated into white society. Douglass advocated the eradication not only of slavery but of all legal restrictions and barriers that perpetuated substandard treatment of blacks. Delany, by contrast, pursued the ultimate goal of relocating African Americans outside the continental United States, first looking to Central America and the Caribbean as the most promising sites of relocation, then finally settling on West African emigration as the final solution to America's racial crisis.

Although I have used the terms "integration" and "black nationalism" frequently in my own writings and research for nearly thirty years, I have never been satisfied with them as ideological labels. It is certainly true that Douglass was a bitter opponent of all back-to-Africa proposals; that he advocated full racial integration in schools and public accommodations; and that he personally embraced racial intermarriage (much to the anger and alienation of his children by his first wife). But the key issue to Douglass, I believe, was not cultural assimilation, or a multiracial fusion breaking across rigid sexual and social taboos established by white supremacy. Douglass's primary objective was actually political, or "state-based": the complete incorporation of the African American as a citizen of the United States, a full partner in the American social contract subject to all of the concomitant rights and responsibilities that are part of citizenship, such as the elective franchise. Racial assimilation was secondary, at best, to this process. Strategically, after the Civil War Douglass became the champion of black political participation through the Republican Party and advocated other liberal reforms, such as women's suffrage and the development of labor unions. It was through protracted democratic struggles within the American state, Douglass recognized, that Negroes could ultimately win the power to become part of the institutional apparatuses, political culture, and civil society of the United States. Racial integration, in itself, was only a useful tool for achieving this larger objective. Far more important to Douglass was the effort to make white Americans understand and acknowledge that black people were "more American" than they themselves were; that black folk possessed, through generations of pain and struggle, a deeper, clearer understanding of the democratic ideal than Jefferson or any of the other Founding Fathers.

Douglass's "state-based" approach conflicted in several ways with Delany's essentialist, "race-based" strategy. Delany's political perspective starts not from the confines of America's political system, but from the black world—Africa and the entire black diaspora. Delany agreed with Douglass that slavery had to be destroyed and that black men must win the right to vote and hold elective office. But he seriously doubted that most white people, even the liberal abolitionists and suffragists, had the capacity to recognize the humanity of people of African descent. Blacks might become formal citizens, but they would never be incorporated fully into white civil society and its institutions. Therefore, it made complete sense to Delany to aggressively pursue all efforts to build black organizational and infrastructural capacity—i.e., black power—because it was only through such means that white, race-based institutions could be forced to concede resources and privileges. Delany held out little hope that whites could be persuaded by moral appeals or arguments about fairness. Race itself had to be used as a site for black capacity-building and collective resistance.

The characterization of the Douglass-Delany debate as a conflict between state-based and race-based strategies of black empowerment also helps to clarify many important conflicts that occurred during and after the Reconstruction period. The vast majority of African-American elected officials during Reconstruction never called for the general expropriation of lands from the former slaveholding class. They frequently restored businesses and presidential properties to the ex-Confederates. They believed, however, that democratic government should be actively used to carry out internal improvements (roads, railroads, canals) and social development (health, education, housing) and to preserve civil rights and individual liberties. For them, the issue was not "integration" versus "racial separatism." The central question was whether and how the African-American people could be fully incorporated into civil and political society, participating fairly in the economic life of the nation, while preserving their own unique cultural and racial heritage that had been historically constructed during more than two centuries of chattel enslavement. It was, after all, only through governmental action that the transatlantic slave trade had been suppressed, the Confederacy defeated, and the right of black male suffrage won. Black leadership certainly believed in the marketplace, entrepreneurship, and the sanctity of private property, but it also knew that capitalism would never sacrifice its profits for the protection of black people's rights. It was chiefly through reforms within the state, and the art of politics, that black people would eventually win their full freedom.

Black people, both slaves and free women and men, actively participated in their successful struggle for freedom during the Civil War. More than 180,000 African Americans joined the Union army, and 38,000 were killed in the conflict. For several decades after the Civil War, hundreds of thousands of black men voted, electing hundreds of African Americans into state legislatures and Congress. But with the Compromise of 1877 and the withdrawal of federal troops from the South, a new racial domain soon consolidated itself across the region—Jim Crow segregation. Certain victories that had been won during Reconstruction still remained: African Americans were no longer described or defined by law as someone else's property, as they had been under slavery. And under the Jim Crow system, in most southern cities there was no extreme pattern of residential segregation—that is, the concentration of neighborhoods exclusively inhabited by members of one racialized ethnic group. However, the racial hierarchy was maintained by other means: the political disfranchisement of black males, the inability to run for public office, the imposition of local and state laws requiring the rigid separation of the races in schools and all types of public accommodation, and the erosion of basic constitutional rights such as the freedom of speech and public assembly. Behind and reinforcing this structure of white supremacy and black subordination was the reality of mass violence and terror. In rural areas, social control of the black population occurred primarily through a brutal control of labor by means of sharecropping, debt peonage, and the widespread use of convict labor. Lynching was also an essential feature in the social exploitation of African Americans across the region. Between 1882 and 1927, an estimated 3,513 African Americans were lynched, about 95 percent of whom were in the South.

As with slavery, whiteness and blackness still defined the social hierarchy of the South. But the essential defining factor of racial domination was no longer primarily economic, but political. African-American entrepreneurs soon learned to use racial segregation as a barrier permitting the construction of black producer and consumer markets. Blacks established banks, schools, and dozens of all-black towns in the rural South, and within two generations after slavery ended had acquired more than 15 million acres of land. Booker T. Washington, the famous Negro educator and founder of Tuskegee Institute, was the principal spokesman for this emerging black entrepreneurship. But there was always a crude racial ceiling imposed on black upward mobility across the region by the Jim Crow system.

Describing race relations in the South in the 1940s, Gunnar Myrdal observed that the Negro's "name is the antonym of white. As the color white is associated with everything good, with Christ and the angels, with heaven, fairness, cleanliness, virtue, intelligence, courage, progress, so black has, through the ages, carried associations with all that is bad and low. . . . The Negro is believed to be stupid, immoral, diseased, lazy, incompetent, and dangerous—*dangerous* to the white man's virtue and social order." The racial hierarchy was most clearly and unambiguously expressed, as it also had been under the slavery regime, in the South's legal system. Writing in 1941, sociologists Allison Davis, Burleigh Gardner, and Mary Gardner observed that the southern "Negro is, from the very beginning, in a position subordinate to both the police and the court. . . . There are no Negro officers, judges, lawyers, or jurymen. The only role a Negro can take is that of defendant or witness, except in a few types of civil cases. Furthermore, the Negro has no part in making the laws which the court system enforces. As a defendant, he faces the white man's court. . . . The law is white."

The white supremacist regime under the racial domain of Jim Crow segregation was totalitarian in the purest sense of this political term. Its cruel logic embraced all aspects of human interaction. The new racial domain was even in some respects more repressive than slavery in an existential way, because at least when black people were viewed by whites as their property they merited some consideration for their potential market value. A slave owner who had invested $1,000 to buy a prime field hand could only receive a decent return on his investment if the slave worked hard and steadily for at least seven years. But in this new racial universe, blacks as a group were deemed to have no value, and a grotesque system of racial discrimination evolved in the South. As historian Paul Gaston wrote,

Racial discrimination, in its historic sense, meant that black people, not individually but as a race, could not:

- Attend schools attended by white people;
- Attend schools equal to those of white people;

- Drink from the same water fountains, relieve themselves in the same toilets, or wash their hands in the same basins used by white people;
- Eat in the same restaurants as white people;
- Sleep in the same motels and hotels; swim at the same pools and beaches as white people;
- Sit next to white people in lecture halls, concerts, or other public auditoriums;
- Sit next to white people on buses or streetcars or other means of public transportation;
- Be born or treated in the same hospitals or buried in the same graveyards as white people;
- Vote or hold public office;
- Expect to live in the same neighborhoods, hold the same jobs, or attain the same standards of living as white people.

This American version of apartheid, reinforced through terror and lynching, produced among the great majority of whites an unquestioned conviction in the inhumanity of blackness. As Gaston put it, "The values and beliefs of the white supremacy culture . . . included the belief that black people, not individually but as a race, were genetically inferior to white people and that this genetic deficiency was responsible for the fact that black people were: less intelligent than white people; more prone to crime than white people; diseased; unclean; untruthful; unreliable; immoral; violent; sexually promiscuous; and sexually threatening, through their men, to white women."

C. Vann Woodward, Louis R. Harlan, and many other southern historians have frequently noted another cultural dimension of the Jim Crow regime: the deliberate rewriting of the public memory. As in Nazi Germany and apartheid South Africa, white supremacy could only be justified by creating a fictive history of race relations. It was not sufficient merely to claim that blacks were incompetent; it had to be shown that blacks had always been excluded from certain categories of employment, that they had never achieved certain levels of academic excellence or professional success, that they were physically and intellectually so inferior that they were responsible for their own degradation. For example, blacks participated in professional baseball and collegiate sports in the late nineteenth century, and blacks even dominated in certain types of sports, such as cycling and horse racing. The cast iron black jockeys that still today grace the front lawns of thousands of estates and affluent mansions across the South are no fluke or aberration of history. Black jockeys had dominated horse racing in the 1870s and 1880s. By 1900, however, most black jockeys were eliminated from horse-racing competition, and by 1950, whites believed that they had never existed. Most white Americans (and the majority of African Americans, sadly) believe that Jackie Robinson, who signed a contract with the Brooklyn Dodgers in 1947, was the first Negro to play in professional baseball. That same rewriting of public memory occurred in virtually every occupation. Large numbers of blacks, for example, were employed in the southern textile industry in 1900, but within forty years black textile workers virtually disappeared. According to the 1940 Census, white males were almost twenty times more likely than black men to be employed as factory foremen in the South. They were seven times more likely to be physicians, five times more likely to be machinists, and three times more likely to be employed as plumbers. Moreover, southern blacks were virtually nonexistent in white-collar occupations, regardless of their education and training. Clerical positions, sales personnel, telephone operators, and office managers were almost always white. Conversely, black men in the South in 1940 were more than six times more likely than white men to be laborers, more than five times more likely to be service workers, and more than forty times more likely to be employed in domestic services.

In the northern states, by the first half of the twentieth century a third racial domain evolved into a strikingly different pattern of white hegemony and black oppression. The percentage of blacks living in the South fell from 89 percent in 1910 to 53 percent in 1970 as millions migrated to the Northeast and Midwest to escape Jim Crow and acquire a better standard of life. During the same period, the proportion of African Americans living in urban areas rose from 27 percent to 81 percent. Blacks again encountered racial segregation in the North, but of a much milder variety. Blacks were usually permitted to vote, to serve on juries, and to exercise their constitutional rights. They were not barred from state-funded universities and professional schools, although in some states these institutions were segregated. Patterns of exclusion at restaurants and hotels existed but were not uniform. There was a deep pattern of employment discrimination, with many unions refusing to extend membership to African Americans, and many employers drawing the color line, especially in professional and managerial positions. But the central defining factor of northern racial formation was the near-universal pattern of residential segregation.

As documented by sociologists Douglas S. Massey and Nancy A. Denton in *American Apartheid,* the American ghetto was first constructed primarily in the North. Restrictive covenants, widespread racial discrimination by banks and financial lending institutions, and even the loan policies by the Federal Housing Administration and the Veterans Administration led to an extreme concentration of racialized minorities in most U.S. cities. Between 1950 and 1970, the percentage of African Americans more than doubled in most major urban areas—going from 18 percent to 34 percent in Philadelphia, from 16 percent to 44 percent in Detroit, and from 14 percent to 33 percent in Chicago. Usually, 80 percent to 90 percent of all blacks living in any city resided in virtually all-black neighborhoods.

The construction of the modern northern ghetto created some benefits but also generated many more liabilities for urban African Americans. The super-concentration of blacks in specific geographical districts made it easier to elect African Americans to local and national offices. It is not surprising, for example, that Chicago, the first major city to elect an African American to Congress, Oscar DePriest in 1928, had by far the most extensive pattern of residential segregation in the country. Ghettoization also created the social and cultural context for race-based protest institutions, and to a limited extent, ethnically oriented consumer markets, which served as the basis for minority entrepreneurship in the North just as they had in the South.

The downside to ghettoization, however, was devastating. Extreme concentrations of poverty created a series of vast social problems, including rampant crime and violence, the undermining of civic institutions of all kinds, and growing social alienation among youth. As middle-class outmigration increased, many businesses relocated outside of the central city or simply shut down. The quality of urban schools rapidly deteriorated as the tax base to support public education declined. As Massey and Denton observed, "Barriers to spatial mobility are barriers to social mobility, and by confining blacks to a small set of relatively disadvantaged neighborhoods, segregation constitutes a very powerful impediment to black socioeconomic progress. . . . The segregation of American blacks was no historical accident; it was brought about by actions and practices that had the passive acceptance, if not the active support, of most whites in the United States."

For over a century, the Black Freedom Movement was confronted with the two parallel regimes of racial domination that existed in the North and the South. As in the struggle against slavery, the black community continually devised a wide variety of protest activities and tactics of collective empowerment: for example, consumer boycott campaigns aimed against businesses that refused to hire African Americans; spontaneous urban rebellions and the destruction of white-owned property in black neighborhoods; voter-registration and education campaigns to mobilize the African-American electorate; emphasis on educational reforms and mass literacy efforts to enhance the ability of blacks to compete more effectively for jobs; the construction of political alliances and coalitions with non-black constituencies to influence public policy decisions and the actions of other white-dominated institutions. Despite this incredible diversity in the history of black collective struggles, there were three major strategies that were employed to confront the omnipresent reality of white institutional power.

The "mainstream" approach to black political capacity-building was the strategy of state-based social change, which was first espoused by Douglass. Frequently termed "integrationism," this political approach emphasized the deep American identity of the black community. African Americans had, after all, fought in all of America's wars, and they had made enormous social and economic contributions to the nation's welfare. Blacks believed in the Constitution and the inherent fairness of democratic institutions. Therefore, according to this argument, it only was reasonable to accept blacks as being full civil partners in the construction of the American nation. All structural barriers impeding the free and fair access by African Americans to economic development, political decision making, and individual advancement should be eliminated. The logical path to achieving these objectives was through political action, broadly defined: the use of lawsuits to challenge segregation laws in schools, public accommodations, and residential codes; the fight to remove all restrictions on black electoral political participation; and the establishment of pragmatic coalitions with sympathetic white political organizations and powerful interest groups to shift racial policies and practices toward black interests. Embedded in this strategic approach to racial advancement was the unquestioned belief that the American state could indeed be lifted from its historical foundations of structural racism. Incremental legal and political victories, over time, would lead to qualitative changes in the American state apparatus. In other words, the state could be deracialized through political activism.

These key assumptions formed the basis for the practical politics of the black middle class for several generations. They are all found, for example, in the 1905 program of the Niagara Movement, a group of liberal black intellectuals and professionals led by W.E.B. Du Bois. The Niagara Movement's agenda called on Congress to enforce the Constitution and demanded "upright judges in courts, juries selected without discrimination on account of color and the same measure of punishment and the same efforts at reformation for blacks as for white offenders." On the issue of electoral political participation, the Niagara Movement urged Negroes to "protest emphatically and continually against the curtailment of their political rights. We believe in manhood suffrage; we believe that no man is so good, intelligent or wealthy as to be entrusted wholly with the welfare of his neighbor." And on the issue of Jim Crow, there could be no compromise: "Any discrimination based simply on race or color is barbarous, we care not how hallowed it be by custom, expediency or prejudice . . . discriminations based simply and solely on physical peculiarities, place of birth, color of skin, are relics of that unreasoning human savagery of which the world is and ought to be thoroughly ashamed."

The same strategic approach for achieving black freedom through the implementation of meaningful reforms within America's democratic institutions can be heard in Martin Luther King, Jr.'s, famous "I Have a Dream" speech delivered before an audience of 250,000 civil-rights protesters at the August 28, 1963, March on Washington. King's speech presented the struggle for racial desegregation as the fulfillment of America's democratic creed: "When the architects of our republic wrote the magnificent words of the Constitution and the Declaration of Independence, they were signing a promissory note to which every American was to fall heir. The note was a promise that all men would be guaranteed the unalienable rights of life, liberty and the pursuit of happiness." Martin's greatest political aspiration, his "dream," was not race-based; it was "a dream deeply rooted in the American dream." It was the belief that through legal and political reforms, "We will be able to transform the jangling discords of our nation into a beautiful symphony of brotherhood."

Throughout the twentieth century, African Americans and their political allies within the white community waged a protracted campaign to uproot both domains of racial inequality. In the 1950s in the Deep South, the Black Freedom Movement took the form of nonviolent civil disobedience against the restrictions of Jim Crow. Although its most prominent spokespersons, such as King, were middle class, the vast majority of local leaders and grassroots activists were working class and poor people, and many were women. The Civil Rights Act of 1964 finally outlawed racial segregation in public accommodations throughout the nation, and the Voting Rights Act the following year permitted millions of southern blacks to vote for the first time in their lives. Although racial segregation persisted in private institutions, such as country clubs and fraternal associations, the formal, legal framework for Jim Crow was finally destroyed.

Organized efforts to dismantle structural racism outside of the South, however, proved to be more difficult than civil-rights activists had anticipated. Northern white liberals didn't object to Negroes gaining the right to vote or eating in restaurants, so long as they didn't move next door. The backlash began in "the bastion of California liberalism," Berkeley, in early 1963, when a referendum on a local ordinance banning racial discrimination in all real-estate sales and rentals was defeated with an 83 percent voter turnout. The next year, California voters approved Proposition 14, which proposed to amend the state constitution "to guarantee a home owner's right to sell only to whom he or she wished to sell," by a two-to-one margin. That same year, Detroit voters approved a "Home Owners' Rights Ordinance" that was designed to maintain that city's pattern of residential segregation. When Martin Luther King, Jr., moved the focus of the desegregation struggle from the Deep South to Chicago, emphasizing employment opportunities and fair housing for Negroes, he encountered fierce resistance from the members of white ethnic groups. Thousands of white men, women, and children hurled rocks, bottles, and even knives at unarmed, nonviolent demonstrators. King was so shaken that he later admitted, "I have never seen such hostility and hatred anywhere in my life, even in Selma." Despite the passage of the 1968 Fair Housing Act, blacks of all social classes found themselves increasingly socially isolated from the rest of society. This pattern of residential exclusion was strikingly different from the experience of Asian Americans and Latinos, who could for the most part escape residential segregation by enhancing their income and socioeconomic status. In other words, as education, occupation, and income increase, Latino and Asian-American segregation sharply falls, whereas "only blacks experience a pattern of constant, high segregation that is impervious to socioeconomic influences."

Although the struggles against legal segregation in the South and against residential segregation throughout the rest of the United States defined the mainstream impulse of the Black Freedom Movement, there were other political orientations within the African-American community calling for different tactics and strategies for challenging the system. The integrationists, or advocates of state-based initiatives, relied heavily on the courts as well as on the legislative and executive branches of government to guarantee blacks' constitutional rights and to overturn de jure and de facto patterns of discrimination. That very reliance on white authorities to "do the right thing" on racial policies made many blacks uneasy. The major alternative approach, represented by black nationalists, can be understood as a "race-based" strategy. The nationalists started with the pessimistic (or perhaps realistic) assumption that racism was not an accidental or secondary element in the construction of U.S. society. White racism was no aberration or mistake within the structure of state power. Blacks were merely fooling themselves if they believed that whites as a group would voluntarily surrender part of their power to a people whom they had viciously oppressed for hundreds of years. The proponents of this race-based perspective argued that black people may be "Americans" by birth or citizenship, but that they would never be fully accepted as such and would only continue to be marginalized, socially isolated, and victimized. The only solution, therefore, was to construct strong black-owned and black-operated institutions that could provide goods and services to African Americans. Black producers and consumers should work cooperatively with each other to increase black capital formation and to create jobs. Blacks should construct their own political institutions, which could then negotiate effectively with white interests, even manipulating fissures within the white establishment to gain certain advantages for African Americans. Blacks were an African people, and their cultural rituals, symbols, and traditions should reflect that rich heritage.

With significant variations, this essentially has been the race-based political thesis in black America since Martin R. Delany, 150 years ago, first articulated it. If one reads Marcus Garvey's 1925 manifesto, "An Appeal to the Conscience of the Black Race to See Itself," one finds the same political argument of "race first": "The Negro will have to build his own government, industry, art, science, literature and culture, before the world will stop to consider him. Until then, we are but wards of a superior race and civilization, and the outcasts of a standard social system." A similar thesis was put forward forty years later by Malcolm X, in his famous speech, "The Ballot or the Bullet":

All of us have suffered here, in this country, political oppression at the hands of the white man, economic exploitation at the hands of the white man, and social degradation at the hands of the white man. Now in speaking like this, it doesn't mean that we're anti-white, but it does mean we're anti-exploitation, we're anti-degradation, we're anti-oppression. . . . No, I'm not an American. I'm one of the twenty-two million black people who are the victims of democracy, nothing but disguised hypocrisy. So, I'm not standing here speaking to you as an American. . . . I'm speaking as a victim of this American system. And I see America through the eyes of the victim. I don't see any American dream; I see an American nightmare.

Malcolm X and Martin R. Delany were not alone in this view. The race-based approach to black empowerment has been represented for over a century by a strong tradition of African-American activism: Henry McNeal Turner, an African Methodist Episcopal Church minister, Georgia state legislator during Reconstruction, and founder and first president of Morris Brown College of Atlanta; Alexander Crummell, an Episcopal priest, proponent of African emigration, and cofounder of the American Negro Academy in 1897; Hubert H. Harrison, an early black leader of the Socialist Party who had been born in St. Croix in the Danish Virgin Islands and had migrated to the United States, and who later served as editor of Garvey's *Negro World* newspaper; Elijah Muhammad, leader of the Nation of Islam (NOI) and "Messenger of Allah," who preached strict racial separation and the establishment of a separate, all-black state; Stokely Carmicheal, the Trinidad-born leader of the Student Nonviolent Coordinating Committee in the mid-1960s and a charismatic proponent of "Black Power"; Maulana Karenga, a black cultural nationalist theoretician and creator of the black cultural rituals of Kwanzaa; Molefi Asante, a prolific scholar and the originator of Afrocentricity, a black-nationalist approach to philosophy and social analysis; and Minister Louis Farrakhan, the controversial leader of the Nation of Islam during the past quarter-century and the initiator of the October 1995 Million Man March, the largest mass demonstration of African Americans in U.S. history. These leaders and the institutions they established were critically important for the survival of the African-American people. Their critics might suggest correctly that simplistic race-based politics never received strong support from the majority of both black middle-class professionals and black trade unionists; that black nationalism has usually

expressed itself in gender politics that are deeply male chauvinistic, oppressive, and homophobic; and that its overemphasis on Africa-centered
concepts of social reality ignored how profoundly "American" black
Americans have become in their group psychology, cultural and social
norms, and material expectations. The clear majority of African Americans have implicitly understood that if they embraced a political strategy
of racial essentialism, of "us against them," that their movement would
run into a dead end.

With the rise of working-class mass organizations and the socialist
movement of the late nineteenth century, a third approach to the struggle against structural racism in the United States emerged within the
black community: class-based politics. One of the earliest proponents of
a class analysis was the brilliant journalist and editor T. Thomas Fortune,
author of *Black and White: Land, Labor and Politics in the South*, first published in 1884. Fortune argued, "Everywhere labor and capital are in
deadly conflict. . . . Indeed the wall of industrial discontent encircles the
civilized globe. The iniquity of privileged class and concentrated wealth
has become so glaring and grievous to be borne that a thorough agitation and an early readjustment of the relation which they sustain to labor can no longer be delayed." For Fortune, racial discrimination was
secondary to the more fundamental contradiction of class inequality.

As in the case of race-based, black nationalism, class-based, or "transformationist," politics was predicated on a distinct set of presumptions
about the relationship between race, capital, and state power. The proponents of class-based politics argued that "race" was neither biologically
nor genetically based, and that in practical, material terms, the poor and
working classes, despite their racial and ethnic differences, had much in
common. They argued that the political and business elites manipulated
racial fears to divide working people's organizations and movements.
Therefore, the true goal of the Black Freedom Movement should not be
the achievement of "black faces in high places," or symbolic racial representation within the existing institutional arrangements of power. Racial
discrimination had come about from the expansion of European capitalism into the Western hemisphere and the coerced migration of millions
of enslaved Africans across the Atlantic. Given the brutal history of capi-

talism, the class-based activists and theorists argued, racial discrimination cannot be eliminated until the exploitation of working people ends and the democratic reorganization of resources and property is actually put into effect. In short, race matters, but class is prefiguration in the evolution of human societies based on class hierarchy.

The transformationist, class-based tradition in the Black Freedom Movement also has an extraordinary leadership tradition. Just a short list would include: Cyril V. Briggs, founder in 1921 of the African Blood Brotherhood, and an early black leader of the U.S. Communist Party; Claude McKay, brilliant Jamaican writer and author of the fiery 1919 protest poem, "If We Must Die," which so outraged conservative Massachusetts Senator Henry Cabot Lodge that he read it into the Congressional Record as an example of black "bolshevism"; Hosea Hudson, steel worker and Communist organizer of black southern workers during the Great Depression; Claudia Jones, a Trinidadian who became national chair of the Young Communist League in the United States at the age of twenty-five, a fighter for women's rights and racial equality who was expelled from this country in 1951 for the "crime" of advocating Marxism; Paul Robeson, an all-American athlete, lawyer, scholar, and the most prominent black singer and actor in the world in the 1930s and 1940s, who had his passport illegally seized by the State Department for advocating peaceful coexistence with the Soviet Union; Huey P. Newton, Bobby Seale, and the other young militants who founded the Black Panther Party in October 1966; Angela Y. Davis, a brilliant feminist scholar and Marxist who was placed on the FBI's "Ten Most Wanted List" for her political activities, but was released from prison after a mass movement demanding her freedom achieved international prominence; and the generation of black radical intellectuals of the 1980s and 1990s, which included Cornel West, bell hooks, Gerald Horne, Adolph Reed, Audre Lorde, Cathy Cohen, Charles Ogletree, Patricia Williams, Kimberlé Crenshaw, Robin D.G. Kelley, and Leith Patricia Mullings.

These activists were dedicated to the transformation of the total structure—political economy, social institutions, civil society, and cultural values—of the entire American society. The difficulties in this strategic approach, however, were many. The white working class has a terribly long history of thinking and acting like "white people" instead of "workers." Class solidarity has periodically expressed itself in the American proletariat, but the "wages of whiteness," the privileges that are bestowed simply by one's racial category, have powerfully affected the white working class. The strategy of class-based politics probably underestimates the psychological and cultural foundations of white supremacist behavior and practices. Black radicals, like the state-based, integrationist reformers, have assumed that the achievement of institutional change would produce a "new" kind of white American, a citizen who would judge others "not by the color of their skin but by the content of their character," as King hopefully declared in his 1963 March on Washington address. The terrible and tragic difficulty with this idealistic approach is that the American state itself was constructed, as I have attempted to illustrate, on a racial foundation. Apartheid-like categories for who qualified as a potential citizen and who did not became the legal template for our political and civic relations today. Perhaps the benefits and privileges—material, political, psychological—of whiteness are so overwhelming and ingrained that a class-based project grounded in a belief that "race" really doesn't exist cannot change American society or its institutions for many more years.

Each of these three strategic approaches had in common a deep humanistic belief in African Americans as a people—their courage in the face of oppression, their music, laughter, and poetry in the depths of their despair, their capacity constantly to rebuild their institutions, to inspire new generations to resist, to sacrifice their individual interests to achieve what was best for the entire community. Blackness was, in this sense, a site of personal and collective validation, a place of pride and hope, an attitude of defiance. Although these were different strategies for black empowerment, they all shared the subaltern view of American history: that the national narrative of inevitable progress, individual liberty, expanding opportunity, and equality under the law had never been achieved, even in part, by African Americans. At a Yale University lecture in 1951, W.E.B. Du Bois spoke to this sense of racial stigmatization and exclusion felt by every African American. "Negroes are not fond of posing before the world as step-children and outcasts in their native land,"

Du Bois observed sadly. Through more than 300 years of struggle, he said, black Americans "have progressed but in the name of God never forget the distance they still have to go. And remember that the man who is climbing out of a well would best not waste too much time, celebrating, when first he see light above."

III

Within each successive racial domain in American history, the boundaries of "whiteness" and "blackness" have never been fixed. They have been continually rearticulated and renegotiated as the political economy of American society was transformed successively from agricultural to industrial production, and as civil society and political institutions were increasingly forced to incorporate racialized minorities as participants in democratic life. With the growth of class stratification and the abandonment of the most impoverished and crime-ridden neighborhoods by millions of African-American middle-class and stable working-class households, the boundaries of race were reconfigured again in new ways by the end of the twentieth century. The professional and managerial black middle class experienced unprecedented affluence and growing political access within government and both major political parties. To a certain extent, this new black elite still perceived its interests as being linked to those of the "truly disadvantaged," in the words of William Julius Wilson. The fates or life chances of those who had achieved this level were in many ways still bound by the continuing burden of race. But the decisive manifestations of racism in daily life for college-educated black professionals and the black working poor began increasingly to diverge.

Sociologist Lawrence D. Bobo has argued that the traditional color line in American life has not "vanished," but instead has been "merely reconfigured." Jim Crow segregation has been destroyed, and the nation broadly "endorses the goal of racial integration and equal treatment" under the law. "The death of Jim Crow Racism has left us in an uncomfortable place . . . that I sometimes call a state of Laissez Faire racism," he wrote. Bobo described laissez-faire racism "as the case when society has ideals, but openness to very limited amounts of integration at the personal level remains, there is political stagnation over some types of affirmative action, quite negative stereotypes of racial minorities persist, and a wide gulf in perceptions regarding the importance of racial discrimination remains." Middle-class blacks and Latinos largely accept the national political narrative about the pluralistic promise of American democracy: Through individual initiative and personal responsibility, success and upward mobility are possible, and through the acquisition of wealth and private property, the residual effects of racism can be minimized.

The fundamental problem with this perspective is that laissez-faire racism is *still racism,* albeit less overt and articulated in the race-neutral language of fairness. The continuing existence of racial inequalities that can be measured in social outcomes is not a product of the lack of individual initiative but of deep structural barriers that continue to be maintained through the pervasive power of white privilege. Racial inequality therefore presents itself, in the post–Second Reconstruction era, as a "normal" aspect of the general social fabric of American society. There are always "winners" and "losers" in the competition for resources and power. If African Americans still find themselves at the lower end of society's totem pole, the overwhelming logic of common sense is that they have no one to blame but themselves.

There are two essential categories used by most social scientists to help calculate the socioeconomic status and well-being of any population—wealth and health. Wealth represents the sum total of the vitality of any people's economic life, including wages, the ownership of property, investments, and savings. Health-related statistics, such as overall life expectancy, age-adjusted death rates due to specific diseases, access to quality health services, and infant mortality rates, provide a critical perspective on the quality of life of any group.

Much of the economic literature about disparities between black and white Americans focuses narrowly on wages, household incomes, and unemployment levels. Using those specific categories, the distance separating African Americans and whites doesn't appear to be too bad. In the period of the Second Reconstruction, from 1954 to 1970, there was a substantial narrowing of the economic gap between blacks and whites.

Progress came to a halt during much of the next two decades. By 1999 the median weekly earnings of African Americans, at $387, was about three-fourths that of whites. The median family income, adjusted for family size in constant 1999 dollars, in 1973 was $47,579 for white families, $28,428 for Hispanics, and $24,112 for African Americans, which was roughly 51 percent of the white family's income. By 1992, the income ratios had stayed about the same, with the median family incomes standing at $54,226 for whites, $27,353 for Hispanics, and $27,416 for blacks. The mid-to-late 1990s, however, finally witnessed real-income growth rates for many minority households. Black median family incomes grew 36 percent in seven years, reaching $35,999 in 1999, about 59 percent of the white median income of $61,284. The Hispanic median income rose only slightly, to $31,062. The recent lag in Hispanic family income can be explained largely by the growth of Latino immigration in recent decades. In 1999, approximately 43 percent of Latinos in the United States had been born outside of the country. The Latino families whose chief income-earner had been born in the United States had median incomes exceeding $38,000, several thousand dollars more than the African-Americans. Latino immigrant families, by contrast, earned a median family income of less than $28,000 in 1999.

Similar trends can be seen in U.S. poverty rates over the past three decades. In 1970, more than one out of three African Americans lived in poverty, 35 percent, compared to one-quarter of all Hispanics and only 9 percent of white Americans. For twenty years, these statistics remained static. With the economic growth during the 1990s, poverty rates for all racial groups declined, particularly for African Americans. By 1999, poverty rates had fallen to 7 percent for whites, 20 percent for Hispanics, and 21 percent for black Americans. Few observers noted, however, that this relatively good economic news for blacks and Latinos still left them at poverty levels white America had not experienced since the Great Depression of the 1930s.

The relatively modest gains for blacks measured by income statistics and poverty rates obscured other real problems. There were, first of all, disturbing indications that millions of racialized minorities had fallen completely out of the formal labor market, and that the U.S. government's official unemployment statistics were increasingly at odds with the actual economic realities of daily life in America's ghettoes and barrios. In the mid-1960s, for example, African-American labor-force participation rates roughly paralleled those for whites. In 1970, among adult males aged twenty-five to fifty-four, 92 percent of all whites and 85 percent of all blacks and Hispanics held jobs. By 1992, white and Hispanic employment rates had declined by about 10 percent, but for African Americans the drop was almost 20 percent. Sociologists such as William Julius Wilson began to observe that white employers had become increasingly reluctant to hire African-American males. White employers in urban areas frequently advertised only in white ethnic and neighborhood publications, and almost never in black-owned newspapers. White employers who were worried about following equal-opportunity guidelines would make half-hearted gestures to recruit employees from black communities, but African-American applicants frequently found that they were not taken seriously as credible job candidates.

For example, in 1998, in testimony before President Bill Clinton's Race Initiative, Claudia Withers, executive director of the Fair Employment Council of Greater Washington, described employment discrimination as a chronic problem. Withers's Employment Council tested for racial discrimination by sending out white and minority "testers" for job interviews. Although the testers had virtually identical resumes and were equally qualified, 20 to 25 percent of the time minorities were "treated less well," Withers stated. Blacks and Latinos were often "not called back for interviews." When they were invited back, they "were offered lesser jobs at lower pay than their white counterparts, who on paper had identical credentials." At the same hearing, economist Harry J. Holzer testified, "It is clear that American employers are more reluctant to hire blacks than any other group." According to William Julius Wilson, "Black inner-city applicants are never given the chance to prove their qualifications on an individual level because they are systematically screened out by the selective recruitment process." The social consequences for African Americans are devastating. "Inner-city black men" in particular, Wilson observed, "grow bitter and resentful in their harsh, often dehumanizing, low-wage work settings."

Statistics about median family income and unemployment levels tell us relatively little about the amount of real wealth a household owns. Economist Henry S. Terrell observed that wealth accumulation in general depends on at least five key factors: "(1) the size of the stream of past income, (2) the rate of savings out of this past income stream, (3) the length of time of accumulation, (4) the rate at which accumulated wealth compounds itself, and (5) any influences of inherited wealth." Thirty years ago, Terrell noted, the empirical literature was "rather convincing that black families tend to save more out of given observed income than white families. This observation *alone* would suggest that black families at similar levels of income ought to have more wealth than whites." Clearly, however, that's not the case. In 1970, the typical black family held $4,384, or about 10 percent of its total wealth, in financial assets. This amount was only 6 percent of the total amount of accumulated wealth of the average white family. At the end of the 1990s, the wealth disparity between black and white households was still enormous. The President's Race Initiative found that black families owned, on average, one-tenth of the wealth that white families owned. One-third of all black households actually have a *negative* net wealth.

What are the factors that retard black capital formation? In September 1999, Freddie Mac, a federally chartered agency that provides capital for mortgage lending, released a comprehensive national study that found, not surprisingly, rampant discrimination in access to credit and capital. The study discovered that whites earning less than $25,000 were given better credit histories than middle-class African Americans earning between $65,000 and $75,000 annually. For middle-class Americans earning between $45,000 and $65,000, 48 percent of the African Americans had bad credit, compared to only 21.6 percent for whites, 28 percent for Hispanics, and 15.7 percent for Asian Americans.

Credit ratings in the United States generally reflect the history of accumulated class inequality and racial disadvantage. Higher unemployment rates and lower wages usually mean that black people are much more likely than whites to fall behind on their credit-card bills and mortgage payments. Whites who lose their jobs usually have ample resources to fall back on, such as the equity in their homes, family savings, stocks, and other investments. The single greatest source of wealth American families have is represented by their home. More than 67 percent of whites own their homes, compared to 45 percent of all African-American households. Poverty is also a drain on the accumulation of wealth. Only 7 percent of all white households are below the poverty level today, which means that most whites experiencing financial trouble have relatives to tide them over and middle-class friends to connect them to new job opportunities. Almost one-third of all African Americans today live in single-parent families, compared to 16 percent of Hispanics and 7 percent of whites. The large number of single-parent households, combined with chronically higher jobless rates, means that middle-class African Americans are frequently responsible for providing significant financial support to significantly larger numbers of individuals—their children, parents, distant relatives, neighbors, and fictive kin. The economics of day-to-day survival always trumps the economics of wealth accumulation.

In April 2000, the staff of New York Senator Charles Schumer released a study that found that most banks largely ignored African-American neighborhoods, even those with above-average incomes, forcing many blacks to depend on "high cost and often abusive lenders." The study reviewed nearly 240,000 home loan applications that had been made in New York City in 1998. The survey showed that African Americans in New York City were denied loan applications by banks at almost twice the rate of whites, even when they had identical incomes. The actual rejection rate was 21.6 percent for African Americans, compared to only 11.4 percent for whites. But what's even more striking was that even African Americans earning more than $60,000 annually had a higher rejection rate (20 percent) than whites earning less than $40,000 (17 percent). In order to buy homes, the majority of black New Yorkers are forced to turn to so-called "subprime lenders," financial firms that loan mortgage money at exorbitantly high interest rates. Such companies routinely force tens of thousands of homeowners into bankruptcy and foreclosure. Only 9 percent of all mortgage loans in the white areas of New York City are provided by those subprime companies; in black neighborhoods, they supply 55 percent of all home loans.

Occupational segregation also persists at all income levels, and African Americans still frequently find that they are the first fired during periods of economic recession. During the 1990–1991 recession, according to the *Wall Street Journal*, a significant number of major corporations cut blacks' jobs at much higher rates than for white employees. For example, J. P. Morgan, in which blacks represented 16.6 percent of the labor force in 1990, responded to the recession, in part, by relocating its clerical and data-processing operations from New York City to Delaware. Black employees consequently suffered 29.6 percent of the total jobs lost. Coca Cola Enterprises, headquartered in predominantly black Atlanta, had a labor force that was 17.9 percent black in 1990. When the company decided to cut its blue-collar workforce, African Americans were disproportionately hit. Over 42 percent of all Coca Cola employees losing their jobs in 1990–1991 were African American. Sears, a corporation that in 1990 had a black workforce of 15.9 percent, made the decision to shut down its distribution centers in central cities and to reduce its clerical staff. As a result, 54.3 percent of all Sears employees who lost their jobs in the 1990–1991 recession were black, nearly 3.5 times the rate of job loss for whites in the company. Of course, these corporations vigorously contested the suggestion that these actions were in any way "racist." The elimination of jobs in central cities, for example, was done to increase competitiveness and profitability. African-American workers frequently had less job seniority and thus were particularly vulnerable to layoffs. In any case, no clear racial intent could be proven. This is laissez-faire racism at work.

If measures of wealth reflect the glaring fact of continuing discrimination in American life, measures of health only reinforce that picture. And measuring the effects of structural racism on the health of black America starts with a consideration of life expectancy. As long as public health records have been kept in the United States, African Americans consistently have had significantly shorter life spans than white Americans. In 1995, the life expectancy for whites was 76.5 years, but for African Americans it was 69.6. The age-adjusted death rate per 100,000, however, was 466.8 for whites and 738.3 for blacks, 58 percent higher. When compared to white people, African Americans were 6.6 times more likely to become victims of homicide. In 1996, African Americans were 5.8 times more likely to die from AIDS/HIV infection than whites, 2.4 times more likely to die from diabetes mellitus, 2.8 times more likely to die from septicemia, and 1.5 times more likely to die from heart disease. Blacks are consistently over-represented in twelve of the fifteen leading causes of death in the United States. These statistical racial disparities have been so outrageous that even the conservative Reagan administration could not ignore them. In 1985, the Department of Health and Human Services, then under Margaret M. Heckler, issued a report on the Secretary's Task Force on Black and Minority Health. It warned that there was clear danger of creating a permanent "health and health care underclass." Sadly, Heckler's report also "glibly prescribed more healthful diets, life style changes, exercise promotions, and health education to reverse mounting black mortality."

There are some obvious explanations for the health deficits that African Americans experience. About 23 percent of all black Americans lack medical insurance, about twice the percentage for whites. Low-income people, regardless of race, are much less likely to have access to regular medical and dental services. The decline in funding for public hospitals and health clinics is sometimes cited as a factor. HMOs and other managed health-care providers have been frequently accused of providing culturally insensitive care and unequal services to blacks and other racialized minorities. Yet even when racial differences in health outcomes can be documented and made public, the impression is left that such disparities are not a consequence of deliberate racial discrimination. A good example of this was a 2000 survey of 347 pharmacies in New York City conducted by the Mount Sinai School of Medicine, which found that in black and brown neighborhoods only 25 percent of pharmacies carried enough morphine or morphine-like drugs to treat severe pain, whereas in white neighborhoods 72 percent did. Because blacks have higher rates of cancer than whites, there actually should be a greater need for medicines treating severe pain. Some pharmacies have explained away these statistics by suggesting that demand was lower in poor neighborhoods because they had higher proportions of uninsured people who could not afford to fill prescriptions. This sounds like a reasonable explanation. The problem becomes more complicated, however, when we learn that white physicians, according to another study reported in the *New York Times,* are much "less likely to prescribe pain killers for blacks and Latinos with broken bones or post-operative pain."

A surprisingly large number of white physicians have limited contact with black patients. The National Medical Association has observed that "African-American physicians are five times more likely to treat African-American patients and four times more likely to treat poor and underserved patients." One 1999 study published in the *New England Journal of Medicine* indicated that white physicians referred African Americans to medically necessary cardiac workups and treatment only 60 percent as often as they referred white males. Based on an extensive survey of 193 physicians, the researchers found that white doctors tended to perceive African-American patients and poor people generally "more negatively than their white counterparts" and upper-class patients. A patient's socioeconomic status "was associated with physicians' perceptions of patient personality, abilities, behavioral tendencies and role demands." A survey of 600 minority-based health-care studies found that black Americans consistently received "less care and less intensive care than do white counterparts." It noted, "This pattern was found not only for such high technology interventions as coronary artery bypass grafting, advanced cancer treatment, renal transplantation, and hip and knee replacement, but also in basic clinical care such as adequacy of physical examinations, histories and laboratory tests."

Despite this overwhelming evidence, most white Americans are unable or unwilling to acknowledge racial health disparities. According to one 1999 national survey funded by the Kaiser Family Foundation, 61 percent of all whites surveyed believed that "African Americans with heart disease were as likely as their white counterparts to receive specialized medical procedures and surgery." When asked if racial discrimination could be a "major problem" for blacks attempting to receive quality health care, "77 percent of whites responded that it was a minor or nonexistent problem." It seems that the white majority is still incapable of judging black people "not by the color of their skin but by the content of their character"—and recognizing the inequality of their lives.

IV

Throughout the long and difficult experience of black people in the United States, and through all the different systems of structural racism, each domain has had its own peculiar characteristics, but all have maintained and perpetuated the hegemony of white over nonwhite. In each of these racial domains, African Americans and other Americans who opposed the inhumanity of racial inequality fashioned tools of resistance, building new protest organizations and thinking creatively to put forward strategies to challenge the institutions that oppressed them. The concept behind all of this activity was the simple belief in human fairness and dignity, and the effort to destroy the burden of history, their continuing status of the Other in their own country.

Although the features and characteristics of twenty-first-century structural racism have been reconfigured once more in some important ways, the lessons of the racial past should not be forgotten in our own time. Democratic transformation along the contemporary boundaries of color, gender, and class will require new kinds of strategies, new approaches, and new thinking. The only way forward is for us to assist the development of initiatives that have the capacity to educate and mobilize those who suffer most from today's racial oppression. In so doing, we must transcend the earlier paradigms of our racial politics. Through this effort, we may make an important contribution toward the reconfiguration of American democracy itself, which could conceivably, in some distant future, finally include us all.

PART TWO

The Retreat from Equality

Chapter 3

The Politics of Race and
the Limits of Electoral Reform

I feel that someone must remain in the position of nonalignment, so that he can look objectively at both parties and be the conscience of both—not the servant or master of either.

—Martin Luther King, Jr., 1960

I

America's political system was originally designed to restrict democratic decision making to a relatively small elite of white merchants, bankers, and slaveholding plantation owners, excluding the great majority of the country's adult population. Property restrictions and other elitist qualifications even eliminated approximately three-fourths of white male adults from the electorate when the American state was established. The first electoral revolution-from-below, described by historians as "Jacksonian Democracy," significantly expanded the national electorate in the 1820s and 1830s to include the majority of white males. Subsequently, over an extended period of nearly 150 years, women, African Americans, and other racialized ethnic minorities also won the right to vote through a series of difficult and hard fought social-protest movements. At every stage of our political history, the battle to redefine America's democratic project was vigorously opposed by broad sectors of the nation's most powerful elites, who feared that they would lose control of the political process. Reforms came gradually, and almost always, not without tremendous human sacrifices by the most marginalized and disadvantaged groups within our society.

From the end of the Civil War to the beginning of the Great Depression, the overwhelming majority of African Americans considered themselves Republicans. The solid partisan identification was not based on gratitude for the Emancipation but on pragmatic political considerations. On issues affecting race relations, the Republicans had been consistently more liberal than the Democratic Party for many years. Frederick Douglass, the premier spokesperson for the Black Freedom Movement in the nineteenth century, had been a loyal leader of the Republican Party for four decades. Booker T. Washington's Tuskegee Machine in the early twentieth century benefited enormously from the political patronage provided by the Republican administrations of Theodore Roosevelt and William Howard Taft. In a number of municipal elections, such as in Cincinnati and Kansas City, blacks developed pragmatic coalitions with Democratic Party organizations and local bosses in return for patronage positions. Relatively few African Americans, with notable exceptions, such as W.E.B. Du Bois and A. Philip Randolph, joined the Socialist Party or other third-party movements. Black people understood the limited alternatives they had under America's system of representative democracy, and they negotiated the best deal they could under the circumstances.

The Great Depression and the election of Franklin D. Roosevelt altered the political landscape for both black and white America. Blacks generally approved of the Roosevelt administration's policies, and in the presidential elections of 1936, 1940, and 1944, the share of the African-American electorate supporting Roosevelt ranged from 67 to 72 percent. However, most black voters continued to reject any firm identification with the Democratic Party. For example, in the election of 1940, their identification with the two major parties was divided equally (with both at 42 percent), and the remainder (16 percent) classified themselves as independent and/or members of other political parties. African Americans in record numbers voted for incumbent Democratic President Harry S. Truman in 1948, with 77 percent supporting his candidacy. Truman's personal popularity, however, did not fully translate into overwhelming levels of support for the Democratic Party as a political organization. Fifty-six percent of all blacks now identified themselves as Democrats, while 25 percent called themselves Republicans and 15 percent said they were independents or claimed other political affiliations.

The Democratic Party during the 1930s, 1940s, and 1950s was essentially dominated by two powerful political blocs—conservative southern Democrats who defended and maintained the system of racial segregation, and big-city political bosses and machines that were based largely on ethnic white constituencies. Blacks had absolutely no leverage within the leadership levels of the party's hierarchy. This is strikingly apparent in view of the minuscule numbers of blacks who were credentialed, voting delegates at Democratic National Conventions. When Roosevelt first won his party's presidential nomination in 1932, not a single African American was among the 1,154 official convention delegates. Ten blacks were permitted to attend the convention as alternates, who were not allowed to cast votes. In 1944, the number of black delegates reached eleven, just under 1 percent of the convention's voting delegates. The black electorate was crucial to the election of Truman in 1948 and of

John F. Kennedy twelve years later, but its political clout was still not reflected in its decision-making capacity at party conventions. There were only 17 black delegates out of 1,234 at the 1948 convention, and only 46 out of 1,521 at the Los Angeles convention in 1960, representing just 3 percent.

The New Deal and its legislative legacy turned the Republicans into a minority party among black voters, but this realignment only happened gradually. For example, in the presidential election of 1936, Republican presidential candidate Alf Landon received the endorsements of twelve of the fourteen bishops of the African Methodist Episcopal (AME) Church. Throughout the 1930s, a significant number of African-American leaders, on the Left as well as on the Right, were intensely critical of the Roosevelt administration's actions, such as the strict racial segregationist policies implemented by the Civilian Conservation Corps and the president's refusal to integrate the armed forces. About one-third of all African Americans supported Republican presidential candidates Wendell Wilkie in 1940 and Thomas Dewey in 1944, largely on the grounds that the Roosevelt administration had persisted in its refusal or inability to implement meaningful racial reforms. Nearly 40 percent of all African-American voters supported the reelection of President Dwight D. Eisenhower in 1956. Even Richard M. Nixon received a respectable 32 percent of the black vote in 1960.

The real political revolution in African-American political culture only occurred in 1964. In the presidential race between incumbent President Lyndon B. Johnson and conservative Republican Barry Goldwater, two strikingly different visions of the country's racial future were presented. In the Senate, Goldwater had voted against the passage of the 1964 Civil Rights Act outlawing racial segregation in public accommodations. Faced with such clear-cut alternatives, the overwhelming majority of blacks went Democratic and never looked back. Ninety-four percent of black voters supported Johnson, and 82 percent now identified themselves as Democrats. Four years later, in a three-way contest for the presidency, Hubert Humphrey won 85 percent of the African-American vote, with 15 percent going to Nixon, and not surprisingly, virtually nothing to Alabama Governor George Wallace.

The enactment of the 1965 Voting Rights Act, and the imposition of federal registrars in states that for decades had restricted the size of the black electorate, almost immediately changed the South's politics, as well as the nation's politics. Between 1964 and 1969, the number of black adults who were registered to vote rose in Mississippi from 6.7 percent to 66.5 percent, and in Alabama from 19.3 percent to 61.3 percent. In 1966, only six African-American representatives sat in Congress, and less than 100 blacks were members of state legislatures throughout the country. Seven years later, more than 200 blacks were in the state legislatures of thirty-seven states, and sixteen African Americans were in Congress. Black mayors presided over Detroit, Newark, Los Angeles, Atlanta, Washington, D.C., and Gary, Indiana. By 1975, there were nearly 400 African-American judges and elected law-enforcement officers, 305 county executives, 135 mayors, 939 blacks elected to city and county boards of education, and more than 1,400 blacks elected to other municipal governmental positions.

Nationally, black electoral clout became fully apparent with the presidential election of November 1976. Former Georgia Governor Jimmy Carter defeated incumbent President Gerald R. Ford by a popular margin of 40.3 million to 38.5 million votes. In the Electoral College, however, the vote margin was much smaller, 297 to 241 votes. The African-American national electorate endorsed Carter overwhelmingly, with 93 percent of their votes. In New York, Texas, Alabama, Ohio, and several other states, black voters represented the crucial margin of victory for the Democratic candidate. In Mississippi, for example, 57 percent of the state's white electorate supported Ford, while over 90 percent of the nearly 190,000 black voters cast their votes for Carter, giving the Democrat a statewide margin of 7,600 total votes. Carter named Atlanta Congressman Andrew Young as United Nations Ambassador, and African Americans in unprecedented numbers were appointed in the federal bureaucracy. Carter's 1976 victory confirmed the realignment of the Democratic Party, which for much of its history had been thoroughly dominated by segregationist southern conservatives and white ethnic, urban political machines. The new core constituencies of the national party, its most reliable electoral base, were now African Americans, Latinos (with the notable exception of the Cubans), feminists, environmentalists, lesbian- and gay-rights activists, and the majority of organized labor.

The remarkable racial realignment within the national Democratic Party unfortunately created the context for the ideological and organizational transformation of the Republican Party as well. The stage for the triumph of racial conservatism in the Republican Party was set by Nixon, who successfully put together a center-right coalition, the so-called "Silent Majority," winning a little more than 60 percent of the popular vote against liberal Democratic presidential candidate George McGovern in 1972. The Watergate scandal slowed, but did not stop, the acceleration of the Republicans to the Far Right, especially on issues of race. The former Dixiecrats and supporters of George Wallace gravitated to the Republican Party and within a decade began to assume leadership positions in Congress. Cultural and religious conservatives represented by the Christian Coalition and other fundamentalist groups became activists in thousands of local Republican organizations across the country. White middle-class suburban voters and white ethnic voters in urban areas, concerned about issues such as busing to achieve school desegregation, affirmative action, welfare, and crime, began consistently to vote Republican. "Sunbelt" entrepreneurial capitalism, which had long opposed government regulations like environmental protection enforcement, joined the ranks of what could be called "mass conservatism."

This New Right chose as its national spokesperson an ex–movie actor and former California governor, Ronald Reagan, who astutely and effectively appealed to the racial fears and concerns of the majority of white Americans, yet without resorting to overtly racist rhetoric. In the presidential elections of 1980 and 1984, Reagan won landslide victories. In the Reagan-Mondale contest of 1984, two-thirds of all white voters, and over 80 percent of white southerners, endorsed the Republican ticket. These victories represented the triumph of white racial politics without the overtly racist rhetoric of the previous generation. The unspoken assumption that formed the ideological glue for this middle- and upper-class white united front was the preservation of white privilege. The New Right's political victories in the 1980s, and later in the congressional elections of 1994, effectively closed the door to America's Second Reconstruction, pushing the black American electorate into the post–Civil Rights era.

Reagan rarely spoke to, or even about, African Americans. When, on rare occasions, he did, he had a capacity to offend black people more than any chief executive of the nation since Woodrow Wilson. One outrageous example occurred in September 1992 at a meeting of the National Black Republican Council. The president lectured his audience that blacks would be collectively much "better off" if Lyndon Johnson's Great Society programs had never existed. "With the coming of the Great Society," Reagan explained, "government began eating away at the underpinnings of the private enterprise system. . . . By the time the full weight of Great Society programs was felt, economic progress for America's poor had come to a tragic halt. The poor and disadvantaged are better off today than if we had allowed runaway government spending, interest rates and inflation to continue ravaging the American economy." Statements such as these, which were completely contradicted by all historical and socioeconomic evidence, were rarely interrogated by the media or even by white leaders of the Democratic Party.

Reagan never used blatantly racist language, because he didn't have to. As sociologist Howard Winant astutely observed, the New Right's approach to the public discourse of race was characterized by an "authoritarian version of color-blindness," an opposition to any government policies designed to redress blacks' grievances or to compensate them for either the historical or contemporary effects of discrimination, and the subtle manipulation of white's racial fears. The New Right discourse strove to protect white privilege and power by pretending that racial inequality no longer existed. "The new right understands perfectly well that its mass base is white," Winant observed, "and that its political success depends on its ability to interpret white identity in positive political terms."

Although race was absolutely central to the construction and consolidation of the conservative Republican Party's hegemony in national politics, it was not the fundamental driving force that determined the material and social conditions of life for most Americans in the 1980s and 1990s. The popular perception is that this period brought unprecedented affluence and expanding opportunity for all. The reality was far different. What both major political parties refused to talk about, the proverbial "elephant in the middle of the room" that no one sees, was the growth of *inequality* within American society.

The Reagan administration's guiding political philosophy could be summarized in one single phrase: total, unconditional war against public institutions. "Government," Reagan repeatedly told white America, "is not the solution to our problems; government is the problem." Reaganites believed that the free market could determine the quality and availability of goods and services far better than the public sector could. Government regulations, they argued, were responsible for adding billions of dollars of unnecessary costs to business, destroying millions of jobs in the process. The government had no business constructing public housing when private enterprise could provide the same housing more efficiently and more economically. Environmental safeguards and health and safety standards were unnecessary and retarded economic growth. The quality of social services would be improved, the administration argued, if private corporations rather than government provided them.

This laissez-faire approach to economic development was of course not new. But under Reagan, it was carried to its logical extreme, well to the Right of traditional Republican social and economic policies under Eisenhower, Nixon, and Ford. This extreme agenda of downsizing, if not abolishing, the public sector also had the effect of increasing racial inequality throughout American society. In the Reagan administration's 1981 tax cut legislation, the 12.5 million Americans who at the time earned $50,000 and above per year received 35 percent of the reduction; the 31.7 million Americans earning $15,000 or less received 8 percent of the total amount of the tax cut. Because blacks and Latinos earned only 60 percent of the income of the average white household, they received less tax relief. Severe reductions in federal aid to education, public housing, school lunch programs, Medicaid, and unemployment compensation all had a disproportionately negative impact on racialized minorities. Such policies dramatically reversed most of the economic gains achieved by African Americans in the previous quarter-century. By 1985, African-American unemployment was 16.3 percent, well above the white jobless rate of 6.2 percent. Black youth unemployment soared to 50 percent. The growing economic pain of black poor and working people was also felt by sectors of the African-American middle class. More than one out of four black householders was employed by the public sector nationwide. For many years, government jobs were the principal source for black advancement into the middle class. The Reagan administration's mandate for governmental devolution destroyed hundreds of thousands of jobs that would have represented employment opportunities for African Americans.

Although Reagan left the presidency in 1989, the political landscape of the country had fundamentally realigned to the Right. His successor, Republican President George H.W. Bush, modified the Republicans' racial agenda in public policy but did not basically retreat from the previous administration's economic program. Reagan, for example, had met with African-American interest groups and leaders only eight times during his eight years as president. In contrast, Bush met with black leaders in business, government, and civic organizations forty times in his first two years in office. Bush allocated $185 million to the Equal Employment Opportunity Commission (EEOC), its largest increase in history. The Bush administration financed new initiatives to support historically black colleges and universities. It appointed liberal Republican Arthur A. Fletcher, the former head of the United Negro College Fund, to chair the U.S. Civil Rights Commission, and ended the Reagan administration's supportive policy of "constructive engagement" with apartheid South Africa, thus assisting the democratic transition, which made Nelson Mandela president in 1994.

Nevertheless, Bush never lost sight of the fact that his Republican base was largely hostile to blacks' interests, and he was not above manipulating racial fears and prejudices when it served his purposes. In the presidential election of 1988, Bush's campaign adviser, Lee Atwater, manipulated the image of a black criminal, Willie Horton, to imply that Democratic challenger Michael Dukakis was "soft on crime." Bush's Office of Civil Rights in the Department of Education halted all compliance investigations of universities that had been in violation of enforcing civil-rights laws. His nomination of reactionary black Republican

Clarence Thomas to the Supreme Court to replace the conscience of civil rights, Thurgood Marshall, in many ways repudiated the last vestiges of the moderate position on civil rights that mainstream Republicanism once represented.

II

There were ten presidential elections between the years 1952 and 1988. The majority of the white American electorate, in these ten electoral contests, voted for the Democratic candidate only once: Lyndon B. Johnson's landslide election of 1964. Since the late 1960s, white male adults, regardless of their education, income, and religious affiliation, have consistently voted Republican in national elections. In Reagan's reelection of 1984, 68 percent of white male voters supported him. A significant bloc of this vote nationally could be attributed to white male voters in the South and in the farming regions of the Midwest, where Reagan and Bush recorded voting margins of better than two to one among white males. As a consequence, in national races Democrats were increasingly forced to rely on a strong voter turnout by African Americans to remain even marginally competitive. For example, in 1968 blacks made up 20 percent of all the votes for Humphrey. Conversely, when black voter turnout was below expectations, it became almost impossible for any white Democratic presidential candidate to win. In the general election of 1988, for example, only 44 percent of eligible black registered voters came out on Election Day, and Michael Dukakis was easily defeated by George Bush.

From the vantage point of most white Democratic Party leaders, the inability to appeal to the white electorate was made far more difficult by the unexpected electoral successes of Jesse Jackson. Despite the strong endorsements of Walter Mondale by many prominent African-American elected officials and civil-rights leaders, Jackson received 3.5 million popular votes in the primaries of 1984, with 3 million African Americans turning out to vote. Four years later, Jackson's total popular vote doubled, accumulating more than 7 million votes in the 1988 primaries. Jackson even won state caucuses and primary elections in states such as Alaska that had virtually no black voters. Most Jackson supporters did not anticipate that their candidate would win the Democratic presidential nomination, but they attempted to use the primary elections process to push their party further to the left of center. Jackson's efforts also registered several million new voters, which significantly increased the size of the Democratic electorate. White centrist Democrats feared that the image of the party would suffer among white male voters, who might feel that it was being held hostage by "special interests."

These two factors—the Reagan administration's success in pushing the public discourse significantly to the Right, and the impact of Jackson's Rainbow Coalition in pulling a significant share of the party's core constituency to the Left—created a crisis of leadership. Centrist and conservative white Democrats, such as Georgia Senator Sam Nunn, Missouri Congressman Richard Gephardt, Virginia Governor Charles Robb, Arkansas Governor Bill Clinton, and Tennessee Senator Al Gore, concluded that the party's core agenda and its image had to be moved sharply to the Right to incorporate many of the antigovernment themes that Reagan had used so effectively. In 1985, these centrist leaders established the Democratic Leadership Council (DLC), which publicly announced its determination to "move the party—both in substance and perception—back into the mainstream of American political life." The DLC essentially repudiated the liberal statism of Johnson's Great Society programs, calling instead for market-based initiatives and the devolution of government services. Its leaders talked vaguely about finding a "Third Way," declaring that "government's role is to promote growth and equip Americans with the tools they need to prosper in the New Economy."

These self-proclaimed "New Democrats" disengaged themselves from the language of class conflict, which they saw as the failed rhetoric of "tax and spend" liberalism. They favored a discourse of "opportunity" over the language of "entitlements" and "rights." New Democrats no longer spoke to the core constituency of their party—blacks, Latinos, people of fixed incomes, the unemployed, and the working poor—but talked instead about "the forgotten middle class." They distanced them-

selves from the liberal wing of organized labor, telling trade unionists
that they needed to become "more competitive," "more realistic," in
their wage demands while preparing for the new demands of global economic markets. Industrial and manufacturing workers were told that
they had to return to school and become retrained to compete for new
jobs in high-technology fields. Behind much of the New Democratic
agenda was a subtle manipulation of race. New Democrats agreed with
Reagan conservatives that traditional welfare policies had produced an
urban underclass that lacked incentives for assuming personal responsibility. They favored tougher laws, mandatory minimum sentencing of
convicted felons, and the death penalty. They rejected "racial quotas"
and urged the adoption of "race-neutral" policies that could advance the
material conditions of the truly disadvantaged.

In 1988, the New Democrats supported the presidential candidacy of
DLC member Al Gore in the Democratic primaries. Gore's campaign,
however, was poorly organized and never really got off the ground.
Gore's voting record in Congress was essentially to the Right of liberal
Republicans such as Lowell Weiker of Connecticut. In the controversial
New York primary, Gore permitted himself to become the spokesman
for the anti-Jackson forces, alienating the black electorate. In 1990, however, Bill Clinton assumed the DLC leadership, with the goal of winning
his party's presidential nomination two years later. He astutely cam-
paigned actively for centrist Democrats, while distancing himself from
the Left at every possible opportunity.

In the Democratic Party primaries, Clinton proved to be an effective
and articulate candidate, far better than Gore had been four years before. Clinton was also lucky: Unlike in 1984 and 1988, Jackson had made
the decision to stay out of the 1992 Democratic race, which meant that
there would be no insurgent challenger to Clinton's Left, and that the
African-American electorate would have nowhere to go. Clinton also understood African-American political culture, having run statewide campaigns in Arkansas, where black voters were a critical constituency. By
late May 1992, Clinton had all but sown up his party's presidential nomination, but in national polls he was running a poor third in the projected
general election that was only months away, behind the incumbent pres-

ident, George Bush, and independent candidate H. Ross Perot. What Clinton needed was an event to distinguish himself as a "different kind of Democrat." Following Reagan's model, he decided to manipulate the politics of race.

In late April and early May 1992, Los Angeles erupted in widespread civil disturbance generated by the black community's outrage in response to the not-guilty verdicts of white police officers involved in the Rodney King case. With thousands of arrests and the destruction of more than $1 billion in property, the racial divide to many whites and blacks seemed further apart than it had been since the 1960s. Clinton had been scheduled to speak before the national convention of the Rainbow Coalition and, without informing Jackson in advance, decided to distance himself from the black community. Although the speech was designed to focus on issues such as urban enterprise zones and the earned-income tax credit, Clinton unexpectedly attacked the Rainbow Coalition's invitation to rap artist Sister Souljah to speak the previous evening. "You had a rap singer here last night named Sister Souljah," Clinton stated: "Her comments before and after Los Angeles were filled with a kind of hatred that you do not honor today and tonight. Just listen to this, what she said: She told the *Washington Post* about a month ago, and I quote, 'If black people kill black people every day, why not have a week and kill white people? . . . So if you're a gang member and you would normally be killing somebody, why not kill a white person?'"

Sister Souljah's original comments as reported in the press were taken out of context, not unlike Malcolm X's "chickens come home to roost" statements in the aftermath of John F. Kennedy's assassination in 1963. Despite her unfortunate choice of words, Souljah was not advocating the "killing" of white people; rather, she was making the point that black-on-black crime and violence was destroying African-American communities. Moreover, Sister Souljah was not an elected official or running for elective office; she was attempting to use her prominence in the hip-hop culture to stem the violence that had ended the lives of thousands of young black people. Clinton and his campaign handlers, however, manipulated the quotation to create the appearance of an association between Souljah's political opinions and those of Jackson and the

Rainbow Coalition. Clinton's rhetorical maneuver paralleled Ronald Reagan's attack against "welfare queens" and George Bush's "Willie Horton" advertisements. It was a strategically planned stunt, and it worked. Clinton followed it up with national interviews, explaining that "If you want to be president, you've got to stand up for what you think is right." His critics in the black community "have chosen to react against me," he said, noting that they felt "that because I'm white I shouldn't have said it, and I just disagree with that." Within two weeks, white levels of support for Clinton markedly increased, and the Democratic candidate jumped from third place to first in national polls. Bush never regained his lead, and Clinton won in November, although with only 43 percent of the popular vote.

The black vote for Clinton in 1992 was 82 percent, the lowest percentage of the black electorate a Democratic candidate had received since 1960. Bush received about 11 percent of the African-American vote, with the rest divided between H. Ross Perot and other third-party candidates. Nationwide, black voter turnout increased slightly, but with the greatest gains measured in the South, with a 54.3 percent turnout in 1992 vs. 48 percent in 1988. Clinton had no high-ranking African Americans in his 1992 presidential campaign, and his decision that same year to go on a golfing excursion at a whites-only, private country club was widely condemned by black Democrats. Nevertheless, the African-American electorate was absolutely critical in determining the outcome of the election. In a series of states Clinton managed to carry by small margins, such as Louisiana (46 percent vs. 42 percent), Tennessee (44 percent vs. 43 percent), Ohio (40 percent vs. 39 percent), and Georgia (44 percent vs. 43 percent), the black electorate was the key difference. Mexican-American voters played a similar role, providing Clinton with the margin of victory in Colorado and New Mexico. Nationally, Clinton also drew well from Jewish voters (78 percent), Hispanics (62 percent), Americans earning less than $15,000 annual income (59 percent), members of labor unions and voters in their households (55 percent), and the unemployed (56 percent). The most instructive statistic is that only 39 percent of all white voters actually voted for Bill Clinton. Forty-one percent, a plurality, had supported Bush's reelection, with another 20 percent of all whites casting ballots for Perot. Blacks now found themselves in a para-doxical situation: They were largely responsible for electing a president who in many ways ran on a campaign that tried to distance itself from the party's strongest core constituency.

In his first term in the White House, Clinton squandered the political capital he had won during his successful national campaign. Johnnetta Cole, president of Spelman College who had served as chair of Clinton's transition team on education, was first rumored to be the president-elect's choice as Secretary of Education. But when she was unfairly at-tacked by conservatives and neoliberals at the *New Republic,* Clinton re-fused to support her. When brilliant legal scholar Lani Guinier, proposed as the new assistant attorney general for civil rights, was pilloried by the extreme Right as the "Quota Queen," Clinton offered first a lukewarm defense, and then withdrew the nomination. Clinton later fired his friend Jocelyn Elders as surgeon general when she came under attack by the Christian Coalition and conservative extremists.

He played no role in shaping the national debate over affirmative ac-tion. Indeed, in his second 1996 debate with Republican challenger Robert Dole, Clinton stated, "I've done more to eliminate affirmative ac-tion programs I didn't think were fair and tighten others up than my predecessors have since affirmative action has been around." Legisla-tively, Clinton practiced the DLC-inspired strategy of "triangulation," keeping a pragmatic distance between the two parties in Congress and the administration, presenting himself to the electorate as an "independ-ent" and "centrist" leader above partisan politics. Such tactics frustrated Clinton's friends and gave legitimacy to the attacks of the Far Right against African-American interests. Largely for these reasons, black turnout in the congressional elections of 1994 was only 37 percent, the lowest voter turnout in a non-presidential year since the 1960s. Nation-ally, the white turnout was 46.9 percent, and much of this gain was reg-istered in the South, where 52.7 percent of all whites voted.

This huge white turnout spelled disaster for the Democratic Party. Nationwide, white males voted overwhelmingly in favor of Republican congressional candidates, by a margin of 63 to 37 percent. For more priv-ileged classes of white males, the support for the Republicans was even

higher. About 70 percent of all white males earning $75,000 or more an-
nually voted for Republican candidates, as did 67 percent of all white
male college graduates. Although white support for the Republican
Party was especially strong in the white South, white males regardless of
geographical region expressed the same political views. In California's
1994 gubernatorial election, two-thirds of all white male voters supported incumbent Republican Governor Pete Wilson, the prime mover
behind Proposition 187, which outlawed access to public services to undocumented immigrants. Blacks voted 75 percent for Wilson's Democratic opponent Kathleen Brown, as did 69 percent of Latino voters. Unfortunately, it just wasn't enough.

With Republicans in control of both houses of Congress for the first
time in four decades, they wasted little time in pushing aggressively for
the adoption of their "Contract with America," a reactionary policy
agenda. Predictably, Clinton pursued a strategy of accommodation to
the Far Right. In the presidential election of 1996, Clinton was determined not to allow Dole to present himself to the national electorate as
the Great White Hope. For purely opportunistic reasons, Clinton decided to use the issue of welfare as the vehicle to shore up his support
among white male voters. Only days before the 1996 Democratic National Convention, Clinton signed the "Personal Responsibility and
Work Opportunity Act," with the stated goal of "ending welfare as we
know it." In his campaign speeches, and in his book *Between Hope and
History*, the president repeatedly employed kinder, gentler versions of
Reagan's racial clichés, celebrating the fact that "1.8 million fewer people
are on welfare than there were on the day I took the oath of office."
Clinton repeatedly criticized the lack of "personal responsibility" of
those on public assistance, because "a mentality of entitlement creates a
narrow interest group politically, a rhetoric of helplessness, and an inability to serve the larger public interest."

On economic issues, Clinton was a free trader who favored neoliberal
policies and opposed protectionism. He ran for reelection as what a generation ago was termed a "liberal Republican," appealing to the white
electorate in a language it understood. The gambit worked, to an extent.
White turnout fell significantly, down to 53.4 percent of registered vot-

ers, the lowest in any presidential year in three decades. The percentage of the turnout was actually higher for blacks than for whites in several key states: California, Texas, Illinois, Maryland, Pennsylvania, and Michigan. Clinton's defeat of Dole only became decisive because of the African-American vote, with black voters representing 17.1 percent of Clinton's total popular vote. In Louisiana and Georgia, more than half Clinton's statewide vote came from African Americans. Blacks were more than 20 percent of Clinton's statewide totals in New Jersey, Michigan, Alabama, Illinois, and Tennessee. Overall, 84 percent of the black electorate supported Clinton, while fewer than one-half of all whites did. The Republicans maintained their control of both houses of Congress. Clinton's failure to articulate an alternative public policy agenda to congressional conservatives in 1996 created the political conditions that led to his impeachment. Had the Democrats regained control of the House of Representatives, impeachment would have never occurred, and George W. Bush probably would not have become president.

Ultimately, however, the real victims of Clinton's neoliberal politics of triangulation were the truly disadvantaged—working women with children, the chronically unemployed, people on fixed incomes, and children living in poverty. According to Peter Edelman, Clinton's assistant secretary of Health and Human Services, the Temporary Assistance to Needy Families (TANF), implemented in 1996 under Clinton, produced some fundamental changes for the poor and working poor, most of them for the worse. From 1995 to 1999, 2 million low-income families, who averaged annual incomes of approximately $7,500, lost 8 percent of their overall household income. The reason is simple: The additional earnings they received from working fell far short of the benefits they had to surrender, such as food stamps and welfare payments.

Most of the former welfare recipients who have been able to obtain full-time employment are only earning about $7.00 per hour, barely enough to keep a single-parent household with two children above the poverty level. The workfare program in New York City, Edelman observed, "teaches no skills, provides no help in finding a job, pays no wage (and therefore allows no access to the earned-income tax credit), often denies necessary safety equipment and applies sanctions for the slightest fraction, real or alleged." By early 2002, about 60 percent of all poor children were receiving no help. Benefits for those who still receive public assistance "are below the poverty line everywhere and below half the poverty line in many states." Edelman resigned from the Clinton administration in 1996, when TANF was approved for purely tactical advantage against Dole. Yet from the vantage point of the most economically marginalized Americans, it was difficult to see what difference it made.

III

In 2000, the American people witnessed the massive and wholesale theft of our presidency. Yet the fraudulent political dynamics that propelled loser George W. Bush into the White House have happened before. Marx once observed that history always repeats itself twice—the first time as tragedy, and the second time as farce. The seeds of the 2000 electoral debacle are found in America's tragic political history.

In 1876, the Civil War had been over for only eleven years. Black men had finally won the right to vote, but southern whites were vigorously attempting to regain power over their state legislatures. Deep sectional antagonisms still divided the nation, with the industrial and commercial North mostly supporting Republicans, and the white South supporting the Democrats. The Republican presidential candidate that year was Rutherford B. Hayes, the governor of Ohio. Hayes was widely viewed as being handicapped by the scandals and corruption that plagued the administration of two-term President Ulysses S. Grant. The Democratic challenger, Governor Samuel J. Tilden of New York, was widely favored to defeat Hayes. In the general election in November 1876, Tilden appeared to be the victor. He carried the national popular vote by 300,000. In the Electoral College, Tilden won 184 votes, to only 165 votes for Hayes, with twenty disputed electoral votes hanging in the balance. If Tilden had received only one of the disputed electoral votes, he would have been declared the winner. Hayes needed to win all twenty disputed electoral votes to become president. Compounding the national crisis were widespread allegations of voter fraud, especially in Florida. There was evidence of ballot tampering, with hundreds of ballots being destroyed or never counted. The political stalemate over who would become president threatened to plunge the country into a second Civil War. Only several days prior to the date set for the presidential inauguration, a deal was reached between Republicans and Democrats.

The "Compromise" of the election of 1876 actually represented a kind of electoral coup d'état. The Republican candidate, Hayes, was selected to become president. The federal government pulled thousands of Union troops out of the South, where they had been stationed since the fall of the Confederacy more than a decade earlier. The Compromise stated that the principle of states' rights would determine the future legal and political status of African Americans. In the language of that era, the so-called "Negro Question" was to become a "southern Question." The white South was given a free hand to set the parameters of black freedom.

The consequences of the Compromise of 1876–1877 were profound and long-lasting. A Civil Rights Act that had been passed by Congress in 1875 was repealed in 1883. Jim Crow segregation was soon institutionalized throughout the South. Hundreds of thousands of African-American men were purged from voters rolls or denied the right to cast ballots by local police intimidation and literacy restrictions. White vigilante violence was widely employed to suppress the black community as 5,000 African Americans were lynched in the South over the next four decades. The Supreme Court confirmed the racist principle of "separate but equal" with its legal decision *Plessy v. Ferguson* in 1896. It would take nearly a century for black America to recover.

The political parallels between 1876 and the presidential election of 2000 are significant. Once again, deep sectional and demographic divisions were reflected within the national electorate. The industrial Northeast, Midwest, and Pacific states were heavily Democratic; the South, the West, and rural America were overwhelmingly Republican. Al Gore, the Democratic presidential candidate in 2000, had served nearly his entire adult life as a public official—first as congressman and senator from Tennessee, and subsequently as vice president. He was, however, widely viewed as being handicapped by the scandals connected with the two-term president then in office, Bill Clinton. George W. Bush, the governor of Texas, was chosen as the Republican presidential candidate, and was largely assumed to be the favorite to win.

In the presidential election of 2000, most exit polls indicated that Gore had won. He carried the national popular vote by nearly half a million votes over Bush. Gore's lead in the Electoral College was 267 to 246, with Florida's 25 electoral votes in dispute. It was as if two distinctly separate nations had voted in America in November 2000. There was a "gender gap," as Gore received 12 percentage points more votes from women than from male voters. The "racial gap" was even more profound. Ninety percent of all African-American voters supported Gore, versus a meager 8 percent endorsing Bush. About two-thirds of all Latinos and the majority of Asian Americans voted for Gore. By contrast, white America clearly saw Bush as its favorite son. Fifty-three percent of all whites supported Bush. More than 70 percent of all southern whites voted for Bush, and religious conservatives endorsed the Republicans by a four-to-one margin. Just as in the election of 1876, there was evidence of massive voter fraud across the South, especially in Florida. In Florida's Palm Beach County, 19,000 ballots were thrown out. In Duval County, 27,000 ballots were declared void. More than 12,000 of these discounted votes came from only four districts where more than 90 percent of the voters were African Americans. In some majority black precincts, more than 30 percent of all votes were actually thrown out. Thousands of African Americans who had registered and were legally qualified to vote were not permitted to do so because they were erroneously listed as having been convicted of a felony. There were dozens of documented cases of blacks going to the polls who were stopped or harassed by local cops.

Over 30 percent of all African-American adult males in Florida are disfranchised for life because of the antidemocratic restrictions against ex-felons. Most Florida Republicans would like to restrict the voting rights of the other 70 percent as well. In fact, Florida State House Speaker Tom Feeney, who had insisted that the Republican-controlled legislature should select a Bush slate of Electors no matter who actually won the state's popular vote, also suggested the reinstatement of "literacy tests," the legal tool of segregationists. Feeney stated to reporters: "Voter confusion is not a reason for whining or crying or having a revote. It may be a reason to require literacy tests."

The election of 2000 was in the end decided not by the popular will of voters, but in Washington, D.C., by a narrow 5–4 conservative majority of Supreme Court justices. Chief Justice William Rehnquist's refusal to acknowledge evidence of blatant voter fraud against African Americans was no surprise. Back in 1962, when Rehnquist was a young attorney in Arizona, he led a group of Republican lawyers who systematically challenged the right of minority voters to cast their ballots in that state. Through his participation in this project, called "Operation Eagle Eye," Rehnquist successfully disfranchised hundreds of black and brown voters in Phoenix's poor and working-class precincts. In 2000, Rehnquist supervised the disfranchisement, in effect, of the *majority of American voters.*

Black America tried its best to keep George W. Bush out of the White House. Its inability to do so did not negate the many significant gains it actually achieved in the electoral arena. The 2000 presidential election was by far the closest in terms of the Electoral College since 1876, and the closest in terms of the popular vote since Kennedy's narrow margin of victory over Nixon forty years previously. Yet despite widespread reports that voter turnout was heavy, the actual number of votes cast was about 104 million, only 1 million more than in 1996. Less than 51 percent of all eligible voters cast ballots, compared to 49 percent in 1996 and 50 percent in 1988. Considering that both major parties spent more than $1 billion in the general election, with millions of phone calls and direct mailings, the turnout was remarkably weak. The lackluster major presidential candidates, Bush and Gore, failed to generate any enthusiasm or deep commitment among the general population.

The African-American electorate, however, was the exception to the rule. In state after state, black turnout was stronger than anticipated. It formed the critical margin of difference for Gore and hundreds of Democratic candidates in Senate, House, and local races. Nationwide, a clear majority of white voters went for Bush over Gore, 53 percent versus 42 percent. African Americans, however, went overwhelmingly for Gore, 90 percent versus 8 percent. Bush's feeble share of the black vote was actually less than his father's had been in 1992, and less than Bob Dole garnered in 1996. Bush's 2000 black vote was the lowest total received by any Republican presidential candidate since 1964, when Barry Goldwater received only 6 percent. In Florida alone, the African-American turnout jumped from 527,000 in 1996 to 952,000 in 2000. In Missouri, more than 283,000 blacks voted, compared to only 106,000 four years ago.

In state after state, African Americans supplied the critical margin of victory for the Gore-Lieberman ticket. In Maryland, Bush defeated Gore among white voters by a margin of 51 to 45 percent. But African-American turnout represented a substantial 22 percent of Maryland's total statewide vote. Because black Maryland voters supported Gore by 90 percent, Gore cruised to a 17 point victory in the state. In Michigan, the white electorate backed Bush 51 to 46 percent, but African Americans came out for Gore at 90 percent, giving the state to the Democrats. In Illinois, a massive turnout of African-American voters in Chicago helped to give Gore 56 percent of the statewide total vote, and a plurality of more than 600,000 votes. The NAACP's National Voter Fund, and its $12 million investment in the elections, was the principal factor behind the surge in the African-American electorate. The NAACP financed a political "command center" with dozens of full-time staff members and volunteers running telephone banks and a satellite TV uplink. Thousands of black churches, community-based organizations, and labor groups mobilized African Americans to turn out on Election Day. Jesse Jackson's campaigning was also critical to Gore's success in the swing states of Michigan and Pennsylvania.

Less publicized, but potentially just as important as the African-American vote, was the electoral response by organized labor. The AFL-CIO devoted millions of dollars to the effort to defeat Bush. In Michigan, for example, where labor households represented roughly 30 percent of the statewide vote in 1992, the union vote eight years later totaled 44 percent of the state's electorate. In Pennsylvania, union households represented 19 percent of the statewide vote in 1992, but increased to 26 percent of all voters in 2000.

The greatest tragedy of the 2000 presidential race, from the vantage point of the African-American electorate, was that the black vote would have been substantially larger if the criminal-justice policies put in place by the Clinton-Gore administration had been different. As noted by the Washington, D.C.–based Sentencing Project and the group Human Rights Watch, more than 4.2 million Americans were prohibited from voting in the 2000 presidential election because they were in prison or had in the past been convicted of a felony. Of that number, more than one-third, or 1.8 million voters who are disfranchised, are African Americans. This represents 13 percent of all black males of voting age in the United States. In Florida and Alabama, 31 percent of all black men, as of 1998, were permanently disfranchised because of felony convictions, many for nonviolent crimes. In New Mexico and Iowa, one in every four African-American males is permanently disfranchised. In Texas, one in five black men are not allowed to vote. In effect, it was the repressive policies of the Clinton-Gore administration that helped to give the White House to the Republicans.

IV

The lost opportunities of the Clinton years and Gore's lackluster campaign were really symptoms of a deeper structural problem within our political system as it relates to issues of race. Neither the Republican nor the Democratic Party, as a political organization, is interested in transforming the public discourse on race, though for different reasons. The Republicans deliberately use racial fears and white opposition to civil rights–related issues like affirmative action to mobilize their conservative base. The national Democratic Party mobilizes its black voter base, in order to win elections, but in a way that limits the emergence of progressive and Left leadership and independent actions by grassroots constituencies. Both parties oppose fundamental reforms within our electoral political system, such as proportional representation voting or the liberalization of election laws to permit easier ballot access to third parties.

In the 2000 election I endorsed the Green Party presidential candidacy of Ralph Nader, but only in those states where the projected majority vote for either Gore or Bush had already been decided. Because of our archaic Electoral College system, voting for Nader in states like California, New York, and Texas would not negatively affect the outcome of the national election. Many progressives and liberals who also took this approach called it the "Nader where you can, Gore where you must" strategy. We felt that a significant national vote for Nader would be interpreted within the Democratic Party as a warning from the Left that could push the party away from its disastrous DLC policies and neo-liberal orientation. In retrospect, however, I think that the emphasis that progressives placed on the symbolic value of running an independent campaign for the presidency was not the most effective use of our resources. The Nader campaign failed to attract any significant support from African-American voters, and the campaign was virtually invisible in predominantly black and Latino urban neighborhoods. Ralph Nader is a great visionary and advocate for social justice, and in a more just and democratic society, his message would have found a receptive audience. But the fundamental problem of the politics of race, I believe, cannot be addressed through a national campaign for elective office. Too many legal and institutional barriers exist, making any serious left-of-center political campaign at the national level virtually impossible.

I agree with Lani Guinier and others who suggest that the real problem is not with the personalities who seek public office, but with the electoral political system itself. Pushing for reforms such as "instant run-off voting" would make it possible to run a progressive third-party candidate for an office without throwing the election to a conservative candidate. The larger problem that African Americans and other progressive constituencies must confront is that the Democratic Party as it presently is constructed will never embrace policies leading to fundamental changes in the country's racial hierarchy. The only way to force the Democrats to change is to challenge them in their own districts, from the outside, especially in predominantly black and Latino congressional districts.

I'm not in favor of an all-black political party, or any political organization that is essentially race-based. What we need is to revive the vision of what the Rainbow Coalition campaigns of 1984 and 1988 could have become. A multiracial, multiclass political movement with strong participation and leadership from racial minorities, labor, women's organizations, and other left-of-center groups could effectively articulate important interests and concerns of the most marginalized and oppressed sectors of society. It would certainly push the boundaries of political discourse to the eft, even if it was unsuccessful at first in winning congressional elections. Such an effort could only be successful, however, if progressives understood the structural limits of electoral politics and built working alliances with community-based and social-justice constituencies that focus their activities outside of the electoral system.

Chapter 4

Losing the Initiative on Race

Can we all get along?
            —Rodney King, 1992

Now, let us not be conformed to this world, but let us go home transformed by the renewing of our minds and let the idea of atonement ring throughout America. That America may see that the slave has come up with power. The slave has been restored, delivered, and redeemed. And now call this nation to repentance.
                        —Minister Louis Farrakhan,
            Million Man March Address, October 16, 1995

I

The basic theory behind America's pluralistic political system was best expressed by Founding Father James Madison in the tenth essay of the *Federalist Papers*. Madison observed that it is the "propensity of mankind to fall into mutual animosities" based on divergent material interests they may have. "But the most common and durable source of factions," Madison added, "has been the various and unequal distribution of property. Those who hold and those who are without property have ever formed distinct interests in society." The task of representative democracy, therefore, is to reduce "mankind to a perfect equality in their political rights" while preserving the "rights of property," which "is the first object of government." Elections then become sites of political contestation, where coalitions of groups reflecting different interests seek to influence the directions of society.

Madison's theme is echoed in the work of political scientist Lucius Barker, who has explained, "Pluralist politics illuminates clearly . . . that there are always winners and losers in elections and that some interests are furthered and others retarded depending on who wins. But the interdependent and incremental nature of our system usually mitigates the loss of the losers." The better organized a group is, he continued, the greater the likelihood that it can affect the outcome of any election. Even if a group loses a contest, however, if it maintains its capacity for electoral engagement it can to a great extent minimize its losses. This theory of political pluralism is used to explain why political disagreements within representative democracies can usually be resolved amicably, without resorting to violence. All parties are "stakeholders" in a fair process of competition where the political ground rules are set and agreed upon in advance. The better a particular constituency is mobilized—for example, through voter registration and high percentages of turnout, extensive lobbying, and political educational outreach—the greater the influence that group will exert on the political system.

The problem for African Americans, however, is that American pluralist politics does not seem to work for them. Political scientists Dianne Pinderhughes, Rodney Hero, Michael Dawson, Aldon Morris, Lucius

Barker, and others in recent years have described this frustrating contradiction. Barker noted, "After the threshold surge in the 1960s, as black electoral involvement became stronger, the policies that would have favored them (at least on the national level) became weaker, having been quite steadily—even systematically—eroded, with the prospects for improvement becoming dimmer." He concluded that "the two broad coalitions that give life and vitality to the governing system—the major political parties—have been unable or unwilling, for the most part, to deal forthrightly with matters of race."

During the 1988 Jackson campaign, for example, wherever African Americans extensively mobilized their communities to participate in the political process, white voters were more likely to express their anti-black bigotry at the polls, thus negating any tangible gains blacks might have achieved. An analysis of twenty-two Democratic Party presidential primaries and caucuses by Amihai Glazer documented this backlash phenomenon. A state-by-state analysis showed that the greater the percentage of black voters in a state, the less likely it was for whites to vote for Jackson. In Vermont, where less than 1 percent of the electorate is African American, Jackson recorded over 35 percent of the vote. In Ohio, where 12 percent of the registered Democratic voters are black, Jackson received 17 percent of whites' votes. In New York, where the Democratic electorate is 14 percent black, the white vote for Jackson fell to 14 percent. And in New Jersey, where 20 percent of the Democratic voters are black, the white vote for Jackson dropped off to 13 percent.

What can explain this frustrating pattern? By the late 1980s, political scientist James Jennings noted, white voters, especially in major urban areas, may have felt "surrounded by increasing numbers of blacks." When African-American "demands do not question the foundation of power and if the system is elastic enough to provide minimally satisfactory responses to actual and potential black insurgents," Jennings argued, racial tension can be reduced. However, when blacks collectively mobilize through the democratic process with the objective of achieving structural change, vigorous white opposition develops. "Ultimately, despite a group's liberal or conservative tendencies, the more powerful must ensure that these groups without access to power do not present threats to social, economic, or political arrangements that may disrupt the hierarchy of power. Systemic restrictions are placed on urban political activism that points to social change."

In the generation of black elected officials since the Civil Rights Movement, one approach for circumventing this racial conundrum in American politics has been what can be termed a "post-black strategy." A number of black elected officials, that is, eschew the goal of African-American empowerment rhetorically and establish clientage relationships with white corporate or political interests. This is a type of "selective integration" in which blacks are assimilated, Jennings said, "on a token basis in the political corridors of power while ensuring that whites—whether machine supporters or reformers—retained control of the contents of a black public agenda." The black official is no longer the "agent" or representative of a specific racialized constituency, a spokesperson for the expression of grievances and interests of black people, along the parameters of Madison's political pluralism model. He/she becomes a politician "who happens to be black" rather than a "black politician." The politician feels no sense of loyalty or responsibility to the members of his/her racial group or to their history, seemingly having nothing in common with them beyond the rather secondary fact of skin color, hair texture, and physical appearance. The objective of such officials is to serve the broader public interest rather than a narrowly defined racial interest, which may frequently be at odds with what white Americans would define as the "national interest."

For most black Americans, the phenomenon of "post-black politics" is tremendously frustrating because there is ultimately a zero-sum game involved in scaling the hierarchy of power. The more successful the African-American elected official becomes, the less likely it is that he/she can be held accountable to black interests. At the level of national politics, a black politician who wants to advance must distance him/herself from being perceived as essentially "black." This is the ambiguous paradox of integration; or, as in the prophetic words of Martin Luther King, Jr., the notion that blacks may live "in a nation where they will not be judged by the color of their skin but by the content of their character." But to be truly color-blind in a nation that aggressively maintains structural racism and oppressive social hierarchies is to become blind to the reality and living consequences of American history. It is to become "invisible" at a moment when racism as a destructive social force is still all too visible.

It is this paradox of integration—the apparently inescapable contradiction that the stronger we become, the less leverage we seem to have as a group—that has forced black Americans to search for alternative models for renegotiating the political reality of race. If not electoral politics, then what? This was the central question that shaped the April 21–23, 1989, African American Summit organized in New Orleans, which was at that time the most important conference of black political leaders since the historic black convention at Gary, Indiana, in March 1972. Attracting 1,200 delegates, observers, and representatives of the media, the key organizer of the New Orleans conference was Richard Hatcher, the former mayor of Gary, Indiana, and the host of the previous convention. The explicit goal of the summit was to construct a broad, united front of black leadership that reflected all significant political and philosophical tendencies within the African-American community, from Republicans to Communists. Hatcher explicitly saw this gathering as an extension of the black political convention movement that first began in Philadelphia in 1830. "This Summit," Hatcher stated, "would not be possible were it not for the landmark meetings of the past, those gatherings where agendas were set, strategies were fixed, and the African American cause advanced." The summit's steering committee and planning group reflected a surprising degree of diversity. Honorary chairs included Coretta Scott King, NAACP Executive Secretary Benjamin Hooks, Urban League Director John Jacob, and Jesse Jackson. Key conference planners included political scientist Ronald Walters, California State Senator (soon Congresswoman) Maxine Waters, Republican leader Gloria Toote, and Romana H. Edelin, head of the National Urban Coalition.

I spoke and participated in the New Orleans summit, and from my perspective the event stood out as a concerted effort to find the appropriate political mechanism to enhance black political capacity as well as to make black leaders more accountable to black constituencies and civic institutions. A number of effective workshops were held on a range of relevant

topics, such as criminal justice, the labor movement, civil-rights enforcement, public education, and economic development. The most interesting and, in retrospect, prescient commentary was provided by Republican
Gloria Toote, who bravely went to the podium to speak before a mass audience consisting largely of Democrats. Wearing a flowing African textile
garment, she deliberately presented herself in the tradition of Du Bois,
Garvey, and Malcolm X. "We have no permanent friends, no permanent
enemies, only permanent interests," Toote declared. "We must cease to
place party labels above our racial interests." Jesse Jackson spoke in a similar vein. "This conference was devised as a free marketplace of ideas,"
Jackson stated. "If we ever as a family needed to come together, we certainly need to come together now. We must seek common ground."

The most significant controversy at the New Orleans summit, spark-
ing a debate that nearly disrupted the proceedings, was whether to extend an invitation to Nation of Islam leader Louis Farrakhan to speak.
Black Republicans and mainstream civil-rights leaders threatened to bolt
if the controversial Muslim minister was permitted to address the convention. After considerable negotiations, Farrakhan was invited to
speak, but at the worst time for a presentation—early on Sunday morning. Farrakhan's reception, as James Jennings observed,

> was far more enthusiastic than it had been for any previous
> speaker. . . . By the time this black leader approached the podium,
> many leaders holding and representing organizational positions in
> the Democratic party and the Republican party had left the sum-
> mit; but many of the rank and file decided to stay for what they
> considered the highlight of the African American Summit of 1989.
> This incident reflected the political bifurcation that exists in the
> black community regarding issues of philosophy, values, and orga-
> nizational relationships to white-dominated political and social
> mainstream processes within American society.

I did not know it at the time, but the New Orleans summit sparked
the beginning of a new process—the search for a "race-based initiative"

to answer the paradox of integration. How could black representation within the institutions of state power and through public policy actually enhance the political capacity on the ground inside predominantly black communities? To maneuver around post-black politics, a race-based initiative had to be constructed nationally, but in a way that would transcend the two-party system, operating largely outside of it.

The subsequent political events of 1990–1994 reinforced and accelerated the search for a new race-based initiative for black empowerment. For reasons known only to himself, Jesse Jackson largely dismantled his own organization, the national Rainbow Coalition, by insisting that he should have the sole authority to name the state leaders of the organization. Hundreds of activists who had loyally worked to construct the Rainbow Coalition at the grassroots level, and who had devoted thousands of hours promoting Jackson's presidential bids in 1984 and 1988, felt disillusioned and betrayed. The Rainbow Coalition's chaotic structure, and Jackson's egocentric personality, all contributed to a lack of democratic accountability within the organization. Ideologically, Jackson had already shifted closer to the center in his 1988 campaign, which contrasted sharply with the more insurgent, radical electoral movement that had disrupted the Democratic primaries four years earlier. By muzzling democratic debate and local initiative, and by suppressing independent Rainbow campaigns outside of the Democratic Party, Jackson pushed his organization virtually into oblivion.

Meanwhile, the social crisis within African-American urban communities seemed to accelerate out of control. The devastation of crack cocaine was at its peak; levels of violence between heavily armed rival street gangs fighting to control drug markets reached unprecedented levels. In the five years between 1989 and 1994, more black males were killed in street violence than all the African-American troops who died in the Vietnam War. In 1990, the statistical likelihood that a black male would become a murder victim was one in twenty. Murder became the fourth leading cause of death in the black community and the number one cause of death for black males between the ages of twenty and twenty-nine.

It was these grim new statistics that prompted Cornel West in 1991 to write his influential essay "Nihilism in Black America." West argued that liberals who advanced "structuralist" interpretations for black oppression, and "conservative behavioralists" who promoted self-help and free-market models for group upliftment, were equally responsible for nearly suffocating "the crucial debate that should be taking place about the prospects for black America." To West, the central challenge confronting the black community was "the nihilistic threat to its very existence. This threat is not simply a matter of relative economic deprivation and political powerlessness. . . . It is primarily a question of speaking to the profound sense of psychological depression, personal worthlessness, and social despair so widespread in black America." The reality of nihilism among blacks was not new, West explained, but it had become much worse in recent years because of the failure of effective black leadership and the destructive impact of "corporate market institutions." Of the latter, he said, "Their primary motivation . . . is to make profits, and their basic strategy is to convince the public to consume." This bottom line has culminated, in West's words, in a widespread "sense of worthlessness and self-loathing in black America. The angst resembles a kind of collective clinical depression in significant pockets of black America." The only way to transform the crisis of nihilistic behavior, he advised, was to actively foster an alternative, humanistic set of values, which he described as the "politics of conversion":

> Nihilism is not overcome by arguments or analyses; it is tamed by love and care. Any disease of the soul must be conquered by a turning of one's soul. This turning is done by one's own affirmation of one's worth—an affirmation fueled by the concern of others. This is why a love ethic must be at the center of a politics of conversion. . . . Work must get done. Decisions must be made. But charismatic presence is no legitimate substitute for collective responsibility. Only a charisma of humility and accountability is worthy of a leadership grounded in a genuine democratic struggle for greater freedom and equality. This indeed may be the best— and last—hope to hold back the nihilistic threat to black America.

West's nihilism thesis provoked considerable debate and critical commentary. Some black leftists accused West of advancing a neo-culture-of-poverty thesis, blaming the internal psychological and sociocultural contradictions within black civil society for the systemic reality of black oppression. Many others, however, felt that West's argument made sense, given the new levels of violence, fear, and social devastation that scarred the urban landscape of black America.

The Los Angeles uprising of 1992 fed into the perception that there was a crisis of black nihilism in our nation. Following the acquittal of four Los Angeles white police officers who had brutally beaten black motorist Rodney King, civil unrest exploded—not only in Los Angeles ghettoes and barrios but also, albeit to a lesser extent, in other U.S. cities with significant populations of racialized minorities. In Los Angeles, in the first three days of rioting more than 3,600 fires were reported. After six days, 42 people had died, 700 buildings had been completely destroyed by fire, more than 5,000 people had been arrested, and more than $1 billion in property damage had been reported. Significantly, the majority of people arrested for looting and rioting were Latinos, not African Americans—indicative of the alienation and resentment about police brutality that also existed in Hispanic neighborhoods. In San Francisco, about 1,400 people were arrested as rioting spread through urban districts. In Las Vegas, several hundred people set fires and destroyed private property. After incidents of sniper fire were reported, the Nevada National Guard was requested by local authorities to restore order. According to researcher Robert Garcia, "Thoughtful observers agreed that racial intolerance and a siege mentality by many police officers towards the communities they were supposed to protect and to serve exacerbated the use of excessive force by the police. Police abuse, racism, poverty, lack of opportunity, crime, drugs, and the loss of hope in the nation's inner cities were fundamental problems of the society as a whole that lay at the core of civil unrest."

At a critical moment, when effective black leadership seemed to be desperately needed, African-American political organizations seemed to be experiencing moral meltdown and a crisis of accountability. There was a growing perception among increasing numbers of African Americans that their own leaders had failed them: In short, confidence in the official representatives of the black establishment, and its traditional liberal, integrationist, "let's-work-within-the-system" credo, was crumbling.

The reasons were not difficult to root out. Poverty and joblessness were distressingly high in areas heavily populated by blacks. As of 1994, for example, in the thirty-nine House districts held by African-American congressional representatives, the black population averaged 53.2 percent, compared to the national African-American population of 12 percent. The average poverty rate in these districts was 23.1 percent; for blacks living in these districts, however, the poverty rate was 29.8 percent. The jobless rate in black-represented districts, 10.3 percent, was significantly higher than the national average of 6.3 percent. And despite the many significant social problems of their districts—or perhaps because such problems appeared so overwhelming that no policy solutions seemed achievable—many black representatives seemed detached and unaccountable to their constituents.

To some extent, this trend had to do with the change in the personal histories and political ideologies of black leaders: The activists of the 1950s civil-rights era had given way to the political conservatism of the 1990s. The first black politicians to be elected to important posts in the 1960s were frequently veterans of the Civil Rights Movement or had closely identified with the militant protests of Black Power. Many either came out of churches or trade unions, where there were large black constituencies involved in activist struggles. Few had prior legislative experience. In contrast, many of today's black officials are professional politicians who have few personal connections with activism. As political scientist Clarence Lusane has noted, among the seventeen blacks newly elected to Congress in 1994, there were eight attorneys, eight former state senators, "three who were state representatives, one former Mayor, one former alderman, one former US District Judge, and two who were long-time appointed government officials."

Most of these black elected officials were decent and well-meaning enough, but they nevertheless were either unwilling or unable to articulate a coherent alternative program for challenging both Clinton's neoliberalism and the reactionary policy agenda of the conservative Republicans. Politically, their top priority, like that of their white colleagues, was to get reelected. Many were prepared to sacrifice political principles for the sake of personal advancement at their constituents' expense. For example, in 1993 the Congressional Black Caucus (CBC) pledged unanimous opposition to the North American Free Trade Agreement (NAFTA). This decision was partly an effort to support organized labor and the AFL-CIO, which had contributed more than $7.9 million to CBC members during the previous decade. There was every expectation that black members of Congress would uphold this decision. In the final vote, however, eight black House representatives and one senator voted in favor of NAFTA. Black elected officials had openly adopted a strategy that went against what the CBC saw as being in the best interests of black constituents. The terms "cross-over" and "racial neutrality" were used to describe what had happened: Those who voted in favor of NAFTA had presented themselves not as representatives of predominately black constituencies, but as elected officials who merely happened to be racially black. Race was now only one of many different variables that could influence political behavior and decision making. Increasingly, black voters were faced with the difficult situation of supporting and defending black officials who employed "race-neutral" approaches in their politics and who expressed no special accountability or responsibility to them as blacks.

The crisis of confidence within black politics was rooted primarily in the deliberate retreat by the leaders of liberal integrationism from initiating, sponsoring, and providing resources to grassroots insurgencies and community-based protest movements. Civil Rights Movement historian and King biographer Clayborne Carson has observed: "The most successful black organizers of the 1960s established a model of community mobilization that emphasized the nurturing of grassroots leaders and organizations. . . . The most effective organizers of the 1960s realized that their job was to work themselves out of a job. They avoided replacing old dependencies with new ones." A belief in the strategies of community-based organizing, economic boycotts, and civil disobedience was supplanted by a blind adherence to electoral politics, lobbying, and collaboration with corporate and philanthropic interests. Instead of

pushing the boundaries of what was once called the "liberal establishment," the post-black politics of the post–civil rights era increasingly
spoke the language of state power, becoming devoid of genuine passion
for activism and resistance. In many ways, ironically, the successful
achievement of major state-based reforms, such as the Civil Rights Act
of 1964 and the Voting Rights Act of 1965, created the conditions for the
rise of a black leadership that was largely incapable of renewing and redefining the continuing struggle for freedom.

II

The historical stage was therefore set for a different kind of black political initiative, one that would address the problem of "nihilism," the
plague of violence, and the so-called absence of political and moral responsibility within African-American public and private life popularized
by West and other black writers to his Right, notably Glenn Loury and
Shelby Steele. The moment had come to face down the black community's "spiritual crisis" by returning to traditional family values and principles of self-love and mutual respect: It was time for a new summit. The
crystallization of this new initiative on race really occurred at the Congressional Black Caucus weekend meeting of September 1993. CBC
leader Kweisi Mfume, then a Democratic congressman from Baltimore,
reached a public agreement with the newly elected executive director of
the NAACP, the Reverend Benjamin Chavis, and NOI leader Louis Farrakhan, to establish an ongoing leadership "dialogue" that would draw
upon the preliminary model of the 1989 New Orleans conference as well
as similar, less publicized exchanges that had occurred throughout the
country, especially in the aftermath of the Los Angeles rebellion. Chavis
then convinced the NAACP board to approve the establishment of a National African American Leadership Summit. The first session would be
held at the NAACP's national headquarters in Baltimore in June 1994.
The decision to invite Farrakhan, as in 1989, prompted considerable debate. NAACP officials were warned privately by foundations and private
donors that they risked the financial survival of the association if they

went ahead with Farrakhan's participation. Mainstream civil-rights leaders such as Coretta Scott King, Julian Bond, and Mary Frances Berry distanced themselves from the summit. Nearly all of the CBC members stayed away, with the prominent exception of Mfume.

But Chavis was adamant that he had been right to proceed with the invitation. As he would later explain to me in a public dialogue, "You cannot get black leaders to sit down around one table, primarily because most of our organizations are not funded by us. . . . That is why we have such profound disunity among our leadership. I felt the NAACP was safe enough to sponsor a summit and then invite everybody to the summit. And that's exactly what we did." Jackson was privately critical of Chavis and the summit and was rumored to have convinced black labor leaders and other allies involved in the Rainbow Coalition not to attend. But at the last minute, both Jackson and his protégé, the Reverend Al Sharpton of New York, did show up at the Baltimore summit—arriving late. Unlike New Orleans, the 1994 summit was an invitation-only event. The approximately ninety participants in attendance represented black civic organizations, fraternities, sororities, business groups, community-based activist groups, faith-based institutions, and the Nation of Islam. The general theme was the development of a national agenda for united action around common social, economic, and political issues. Unfortunately, the media focused almost exclusively on Farrakhan's prominent role at the gathering.

It did not surprise me that only two months later, Chavis was fired from his position at the NAACP, ostensibly not because of the summit but on the grounds of using the association's funds to settle a sexual-harassment lawsuit that had been filed against him by a former employee. While the charge may have been technically true, the major reason that Chavis was dismissed was fierce political opposition to his efforts to broaden the base of the NAACP. He had reached out to the hip-hop generation and even urban youth gangs, and now he seemed to be developing a cooperative association with Farrakhan and the NOI. The NAACP was more than $1 million in debt and was in organizational chaos internally; many of its principal donors threatened the organization with bankruptcy unless Chavis and the National African American

Leadership Summit were jettisoned. Farrakhan almost immediately, and astutely, stepped in, taking administrative control of the summit process and hiring Chavis to lead the development of this new black united front.

Toward the end of 1994, Farrakhan and other NOI leaders came up with a brilliant idea for developing a mass, popular constituency to sustain the National African American Leadership Summit. In the aftermath of the public controversy surrounding the NAACP's ouster of Chavis, there was a growing sentiment among African Americans for some kind of mass public statement or demonstration that would reaffirm the humanity of all black people, bring us together in a unifying event, and provide a public forum for expressing outrage at the assaults undermining our people. In the wake of what seemed like an endless series of public controversies and conflicts—the beating of Rodney King and the initial acquittal of his police attackers, the Los Angeles rebellion, the appointment of Clarence Thomas to the Supreme Court, the refusal of the Clinton White House to fight for the confirmation of Lani Guinier as assistant attorney general for civil rights, the sordid soap opera of O. J. Simpson's murder trial—the popular conditions for black mass action were at a height.

Although the call for a national march received broad and popular support within the black community, a significant minority sharply condemned the mobilization. Some critics felt that Farrakhan's public history of making homophobic, sexist, and anti-Semitic statements made any association with the effort too controversial. Many political progressives and activists on the Left were puzzled by Farrakhan's emphasis on the necessity for blacks to "atone" for their sins. In the face of a Republican-controlled Congress, which had recently passed repressive policies under its "Contract with America" agenda, why should African Americans travel to Washington, D.C., to "denounce" themselves in the shadow of the national Capitol?

The most vocal criticisms, however, came from black women's and feminist groups, who were disgusted and appalled by the deeply heterosexist and misogynistic orientation of much of the Million Man March's literature and public outreach efforts. Farrakhan himself intensified their criticisms by making a series of sexist excuses to explain why the march had to be for males only. "We are asking the black woman, particularly our mothers, to be with our children, teaching them the value of home, self-esteem, family and unity; and to work with us to ensure the success of the March and our mission to improve the quality of life for our people," Farrakhan explained in his newspaper, the *Final Call.* "The March is not against females, it's not to say we don't love our women. But we must do something to atone for what we have done to our women and atone for the abuse we have heaped on our women."

Farrakhan's emphasis on the patriarchal "protection" of black women seemed to many to imply a justification for the physical domination of women by men. In many communities, deliberately or not, that was the real message that the mobilization expressed. In Los Angeles, for example, one march organizer, writing to a local black newspaper, warned that "sisters gotta stay home on this one. I know you ain't used to anybody telling you where you can go. That might be part of the problem. . . . Until the black man regains the respect (and control) of his women, he will never regain the respect of the larger society." Blatant and vulgarly sexist expressions such as these forced Chavis and other march organizers on the defensive. They invited a small number of prominent African-American women to appear on the dais and to speak briefly at the big event. Their limited participation, however, did little to alter the patriarchal character of the march.

Nevertheless, the degree of rage within black America was so overwhelming that the Million Man March mushroomed into an unprecedented, popular, mass mobilization. On October 16, 1995, vast numbers of African-American men, most arriving by caravans of buses and cars, came to bear witness to history. The U.S. Park Service's estimate that 400,000 attended the march grossly underestimated the turnout. A more accurate estimate, by researchers at Boston University for ABC television, placed the number at somewhere in the range of 675,000 to 1.1 million. If the Boston University figures are correct, the Million Man March brought together, on a single day, anywhere from 4 to 6 percent of the total African-American male population of the United States.

The lengthy program featured more than fifty speakers as well as artistic and musical presentations—at least three times longer than the

1963 March on Washington. Although the majority of the CBC stayed away from the gathering, a number of prominent black congressional leaders spoke and offered their support, including Charles Rangel, John Conyers, Faye Williams, Donald Payne, Gus Savage, and Kweisi Mfume. The traditional civil-rights leadership was represented as well, by Joseph Lowery, president of the Southern Christian Leadership Conference, and Dorothy Height, president of the National Council of Negro Women. Black nationalists who had been central to planning the event and conceptualizing its public agenda also spoke, such as Maulana Karenga, Haki Madhubuti, and Conrad Worrill. Although men dominated the program, several prominent African-American women were featured as well. Dr. Betty Shabazz, the widow of Malcolm X, made an appearance at the podium, which for many symbolized a historic reconciliation between the factional divisions that had separated Malcolm X from Elijah Muhammad and his successor, Farrakhan. Poet Maya Angelou and the venerated Rosa Parks offered their praises to the gathering. And after weeks of privately criticizing the moblization, even Jesse Jackson found it prudent and necessary to come to the march and offer words of political solidarity in the cause of black unity. Most of the speakers emphasized the march's central themes of "atonement," personal improvement, moral renewal, and community upliftment.

The high point of the march was expected to be Louis Farrakhan's keynote address. Most of the audience knew about, and some had actually heard firsthand, Martin Luther King, Jr.'s, "I Have a Dream" speech at the Lincoln Memorial on August 28, 1963. Those who anticipated a similarly bold and visionary public statement about the future of race in American life from Farrakhan, however, were disappointed. For two and a half hours, the NOI leader delivered a rambling, poorly organized, and at times even bizarre discourse, from his ruminations about the origins of the Great Seal of the United States to the role of Egyptian Pharoah Akhenaten, who "was the first man of this history period to destroy the pantheon of many gods and bring the people to the worship of one god." The first hour of Farrakhan's speech was filled with conjectures about numerology and the mysterious meanings of Masonic and ancient Egyptian symbols. The Washington Monument, Farrakhan informed the audience, was "555 feet high. But if we put a one in front of that 555, we get 1555, the year that our first fathers landed on the shores of Jamestown, Virginia, as slaves."

Farrakhan was sensitive to the widespread criticism that many, including President Clinton, had "tried to distance the beauty of this idea" of the Million Man March "from the person through whom the idea and the call was made. . . . You can't separate Newton from the law that Newton discovered, nor can you separate Einstein from the theory of relativity. It would be silly to try to separate Moses from the Torah or Jesus from the Gospel or Muhammad from the Koran." Much of the speech avoided any specific criticisms of the Clinton administration's public policies, or even of the Republican-controlled Congress and its Contract with America. Farrakhan emphasized the problems of nihilism and moral poverty as something every American had to address. "We are a wounded people but we're being healed, but President Clinton, America is also wounded. And there's hostility now in the great divide between the people. Socially the fabric of America is being torn apart. . . . Power and wealth has made America spiritually blind and the power and the arrogance of America makes you refuse to hear a child of your slaves pointing out the wrong in your society."

Recognizing that he had a worldwide audience of hundreds of millions of people viewing the televised march, Farrakhan downplayed traditional black nationalist–style, race-based arguments and attempted to transcend the racial divide. "Do you want a solution to the dilemma that America faces? Then," Farrakhan advised, "don't look at our skin color, because racism will cause you to reject salvation if it comes in the skin of a black person. Don't look at the kinkiness of our hair and the broadness of our nose and the thickness of our lips, but listen to the beat of our hearts and the pulsating rhythm of the truth." It was impossible, in the end, to "integrate into white supremacy and hold our dignity as human beings." But white racism also "prevents anyone from becoming one with God. White people have to come out of that idea, which has poisoned them into a false attitude of superiority based on the color of their skins. The doctrine of white supremacy disallows whites to grow to their full potential."

Farrakhan devoted only a few minutes to suggesting practical steps that African-American males could take to empower their communities. He encouraged the development of an "Exodus Economic Fund" to "build an economic infrastructure to nurture businesses within the black community." He urged his audience to join the NAACP, the Urban League, and other black organizations, regardless of their ideology, that were attempting to provide solutions to blacks' problems. Finally, he challenged his mass audience to pledge that "from this day forward I will strive to improve myself spiritually, morally, mentally, socially, politically, and economically for the benefit of myself, my family, and my people."

The gathering was remarkably peaceful, with very few incidents of disorderly conduct and virtually no actions of civil disobedience or political protest. Even President Clinton, who wisely was out of town for the event, offered his praise for the demonstration's emphasis on personal responsibility and family values, as did several Republican congressional leaders.

The march, undeniably, had been a success. But an uncomfortable yet unavoidable question remained: Can a mass rally be equated with a mass movement? We know a considerable amount about who came to the Million Man March from a comprehensive survey of participants completed by Ronald Lester and Associates for the *Washington Post*. Sixty-two African-American researchers randomly conducted more than 1,000 interviews at the event. They found that the typical march participant was more likely to be middle-aged, more affluent, and better educated than most African-American males. Only one-third of all marchers were age thirty and below. Ninety-five percent had at least a high-school education; 59 percent had attended or completed college; and 14 percent had professional school or graduate education. Only 16 percent claimed incomes of below $30,000. One-third earned between $30,000 and $49,999, 17 percent had incomes of $50,000 to $74,999, and an impressive 19 percent had incomes of $75,000 and above. Although march organizers emphasized patriarchal family values and the obligations of black men to support households, only 42 percent of the respondents were married. Politically, the typical marcher was involved in civic affairs, with 80 percent of all men surveyed registered to vote. This socioeconomic profile indicates that the base of support for the march came from the middle and upper middle class, the professional managerial and entrepreneurial elite of black America. These statistics are all the more striking when one considers that the average black household's income in 1997 was only $25,050 and that even the average white household income was $38,972. The number of black families reporting incomes above $50,000 per year actually increased by one-fifth in the years between 1992 and 1997. Low-wage workers, the unemployed, and people living on public assistance, while certainly present at the Million Man March, were not the primary constituency on the Mall that day.

What made black middle-class males, most of whom were middle-aged, turn out in such numbers? Certainly it was not the personal appeal of Farrakhan himself. Only 5 percent of those surveyed stated that their primary reason for coming was to express support for the NOI leader. Almost one-third attributed their presence to their support for the African-American family. One-fourth replied that they went to Washington, D.C., to display "black unity," and another 25 percent said they wanted "to show support for black men taking more responsibility for their families and communities." I believe that most politically active middle-class African Americans no longer believe that the strategies of liberal integrationism and/or post-black politics will produce meaningful, long-term socioeconomic and political changes for the African-American community. There is a deep understanding that something much more is needed, an initiative anchored to the historical struggle for black collective empowerment and capacity-building. That's why so many black people came to Washington, D.C.

It was only after the Million Man March that the serious limitations and contradictions of Farrakhan himself became readily apparent to many African Americans who had supported and even attended the mass event. Farrakhan ideologically was committed to a black political project that can best be described as "conservative black nationalism." Like liberal integrationism, it supports the development of strong black institutions. Philosophically, it has long been suspicious of alliances with whites, especially liberals, organized labor, and the radical Left. On economic issues, conservative black nationalism has strongly advocated the capitalist system and entrepreneurship in the tradition of Booker T. Washington. Polemically, it has often used the label "Uncle Tom" to pillory both black leftists and liberal integrationists who reject racial separatism and social intolerance. But despite his elaborate masquerade of pro-black militancy, Farrakhan was essentially an advocate of "Reaganomics" and the conservative social policy orientation embedded in the Contract with America. He personally supports supply-side economic policies and even the gold standard. Throughout 1996 he extended his collaboration with fascist political cult leader Lyndon La Rouche. After he attended a posh political retreat in Boca Raton, Florida, hosted by Republican economic writer Jude Wanniski, Farrakhan was publicly courted by notorious reactionaries, such as journalist Robert Novaks, to make common cause with the Republican Party.

The Nation of Islam had little experience working in concert with independent black political organizations with divergent ideologies. Farrakhan charged Chavis and the National African American Leadership Summit with the responsibility of building the coalition of black groups that had endorsed the March. Despite the continuing support of some black progressives, such as West, enthusiasm for the summit gradually diminished in the black community. Only a small group of black cultural nationalists, and some representatives of black fraternal organizations and small business groups, were still active supporters. In late September 1996, when the leadership sponsored a national convention of black activists, delegates were stunned when Lyndon La Rouche was introduced as a featured speaker. A near-riot erupted as Fruit of Islam members and La Rouchites confronted outraged black activists. Most prominent black nationalists who had contributed to the success of the march, such as Haki Madhubuti and Maulana Karenga, withdrew their support from the summit. The final straw for many was Chavis's induction as a member of the Nation of Islam in 1997. Surrendering even the appearance of independence, Chavis acquiesced to the role of loyal subordinate. Many had become convinced that the head of the Nation of Islam could tolerate no independence of thought or action by others around him; this act seemed to confirm that view.

In spearheading the Million Man March, Farrakhan had been astute enough to measure correctly the contemporary mood of black America. But the success of the march, in retrospect, probably owed more to the failure of many mainstream African-American leaders to address the flaws of post-black and race-neutral politics, and the absence of greater militancy and collective resistance, than to the Nation of Islam's organizational and outreach capabilities. Although a minority of black America remains enthusiastic about Farrakhan's conservative black nationalism, many supporters now make a critical distinction between his rhetoric and the actual content of his programs. As many activists who rejected Farrakhan's sexism and social conservatism but nevertheless helped with the march frequently said, "Farrakhan may have called the March, but the March belongs to us." What was urgently required was a different kind of black political initiative, an approach to public policy issues that would once again bring the enthusiasm and energy of the masses of black people into the public arena. What was necessary was the reconstruction of a black movement that rejected the charismatic style of leadership characteristic of both Jesse Jackson and Louis Farrakhan and moved toward a democratic approach promoting "group-centered leaders" rather than "leader-centered groups."

III

By late 1996, the heady aspirations that had been generated within black America had all but disappeared. The NOI had no experience or prior history of building broad-based, nonsectarian organizations or coalitions. Its inflexible, paternalistic hierarchy and conservative social views about gender and sexuality turned off many younger African-American males who had become enthusiastic supporters of Farrakhan during the mass mobilization only twelve months before. Rumors circulated about "what happened" to the hundreds of thousands, perhaps even millions, of dollars that had been donated to help fund the march.

Farrakhan himself was, in a curious and paradoxical way, a victim of his own success. He knew, like Malcolm X before him, that the NOI inevitably had to give up its separatist ideology and merge into the orthodoxy of Sunni Islam. That required making a bold break from the doctrines of Elijah Muhammad, something that Farrakhan found difficult if not impossible to do. Farrakhan wanted, in Malcolm's words, to "turn a corner," to move away from racial fundamentalism toward a more pluralistic, universalist politics that would have permitted him to assume a decisive leadership role in national affairs. But the conservatives within his own organization were not prepared for such a sea change. By the late 1990s there were small but growing defections from the NOI due to its more liberal and inclusive orientation. Serious health problems complicated Farrakhan's dilemma, and his impetus in providing leadership to the entire Black Freedom Movement stalled, then stopped. Farrakhan, like Jesse Jackson and Al Sharpton in different ways, could not distance himself from his own history.

The Million Man March's success, however, was probably a motivating factor prompting President Clinton to advance his own initiative on race, one that would come from the top down rather than from the bottom up. After his convincing reelection to the presidency in 1996, Clinton, as part of an effort to secure his legacy as chief executive, pursued an agenda that included a greater interracial dialogue and constructive civic engagement. Soon after the second inauguration, the Clinton administration drafted preliminary plans to launch a national "race initiative." In a much-publicized commencement address at the University of California at San Diego in June 1997, Clinton delivered what one *New York Times* editorial effusively praised as "a sermon with little sanctimonious preaching. He went beyond the obvious need for racial justice to the practical and even economic reasons why the United States must nurture its increasingly diverse society." Clinton reaffirmed his support for affirmative action but quickly added that opponents of the policy were "without any ill motives." The president then challenged his audience to ask, "Can we fulfill the promise of America by embracing all our citizens of all races, not just at a university, where people have the benefit of enlightened teachers and the time to think and grow and get to know each other, but in the daily life of every American community?"

Clinton's next statement seemed to suggest that government and the enforcement of civil-rights laws by themselves would not uproot racism:

"I know and I've said before that money cannot buy this goal. Power cannot compel it. Technology cannot create it. This is something that can only come from the human spirit." He reflected that, despite the "evidence of bigotry" that still remains, "minorities have more opportunities than ever today." In his concluding remarks, Clinton recalled that at the "high tide of the civil rights movement, the Kerner Commission said we were becoming two Americas, one white, one black, separate and unequal." Today's challenges of race and ethnicity were fundamentally different: "Will we become not two, but many Americas, separate, unequal and isolated? Or will we draw strength for all our people and from our ancient faith in equality and human dignity, to become the world's first truly multiracial democracy?"

The general response from the media was warmly positive, praising Clinton for proposing "a year-long conversation about race." The *New York Times* expressed the hope that, "If Mr. Clinton's speech starts such a process, and leads to concrete actions, it could be remembered as a turning point for him and the country. Let the conversation proceed." Predictably, the Republican Party was critical of the president's address. Speaker of the House Newt Gingrich protested that there was already too "much talk on this issue" of race and not enough action. "We must make America a country with equal opportunity for all and special privilege for none by treating all individuals as equals before the law and doing away with quotas, preferences and set-asides in Government contracts, hiring and university admissions," he said. Gingrich's approach to constructive race relations included policies to push welfare recipients into low-paying jobs, support for minority entrepreneurship, tougher sentences for violent criminals, and the establishment of a "multiracial" category to the census and other government forms as an attempt to phase out "black," "white," and other racial classifications. It was, in short, an abbreviated version of the Republican Contract with America program, essentially a call for the elimination of key reforms achieved by the Civil Rights Movement during a half century of struggle, filtered through his own peculiar notions about blacks.

The confrontative and polemical character of Gingrich's remarks could not entirely obscure the similarities between the two leaders' positions on the issue of race. In his highly publicized address, the president deliberately had proposed no new policies to uproot structural racism. Clinton had been virtually silent when California voters had passed Proposition 209 eliminating that state's affirmative-action programs. In 1996 Clinton signed a welfare bill that threatened to push many black women and children into poverty. His administration had done nothing to respond to the 1996 *Hopwood v. State of Texas* decision of the U.S. Court of Appeals for the Fifth Circuit outlawing the use of race as a factor in admissions to universities. *The Nation* thoughtfully editorialized that Clinton's "lofty rhetoric" was empty and suggested that he lacked the political commitment necessary to challenge racism: "The remedies are no longer as simple as taking down signs by water fountains—not that they ever were. A bold President would educate and lead. He or she would have to be willing to expend resources—dollars or political capital or points in the polls. But this President offers only his words, not his soul."

In the end, neither Clinton, Gingrich, nor their political defenders and supporters were willing to address the "problem of whiteness," of how white privilege remains deeply ingrained into the political and economic structures of society. The deconstruction of "whiteness" is essential in creating the political conditions where honest and constructive racial discourse is possible. In the powerful words of historian David Roediger: "It is not merely that whiteness is oppressive and false; it is that whiteness is *nothing but oppressive and false.* . . . It is the empty and terrifying attempt to build an identity based on what one isn't and on whom one can hold back." In effect, the leaders of both major U.S. political parties still deny the structural reality of white privilege and the continuing burden of racial difference. Both sides grope toward an end to racial hostilities, a modern-day "Appomattox" on the multicultural front, but silently prefer the preservation of whiteness above the realization of racial justice.

One measurement of white privilege can be found in the vastly different ways in which blacks and whites describe the racial contours of daily life. Only days before Clinton's San Diego address, the Gallup Organization released the results of a nationwide poll charting African-American and white perceptions of how blacks are treated. The poll indicated that the vast majority of whites were absolutely convinced that blacks receive at least the same treatment, and perhaps even preferential treatment, in the workplace and other arenas of daily life. For example, only 14 percent of all whites responded that blacks were "treated less fairly than whites on the job," compared to 45 percent of the African Americans interviewed. Nineteen percent of whites and 46 percent of blacks agreed that blacks were "treated less fairly at stores downtown or in malls."

The racial gap extended to virtually every aspect of social intercourse. Those concurring that blacks were treated less fairly than whites tallied up as follows: on public transportation, 25 percent of blacks and 12 percent of whites; in neighborhood shops, 46 percent of blacks compared to 18 percent of whites; in restaurants, 42 percent and 16 percent; and by the police, 60 percent to 30 percent. Significant numbers of the blacks interviewed also asserted that they had personal "experiences of discrimination within the past thirty days": while shopping, 30 percent; dining out, 21 percent; at work, 21 percent; encountering the police, 15 percent; and while on public transportation, 6 percent. To be truly effective, the President's Race Initiative would have to speak openly and honestly to white Americans about this "white blindness" to these continuing patterns of blatant discrimination.

Clinton's initiative was the fourth presidential effort in half a century attempting to engage the nation in a dialogue about issues of race. Following World War II, President Harry S. Truman authorized a commission to examine the state of race relations throughout the United States and make recommendations for public policy reform. Truman's commission produced the document "To Secure These Rights," which for its time was an extraordinary statement advocating the complete "elimination of segregation, based on race, color, creed, or national origin, from American life." The report provided the Truman administration with intellectual justification for eliminating Jim Crow educational facilities. A follow-up committee in 1948 produced a second study, "Freedom to Serve," pointing the way toward outlawing racial segregation in the armed forces. Truman gave moral and political authority to these initiatives by signing an executive order mandating fair-employment policies in the federal government, stating, "The principles on which our Government is based require a policy of fair employment throughout the Federal establishment without discrimination because of race, color, religion, or national origin." Southern Democrats were bitterly opposed to the administration's initiatives, and a number of them broke with the national ticket in 1948 to establish the Dixiecrat Party. Truman was from Missouri, a border state with a long history of racial discrimination, and in some ways he was personally racist. Nevertheless, he used the power of his office to push the country's racial discourse forward.

Truman's successor, Dwight D. Eisenhower, also initiated several less ambitious, but nevertheless constructive, initiatives on race. Eisenhower had received the support of 39 percent of the African-American electorate in his 1956 successful reelection campaign, and at the time the Republican Party had a strong liberal wing that was pressuring the White House to take bolder steps on racial policy. Eisenhower submitted a four-point proposal to Congress for the new implementation of civil rights, with the key reform of granting the attorney general the power to go to federal court to directly assist citizens whose constitutional right to vote had been violated by local registrars in the South. Southern Democrats in the Senate were able to defeat this element of the bill. However, what was produced was the establishment of the U.S. Commission on Civil Rights, which was given the power to make inquiries into local charges of violations of voting rights, to "study and collect information concerning legal developments constituting a denial of equal protection of the laws, and to appraise the laws and policies of the federal government with respect to equal protection." The bill also "elevated the civil rights section of the Department of Justice to the status of a division, with an assistant attorney general over it." In the view of historian John Hope Franklin, "The real significance of the legislation lay not so much in its provisions as in its recognition of federal responsibility and its reflection of a remarkable and historic reversal of that federal policy of hands off in matters involving civil rights."

Ten years later, in the wake of a series of unprecedented urban uprisings, President Lyndon Johnson established the National Advisory Commission on Civil Disorders, chaired by Illinois Governor Otto Kerner. The Kerner Commission studied the underlying factors leading to the black revolts in America's inner cities. The final report documented that in the first nine months of 1967, the nation had experienced 164 civil disturbances, and that the reasons for racial unrest had much more to do with systemic poverty, unemployment, and social inequality than with the activities of political subversives, as law-enforcement authorities claimed. "What white Americans can never fully understand," the Kerner Report stated, "but what the Negro can never forget—is that white society is deeply implicated in the ghetto. White institutions maintain [racism], and white society condones it." The report's prophetic warning challenged white America's historic inertia on matters of race: "Our Nation is moving toward two societies, one black, one white— separate and unequal." Although Johnson distanced himself from the honest and frank judgments of the Kerner Report, he had nevertheless initiated a process that helped to establish the societal justification for reforms such as affirmative action and minority economic set-aside measures.

It is by these historical precedents that Clinton's 1997–1998 President's Race Initiative should be judged. Throughout most of his administration, Clinton's chief accomplishments in promoting the interests of black Americans had been achieved through the power of the executive branch of government. About 15 percent of the administrative appointments in the White House went to blacks. African Americans would serve, at some point of his eight years in office, as heads of the Departments of Agriculture, Commerce, Energy, Labor, and Veterans Affairs. He appointed more African Americans to the federal courts and to other federal posts than any other president in history. After his reelection, I think that Clinton sincerely wanted to leave a permanent legacy of racial liberalism behind and that he believed that a new commission to study an age-old problem that had challenged American democracy for four centuries was the way to do it. At least, that's what the plan was.

On June 13, 1997, President Clinton signed Executive Order 13050 establishing the "Initiative on Race" and authorizing a presidential advisory board to conduct a study and produce a final document. The immediate objective was for the board to hold meetings and conversations about the contemporary role of race in American life, examining all aspects of civil society, including health care, education, housing, and culture. Heads of federal agencies were expected to cooperate fully with the board's inquiries. Clinton's wisest decision was in the selection of the board's chair, the esteemed historian Dr. John Hope Franklin. Franklin had first met Clinton during the 1992 presidential campaign, and after their initial conversation he had come away very impressed with the Arkansas governor's extensive knowledge of African-American history. In 1995, Clinton had awarded Franklin the Presidential Medal of Freedom. In their private conversations at the White House after the awards ceremony, Clinton revealed to Franklin that he considered him to be a "prisoner of American racism"—which the historian interpreted to mean that Clinton believed that all African Americans were still trapped by the structural barriers of discrimination and that the president was personally committed to addressing this great American tragedy.

On the basis of these prior, productive conversations, Franklin agreed to take responsibility for running the board. A prominent Asian-American civil-rights attorney and expert on ethnic discrimination, Angela Oh, was named the board's vice chairperson. The seven-member panel also included former Republican Governor Thomas Kean of New Jersey, who had previously received strong support from African-American voters in his statewide races and had established credentials in the field of education.

Almost immediately, the President's Race Initiative came under attack from the Republican Party leadership and from ideological conservatives. There were other problems, too. There had been remarkably little prior background research or extensive consultation with scholars leading up to the announcement of the president's initiative. The board, which was given no real administrative infrastructure, was widely referred to in the media as a "presidential commission"—which it was not. The board's actual power was extremely limited. It was, for example, not permitted to meet privately to discuss issues as an internal body. Any meetings involving more than three members of the board had to be held publicly, thereby inhibiting any meaningful discussions.

Personal conflicts also interfered with the board's work. Kean would become a constant problem on the board—first through his failure to attend crucial sessions, and later because of his private and public criticisms that the initiative had failed to produce anything of substance. Tensions broke out between Franklin and Oh, and to a lesser extent between other board members, on the degree of emphasis they should give to the black-white paradigm in discussing the future of American race relations. Oh emphasized that "any relevant framework around race relations in this country would have to include the experiences of people who are neither black or white, let alone mixed race people." Franklin's position was that the black-white relationship was the societal template upon which all subsequent multiracial relations and dynamics had been constructed. Both Franklin and Oh later denied that their differences were significant, but in truth, their theoretical division helps to explain many of the conceptual weaknesses in the final report and the absence of clear-cut policy recommendations despite a fifteen-month process of meetings.

These meetings included several major televised public "conversations" and several hundred public gatherings across the country involving tens of thousands of people. But complaints continued to surface from all quarters. In Denver, about 200 American Indians, many of them members of the American Indian Movement, protested the absence of an American Indian on the advisory board. The protests from the floor were so disruptive that the decision was made to divide the community forum in Denver into two sections. In the first group, a number of individuals, who had been "screened" off from the formal proceedings, were given space to vent their concerns—which included everything from the demands of white supremacists to those favoring justice for the Roma people (gypsies). The second, more formal session almost immediately broke down into chaos. Native-American scholar Ward Churchill, a participant in the protests, stated that African Americans in attendance were angered by the insults and lack of decorum that Indian protesters had shown Franklin. Churchill observed:

> In response, an indigenous protester explained that if a native person had been named chair of the board and had then excluded African Americans, not only would blacks be justified in protesting

but Indians would be obliged to join their protest. Since there seemed to be little reciprocation of this position from the Afro-American community, the native activist continued, "It looks like you folks are selling us out and even attacking us to make sure you get a 'slice of pie,' at our expense. Well, later for that, my 'brother.'" "From where we stand," the member of the American Indian Movement of Colorado summed up, "it's still all stolen pie. And John Hope Franklin? He's just today's version of a Buffalo Soldier."

Franklin had personally lobbied for the appointment of an American-Indian representative to the board, but had been unsuccessful. The board did appoint two American-Indian consultants to advise their work, and later the board members met with a series of Indian groups and representatives. Nevertheless, the chaos of the Denver sessions gave the media a legitimate pretext for trashing the President's Race Initiative and its controversial board. It is possible that Clinton himself could have resuscitated the activities of the board by placing the weight and author-ity of his administration behind the effort. Yet by early 1998, White House staffers in many instances were discouraging the president from identifying himself with the initiative. The Monica Lewinsky sex scan-dal, leading to Clinton's subsequent impeachment by the House of Rep-resentatives, overshadowed the constructive work of the board.

The final report of the president's advisory board was entitled, "One America in the Twenty-First Century: Forging a New Future." Despite some important limitations, the report was probably the most progres-sive document to emerge from the Clinton administration during its en-tire tenure. It gave a comprehensive overview of how racial discrimina-tion is perpetuated in a host of policy areas—housing, employment, law enforcement and criminal justice, education, and social services. The re-port defended affirmative-action laws as absolutely essential to sustain-ing the modest gains achieved by racialized minorities. It emphasized the centrality of focusing on the "promising practices" of nongovern-mental organizations and voluntary associations in civil society. Conceptually, it recognized fundamental demographic changes in the ethnic composition of the country.

The report received mixed reviews in academic circles. Sociologist Howard Winant observed that its political orientation of social democracy was remarkable in and of itself, since the board "had to address the centrist Democratic president who had created their council out of a mixed set of political motives." To its credit, according to Winant, the report "ventures into redistributive, human rights oriented territory at a number of points: calling for large-scale state investments in universal health care, high quality education at all levels, a variety of anti-poverty measures such as increasing the minimum wage, and collective bargaining rights for all."

Despite these strengths, "One America" contained many contradictions and weaknesses, especially conceptually and theoretically. Ethnic studies scholar Gary Okihiro criticized the board's "notions of racism as largely an individual, and not a social matter, and of its eradication as a product of reaching a mutual understanding and thereby appreciation though dialogue." Winant suggested that the report broke "virtually no new ground analytically," and was "an articulate throwback to the good old days of civil rights, when indeed the problem seemed to be 'rights' or the lack of them." Embedded in the text was a kind of liberal "color-blindness," implying "race is still seen as something that ought to be 'transcended.'"

Perhaps the report's most surprising critic from the civil-rights community was Mary Frances Berry. Berry charged that the Race Initiative "did not deal with the fundamental issues" and "missed the central crisis in U.S. racial tensions, rooted in the four-centuries-old interactions between blacks and whites." Berry charged that the report's overriding theme was "that African Americans are just another group of 'colored people' with no special place in the pantheon of those who have suffered from subordination, and are at the periphery of discussion." Berry noted, "African Americans have not been in vogue in policy discussions for quite some time, except for self-help projects and admonitions to be responsible, no matter how responsible we believe we already are being." Berry charged that the report ducked the fundamental challenge of identifying the full structural barriers of white supremacy that remain the anchors of anti-black racism:

> In any discussion about racism, beyond a brutal murder such as what occurred in Jasper County, Texas, the predicament of African Americans risks being rejected as insignificant or a case of special pleading. We may be concerned about DWB, driving while black, or being black jelly beans in a jar, but politicians and the public are only sporadically interested at best. Just as the Kerner report caused private institutions, including the media, to become more inclusive of black people, the Clinton initiative gives the seal of approval to a shift in focus to emphasize the inclusion of anyone but African Americans in well-paying jobs, entrepreneurship and educational opportunities, since black people have had "their turn."

At the formal press conference announcing the "One America" report, there were no copies of the study available for distribution. It was so typical of Clinton, who walked away from his commitments in virtually every public-policy arena, that no one was surprised. The president's highly touted Race Initiative ended not with a bang, but a whimper. The tragedy, from the vantage point of black Americans, was that Clinton truly had the political authority to advance the national dialogue on racism but lacked the moral and political will to do so. As in Farrakhan's earlier "race initiative" in the 1990s, the Million Man March, no permanent or structural change came out of the entire process. From both ideological sides—the race-based and the state-based approaches to reshaping the racial discourse of America—little ground was gained, and millions of working-class and low-income black people continued to find themselves sliding further into the abyss.

Chapter 5

Race and Educational Inequality

We must have integrated schools. . . .
That is when our race will gain full equality.
                    —Martin Luther King, Jr.
                        December 23, 1956

I

Education has always been a way for oppressed peoples to improve themselves, to move their families and communities forward. My own family's history is probably similar to that of many other American minority families. My great-grandfather, Morris Marable, was born a slave before the Civil War. But as a slave, and later as a freed man after the Civil War, Morris recognized that knowledge was power. He sent his thirteen children to school. As the superintendent of his Sunday school at church, he led his congregation in reading the scriptures. But my great-grandfather, this former slave, never really mastered the skill of reading himself. Memorizing each passage by heart, Morris could open the Bible and quote chapter and verse with total accuracy without knowing individual words. His illiteracy did not prohibit him from trying to improve his own children's lives.

My father, James Marable, served as a sergeant in the racially segregated Army Air Corps in World War II, fighting to defend a democracy that did not include people of color. Through the GI Bill, he was able to enroll in Wilberforce College, a historically black college in Ohio. But the GI Bill did not guarantee him success, it only gave him the opportunity to achieve. My dad went to school full-time in the day and for years worked the night shift as a maintenance worker in a factory. James Marable worked two full-time jobs for nearly two decades, to make sure that his two sons and daughter could attend college and make something more of their lives.

I have related these stories from my own life because they are both ordinary and exceptional—like that of millions of other oppressed people. African-American people have always overcome the odds against them, using education as a central tool to dismantle the barriers of racial inequality. Yet despite our limited educational victories over the years, the chasm between America's democratic rhetoric and the unequal reality still seems as vast as the Grand Canyon for black, brown, and poor people.

How far has America actually progressed toward more constructive race relations, especially in the area of multicultural education? Judging by some recent events in my own life, not much. Several years ago, I was invited to deliver the Martin Luther King, Jr., holiday speech at a small, predominantly white southern college. For decades, this school had been racially segregated, like other all-white public educational institutions. The college's first black faculty member had been hired only in the early 1980s. Nevertheless, the initial reception I received was friendly and positive, from administrators, faculty, and representatives of the student government association, which had sponsored my visit. Nothing in these introductions prepared me for what I would soon encounter that evening.

My lecture that night was before an audience of perhaps 500 people, consisting mostly of students and a significant number of African Americans from the surrounding community. I spoke about King's enduring legacy, the importance of achieving social justice, and the urgent need for constructive dialogue across America's racial chasm. As I concluded, most of the audience responded favorably to the message, but many sat in silence.

A white male student jumped out of his seat, even before the audience had stopped applauding, and raised his hand to ask the first question. When I acknowledged him, the white student launched into an attack against affirmative action, which he characterized as "reverse discrimination." He insisted that both he and many of his friends had lost scholarships and jobs to unqualified minorities. I replied that statistically less than 2 percent of all university scholarships were "race-based," that is, designated for blacks and Hispanics. Affirmative action and the enforcement of civil rights laws were necessary because job discrimination was still rampant, and blacks frequently were unfairly charged more for goods and services than whites. I cited one major study illustrating that blacks who negotiated and purchased automobiles at white car dealerships were frequently charged significantly more than whites who bought identical cars.

The white student was unimpressed and unapologetic. His precise words were unclear, but his essential response was, "Then the blacks ought to shop somewhere else!" Suddenly, a significant number of white students burst into applause, and a few even cheered. Surprised and saddened, I quickly responded that this discrimination was illegal and morally outrageous, and that blacks should not have to shop in another country in order to be treated fairly in the marketplace.

Don't misunderstand my point here. As a middle-aged black man, I spent many summers in Dixie during the 1960s. I experienced Jim Crow segregation firsthand, and white racism is hardly a new phenomenon to me. But the white students at this formerly segregated college had no personal knowledge of what Jim Crow was about. They had never witnessed black people being denied the right to vote, or signs posted on public restrooms reading "white" and "colored." Yet they felt no hesitation, no restraint, about proclaiming their prerogatives as whites, over and above any claims that black people have made for equality. In effect, this was "white supremacy": The students were blind to the historical dynamics and social consequences of racial oppression, jealous of any benefits achieved by blacks from civil-rights agitation, and outraged by the suggestion that racial minorities should be compensated for their exploitation. The twisted logic of white supremacy is that reformers who champion racial equality and social justice are the "real racists." And as I subsequently learned, a number of white students were e-mailing administrators and others the next morning, demanding to know why this black "racist" was invited to speak at their campus!

What particularly struck me about this incident was the deep anger displayed by some whites in the audience. One can disagree with someone else's political perspective, yet behave in a civil manner. Something I had said, or perhaps, what I represented, had generated white rage bordering on irrational hatred.

Instead of leading the nation in constructive racial change, the field of education seems to be suffering defeats in this arena at every level. The trends in the courts and in electoral politics have been to reverse previous advances. Landmark cases, including *Podberesky v. Kirwan* in 1994 and *Hopwood v. State of Texas* in 1996, have meant lower minority enrollments at the university level. Initiative 200 in the state of Washington and Proposition 209 in California had similar effects. Other universities across the country have faced the same dilemma. Moreover, in the southern states, little progress has been made to desegregate public universities. A recent report by the Southern Education Foundation found that over the past twenty years, black students' access to higher education in the region has remained virtually unchanged. In several southern states, black first-year student enrollment in state-supported universities is today actually lower than it was twenty years ago. The universities are not the only level of our educational system under attack by racist factions. The K–12 public school system is just as affected.

II

Few issues are more controversial in American politics today than the intense debates over privatizing the management of public schools and the
conservative campaign favoring school vouchers, in which public funds
are used to pay for all or part of students' tuition costs at either public or
private schools. Most advocates of public education fear, with considerable justification, that these moves toward privatization will do nothing
to enhance the actual quality of education, especially for black, brown,
and poor children. Conservative Republicans, from President Bush to
former New York Mayor Rudolph Giuliani, preach that market-based
initiatives will provide the necessary incentives to promote higher levels
of educational achievement. Millions of African Americans who usually
support progressive and egalitarian public-policy positions are increasingly divided over these issues. A growing and vocal constituency has become convinced that public education has failed and that privatization is
the only hope for our children.

Nationally, public opinion has also shifted during the past decade toward privatization and "educational choice." In 1990, only about one-
fourth of all Americans supported school vouchers. By 2000, nearly one-
half did. Levels of support varied greatly, however, according to the
wording pollsters used to ask the question of whether public funds
should be used to pay the tuitions of children attending private schools.
Opinion surveys among African Americans and Latinos have indicated
for a number of years that there is a widely held perception that minority students perform better in private schools, especially in parochial
schools. One 1990 educational survey of more than 100,000 students reported that African-American Catholics attending parochial schools
were "more likely to complete high school and college." It is also significant that African Americans, Latinos, and Asians now constitute more
than one-quarter of the 2.6 million children attending Catholic schools
in the United States.

Vouchers have not done well to date when placed on the ballot. In
November 2000, California's voucher initiative, Proposition 38, was

overwhelmingly defeated. Even California's Catholic Bishops refused to campaign for the initiative, complaining that it failed to "serve the poor."

How did we reach this point in the national discourse about public education? The roots of today's debate about vouchers and privatization actually go back a half century, to 1954 when the Supreme Court outlawed "separate but equal" public schools. According to education scholars Robert S. Peterkin and Janice E. Jackson, one response to the *Brown v. Board of Education* decision was the creation of magnet schools, which were originally designed "to draw students across segregated residential areas to desegregated school environments." In the late 1970s, an idea that emerged in Cambridge, Massachusetts, called "controlled choice," was essentially "not only an attempt to voluntarily desegregate the schools but also one of the first district-wide plans to promote parental choice of schools as a major goal." Liberals and many radicals also began advocating the concept of "charter schools," public educational institutions that were given much greater flexibility than traditional public schools in administration and curriculum. These alternative, public-choice models of education rapidly proliferated across the country. The Reagan administration got behind magnet schools in a big way. In 1984, the Magnet Schools Assistance Program was passed as part of Title VII of the Education for Economic Security Act. According to the research of Peterkin and Jackson, the magnet schools grew "from 14 districts nationwide in 1976, to 1,000 schools in 138 districts in 1981, and to 2,652 schools offering a combined total of 3,222 magnet programs at the end of the 1991-92 school year." By 2000, there were also about 1,000 charter schools nationwide.

Criticisms of the public school–choice reforms began surfacing as early as twenty years ago. Critics argued that magnet schools created privileged learning environments primarily for middle-class white students and a much smaller percentage of minority students at the expense of lower-income black and brown students. Others pointed out that these educational reforms did relatively little to stem the growing exodus of white middle-class children from predominantly minority urban school systems. And by the early 1990s, the racial demographics of

America's public schools were almost as striking as the racialized patterns of apartheid in South Africa. According to the National Center of Education Statistics, as of 1993, of the more than 15,000 school districts in the United States, the 100 largest districts enrolled more than 40 percent of the nation's total minority student population. In 19 of these school districts in 1993, more than one-half of all students were African American, and in six, the majority were Latino.

Increasingly, African-American and progressive educators and school administrators face off with a conservative political establishment, corporate interests, and the media, all of which overwhelmingly favor privatization schemes of one type or another. The fight to defend and enhance our public schools is a struggle that we must undertake because we cannot afford to lose. When one objectively analyzes the arguments for vouchers and school privatization, they fall apart, one by one.

Reviews comparing the scholastic performance of students in public versus private and alternative schools can be misleading for a number of reasons. Many "choice" schools achieve their levels of excellence by limiting access to the most "competitive students." Indeed, what researchers are frequently measuring may not be the effectiveness of an educational program, observed education scholars Gary R. George and Walter C. Farrell, Jr., but the process of selectivity "along even more rigid lines of race and class." They wrote, "Private choice schools often recruit differentially, pursuing students from middle-class public schools and other private schools aggressively and in person while sending only promotional brochures or booklets to students in low-income schools." George and Farrell also noted that private schools frequently "do not provide services for handicapped students, and limited-English-proficient students often are discouraged from applying."

There is a widely held belief that students generally do better in private schools than in the public school system, but the evidence for this is at best mixed. One 1992 study assessing the results of private versus public schools with statistical evidence taken from the 1990 National Assessment of Educational Progress actually found that "the longer students stay in private schools, the worse they do, and the longer students stay in public schools, the better they do."

People may have different views on the quality of the public schools, but one thing is clear: Public schools have the greater potential for creating culturally diverse environments that measurably enhance the critical intellectual skills of young people. One 2000 study sponsored by the Harvard Civil Rights Project, in partnership with the National School Boards Association's Council of Urban Boards of Education, found that "high school students in metropolitan Louisville—a particularly diverse and integrated urban school system—reported that they benefited greatly from the diversity of their schools." The survey, which was administered to more than 1,000 students, found that "strong educational benefits" were observable in three key categories: "critical thinking skills, future educational goals, and principles of citizenship." About 90 percent of all students surveyed reported "that exposure in the curriculum to different cultures and experiences of different racial and ethnic groups has helped them to better understand points of view different from their own."

The advocates of school choice fail to comprehend that the purposes and functions of profit-making businesses and education are fundamentally different. Education scholar Alexander Astin of UCLA made this point brilliantly: "Successful profit-making businesses grow to accommodate the increasing demand for their products or services because growth tends to increase profits." What happens when a particular public school becomes very popular or highly successful in the market for students? It doesn't increase its enrollment to accommodate demand, Astin observed, "It becomes 'selective.' Notable examples of such schools would be the Bronx High School of Science, Bronx, New York, or the many 'magnet' schools. In short, since the size of successful schools in the educational marketplace does not usually increase, the least successful schools seldom go out of business. Students have to attend school somewhere."

This process of selectivity concentrates the "best students"—those who are highest achieving and highly motivated—in the elite schools. These are also usually the children of the wealthiest and best-educated households. The net effect of what Astin called "differential selectivity is thus to stratify schools" by socioeconomic status and academic achievement. "These realities suggest that one highly likely consequence of implementing a policy of choice would be to magnify the existing social stratification of the schools." Vouchers will only be financial incentives for more middle-class families to take their children out of public schools; many private schools will simply respond to this increased demand by becoming even more "selective," or by raising their tuitions, or both.

There are alternative practical steps we can and must take to improve the quality of public education. Educator Faustine C. Jones-Wilson, in a spring 1990 article published in the *Journal of Negro Education*, provided an effective orientation for black empowerment:

> We must organize ourselves to affect educational policies and practices in those states and cities in which we are most concentrated. We must use our time and energy to monitor the implementation of appropriate policies, programs and practices. . . . We must resuscitate our heritage of survivalism and self-sufficiency. We must stop the everlasting rhetoric about what we have done and what we are going to do and do more now. . . . Our focus, thus, must not be on theoretical education. Education must be related to the lives of learners. It must be related to political action aimed at improving Black communities. . . . We must emphasize to our young that they have a responsibility to learn—not learning is not a viable choice. We must make it clear to them that what we are teaching relates to their lives and to the potential well-being of their communities.

I believe that real academic excellence can only exist in a democracy within the framework of multicultural diversity. Indeed, our public school systems, despite their serious problems, represent one of the most important institutional safeguards for defending the principles of democracy and equality under the law. There is, in effect, a dual function of public education. As Diane Ketelle, a professor of education at St. Mary's College of California, recently wrote: "A public school has both internal public purposes and external public purposes. The internal purpose is learning, but the external purpose is to build community."

Public education alone has the potential capacity for building pluralistic communities and creating a lively civic culture that promotes the fullest possible engagement and participation of all members of society. In this sense, the public school is a true laboratory for democracy.

III

Higher education is today in the midst of a fundamental transformation even more profound than during the aftermath of World War II, when the passage of the GI Bill greatly increased the number of Americans enrolled in universities. Two of the primary factors behind the current changes in higher education, most educators agree, are the revolution in high technology and the transnational dynamics of globalization. The creation of cyberspace and new information technologies have transformed how we think about everything related to learning, from classroom instruction to knowledge production and research. Globalization, in particular the unprecedented integration of international markets, the vast migrations of labor, and the construction of multinational workforces, also creates a qualitatively new economic environment for colleges. "Competitiveness" can no longer be defined in parochial or traditional terms but must be taken in the context of increasingly international student populations, rapidly changing labor forces, and new global economic developments.

There were at least three other factors that will have equally profound effects on the future development of American higher education, especially in the context of a racially diverse, multicultural society. In brief, these factors are: (1) the triumph of the politics of neoliberalism, which has caused the rapid dismantling of public institutions of all kinds, from human services programs and state universities to public works and public housing; (2) the glaring and unprecedented class stratification in the contemporary United States, with vast concentrations of wealth and affluence among a very small percentage of the population who coexist with millions of working poor people, the unemployed, and people on fixed incomes; and (3) the polarization of racialized ethnicity, including the socioeconomic marginalization of blacks, Latinos, and immigrants from Third World countries, the elimination of affirmative-action and race-based scholarships, and the decline of educational opportunity and access to millions of nonwhite Americans. One could perhaps characterize these three factors as dimensions of a larger social contradiction: the growing problem of human inequality, which now expresses itself as "progress."

In today's neoliberal political environment, federal and state governments have moved to limit and reduce expenditures to public colleges and universities. As education researchers Sheila Slaughter and Gary Rhoades have noted, in 1973 states contributed about one-half of the operating budgets of public colleges. By the mid-1990s, that level of support fell to 33 percent. Tuitions at public universities accounted for roughly 15 percent of institutional revenue streams in 1973 but have increased to 22 percent today. Working-class and low-income families making tremendous sacrifices to send their children to public universities were now expected to assume a significantly greater share of the costs. For example, the total cost of an average undergraduate student to attend a school in the State University of New York system, including tuition, books, and room and board, rose from $7,319 in 1991 to $11,201 by 1997, a 35 percent increase. At the City University of New York (CUNY), a system whose students are overwhelmingly black, Latino, working class, and poor, tuition and fees for undergraduates doubled between 1988 and 1998. At the same time, the state's share of the CUNY operating budget fell from 77 percent to 49 percent. In *Culture of Intolerance*, Mark Nathan Cohen recently observed that such policies in New York and elsewhere are "affirmative action for the affluent because it guarantees that only they will apply for professional positions. Doing away with *official* affirmative action while simultaneously reducing funding for public colleges and schools (except in affluent neighborhoods, which can take care of their own funding) further reduces competition and doubly damages the prospects of minorities and the poor."

This shift in investment and expenditures in education from the state to private individuals is a neoliberal phenomenon that is occurring throughout the world. Australia, a country that charged no tuition at public universities prior to 1989, now requires full-time students to pay

annually between $1,940 and $3,200, depending on their area of study. In
China, which has an annual per capita income of less than $680, yearly
tuition at public universities amounted to $890 in 1998-1999. In Israel,
Canada, Britain, South Africa, Ghana, and Mexico, millions of students
have engaged in mass demonstrations and strikes to protest tuition increases during the past four years. The worldwide retreat in government
subsidies for public higher education has indirectly contributed to increased tuition costs at private research universities and liberal-arts colleges because it raises public expectations of what the price of a four-
year college degree should be.

Federal and state governments have also made it much more difficult
for working-class people and racialized minorities to finance their own
education through state-assisted loans and grants. In 1981, for example,
the maximum amount awarded under the Pell Grant program paid approximately 85 percent of the total cost of attending a public four-year
college. Today, the maximum Pell Grant that the neediest students can
receive is only $3,300, less than one-third of the financial support neces-
sary at most public universities. In the 1980s and 1990s, many state legislatures passed repressive legislation restricting eligibility in state-funded
scholarship programs and for state tax credits for college tuition for residents convicted of a felony or drug-related offense. In South Carolina,
for example, students who are convicted of even minor offenses, such as
violating the state's open-container laws, have been permanently denied
participation in education aid programs. Since about one-third of all
African-American males in their twenties are at any time under the direct supervision of the criminal-justice system—either in jail or prison,
on probation, on parole, or awaiting trial—the impact of disqualifying
convicted felons from educational aid programs is profoundly racial.

The decade of the 1990s also symbolized an unprecedented affluence
for a privileged minority of Americans—whose children are the core
group recruited for admission to elite colleges. As of 1999, the wealthiest
1 percent of all Americans (about 1.2 million families) had average pretax
incomes of $786,000. This affluent class received 15 percent of the total
family income and has a greater combined net wealth than the bottom
90 percent of all U.S. households. The richest 20 percent of the popula-

tion receives about 54 percent of all income, owns more than three-fourths of the society's net wealth, and as of 1999 earned an average of $144,000 annually. Much of this new wealth was of course generated by the growth in equity markets and investments in new technologies and global corporations. By way of a brief comparison, the average African-American household earns less than $35,000 annually, and more than one-quarter of all black families remain below the federal government's poverty line. In this extremely polarized environment of class and race, opportunity and access to higher education are determined primarily by wealth. According to U.S. Census Bureau statistics of 1998, for families with incomes above $75,000 annually, 65 percent of their children aged eighteen to twenty-four enroll in college. Only 24 percent of students from families with incomes under $25,000 attend college. Race also remains a significant factor in college access. The Census Bureau figures indicate that white students in this age category have enrollment rates of 37 percent. The enrollment rates for African-American students in the same age category fall to 30 percent, and are only 20 percent for Hispanics.

As government support for higher education has retreated, public and private colleges and universities alike in recent decades have had to turn to aggressive fundraising strategies, soliciting private gifts to cover their operating costs. In academic year 1998-1999 U.S. colleges and universities collectively raised $20.4 billion. The average raised per institution among research and doctoral universities was $62.7 million, almost eight times the average of $8.3 million raised at liberal-arts colleges. Much of this surge of fundraising is coming directly from corporations, or foundations established by wealthy individuals. The *Chronicle of Higher Education* estimates that corporations and foundations donated 40 percent of all voluntary support for higher education, with aggregate giving rising by 15 percent in 1998-1999, compared to a 7.4 percent increase from alumni, parents, and others.

The pressure to generate external funding is virtually overwhelming, as college presidents increasingly are expected to be primarily fundraisers for their institutions rather than being intimately involved in academic and campus life. An admittedly extreme example of this is provided by former Harvard president Neil L. Rudenstine, who between

1994 and 2000 raised an average of more than $1 million a day. To his credit, Rudenstine claimed that he had personally overseen all tenure decisions at Harvard, handling over 250 cases during his presidency. At large research universities and most public institutions, this is generally no longer the pattern. Presidents function more or less as corporate chief executive officers, rarely seeing the inside of a classroom, and are largely disconnected from student life. Even several private liberal-arts colleges have appointed presidents directly from the corporate world, or with limited academic credentials.

Liberal-arts colleges are also aggressively focused on fundraising and are launching ambitious capital campaigns. In 1996, Vassar College collected $206 million in its capital campaign, the largest amount of any liberal-arts college up to that time. In 2000, Wellesley College announced a fundraising campaign with a goal of $400 million.

Slaughter and Rhoades have characterized these neoliberal-inspired changes in academe as "academic capitalism," a system in which public colleges and universities act like capitalist enterprises, investing in business ventures such as startup companies spun off from faculty research and in research parks and auxiliary units such as residence halls. Virtually all large research universities, both public and private, operate in this manner. In 1998, for example, Columbia University received $61 million in royalties for several drug patents as well as a new technology used in DVD players. The University of California system's nine campuses reported royalty incomes of $73 million on its combined patents in 1998. The University of Rochester's drug patent on the development of Cox–2 inhibitors, commonly termed "super aspirin," is estimated to be worth several billions of dollars.

Investment policies at these institutions also acquire an increasingly speculative character, in sharp contrast to the fiscal conservatism of the mid-twentieth century. New York University (NYU) provides an excellent example. Back in 1990, NYU's then $300 million endowment was 85 percent invested in cash and short-term bonds, and only 15 percent in equities, according to researchers Kimberly Quinn Johnson and Joseph Entin. Between September 1998 and August 1999, NYU raised $247.3 million. Where did it invest its money? About 25 percent was allocated to bonds, and three-fourths in equities, with one-third of the latter amount "into high-risk private equity, including venture capital." While Yale University reinvests much of its endowment in highly speculative but high-yielding areas such as international investments and real estate, between 1985 and 1995 it spent only 3.9 percent of its endowment's growth on immediate operating expenses devoted to education. As Yale Law School professor Henry Hansmann has observed, "A stranger from Mars who looks at private universities would probably say that they are institutions whose business is to manage large pools of money and that they run educational institutions on the side."

While most liberal-arts colleges are largely excluded from full participation in academic capitalism, they are nevertheless deeply influenced by it. Both public and private institutions have also gravitated toward what Slaughter and Rhoades termed "managed professionals," or the "rapid expansion of nonfaculty support professionals and a reduction, through outsourcing, in the number of nonprofessional, traditional blue-and-pink collar employees." Slaughter and Rhoades observed: "These support professionals—in student services, computer services, fundraising, technology transfer, assessment, and instructional support—can be called managerial professionals in that they have some characteristics of traditional professionals such as faculty . . . [but] are more closely linked to and dependent on management than are faculty." Neoliberal management strategies on college campuses include the reduction of salaries and benefits to college employees by aggressively outsourcing services, especially in food service, custodial maintenance, bookstores, and security, and by reducing or eliminating unions.

The impact of neoliberal academic management may be best measured by an examination of what is happening to the faculty. When I entered graduate school at the University of Wisconsin in the fall semester of 1971, I did so with the expectation that if I successfully completed the doctoral requirements in my field of study, I would be employed in a full-time teaching position at a college or university. Further down the road, if I proved to become a productive scholar and an effective teacher, I could anticipate tenure. At that time, the vast majority of faculty members I knew and worked with were full-time, either tenure-track or tenured. According to the National Center for Education Statistics, only 22 percent of all faculty in higher education were employed part-time in 1970. Near the end of the Reagan era, in 1987, that figure had increased to 33 percent; and by 1993, it reached 42 percent. Today, about 60 percent of higher education's teaching workforce is comprised of what education researcher Gary Zabel termed "contingent faculty." These include career academics who teach part-time jobs on multiple campuses, half-time instructors who hold full-time jobs outside of academe, and non–tenure track, full-time faculty hired on term appointments. This latter group by itself comprised 17 percent of all university and college faculty. The elimination of thousands of full-time faculty jobs in recent years has had the effect of greatly increasing the power of the administration at the expense of faculty governance and authority. Decisions over employment and curricula that were once defined solely by faculty have increasingly shifted to academic management.

Finally, there is within the changing politics of American higher education the reconfigured reality of race: the deteriorating public support for affirmative-action and race-based scholarships, a retreat from needs-blind admissions, and the implicit "writing-off" or elimination of most low-income and urban poor students from having access to elite schools. There's also a curious paradox in how racial diversity is perceived as a goal within most colleges and universities. From my anecdotal experiences, I have generally found most administrators to be the strongest supporters of racial and gender diversity in hiring policies and student recruitment. A recent national survey conducted by the American Council on Education and the American Association of University Professors indicated that faculty at major research universities overwhelmingly valued racial diversity on their campuses. About 85 percent of respondents disagreed with the assertion that "racial and ethnic diversity has lowered the quality of their institutions," with less than 6 percent agreeing. More than 90 percent of all faculty said that diversity did not impede "discussions of issues in classrooms," illustrating that "political correctness" is largely an invention of the Far Right. More than one-fourth of all faculty respondents even claimed that racial and ethnic diversity had "caused them to adjust course syllabi to include such issues."

By contrast, white students are far less supportive of affirmative-action and diversity programs designed to recruit and retain minorities. A recent survey of freshmen at the University of California at Los Angeles conducted by the Higher Education Research Institute reported that almost 50 percent "believe affirmative action should be abolished." A national telephone survey commissioned in 2000 by a conservative group, the Foundation for Academic Standards and Tradition, reported that 79 percent of the 1,004 respondents said that "lowering the entrance requirements for some students, regardless of the reason, was unfair to other applicants." Nearly the identical number, 77 percent, stated that it was "not right to give preferential treatment to minority students, if it meant denying admission to other students." The evidence suggests that the majority of white Americans favor multicultural and racial diversity, so long as they don't have to pay for it.

The vast majority of black and Hispanic students continue to function under a kind of educational apartheid, more than a generation after the passage of the 1964 Civil Rights Act. The apartheid begins in the public schools, with the underfunding of urban education. Advanced placement (AP) and honors courses are widely available at private and suburban schools, but frequently unavailable in mostly black and brown public high schools. The so-called "racial achievement gap" in most standardized tests that determine admission to colleges is more than anything else a measurement of "unequal treatment."

Graduate and professional schools are the primary institutions for the reproduction of America's intelligentsia. The good news is that every year since 1984, the number of African Americans enrolled in graduate schools has increased. According to the spring 2002 issue of *The Journal of Blacks in Higher Education,* as of 2002 there were 139,000 African Americans attending graduate programs, representing more than a 100 percent increase since 1984. As of 2000, more than 9,300 African Americans were attending law schools, which was 50 percent more than in 1990. In academic year 1999-2000, blacks received approximately 5,300 professional school degrees, a number constituting 6.7 percent of professional degrees awarded that year. Between 1989 and 2002, the number of African Americans who annually received professional degrees went up about

70 percent. And the number of black Ph.D.'s produced in 2000, 1,656 doc-
torates, is over twice the number of blacks earning Ph.D. degrees in the
late 1980s.

If the sojourn of black scholars in white academe ended there, it
would appear to represent a remarkable multicultural transformation of
higher education. Unfortunately, the story doesn't end there. *The Journal
of Blacks in Higher Education* has also documented numerous recent
trends that undermine access and opportunity for African Americans in
higher education. The overall percentages of African Americans employed in faculty, administrative, and professional managerial positions
remain minuscule. In 2001, the total number of African-American faculty at all institutions was 61,183, a figure representing only 6.1 percent of
all U.S. faculty. The overwhelming majority of black teaching faculty are
located in historically black colleges and universities, in two-year community colleges, and at large, underfunded second- and third-tier public
universities where teaching demands are high and resources for research, laboratories, travel to academic and professional conferences,
and libraries are modest.

The higher up the academic hierarchy one goes, the whiter the institution or scholarly society becomes. A 2001 survey of the twenty-seven
highest-ranked research universities in the United States indicated that
3.6 percent of all faculty were black. African-American educators remain
underrepresented in the upper levels of academic administration. To really obtain a true picture of how "white" higher education is, one must
disaggregate from what is frequently defined as "faculty" those who are
actually adjunct professors, administrators counted as instructors, and
faculty working on limited, term contracts. At Columbia University,
which in 2002 had reported one of the highest percentages of black faculty in the Ivy League, the total number of tenured full professors and
associate professors in the College of Arts and Sciences was eight out of
a total of approximately 440 tenured faculty. Three out of these eight
African-American faculty members only received tenure in 2001 and
2002. We have a long journey to travel before the goal of fairness and
black representation in higher education is realized.

At the highest levels of the American educational hierarchy, African Americans virtually disappear. The American Academy of Arts and Sciences (AAAS) is perhaps the nation's most prestigious academic society. Of the AAAS's more than 3,700 members, only 160 are African Americans, approximately only 1.6 percent of the Academy's membership. There is on the list only one prominent African-American historian, John Hope Franklin; three black sociologists, William Julius Wilson, Kenneth B. Clark, and Orlando Patterson; in anthropology, just Johnnetta Cole; in philosophy, K. Anthony Appiah and Cornel West. With these and other similar exceptions, when one considers the hundreds of outstanding African-American scholars who are today redefining the contours of academic disciplines throughout the humanities and social sciences, their lack of representation in the American Academy of Arts and Sciences is indefensible and outrageous.

How do we reverse the patterns of educational apartheid and class inequality in higher education? How can we achieve the ideal that access to advanced learning should be an entitlement in a democratic society? Liberal-arts colleges have a critical role to play in this regard through fostering the values of hope and opportunity.

Higher education in the twenty-first century will increasingly become an important battleground around issues of class, pitting labor and management around a host of concerns. At Harvard University in May 2000, a coalition of students and faculty rallied in a campaign to increase minimum-wage levels for Harvard employees to $10.25 an hour. Harvard administrators found it difficult to explain to students why an institution that raised $451.7 million in academic year 1998-1999 could not pay many of its employees a living wage. Students at Johns Hopkins University, over a three-year period beginning in 1996, conducted a vigorous campaign to support a living wage for all university employees. More than 100 faculty signed the petition calling for annual cost-of-living adjustments, health benefits, and the establishment of an oversight committee of students, workers, and community representatives to guarantee compliance. In February 1999, the university finally agreed that it would implement an hourly wage rate of $7.75 phased in over three years, but refused to make promises on health or cost-of-living adjustments. Johns Hopkins President William Brody declared publicly that a living wage was "a moral imperative," yet the university maintains its own for-profit subsidiary, Broadway Services, through which it contracts most of its custodial, security, and parking lot services at starting wages of $6 per hour. Meanwhile, in academic year 1998-1999, Johns Hopkins University's fundraising efforts totaled $207 million. What kind of "values" are Hopkins undergraduates learning from university policies toward the working poor?

A college committed to liberal values should address in a thoughtful and creative manner American society's growing racial divide. This requires more than concerted efforts to recruit and retain racialized minorities within its student body. It should also initiate proactive measures to diversify its faculty and administrative staff. It could, for example, establish exchange programs with students and faculty at historically black colleges and universities or predominantly Hispanic institutions. It could reach out to nearby urban communities and, working with public-school officials, create mentorship programs, encouraging minority students to pursue postsecondary education. Administrators should set clear guidelines and expectations for the implementation of diversity policies within their institutions.

A more challenging task for liberal education is the deconstruction of the intricate patterns of social privilege, which are obscured from critical scrutiny by the ideology of meritocracy. Part of the historic difficulty in uprooting racial and gender inequality in the United States is that whites generally, and especially white middle- and upper-class males, must be taught to recognize how the omnipresent structures of white privilege perpetuate inequality for millions of Americans. As Mark Nathan Cohen, in *Culture of Intolerance*, eloquently stated: "If, historically, any working-class or middle-class group has received affirmative action it has been white males with their de facto monopoly of jobs and education. In their world, competition has clearly been limited and quality has suffered as a result. White men . . . have benefited from the fact that women and minorities could not compete on equal footing for a job." The classical liberal ideal of free and fair competition in the marketplace has always been a lie. Private colleges "privilege" the children of their alumni through the policy of legacies, preserving traditional class and racial hierarchies.

IV

More than 150 years ago, African Americans understood that knowledge is power. The new freedmen after Emancipation and the celebration of Jubilee desired two things above all else: land and education. The formerly enslaved African Americans were absolutely clear that knowledge was power, and that the resources of the government were essential in providing the educational context and social space for their collective advancement. It is for this reason that so many of the decisive struggles against Jim Crow segregation in the twentieth century focused around our access to quality public education. It makes absolutely no sense to divert billions of dollars away from struggling public institutions to finance privately owned corporations that consider education merely a profit-making venture. The fight to preserve and enhance public education is inseparable from the struggle for the empowerment of the oppressed, toward the pursuit of human freedom.

At roughly the same time, educators established colleges like Oberlin, Antioch, and Bowdoin with the belief that such institutions could become catalysts for the making of a more racially just society, in which human bondage did not exist. A generation ago, at the height of the Black Freedom Movement, black and white students at Antioch's campus trained to engage in civil disobedience and nonviolent direct action to protest racial segregation across the South. As an undergraduate student at Earlham College in Indiana in the late 1960s and early 1970s, I witnessed the entire campus community—administrators, faculty, and students—critically engaged in teach-ins, discussions, and public demonstrations over the Vietnam War. What example of praxis, the unity of critical theory and principled action, do we now give to the next generation of students, who are entering this brave new world?

Knowledge, from the vantage point of the oppressed, must not only inform, but transform, the real conditions of daily life in which people live. A humanistic, liberal education must do the same thing. It must provide new perspectives and insights for young people, usually of privileged backgrounds, to understand the meaning and reality of hunger and poverty. It should create and nourish a commitment to a society committed to social justice and a culture of human rights, which has the potential for including all of us. It should foster an impatience with all forms of human inequality, whether based on gender, sexual orientation, or race. The knowledge to help to empower those without power, to bridge our social divisions, to define and to enrich our definitions of democracy, should be the central aim of a liberal education for the twenty-first century.

Chapter 6

Facing the Demon Head On

Race and the Prison Industrial Complex

We know through painful experience that freedom is never voluntarily given by the oppressor; it must be demanded by the oppressed.

—Martin Luther King, Jr.
"Letter from Birmingham Jail," April 16, 1963

I

When I was a child, the only two prisons I had ever heard about were Alcatraz and Sing Sing. Alcatraz was the formidable, stone citadel, perched on a small island in the middle of the San Francisco Bay. I saw *The Birdman of Alcatraz* starring Burt Lancaster, and the film left a deep impression about prison life. I suppose my knowledge of Sing Sing was acquired in a similar fashion. My images of crime and punishment were derived from Edgar G. Robinson, or perhaps some obscure character actors who were usually cast as hoodlums. Somehow, though, I knew that the phrase "to send him up the river" meant a one-way trip along the Hudson River to the infamous Sing Sing Prison.

Nothing I have seen or experienced prepared me for the reality of Sing Sing. The prison itself seems literally carved out of the side of a massive cliff that hovers just above the Hudson River. Parking is usually difficult to find near the prison, so you have to walk a good distance before you come to the outer gate, the first of a series of razor sharp barriers. The main entrance looks remarkably small, compared to the vast size of the prison. Entering the front door, you find yourself in a relatively small room, with several guards and a walk-through metal detector. Your clothing and other personal items are carefully checked. Permission to go inside the prison is severely restricted, and you must be approved through a review process well before your visit.

On the other side of the entrance area, shielded by rows of steel bars, is a hallway that is lined with wooden benches on either side. It is here that inmates wait before being summoned to their hearings to determine whether they have merited early release. During my first time visiting Sing Sing, there were about a half dozen young males, all African Americans and mostly in their twenties, who were sitting nervously on the benches. Most would be forced to wait for hours in order to have fifteen minutes before the parole board. In fifteen short minutes, they would learn whether they would be released, or ordered to serve another term of years behind bars. You could see clearly the hopeful anxiety in each man's face, trying to anticipate the queries of their inquisitors. The right answer at the right moment could bring their suffering to an end.

The prisoners also know that the parole board's decisions are directly influenced by authorities in political power. Under former Governor Mario Cuomo, for instance, approximately 54 percent of violent offenders received parole on their first appearance before a parole board. Since 1995 under Governor George Pataki, only one-third of violent offenders were granted parole after their first review. As Robert Gangi, the director of the Correctional Association of New York, observed, "Given the practice of the parole board, there are more and more long-termers that no matter how well they behave, no matter how many programs they complete, the parole board is not going to let them out."

As you walk through the prison, you go down a series of hallways, separated by small containments that have two sets of steel bars on either side, and secured by a prison guard. Only one set of doors opens at a time. The guard must lock and secure the first door before you're permitted to walk through the second door. Because the prison was constructed on a side of a cliff, there are also a series of steps that must be climbed to go from one area to another.

At the end of one hallway is the infamous, seventy-year-old structure, Cell Block B. The guards informed me, with considerable pride, that Cell Block B was one of the largest enclosed incarceration areas of its kind in the world. One must first walk through a series of double barred steel doors separated by a small interlocking security chamber. Once passing through the second door, one enters a vast open space, surrounded by massive concrete walls and ceiling. In the center of this chamber, filling up nearly the entire space, is a solid iron cage, five stories high. Every story or tier contains 68 separate prison cells, front and back, for a total of 136 cells on each level. Each tier is separated by small-railed catwalks and narrow stairwells.

Each cell is a tiny confined space, with barely enough room for a prisoner's toilet, sink, and bed. Prisoners are not allowed to place any clothing or items covering the front of their cells, except when using their toilets. In effect, personal privacy is nonexistent. The massive metal structure is like a huge iron and steel echo chamber, where every sound from tier to tier resonates and can be easily heard. The whole oppressive environment—the pungent smells of sweat and human waste, the absence of fresh air, the lack of privacy, the close quarters of men who have been condemned to live much of their natural lives in tiny steel cages—is so horrific that I find it even now impossible to express in words its awesome reality. Perhaps the only word for it is evil.

Ted Conover, the author of *Newjack: Guarding Sing Sing,* who worked for nine months as a correctional officer at the prison, had a similar experience when he spent his first day on the job in Cell Block B. Conover was immediately overwhelmed by the constant level of noise, the demands of his supervisors, and the general chaos. "Being a new face," Conover noted, "was like being a substitute teacher. They test you. They defy you. And your job is to get them to comply." Conover questioned the ability of anyone to withstand the psychological stresses and physical levels of brutality that permeated the entire character of life in Sing Sing. "Every day is terrifying," Conover observed. "From the first minute, you're presented with challenges no one prepared you for. It's like working in an explosives factory. You think you're going to get killed. But you have to put it out of your mind."

Violence against prisoners is a daily occurrence. Conover described the process of carrying out a "shakedown" of solitary confinement cells. The guards go from cell to cell, demanding that each individual prisoner strip, turn around, raise his arms, and permit himself to be body searched. For prisoners who refused to be humiliated by this demeaning procedure, a group of guards pushed their way into their cells and forcibly carried out body searches. It was months after Conover was working in Sing Sing, however, that he realized that prisoners who resisted being physically searched were trying to hold on to some element of self-respect, to refuse to participate in their own violation. "If enough people did that together," Conover recognized, "the correctional system would come tumbling down."

In this man-made hell-on-earth, something within the human spirit nevertheless flourishes. About two decades ago, the prisoners of Cell Block B somehow managed to overwhelm their guards, protesting their inhumane conditions. For several days seventeen correctional officers were held as hostages. But in the end, the prisoners recognized that escape was impossible, and that this act of resistance was more symbolic than anything else. To demand to be treated as a human being in an inhumane environment is to be a revolutionary.

Seven years ago I received an invitation to visit Sing Sing from the Reverend George William ("Bill") Webber, who in 1982 had started the master's degree program at New York Theological Seminary (NYTS). When Bill began visiting Sing Sing on a regular basis, he observed that there were a small but highly motivated number of prisoners who had finished their bachelor's degrees and wanted to take more advanced courses. NYTS began to offer a graduate program designed for long-term prisoners at the facility. As the NYTS program developed, inmates at various correctional facilities throughout New York State were selected for admission and then transferred to Sing Sing. About fourteen to sixteen men were selected every year, with a waiting list of one or more years.

I was escorted to the rear quarters of the prison, which consist of religious quarters and chapels of different denominations. At the bottom of a stairwell was the entrance to a classroom. The students were already waiting there and were eager to introduce themselves. There was Louis, a twenty-nine-year-old man of Puerto Rican descent, who had already spent twelve years of his brief life inside penal institutions; Kevin, a middle-aged African-American man, articulate and serious, who had been in Sing Sing for nineteen years, and who was now actively involved in AIDS awareness and antiviolence programs within the inmate population; "Doc," a thirteen-year prisoner who planned to be a counselor; Paul, a seventeen-year inmate interested in working with teenagers and young adults after his release; and Felipe, a prisoner for nineteen years, who was preparing himself for the ministry.

The NYTS program is basically designed to prepare these men for community service. There is a rigorous academic program, where lectures and classroom discussions are held three hours a day, five days a week. Forty-two credit hours must be taken to complete the degree. Inmates are also required to perform an additional fifteen credit hours of field service within the prison, which can range from working in the AIDS ward to tutoring other prisoners. Since the program was established, more than 200 men have graduated with master's degrees. Only

5 percent of those inmates who have completed the program and were released were subsequently returned to prison.

The NYTS program is exceptional, in part, because so few educational programs of its type exist in U.S. prisons. In 1995, only one-third of all U.S. prisons provided college course work, and fewer than one in four prisoners were enrolled in some kind of educational or tutorial program behind bars. There are only about 11,000 paid teachers who are currently employed by penal institutions, or about one teacher per ninety-three prisoners.

One can only imagine the personal courage and determination of these men, most of whom entered prison without a high-school diploma or GED. From the first day of their sentences inside Sing Sing, they experienced what the NYTS 1994 program graduates accurately described as "social death": "We are told what we can eat, when we can eat it, and how we must eat it. We are told what type of clothing we can wear, when to wear it, and where we can wear it; when we can sleep and when we cannot sleep; where we can walk and where we cannot walk; when we can show affection to our families and when we cannot show affection; where we can sit and where we cannot sit; where we can stand and where we cannot stand." Despite the hostility of many prison guards, most of whom come from the same oppressed classes of those whom they are employed to guard, the men involved in the program withstand the daily abuse and harassment. In their own words, "We see ourselves as agents of change."

II

For a variety of reasons, rates of violent crime, including murder, rape, and robbery, increased dramatically in the 1960s and 1970s. Much of this increase occurred in urban areas. By the late 1970s, nearly one-half of all Americans were afraid to walk within a mile of their homes at night, and 90 percent responded in surveys that the U.S. criminal-justice system was not dealing harshly enough with criminals. Politicians like Richard M. Nixon, George Wallace, and Ronald Reagan began to campaign successfully on the theme of law and order. The death penalty, which was briefly outlawed by the Supreme Court, was reinstated. Local, state, and federal expenditures for law enforcement rose sharply. Behind much of anticrime rhetoric was a not-too-subtle racial dimension, the projection of crude stereotypes about the link between criminality and black people. Rarely did these politicians observe that minority and poor people, not the white middle class, were statistically much more likely to experience violent crimes of all kinds. The argument was made that law-enforcement officers should be given much greater latitude in suppressing crime, that sentences should be lengthened and made mandatory, and that prisons should be designed not for the purpose of rehabilitation, but punishment.

Consequently, there was a rapid expansion in the personnel of the criminal-justice system, as well as the construction of new prisons. What occurred in New York State, for example, was typical of what happened nationally. From 1817 to 1981, New York had opened thirty-three state prisons. From 1982 to 1999, another thirty-eight state prisons were constructed. The state's prison population at the time of the Attica prison revolt in September 1971 was about 12,500. By 1999, there were more than 71,000 prisoners in New York State correctional facilities.

In 1974, the number of Americans incarcerated in all state prisons stood at 187,500. By 1991, the number had reached 711,700. Nearly two-thirds of all state prisoners in 1991 had less than a high-school education. One-third of all prisoners were unemployed at the time of their arrests. Incarceration rates by the end of the 1980s had soared to unprecedented rates, especially for black Americans. As of December 1989, the total U.S. prison population, including federal institutions, exceeded 1 million for the first time in history, an incarceration rate of the general population of 1 out of every 250 citizens. For African Americans, the rate was over 700 per 100,000, or about seven times higher than for whites. About one-half of all prisoners were black. Twenty-three percent of all black males in their twenties were either in prison, on parole, on probation, or awaiting trial. The rate of incarceration of black Americans in 1989 had even surpassed that experienced by blacks who still lived under the apartheid regime of South Africa.

By the early 1990s, rates for all types of violent crime began to plummet. But the laws sending offenders to prison were made even more severe. Children were increasingly viewed in courts as adults and subjected to harsher penalties. Laws like California's "three strikes and you're out" eliminated the possibility of parole for repeat offenders. The vast majority of these new prisoners were nonviolent offenders, and many of these were convicted of drug offenses that carried long prison terms. In New York, African Americans and Latinos make up 25 percent of the total population, but by 1999 they represented 83 percent of all state prisoners and 94 percent of all individuals convicted on drug offenses. The pattern of racial bias in these statistics is confirmed by the research of the U.S. Commission on Civil Rights, which found that while African Americans today constitute only 14 percent of all drug users nationally, they account for 35 percent of all drug arrests, 55 percent of all drug convictions, and 75 percent of all prison admissions for drug offenses. Currently, the racial proportions of those under some type of correctional supervision, including parole and probation, are one in fifteen for young white males, one in ten for young Latino males, and one in three for young African-American males. Statistically today, more than eight out of every ten African-American males will be arrested at some point in their lifetime.

Structural racism is so difficult to dismantle in our nation today, in part, because political leaders in both major parties have deliberately redirected billions of our tax dollars away from investments in public education into the construction of what many scholars now describe as a prison industrial complex. This is the terrible connection between education and incarceration.

A 1998 study produced by the Correctional Association of New York and the Washington, D.C.–based Justice Policy Institute illustrated that in New York State hundreds of millions of dollars have been reallocated from the budgets of public universities to prison construction. The report stated: "Since fiscal year 1988, New York's public universities have seen their operating budgets plummet by 29 percent while funding for prisons has increased by 76 percent. In actual dollars, there has nearly been an equal trade-off, with the Department of Correctional Services receiving a $761 million increase during that time while state funding for New York's city and state university systems has declined by $615 million." By 1998, New York State was spending nearly twice what it had allocated to run its prison system a decade ago. To pay for that massive expansion, tuitions and fees for students at the State University of New York (SUNY) and the City University of New York (CUNY) had to be dramatically hiked.

For black and Latino young adults, these shifts have made it much more difficult to attend college than in the past, but much easier to go to prison. The New York State study found: "There are more blacks (34,809) and Hispanics (22,421) locked up in prison than there are attending the State University of New York, where there are 27,925 black and Hispanic students. Since 1989, there have been more blacks entering the prison system for drug offenses each year than there were graduating from SUNY with undergraduate, masters, and doctoral degrees—combined."

The devastating pattern of schools versus prisons in New York exists throughout our country. In California, thousands of black and Latino young adults were denied access to state universities because of the passage of Proposition 209, which destroyed affirmative action. Thousands more have been driven out by the steadily growing cost of tuition and cutbacks in student loans. Meanwhile, hundreds of millions of dollars have been siphoned away from the state's education budget and spent on building prisons.

In 1977, California had 19,600 inmates in its state prison system. By 2000, the number of that state's prisoners exceeded 163,000. In the past two decades of the twentieth century, California has constructed one new state university, but twenty-one new prisons. California's prison system "holds more inmates in its jails and prisons than do France, Great Britain, Germany, Japan, Singapore, and the Netherlands combined." And future trends are worse. The California Department of Corrections estimated in 2000 that it would need to spend $6.1 billion over the coming decade just to maintain the present prison population. There are more employees at work in the American prison industry than in any Fortune 500 corporation, with the one exception of General Motors.

Instead of funding more teachers, we are hiring extra prison guards. Instead of building new classrooms, we are constructing new jails. Instead of books, we now have bars everywhere.

III

The latest innovation in American corrections is termed "special housing units" (SHUs), but which prisoners also generally refer to as The Box. SHUs are uniquely designed solitary confinement cells in which prisoners are locked down for twenty-three hours a day for months or even years at a time. SHU cell blocks are electronically monitored, prefabricated structures of concrete and steel, about 14 feet long and 8 1/2 feet wide, amounting to 120 square feet of space. The two inmates who are confined in each cell, however, actually have only about 60 square feet of usable space, or 30 square feet per person. All meals are served to prisoners through a thin slot cut into the steel door. The toilet unit, sink, and shower are all located in the cell. Prisoners are permitted one hour "exercise time" each day in a small concrete balcony, surrounded by heavy security wire, directly connected with their SHU cells. Educational and rehabilitation programs for SHU prisoners are prohibited.

As of 1998, New York State had confined 5,700 state prisoners in SHUs, about 8 percent of its total inmate population. Currently under construction in Upstate New York is a new 750-cell maximum-security SHU facility that will cost state taxpayers $180 million. Although Amnesty International and human-rights groups in the United States have widely condemned SHUs, claiming that such forms of imprisonment constitute the definition of torture under international law, other states have followed New York's example. As of 1998, California had constructed 2,942 SHU beds, followed by Mississippi (1,756), Arizona (1,728), Virginia (1,267), Texas (1,229), Louisiana (1,048), and Florida (1,000). Solitary confinement, which historically had been defined even by corrections officials as an extreme disciplinary measure, is becoming increasingly the norm.

The introduction of SHUs reflects a general mood in the country that the growing penal population is essentially beyond redemption. If convicted felons cease to be viewed as human beings, why should they be treated with any humanity? This punitive spirit was behind the Republican-controlled Congress and President Clinton's decision in 1995 to eliminate inmate eligibility for federal Pell Grant awards for higher education. As of 1994, 23,000 prisoners throughout the United States had received Pell Grants, averaging about $1,500 per award. The total amount of educational support granted prisoners, $35 million, represented only 0.6 percent of all Pell Grant funding nationally. Many studies have found that prisoners who participate in higher education programs, and especially those who complete college degrees, have significantly lower rates of recidivism. For all prison inmates, for example, recidivism averages between 50 percent and 70 percent. Federal parolees have a recidivism rate of 40 percent. Prisoners with a college education have recidivism rates of only 5 to 10 percent. Given the high success ratio of prisoners who complete advanced degree work and the relatively low cost of public investment, such educational programs should make sense. But following the federal government's lead, many states have also ended their tuition benefits programs for state prisoners.

The economic consequences of the vast expansion of our prison industrial complex are profound. According to criminal-justice scholar David Barlow at the University of Wisconsin at Milwaukee, between 1980 and 2000 the combined expenditures of federal, state, and local governments on police have increased about 400 percent. Corrections expenditures for building new prisons, upgrading existing facilities, hiring more guards, and related costs increased approximately 1,000 percent. Although it currently costs about $70,000 to construct a typical prison cell, and about $25,000 annually to supervise and maintain each prisoner, the United States is still building hundreds of new prison beds every week.

The driving ideological and cultural force that rationalizes and justifies mass incarceration is the white American public's stereotypical perceptions about race and crime. As Andrew Hacker perceptively noted in 1995, "Quite clearly, 'black crime' does not make people think about tax

evasion or embezzling from brokerage firms. Rather, the offenses generally associated with blacks are those . . . involving violence." A number
of researchers have found that racial stereotypes of African Americans—
as "violent," "aggressive," "hostile," and "short-tempered"—greatly influence whites' judgments about crime. Generally, most whites are in-
clined to give black and Latino defendants more severe judgments of
guilt and lengthier prison sentences than whites who commit identical
crimes. Racial bias has been well established, especially in capital cases,
where killers of white victims are much more likely to receive the death
penalty than those who murder African Americans.

The greatest victims of these racialized processes of unequal justice,
of course, are African-American and Latino young people. In April 2000,
utilizing national and state data compiled by the FBI, the Justice Department and six leading foundations issued a comprehensive study that documented vast racial disparities at every level of the juvenile justice
process. African Americans under age eighteen constitute 15 percent of
their national age group, yet they currently represent 26 percent of all
those who are arrested. After entering the criminal-justice system, white
and black juveniles with the same records are treated in radically different
ways. According to the Justice Department's study, among white youth
offenders, 66 percent are referred to juvenile courts, while only 31 percent
of the African-American youth are taken there. Blacks make up 44 percent of those detained in juvenile jails, 46 percent of all those tried in
adult criminal courts, as well as 58 percent of all juveniles who are warehoused in adult prison. In practical terms, this means that young African
Americans who are arrested and charged with a crime are more than six
times more likely to be assigned to prison than white youth offenders.

For those young people who have never been to prison before,
African Americans are nine times more likely than whites to be sentenced to juvenile prisons. For youths charged with drug offenses, blacks
are forty-eight times more likely than whites to be sentenced to juvenile
prison. White youths charged with violent offenses are incarcerated on
average for 193 days after trial; by contrast, African-American youths are
held 254 days, and Latino youths are incarcerated 305 days.

Even outside of the prison walls, the black community's parameters are largely defined by the agents of state and private power. There are now approximately 600,000 police officers and 1.5 million private security guards in the United States. Increasingly, however, black and poor communities are being "policed" by special paramilitary units, often called SWAT (Special Weapons and Tactics) teams. Researcher Christian Parenti cited studies indicating that "the nation has more than 30,000 such heavily armed, military trained police units." SWAT-team mobilizations, or "call outs," increased 400 percent between 1980 and 1995, with a 34 percent increase in the incidents of deadly force recorded by SWAT teams from 1995 to 1998.

What are the practical political consequences for regulating black and brown bodies through the coercive institutional space of our correctional facilities? Perhaps the greatest impact is on the process of black voting. According to the statistical data of the Sentencing Project, a nonprofit research center in Washington, D.C., forty-eight states and the District of Columbia bar prisoners who have been convicted of a felony from voting. Thirty-two states bar ex-felons who are currently on parole from voting. Twenty-eight states even prohibit adults from voting if they are felony probationers. There are eight states that deny voting rights to former prisoners who had been serving time for felonies, even after they have completed their sentences: Alabama, Florida, Iowa, Kentucky, Mississippi, Nevada, Virginia, and Wyoming. In Arizona, ex-felons are disfranchised for life if they are convicted of a second felony. Delaware disfranchises some ex-felons for five years after they finish their sentences, and Maryland bars them from voting for an additional three years.

The net result to democracy is devastating. The Sentencing Project released these statistics in 2002:

- An estimated 3.9 million Americans, or one in fifty adults, have currently or permanently lost their voting rights as a result of a felony conviction.
- 1.4 million African-American men, or 13 percent of black men, are disfranchised, a rate seven times the national average.

- More than 2 million white Americans (Hispanic and non-Hispanic) are disfranchised.
- Over half a million women have lost their right to vote.
- In seven states that deny the vote to ex-offenders, one in four black men is *permanently* disfranchised.
- Given current rates of incarceration, three in ten of the next generation of black men can expect to be disfranchised at some point in their lifetime. In states that disfranchise ex-offenders, as many as 40 percent of black men may permanently lose their right to vote.
- 1.4 million disfranchised persons are ex-offenders who have completed their sentences. The state of Florida had at least 200,000 ex-felons who were unable to vote in the 2000 presidential elections.

The Sentencing Project adds that "the scale of felony voting disenfranchisement is far greater than in any other nation and has serious implications for democratic processes and racial inclusion." In effect, the Voting Rights Act of 1965, which guaranteed millions of African Americans the right to the electoral franchise, is being gradually repealed by state restrictions on voting for ex-felons. A people who are imprisoned in disproportionately higher numbers, and then systematically denied the right to vote, can in no way claim to live under a democracy.

The consequence of such widespread disfranchisement is what can be called "civil death." The individual who has been convicted of a felony, serves time, and successfully completes parole nevertheless continues to be penalized at every turn. He/she is penalized in the labor force, being denied certain jobs because of a criminal record. He/she has little direct access or influence on the decision-making processes of the political system. He/she may be employed and pay taxes, assuming all of the normal responsibilities of other citizens, yet may be temporarily or permanently barred from the one activity that defines citizenship itself— voting. Individuals who are penalized in this way have little incentive to participate in the normal public activities defining civic life because they exercise no voice in public decision making. Ex-prisoners on parole are also frequently discouraged from participation in public demonstrations or political meetings because of parole restrictions. For many ex-prisoners, there is a retreat from individual political activity; a sense of alienation and frustration easily leads to apathy. Those who experience civic death largely cease to view themselves as "civic actors," as people who possess the independent capacity to make important changes within society and within governmental policies.

Criminal-justice scholars have described prison as a metaphor for the most oppressive and socially destructive conditions of structural racism in America. As Alvin J. Bronstein observed in the *Prisoners' Rights Sourcebook* (1981), edited by Ira Robbins:

> In a very real sense, the prison is the outside world, squeezed into a very small space. The total and largely self-contained society that is prison contains all of the evils of that outside world, only much more concentrated. . . . Hence, militancy is especially great in prison, not because of a few agitators, but because the repression—whether justified or not—is harsh and undiluted. Because prison is one of the most severe sanctions in our society, the subjects of that sanction include the most alienated and the most aggressive members of society. And since the sense of injustice is most developed where the penalties are the greatest, the resentment and bitterness . . . [are] deep and pervasive.

Many women and men who do manage to survive incarceration often acquire critical insights about the nature of the legal process and the criminal-justice system that could provide important and powerful lessons for young people in racialized minority communities. Like Frederick Douglass and Fannie Lou Hamer before them, they frequently do not have formal educational credentials or middle-class privileges. Yet from theorizing about their practical day-to-day experiences within the prison system, they come to a richer understanding of how that system actually works and how to develop innovative and creative ways to subvert it. As Bronstein noted, "It is no coincidence that many of the classics of black literature, such as those by Malcolm X, Eldridge Cleaver, Bobby

Seale, and George Jackson, are prison memoirs, in whole or in part."
Paradoxically, such strong personalities, who were able to survive the
system, found ways to learn its lessons and to become empowered in the
process. An essential step in transforming this system is in "reproducing"
leaders like Malcolm X. The site of the most extreme oppression could
have the greatest potential for creating the most effective leadership.

IV

It is absolutely clear that a new leviathan of racial inequality has been
constructed across our country. It lacks the brutal simplicity of the old
Jim Crow system, with its omnipresent "white" and "colored" signs. Yet
it is in many respects potentially far more brutalizing, because it presents
itself to the world as a correctional system that is theoretically fair and
essentially color-blind. The Black Freedom Movement of the 1960s was
successful largely because it convinced a majority of white middle-class
Americans that racial segregation was economically inefficient and that
politically it could neither be sustained nor justified. The movement uti-
lized the power of creative disruption, making it impossible for the old
system of white prejudice, power, and privilege to function in the same
old ways it had for nearly a century. How can Americans who still believe in racial equality and social justice stand silently while millions of
our fellow citizens are being destroyed all around us?

It is abundantly clear that the political demand for mass incarceration
and the draconian termination of voting rights to ex-felons will only
contribute toward a more dangerous society. No walls can be constructed high enough, and no electronic surveillance cameras and
alarms sophisticated enough, to protect white middle- and upper-class
American families from the consequences of these policies. Keep in
mind that approximately 600,000 people are released from prison every
year; that about one-sixth of all reentering ex-prisoners, 100,000 people,
are being released without any form of community correctional supervision; that about 75 percent of reentering prisoners have substance
abuse histories; and that an estimated 16 percent suffer from mental ill-

ness. Nearly two-thirds of this reentering prison population will be arrested again within three years. The madness of our penal policies and of the criminal-justice system places the entire society at risk. Dismantling the prison industrial complex represents the great moral assignment and political challenge of our time.

During my last visit to Sing Sing, I noticed something new. The prison's correctional officials had erected a large, bright yellow sign over the door at the prison's public entrance. The colorful sign reads: "Through these doors pass some of the finest corrections professionals in the world."

I stood frozen for a second, immediately recalling the chillingly brutal sign posted above the entrance gate at Auschwitz and other concentration camps: *Arbeit Macht Frei* ("Work Makes Us Free"). I later asked Bill Webber and a few prisoners what they thought about the new sign. Bill thought a moment, then said simply, "demonic." One of the M.A. students, a thirty-five-year-old Latino named Tony, agreed with Bill's blunt assessment. But Tony added, "Let us face the demon head on." With more than 2 million Americans who are now incarcerated, it is time to face the demon head on.

Chapter 7

The Death of the Talented Tenth

The middle-class Negroes are our problem. They've all gone to Shaker Heights and don't give a damn about being Negro anymore.

—Martin Luther King, Jr., 1967

I

At Fisk University's 1898 graduation ceremonies, W.E.B. Du Bois, an 1888 alumnus of that historically black institution, was invited to deliver the commencement address. Du Bois used the occasion to set forth a challenge to the new graduates of his beloved university and to instill within them a passionate commitment for using their intellectual talents and training for the general advancement of humanity. "We must not only work and sacrifice for ourselves and others, but also render each other mutual service," Du Bois observed. "The physician must heal not himself, but all men; the tailor must mend the whole village; the farmer must plant for all. Thus in the civilized world each serves all, and all serve each, and the binding force is faith and skill, and the skill is bounded only by human possibility and genius, and the faith is faithful even to the untrue."

This was, in effect, the concept that the purpose of advanced learning was the linking of theory to practice, from knowledge as an abstraction to its application in the real world. For people of African descent, Du Bois suggested, there is an even greater responsibility to provide leadership and service. "You are Negroes," Du Bois stated, "members of that dark, historic race that from the world's dawn has slept to hear the trumpet summons sound through our ears. Cherish unwavering faith in the blood of your fathers, and make sure this last triumph of humanity." Such a commitment to an oppressed people would require some sacrifice. However, for those "who will work and dig and starve there is a chance to do here incalculable good for the Negro race."

Du Bois's 1898 address established the rationale for what several years later would become his theory of the "Talented Tenth." In his classic debate with conservative educator Booker T. Washington, Du Bois did not oppose vocational training for the majority of African Americans. He did insist, however, that the training of a group of black men and women in the humanities and in the arts and sciences, was essential for the advancement of the entire group. Embedded in Du Bois's "Talented Tenth" concept was the assumption of "linked fates." African Americans who one hundred years ago were fortunate enough to gain access to a higher education were obligated to serve those who were economically and socially disadvantaged. The black sharecropper and the black convict laboring on a chain gang did not live in a separate racial universe from the African-American entrepreneur or university professor. Everyone who was "black," by the definitions of the South, sat in the Jim Crow section of the train; "college-bred Negroes" to use Du Bois's term, were just as subjected to political disfranchisement, verbal abuse, and even lynching as their poorer sisters and brothers. Du Bois elaborated this point in his 1903 address, "The Training of Negroes for Social Power":

> The history of civilization seems to prove that no group or nation which seeks advancement and true development can despise or neglect the power of well-trained minds; and this power of intellectual leadership must be given to the talented tenth among American Negroes before this race can seriously be asked to assume the responsibility of dispelling its own ignorance. Upon the foundation stone of a few well-equipped Negro colleges of high and honest standards can be built a proper system of free common schools in the South for the masses of the Negro people; any attempt to found a system of public schools on anything less than this—on narrow ideals, limited or merely technical training—is to call blind leaders for the blind.

Three generations of black intellectuals and college-trained professional men and women who were produced by historically black colleges and universities lived and worked in a racially segregated world. The size of the early black intelligentsia was incredibly small. In *Dusk of Dawn*, Du Bois noted that there were exactly 215 African Americans who had graduated from college as of 1876; by the Great Depression, in the four-year period from 1931 to 1935, a total of 10,000 black college graduates were produced. In academic year 1945-1946, there were about 45,000 black undergraduate students then attending more than 100 black colleges and universities. Only four of these institutions at the time were accredited by the Association of American Universities. About 1,800 blacks were enrolled in graduate and professional schools across the United States. The number of African Americans enrolled in all law schools, including Howard University, was 118. The GI Bill greatly increased the opportunities for black veterans of World War II to attend colleges. My father, a master sergeant in the segregated Army Air Corps, used the GI Bill to attend Wilberforce University, enrolling there in the fall semester, 1946. The Census of 1950 reported that the total number of nonwhites between ages eighteen and twenty-four enrolled in America's colleges and universities was 83,000. Only 4.5 percent of all blacks in the same age group were enrolled in college, compared to 15 percent of the same cohort for white males and 8 percent for white females.

For all practical purposes, as these statistics indicate, in the Talented Tenth, almost *everybody* knew everybody else. The black elite in the segregation era belonged to the same sororities, fraternities, and social clubs. They vacationed together at summer resorts such as Sag Harbor, New York, and Oak Bluffs, Martha's Vineyard. All of the historians belonged to the Association for the Study of Negro Life and History, founded by Carter G. Woodson in 1916. Black educators relied on the *Journal of Negro Education,* established in 1930, because many white academic journals would not usually accept or publish works by blacks in higher education. As late as 1960, three-fourths of all African Americans enrolled in colleges and universities were attending predominantly black institutions. As of 1980, over 60 percent of all African-American M.D.'s and nearly three-fourths of all black Ph.D.'s had been produced by historically black academic institutions.

What kept the Talented Tenth accountable to the rest of the African-American community, more than anything else, were the structural barriers of Jim Crow segregation. Author bell hooks has recalled, "On some level, the masses of black people have asked our talented groups to register their power through materiality. We have not demanded that they register it through service." However, hooks wrote, "In the days of strict racial apartheid, it was much easier to do both—that is, be of service to the community and reap a reward or status for what one did." "With assimilation and racial integration," she observed, "so many of our talented groups of people live outside of black communities, including myself." What was true for the black intelligentsia was also the case for the black middle class as a whole. Economist Julianne Malveaux noted that in "the historical development of the black middle class . . . the cohort that arose after the Civil War basically depended on the community and so had to respond to it directly." In the twentieth century this sense of shared community gradually became less the case, as "elements of the black middle class strayed farther and farther away from the community."

Growing up in a black neighborhood in the 1960s, as I did, still meant that the bonds of linked fates were strong. When black people needed to talk to a lawyer, they routinely solicited advice from one of the few African-American attorneys in our community. Our physician was black; the architect and construction company my father hired to build our home were black; my mother's sorority meetings for Alpha Kappa Alpha held in our home included only African-American women; my dad belonged to the Prince Hall Masonic lodge, which had been founded by an African American two centuries before. Our church was almost entirely black, with the exception of several liberal whites who were married to African Americans. Growing up, I cannot recall a single white classmate ever visiting or playing basketball at my home. The magazines and newspapers in our home were *Ebony, Jet,* the *Cleveland Call and Post,* and the *Dayton Express.* My dad was employed at the predominantly black public high school, which, appropriately, was named for Paul Laurence Dunbar. We lived in a world apart.

I'm not suggesting that we should become nostalgic for Jim Crow segregation, not for a minute. But it is undeniable that with the introduction of integration came a process of cultural fragmentation and class stratification. As novelists like Chinua Achebe have illustrated, in the period when European colonialism was imposed on traditional African societies, the latter experienced profound changes in how they saw themselves culturally and psychologically. As African political theorist Amilcar Cabral once suggested, the rule of Europe created a new social environment in which African people left their own history and became part of someone else's. A similar process happened here in the United States in the mid-twentieth century. Under Jim Crow, the social norms and rules for navigating the color line were clear; with the introduction of desegregation, there were unexpected problems as well as new opportunities.

One of the greatest changes that happened to the Talented Tenth was the desegregation of higher education. By 1970, 417,000 African Americans were enrolled in U.S. colleges, about 15.5 percent of all young black adults eighteen to twenty-four years old, compared to 34 percent of all white males and 21 percent of white females in that same cohort. Three-fourths of these black students were now enrolled in predominantly white schools. By 1980, black college enrollment had more than doubled, exceeding 1.1 million, with slightly more than 80 percent attending largely white institutions. My point here is that most white Americans really do not comprehend how recently desegregation occurred in American cultural, civic, and educational institutions, and that without affirmative-action programs, such as minority-based academic scholarships and the expansion of needs-blind admissions initiatives, the explosion in the size of the African-American middle class would not have occurred. Black graduate and professional-school students in the 1960s and 1970s frequently felt themselves to be strangers in a strange land of white higher education. We had few black role models available to provide mentorship. Much of what we were taught, or were expected to learn, was at odds with what most people within our neighborhoods knew to be true. "Merit" was the masquerade for what in reality was white privilege, as hundreds of thousands of the children of white affluent households benefited from legacy programs and college preparatory courses that gave them real advantages. I received my Ph.D. at the University of Maryland in the department of history in 1976, and to my knowledge, I was the first American of African descent awarded a Ph.D. in that department. It was a terribly lonely place for us.

But from the perspective of liberal integrationism, black people generally believed that the total desegregation of white institutions was identical with the pursuit of racial progress and individual upward mobility. We were, in effect, obligated by the weight of our own history to boldly go where no Negroes had gone before. Almost immediately, this exodus created real problems within historically black colleges and universities. There was undeniably a "brain drain" of scholars from small black institutions into major research universities, where access to research stipends, graduate students, and institutional resources was the norm. In thousands of African-American, second-generation, middle-class households, the parents who had graduated in the 1940s and 1950s from Howard, Spelman, and Prairie View now sent their children to Harvard, Stanford, and Princeton in the 1970s.

A curious dimension of this process was the relative lack of black institutionalization and capacity-building, even during the period of Black Power. Relatively few black publishing houses, national magazines, journals, and artistic and cultural nonprofit groups that were established in the 1960s made it to the 1990s. When they did in rare cases, they usually were successful because they departed from their original cultural and political vision to attract advertising dollars, corporate, and/or philanthropic support. The rising black bourgeoisie, for the most part, did not adequately support or raise money for the construction of new black cultural institutions. Harold Cruse identified this problem in *The Crisis of the Negro Intellectual:* "The black world cannot and does not, support the Negro creative intellectual. The black bourgeoisie does not publish books, does not own and operate theatres or music halls. . . . Add to the Negro intelligentsia who have no firm cultural base in the reality of either the black world or the white (even when they *have* achieved recognition), a large fluctuating contingent who make up the bulk of new aspirants to integrated cultural achievements. The result," said Cruse, is "a rootless class of displaced persons who are refugees from the social poverty of the black world."

The weakness of the black community's cultural and public intellectual infrastructure, as well as the prestige and material benefits to be derived by assimilation into or cooperation with white established institutions, has produced a growing elite of black "intercessors" or go-between facilitators along society's color line. "They now become interpreters for the black world to the white—a new role for them," Cruse wrote sadly. "But this new dialogue between the black and white intelligentsia somehow sounds flat and unconvincing to the ear. While Negro intellectuals are busy trying to interpret the nature of the black world and its aspirations to the whites, they should, in fact, be defining their own roles as intellectuals within *both* worlds."

Fifty years ago, this group had no alternative but to accept its linked fate with the black working class, the poor, the imprisoned, and the dispossessed. "Racial advancement" in a Jim Crow social order could only have real meaning when it was defined in collective terms. The Talented

Tenth was not a privileged elite within the *white* world; it existed and was conscious of itself largely as it functioned within the extensive networks and voluntary organizations of black civil society. There were inescapable bonds of loyalty, friendship, and obligation that created an intimate context for social interaction. Growing up in this segregated world, we had to navigate the racial boundaries while recognizing our common tie to a people who had their own national consciousness and unique historical memory. The true paradox of integration is found in this: As the scope, complexity, and size of the black elite grew to unprecedented dimensions, the bonds that tied it to the bulk of the African-American majority fragmented and in many instances ceased to exist.

II

The greatest struggle of any oppressed group in a racist society is the struggle to reclaim collective memory and identity. At the level of culture, racism seeks to deny people of African, American Indian, Asian, and Latino descent their own voices, histories, and traditions. From the vantage point of racism, black people have no "story" worth telling; the master narrative woven into the national hierarchy of white prejudice, privilege, and power represents the only legitimate experience worth knowing. Frantz Fanon once observed that the greatest triumph of racism is when black people lose touch with their own culture and identity, seeking to transcend their oppressed condition as the Other by becoming something they are not.

Under colonialism and Jim Crow segregation, people of African descent were constantly pressured to conform to the racist stereotypes held of them by the dominant society. Some succumbed to this pressure, assuming the mask of "Sambo" in order to survive, or to ensure that their children's lives would go forward. Others sacrificed themselves to achieve a higher ideal, the struggle to claim their own humanity and cultural traditions and to build communities grounded in the integrity of one's own truths. The knowledge of blackness is not found in genetics, and only indirectly in the color of one's skin. It is found in that connection to symbols, living traditions, and histories of collective resistance, renewal, and transformation.

We now live in a time when legal segregation, colonialism, and even apartheid have been dismantled. The "white" and "colored" signs across the South that I remember so vividly from my childhood have been taken down for over a generation. Perhaps it is not surprising that a growing number of black intellectuals casually take for granted the democratic victories achieved—the right to vote and hold elective office, access to fair employment, the abolition of racially segregated public accommodations, opportunities in higher education through affirmative action—failing to recognize that what has been won over centuries of struggle can be taken away. Although they are the prime beneficiaries of the freedom struggle, they distance themselves from it. They have come to the false conclusion that what they have accomplished was by their own individual talents and effort. And they actively attack the thesis that blackness, in and of itself, has any cultural value.

Debra Dickerson, a Senior Fellow at the New America Foundation, is one example of this unfortunate trend. In *An American Story*, she argued, "It's long past time blacks opted out of blackness." In a 2000 op-ed essay appearing in the *Washington Post*, Dickerson criticized Howard University's African DNA database project for attempting to link black Americans to African ancestors. For Dickerson, the DNA research only has value because "we who were swindled out of every link to the past except skin color will be able to find out more about our [European] heritage." Dickerson has no patience for African Americans who identify themselves as part of the African diaspora. "A Nigerian who immigrates to America in 2000 has virtually nothing in common with the descendants of American slaves, but we're both conceptually freeze-dried down to that one aspect of our selves." Besides, she noted, "There are few black families who don't brag about the whites and Indians (all chiefs) in their lineage and lie about how hard it was to make their hair stand up 'like that' during the reign of the Afro."

At the conclusion of her essay, in a passage that is both politically and ethically confused, Dickerson claimed that black Americans should not "despise" the white men who raped their foremothers. "Without slavery, there would be no Jesse Jackson," she insists, "no Leontyne Price," "Tiger Woods," "jazz or gospel," and "no me." Should the NAACP halt its campaign against the public display of the Confederate battle flag over the South Carolina statehouse because its part of "our" heritage, too? Should the descendants of those who were raped find identity and meaning for themselves by coming to a new appreciation of the rapists? Dickerson confused genetics with culture. We may share a genetic tie to the slaveholders, but their only vital contribution to our historical identity was the struggle we waged against them. We share no morals, and no common history. We owe them nothing except contempt.

More academic in style, but no less self-hating, is the book *Losing the Race: Self-Sabotage in Black America*, by University of California linguistics professor John H. McWhorter. In it he argued that affirmative action cripples African-American students by contributing to a spirit of black "anti-intellectualism" and a "deep-reaching inferiority complex" that discourages learning. "In my years of teaching," McWhorter declared, "I have never had a student disappear without explanation, or turn in a test that made me wonder how she could have attended class and done so badly, who was not African American."

McWhorter's central point was that black people as a group are unprepared and unworthy of being admitted to elite white institutions. Black Berkeley students, however, aren't a total loss. None of them "would be uncomfortable in a nice restaurant," and most "probably do know what wine goes with chicken." Nevertheless, they clearly cannot compete with their white counterparts and are trapped by their "defeatist thought patterns." McWhorter did admit that his race helped him to win academic fellowships and to achieve his faculty positions at Cornell and now at Berkeley. But like the proverbial man who escapes from a pit and pulls up the ladder behind him, trapping others at the bottom, McWhorter desperately wants to distance himself from his oppressed sisters and brothers. The price for admission into the white establishment is to denounce blacks in stereotypical terms.

Dickerson and McWhorter are cultural casualties in the centuries-old struggle against racism. But it would be a mistake to conclude that these black intellectuals are aberrations. The death of legal segregation, and the explosion in the size of the black professional-managerial class, creates the political space for the emergence of black intellectuals who desperately want to escape their blackness. They may be prepared to denounce their own people in order to advance their careers, but African Americans should not permit them to go unnoticed or unchallenged. To uproot racism, black Americans must constantly remember that the first step is in appreciating our history and culture. As white Americans acquire a better understanding of the lessons and the meaning of the black experience, the possibilities for interracial dialogue increase.

III

For over one hundred years, the black bourgeoisie has generally held a racial philosophy of "liberal integrationism," the attempt to assimilate African Americans into the dominant institutions of American society. To achieve this goal of "color-blindness," the middle-class generally relied on what I have described previously as "state-based politics," that is, the use of influence within the government and its affiliated agencies within civil society (such as major foundations) to redirect public policies toward goals favoring blacks generally and, more narrowly, their own individual career advancement. Throughout much of our recent history, liberal integrationists have allied themselves with the Democratic Party, pursuing reform strategies such as affirmative action and minority economic set-asides that promoted capital formation and the long-term expansion of the middle class within the black community. This liberal approach to racial policy, however, has never been universally accepted within the black bourgeoisie as a class.

A minority segment of the black bourgeoisie, those elements most extremely hostile to black nationalism, have argued that pluralist-style, interest-group politics have not and do not advance blacks' interests as individuals. The ultimate goal of "integration" should be, ideally, the complete elimination of separate black and white institutions and the end of race-based criteria for directing public policy. This wing of the black bourgeoisie has relied heavily on white corporate and philanthropic support to advance its goals. Since the 1970s, many in this group have developed a strategic dependency on Republican administrations in the White House, as well as the Republican-controlled Congress, to advance their own careers. They shift back and forth between state-based positions within conservative administrations and private-sector managerial and executive positions for personal wealth accumulation. Arguing against "racial quotas," they generally believe that private enterprise and the free market, if left alone without excessive governmental regulations, will ultimately solve the country's race problem.

During the long nightmare of Jim Crow segregation, it would have been difficult for any sane Negro to advocate such an individualistic and conservative version of the integrationist philosophy. The hegemonic nature of Jim Crow as a social system based on white supremacy made absolutely necessary the use of black collective strategies and race-conscious organizations to defeat it. It was only with the passage of the 1964 Civil Rights Act, which outlawed legal segregation—but significantly, did not destroy racial restrictions in private clubs and institutions—that this conservative element of the black bourgeoisie found its true voice. In electoral politics, black Republican Edward Brooke emerged after winning the election as Massachusetts attorney general in 1962; four years later, he became a U.S. senator. Brooke rarely, during his twelve-year career in the Senate, identified himself as a "black politician." After his 1966 election, he hired only two blacks out of a nineteen-member staff. He supported affirmative action, but he took other economic and social policy positions to the Right of many mainstream white Democrats. Brooke had no problem campaigning twice for the election of Richard M. Nixon. Political scientist Chuck Stone described Brooke as "Mr. Non-Negro Politics."

Brooke's success in the Republican Party created a model to which others within the most conservative wing of the black bourgeoisie would aspire. Floyd McKissick, the former head of the Congress of Racial Equality, endorsed Nixon's reelection in 1972 in return for federal support for "Soul City," a planned community located in North Carolina. With Reagan's election to the presidency in 1980, a new generation of black conservatives found their way into power: Melvin Bradley, minority business development and black-college adviser to Reagan; Thaddeus Garret, domestic policy adviser to Vice President George Bush; Thelma Duggin, who was involved in the GOP's national black voter program in 1980, and subsequently served as a deputy to Reagan cabinet member Elizabeth Dole; Clarence Thomas, who in 1981 was appointed the Education Department's assistant secretary for civil rights and later became associate justice of the U.S. Supreme Court; and Clarence Pendleton, former head of the San Diego branch of the Urban League, who was selected as chairman of the U.S. Civil Rights Commission. This group of opportunists was provided ideological cover by a group of conservative intellectuals, prominently including economists Thomas Sowell, Walter Williams, Glenn Loury, and later in the 1980s, author Shelby Steele. In theory, Sowell and his conservative cohort argue, racial discrimination in market exchange is essentially irrational. Racial inequality may privilege some whites, they admit, but not the majority.

As sociologists Michael Omi and Howard Winant have explained, conservative economists generally believe that

> state policies such as minimum wage laws, labor law, licensing procedures in labor-intensive trades (barbering, taxi-driving, trucking, etc.) are undertaken in response to the demands of white workers (or, often, white-dominated trade unions) anxious to protect their jobs from open competition with non-whites. Thus the opportunities which white workers' immigrant parents and grandparents seized to lift themselves out of poverty and to create viable ethnic community institutions (particularly small businesses and trades) are denied to minorities today.

Economists like Sowell and Williams therefore believe "that racial policies should be guided by principles of individualism," and not by programs like affirmative action, which strive for what could be termed "equality of result." The practical implications of this conservative, market-based theory of race point the way toward embracing the complete Reaganite agenda: reduced federal expenditures for social programs, deregulation of business, elimination of environmental safeguards and health safety standards in the workplace, the privatization of public schools, and the abolition of affirmative action and other racially based tools that attempt to create more equal outcomes between racial groups.

This conservative wing of what thought of itself as the political Talented Tenth in black America has, in effect, committed "racial suicide," in the sense that it has no sense of linked fates that are dependent on what happens to the masses of disadvantaged African Americans. There is no sense of personal responsibility or accountability to a political project that is centered around the survival and development of the black community. These black conservatives wish to be judged as raceless individuals, not as part of a larger racialized group. They explicitly reject notions that their own career advancement was largely a product of a mass, democratic movement to challenge structural racism. So in this limited sense, these reactionary members of the black political elite have ceased to be black in terms of a historical, oppositional social category of resistance. They are "race traitors": dedicated to the destruction of all racial categories, or even, for some, the collection of data indicating racial discrimination; critical of the liberal integrationist establishment; defenders of the cultural standards of "whiteness" as the norm for excellence; and enthusiastic boosters of corporate capitalism as we know it.

The preeminent "race traitor" remains unquestionably Clarence Thomas. For more than a decade as an Associate Justice on the Supreme Court, Thomas has consistently voted against affirmative action, civil rights, and social policies designed to advance the interests of the truly disadvantaged. Some of his closest personal friends are Attorney General John Ashcroft and Solicitor General Theodore Olson in the Bush administration—in fact, Thomas even officiated at Olson's wedding. In a confused and angry tirade delivered at the conservative American Enterprise Institute's Francis Boyer Award dinner in Washington, D.C., on February 13, 2001, Thomas defended his dissenting opinion that argued that the beating of a handcuffed prisoner was not tantamount to "cruel and unusual punishment" as defined by the Eighth Amendment. He praised as his "friend and mentor" Jay Parker, formerly a registered agent for the white minority apartheid regime in South Africa. He then cited the work of conservative historian Gertrude Himmelfarb to attack the ideal of maintaining "civility" as "the governing principle of citizenship or leadership."

For Thomas, conservatives have a moral obligation to vigorously oppose left-of-center politics. "The war in which we are engaged is cultural, not civil," Thomas declared, and "tests whether this 'nation conceived in liberty . . . can long endure.'" The spirit of political intolerance, the refusal to compromise or to reach halfway toward a political opponent, was for Thomas essential for the defense of a free society. "An overemphasis on civility," Thomas warned, "allows our critics to intimidate us. As I have said, active citizens are often subjected to truly vile attacks; they are branded as mean-spirited, racist, Uncle Tom, homophobic, sexist, etc." The challenge to conservatives was not to "be tolerant and nonjudgmental," but to fight back hard. Compromise, Thomas implied, "is cowardice, or well-intentioned self-deception." Thomas's ideological commitment to evangelical, free-market racial assimilationism knows no boundaries. Even as reported in USA Today, Thomas once declared, "If I type one word in my word processor" in favor of affirmative action, "I break God's law."

In the field of education, the leading race traitor is Bush's Secretary of Education Roderick Raynor Paige. Born in 1933 in Monticello, Mississippi, Paige received his bachelor's degree from the historically black Jackson State University and his doctorate in physical education at Indiana University. He spent part of his professional life as a football coach and college athletic director, and served as dean of Texas Southern University's School of Education from 1984 to 1990. Elected to Houston's school board in 1989, Paige was named superintendent in 1994, the same year George W. Bush won the election as Texas governor. As Houston's superintendent, Paige pushed classroom teachers to "teach to the test," reinforcing memorization and rote learning rather than actual comprehension. He was also responsible, according to education scholar Linda McNeil of Rice University, for a "systematic effort to drive out students who appeared unable to make the grade." He initiated a limited voucher program, using state education funds to permit children from the city's lowest-performing schools to attend private but nonsectarian schools.

Over the past two decades, much of Paige's career advancement was owed directly to the Bush family. In early 1980, Paige volunteered to support the senior Bush's effort to win the Republican Party's presidential nomination. When Reagan won the nomination and asked Bush to join his ticket, Paige ended up as a delegate to the 1980 Republican National Convention. Paige's closest associates suggest that his decision to join the Republican Party was "opportunist"—and Paige doesn't disagree. "I wouldn't discount that," Paige stated to the *Washington Post.* "In fact, some of my friends, we've discussed it and said this: 'The lines are shorter.'"

In the field of foreign affairs, the leading race traitor, hands down, is Condoleezza Rice, Bush's national security adviser. Born in Birmingham, Alabama, in 1954, Rice grew up under Jim Crow segregation. She earned her bachelor's degree at the University of Denver in 1974, followed quickly by her master's from Notre Dame in 1975 and her doctorate at Denver in 1981. Rice was hired as an assistant professor of political science at Stanford University that same year, and she left the Democratic Party to become a Republican the next year. Rice's partisan political conversion during the Reagan-Bush years accelerated her career advancement. Rice served on the National Security Council, then returned to Stanford when in 1993 she became the first woman and first African American to become the university's provost.

It didn't take long before the offers poured in. Rice was briefly touted as a Republican candidate for the U.S. Senate in California. She became a board member of the Chevron Corporation, where she so impressed and charmed her fellow board members that they actually named an oil supertanker after her—"the *Condoleezza.*" At Stanford, she earned a reputation for cutting personnel and reducing university services with minimal faculty input. When challenged on her failure to promote diversity in university hiring, Rice publicly repudiated her previous support for affirmative action when she had been a member of the faculty. "I'm the chief academic officer now," Rice asserted to the press. "I say in principle that I don't believe in and in fact will not apply affirmative action [in university appointments]."

Rice's emergence as a major black figure in the Republican Party occurred at the 2000 National Convention. In her convention address, she justified her membership in the party, saying that "the Democrats in Jim Crow Alabama of 1952 would not register" her father, but "the Republicans did. I want you to know," Rice declared to the cheering, predominantly white audience, "that my father has never forgotten that day, and neither have I." The fact that the majority of these white racist Democrats two decades later now constituted the South's Republican Party was conveniently ignored. Rice continued: "I joined the party for different reasons. I found a party that sees me as an individual, not as part of a group. I found a party that puts family first. I found a party that has love of liberty at its core. And I found a party that believes that peace begins with strength."

The Bush administration's most prominent African American, Secretary of State Colin Powell, falls far short of the race-traitor category because he is too principled. The son of Jamaican immigrants, Powell attended a working-class school, the City College of New York, and joined the army as a second lieutenant in 1958. After a thirty-year plus career in the military, Powell served as the commander of the Army's Fifth Corps in Western Europe; he was national security adviser under Reagan and subsequently George Bush's chairman of the Joint Chiefs of Staff, the youngest ever. It's true that Powell has earned millions from his speeches, at $75,000 per appearance, and received a $6 million advance for his 1995 autobiography. But it also is true that his project "America's Promise: The Alliance for Youth," started in 1998, raised $300 million for youth community-based programs. Powell had the integrity to speak before the Republican National Convention in defense of affirmative action: "Some of our party miss no opportunity to roundly and loudly condemn affirmative action that helped a few thousand kids get an education, but you hardly hear a whimper when it's affirmative action for lobbyists who load our federal tax code with preferences for special interests." He serves a president who joined the Texas Air National Guard to avoid serving in Vietnam, and who advances a domestic policy agenda that in many respects Powell privately opposes.

Powell is the last of a long line of African-American liberal Republicans, from the historical tradition of Frederick Douglass; through William T. Coleman, secretary of transportation in the Ford administration; and baseball star Jackie Robinson. The great dilemma for Powell and the few others in this remnant of the black managerial and professional elite is that the conservative core of their party implacably opposes blacks' interests. Even conservative black commentator Armstrong Williams admitted, in late 2000: "White people don't choose their political affiliation based on affirmative action; countless black people do. . . . The only thing that the Republicans accomplish by digging their heels in opposition to the affirmative action issue, is the widespread alienation of black voters." White supremacy is a central component of the core ideology of modern Republicanism, and one thousand Colin Powells would not change that reality.

At the end of the day, the conservative race traitors have nothing to offer the African-American community. They are symbols of personal upward mobility without the substance of collective empowerment and group development. There is no longer a sense of allegiance or obligation to link these public figures to black civil society. In his 1972 study *Black Politics: A Theoretical and Structural Analysis*, Hanes Walton, Jr., observed: "Though the appointment of blacks to high level federal positions does not improve the economic, educational, or political condition of the black masses, they are nevertheless impressive to black people. Such appointments revitalize the American dream and reawaken the black community to the possibility that with significant individual achievement, the 'American dream' is still workable. These positions, however, are usually more symbolic, honorific, and promotional than substantial and meaningful."

IV

Does the black bourgeoisie possess the capacity to assume a leadership role in the reconstruction of American democracy, and a new national discourse about racism? The great bastion of liberalism in the black community is found within the NAACP. I had the opportunity to assess the political strengths and weaknesses of the association by attending and participating in its 93rd annual convention, held in Houston, Texas, on July 6–11, 2002. Most observers described the convention, which was held in the George R. Brown Convention Center and attracted 20,000 delegates and participants, as the NAACP's most successful conference to date. Its theme, "Freedom Under Fire," evoked the still vivid images of the terrorist strikes of 9/11, as well as the subsequent challenges that have threatened civil liberties inside the United States. The electoral debacle of 2000 was still perceived by most NAACP stalwarts as Bush's usurpation of the presidency, and the group was determined to use this convention to promote an alternative agenda to counter that of the conservative Republicans.

The Houston convention was also something of a celebration for the venerable civil-rights organization, marking a return to the national power it exerted a generation ago. Most association leaders still blame the decline of the organization on the 1993 selection of the Reverend Benjamin Chavis to replace retiring executive secretary Benjamin Hooks. As I have previously discussed, Chavis was summarily fired, technically for fiscal improprieties, but in reality for political reasons. The internal dissension over Chavis's ouster almost immediately led to a second power struggle between those loyal to NAACP Chairman William Gibson, on one hand, and the reformers who found their spokeswoman in Myrlie Evers-Williams, the widow of civil-rights martyr Medgar Evers, on the other.

With her extensive and cordial contacts in many corporations and foundations, plus the backing of liberal and progressive leaders who favored a democratic revitalization of the NAACP, Evers-Williams narrowly defeated Gibson and became the new chairwoman of the organization in 1995. Her first task was to retire the NAACP's debt, which by then exceeded $5 million. Evers-Williams and her allies persuaded Democratic Congressman Kweisi Mfume, former head of the Congressional Black Caucus, to accept a greatly redefined and expanded leadership post as the NAACP's president and chief executive officer. Several years later, the board chairmanship was passed to veteran civil-rights activist

Julian Bond, despite the fact that his progressive political views were distinctly to the Left of many in the organization. The partnership between Mfume and Bond, both of whom had held elective offices for many years, pushed the NAACP aggressively back into national politics in the 2000 elections.

A review of the NAACP Houston convention's policy 2002 agenda, as reflected by its main resolutions, indicates that the organization continues to be clearly left of center, exactly where the overwhelming majority of the African-American electorate is. The convention reaffirmed its earlier 1992 endorsement of a national, single-payer health-care system to provide comprehensive coverage for all Americans. It rejected the so-called "Racial Privacy Initiative," promoted in California by black conservative Ward Connelly. The proposed ballot initiative, if passed, would eliminate the collection of racial statistics in state agencies, thus making it virtually impossible to document incidents or patterns of racial discrimination. The NAACP endorsed statehood for the District of Columbia and advocated measures promoting environmental justice, women's equality, and urban economic development. It called for the creation of a presidential commission to address the gross racial disparities in sentencing patterns within the criminal-justice system and demanded the abolition of racial profiling by police. The resolutions supported justice and fairness for Haitian undocumented refugees being detained by the U.S. government, and it opposed the eviction of "law-abiding citizens" from public housing under repressive laws that expel families from their homes if a family member has a drug conviction. By any standard, this is a progressive agenda, well within the liberal tradition of the Black Freedom Movement historically.

The Houston convention also achieved two significant breakthroughs addressing strategic weaknesses in its political efforts. For years, the NAACP and many African-American political organizations had done little to cultivate a working relationship with Latino groups around strategic public-policy goals and tactical electoral interests. In 2001, Gary Bledsoe, NAACP Texas state president, and Vincent Ramos, the state leader of the League of United Latin American Citizens (LULAC), had forged a statewide coalition to build a bilingual voter-education and mobilization effort. This attempt to build Latino–African American unity helped to construct the unprecedented coalition ticket of Ron Kirk, the black mayor of Dallas who won the Democratic Party's Senate nomination, and Texas gubernatorial Democratic candidate Tony Sanchez, a Mexican American. The NAACP wisely extended an invitation to LULAC president Hector Flores to speak at its Houston convention, making it the first time ever that a LULAC leader had addressed the association. Mfume informed the media that Flores's appearance went "beyond symbolism. It has everything to do with substance. There are issues that confront Hispanics and African Americans all over the country that are harder to deal with when we're dealing with them individually."

Another strategic problem that has plagued the NAACP, its weakness among black youth and young adults, was also strongly addressed. Critics have noted that at least 80 percent of the NAACP's national membership is over thirty-five years old, and the association has widely been viewed as outdated by the post–civil rights, hip-hop generation of blacks born between 1965 and 1984. Under the effective leadership of its twenty-nine-year-old national youth director Jeffrey Johnson, the youth division has recently grown to 60,000 members, with more than 600 youth councils and college chapters.

I spoke to a youth workshop of several hundred on issues of racism in the juvenile justice system and the destructive impact of mass incarceration and the prison industrial complex on the black community. After my presentation, the workshop split into five working groups to discuss hypothetical examples of how to respond to criminal justice–related conflicts. What particularly impressed me was the range of practical political experience and the level of analysis apparent among a large number of young delegates. Johnson and other young NAACP activists, such as twenty-nine-year-old Education Director John Jackson and thirty-six-year-old National Vice Chairwoman Roslyn Brock, represent a progressive and promising future leadership for the association. Other youth-oriented speakers in Houston included rap artist Lil' Zane, who appeared at a Youth Council seminar on creative ways to promote voter-registration drives; and hip-hop mogul Russell Simmons, who addressed the Youth Freedom Fund Awards Dinner honoring the most outstanding college chapters.

Beneath this apparent show of unanimity, there were also unmistakable fissures within the national group only partially obscured by the language of civil-rights discourse. With the demise of the Democratic Party's liberal wing and the near hegemony exercised by the pragmatic "New Democrats," there has been external pressure on the NAACP to move toward a more neoliberal policy position. The most progressive, social democratic tendencies in the NAACP have vigorously opposed the Democratic Party's capitulation to neoliberalism and globalization; this group's leading personality has been the association's chairman, Julian Bond.

Speaking at the opening of the Houston convention, Bond delivered a blistering condemnation of the Bush administration's entire public record. President Bush "promised to enforce the civil-rights laws," Bond declared. "We knew he was in the oil business—we just didn't know it was snake oil." Bond condemned the appointment of "racially hostile, conservative Republicans" to key civil-rights posts and throughout the Department of Justice. He ridiculed Attorney General John Ashcroft as "a cross between" former FBI director J. Edgar Hoover and conservative fundamentalist preacher Jerry Falwell. Bond rejected the Bush administration's endorsement of school vouchers, calling upon "all freedom loving people and the NAACP" to fight "against transferring tax dollars to private schools." Bond declared, "There's a right-wing conspiracy [against African Americans], and its operating out of the United States Department of Justice." He reminded his audience that thousands of African Americans had been disfranchised in Florida and other states in the 2000 election, and said Bush's "Justice Department whittled 11,000 election complaints down to five potential lawsuits, including a mere three in Florida. . . . The margin of the Justice Department's cynicism is surpassed only by its hostility to civil rights." Bond observed that although many African-American leaders had muted their criticisms of the Bush administration, it would be wrong for the NAACP to do so. When democracy is challenged by external threats, "the first casualty is usually democracy. So both because of and in spite of the war against terrorism," the NAACP chairman declared, "we will insist on our right to dissent, to petition our government for a redress of our grievances. We do so as patriots, not as partisans."

The following day, after Bond's remarks had been reported in the press, Bush reacted with racist condescension. Asked to respond to his refusal to engage in a dialogue with civil-rights leaders, Bush commented: "There I was, sitting around the table with foreign leaders, looking at Colin Powell and Condi Rice. Yeah." Bush's hasty attempt to present Powell and Rice as "civil-rights trophies," in the words of the Reverend Al Sharpton, was "the epitome of insensitivity."

Bond had effectively used the Houston convention's theme, "Freedom Under Fire," to underscore the danger of freedom being "undermined in the name of fighting terrorism" in the aftermath of the September 11, 2001, attacks. He reminded African Americans and other racial minorities that their "freedom is always under fire" because of "constant attempts to limit [our] mobility in voting, economic development, education, access to health care, and in other fields. . . . In the wake of the September 11, 2001, attacks, racial profiling has gained a false legitimacy."

In striking contrast, Mfume's language was markedly more conciliatory and centrist. In his welcoming letter to the convention, Mfume declared: "Now, the freedom of innocents in America and throughout the world is under fire from hate-mongers who would use terror to achieve their ends. We, who have fought for freedom for nearly a century, decry the methods of those who would destroy civilization. . . . We stand proud, in fierce opposition to hatred espoused from any quarter, knowing that freedom will prevail." Nothing in Mfume's welcoming letter condemned the Bush administration's extremist record or addressed the enormous dangers presented by the undermining of civil liberties and voting rights under Ashcroft.

This same thesis formed the basic framework for Mfume's major address at the convention. Mfume declared that though he liked Bush personally, "I don't like his presidential practice of divide and conquer when it comes to black organizations and black people and black thinking."

Mfume also attacked Democrats for "taking our votes for granted," stating that every Republican was "not an enemy" and that every Democrat was "not a friend." The NAACP president condemned "black bigotry" and urged the organization to oppose injustices from the "far, far left" as well as the "far, far right." Since the "far, far left" is not in power anywhere in the United States, it was difficult to know whom Mfume was condemning. The only logical explanation was that he was attempting to give a more centrist image to the NAACP. This may explain the NAACP's decision to invite Texas Senator Kay Bailey Hutchison, a conservative Republican with a long record of hostility to blacks' interests, as a convention speaker.

Another prominent tendency at the NAACP 2002 convention was the almost overwhelming presence of corporate America in every aspect of the gathering. Major conventions are, after all, big business. Houston's Convention and Visitors Bureau predicted that the NAACP conference would generate $6.8 million in profits for the city. Seven of the eight major vendor contracts controlled by the NAACP went to minority-owned businesses. The NAACP also persuaded the Brown Convention Center to employ minority-owned subcontractors for food services, audiovisual services, electrical needs, and other services instead of the larger white-owned contractors that normally control convention business. Far exceeding the presence of black small business, however, was the predominance of major corporations. On the NAACP convention's "2002 Blue Ribbon Committee," chaired by Houston Mayor Lee P. Brown, were: the owners of the Houston Rockets and Houston Astros and the presidents and/or chief executive officers of Shell Oil, Bank One–Houston region, Wells Fargo Bank of Texas, ExxonMobil Production Company, and Reliant Energy. Donating "benefactors" listed in conference literature prominently included Enron, Bank of America, JP Morgan Chase Bank of Texas, Continental Airlines, and Sysco Corporation. In its convention advertisement, ExxonMobil identified its corporate goals with those of the NAACP: "For over ninety years, the NAACP has been a champion for the civil rights of all Americans. Its struggle is our struggle; its success is our success. . . . Diversity is the key to business success and fosters a highly productive work environment in which all employees are treated with respect. ExxonMobil is dedicated to being a partner with our employees and the communities in which they live and work toward a future that leaves no one behind."

Microsoft Corporation announced at the convention a $670,000 donation of cash and software to the NAACP to upgrade its information-technology capacity at its national and regional offices. Mfume stated, "Our constructive relationship with Microsoft has given the NAACP the ability to do more in helping to reduce the gap in technology so evident in poor communities across America." Microsoft and its employees had previously given more than $1.5 million to assist the NAACP. The Bell-South Corporation used the convention to announce its continuing association with the NAACP by providing live Internet broadcasts of plenaries, major speeches, and other events on the organization's Web site. BellSouth's diversity chief, Ronald E. Frieson, declared, "BellSouth's strategic imperative of inclusion is closely aligned with that of the NAACP's."

The Microsoft and BellSouth alliances are only a small part of the NAACP's growing network of corporate sponsorships. Companies as diverse as McDonald's, Wal-Mart, Texaco, GTE, Ford, BMW, 7-Eleven, and AT&T have given funds through grants, gifts, or advertisements in NAACP publications and convention brochures. The growing influence of these large multinational corporations on the daily functioning of the association—from the information technology needed to run its offices to the resources essential to finance its expanded service and educational programs—will inevitably influence its public-policy agenda to the right.

That pressure toward accommodation may already be happening. At the February 23, 2002, NAACP "Image Awards" honoring people of color primarily in the entertainment industry, the organization stunned members and critics alike by selecting as one of its recipients National Security Adviser Condoleezza Rice. At the televised black-tie event sponsored by Nationwide Insurance, Mfume praised Rice as a "role model." Rice accepted the honor, stating that America "still struggles with the true meaning of multi-ethnic democracy, . . . still struggles with how to accommodate and indeed, how to celebrate diversity." Nevertheless, Rice declared, "It does struggle to become better. It is not perfect but it is a long, long way from where we were."

Rice's award from the nation's oldest and largest civil-rights organization represents the continuing dilemma of the liberal integrationist philosophy. The black middle class overwhelmingly rejects Condoleezza Rice's politically conservative ideology, but it admires the personal accomplishments and achievements that her academic and public career represents. Rice is the perfect "symbolic representative" of black upward mobility and career advancement. But advancement toward what goals, and for what ends? What does it mean when blacks uncritically celebrate a key representative of an administration that works overtime to reverse the historic gains of the Black Freedom Movement, simply because she shares the color of our skin? The powerful dependency on corporate and philanthropic support may make it increasingly difficult for the NAACP to offer a clear, consistent voice against both the Far Right and globalization.

Despite these constraints and contradictions, the NAACP remains the most important mass organization with the capacity to mobilize millions of African Americans, with the exception of the black church. There are significant variations in political orientation between national leadership and grassroots activists in local branch organizations. In cities like Detroit, for example, the NAACP has a militant, black nationalist membership and an experienced, progressive local leadership. On many white college campuses, black student unions have evolved into apolitical social clubs; the campus NAACP chapters are frequently the only site where activist black youth can become directly involved in antiracist issues. A number of younger NAACP leaders not only share Bond's radical democratic views, but would move the organization further toward broad popular coalitions with other black groups, even including the Nation of Islam, that do not share all of their views. Consequently, it is unclear which direction the NAACP will take; what is absolutely clear, however, is that the NAACP will remain central to any future project in the reconstruction of black politics.

In the post–civil rights era, the Talented Tenth—however it may be defined as a relatively privileged social category within the African-American community—can no longer play the leading role in the next campaign to democratically restructure American race relations. It has in many ways become a class for itself, weakened as a force for real change through the wholesale defection of many of its members to the ranks of white conservatism, or at least the capitulation to outside influences whose goals may often be at odds with those of black America. It possesses a class consciousness that has come to terms with the collapse of communism and European social democracy, and with the new hegemony of globalization, capitalist markets, and the devolution of state authority and programs to the private sector.

Nevertheless, the great majority of the black bourgeoisie still adhere to left-of-center politics because in their practical, collective experiences over several generations, they have learned that the state, and only the state, is the best guarantor of black freedom within a structurally racist and class-stratified social order. Unregulated private markets, without state sanctions, would never have overturned racial discrimination in economic life. Large private institutions opened their white-collar offices to blacks and Latinos not out of some abstract moral commitment to multiculturalism, but because a powerful antiracist movement had pressured them to negotiate new terms. Blacks have always advanced in far greater numbers in the public sector than in the private sector; by the mid-twentieth century, we had become a political force that possessed the capacity to alter the outcome of national elections and used the state as a vehicle to foster black capital accumulation. The modern black professional and managerial class was largely constructed from this process.

Now, in the period of neoliberalism, the political context has changed. The black bourgeoisie's connections with the fates of the black working class and poor have gradually become more tenuous. The likelihood of a return to the welfare state and liberal Keynesianism seems bleak. Markets rule, and even liberal and progressive elements within civil-rights constituencies like the NAACP are pressured to adapt themselves to the New World Order. Political realities require a new historic compromise—not unlike those of 1877 and 1895. To preserve and to protect their relatively modest gains, the black elite has established partnerships with global, multinational capital. The race traitors, a much smaller segment of that elite, are even prepared to liquidate their historical ties of obligation and group upliftment to further their own personal aspirations. The question thus must be posed: Which trend is most indicative of what the politics of the black middle class may become in the next half century—that of the race traitors, represented by Condoleezza Rice, or that of moderate or pragmatic liberals, represented by Kweisi Mfume? The Talented Tenth, of its own accord, will not and cannot break its partnerships with multinational capital unless it is pressured from below by those social forces that have experienced the greatest economic and political marginalization. The basic strategy of affirmative action as a tool for implementing enlightened racial change within the public sector has largely been dismantled. A new approach, one that recasts the public discourse on race in a radically different way, remains to be constructed.

PART THREE

Reconstructing Racial Politics

Chapter 8

Building Democracy from Below

Community Empowerment

We must come to see that, as the federal courts have consistently affirmed, it is wrong to urge an individual to cease his efforts to gain his basic constitutional rights because the quest may precipitate violence. Society must protect the robbed and punish the robber.

—Martin Luther King, Jr.
"Letter from Birmingham Jail," April 16, 1963

I

Two hours after midnight on April 7, 2001, nineteen-year-old Timothy Dewayne Thomas left his apartment, which was located in Cincinnati's inner-city neighborhood called Over-the-Rhine, and walked to a nearby convenience store to buy some cigarettes. Although Over-the-Rhine was less than twelve city blocks from Cincinnati's central business district and impressive new Convention Center, it was generally considered by most of the city's white population a dangerous, drug-filled ghetto. For most African-American residents of Over-the-Rhine, the district's petty dealers, prostitutes, and grifters who came out after dark posed no threat to personal safety. Thomas's only worry was the possibility of running into the police, who had a habit of stopping and frisking black men out at night without probable cause. Thomas had been stopped eleven times since March 2000, mostly on suspected driving infractions, such as driving without a seat belt, and other petty misdemeanors. Twice he had managed to run away, darting into familiar neighborhood alleys and one-way streets. All he wanted was to pick up some cigarettes and go home to his girlfriend and their newborn baby boy.

Several Cincinnati police officers, including Stephen Roach, twenty-seven years old, saw Thomas returning home on foot and decided to check him out. When they confronted Thomas, the young laborer decided that the only prudent course of action was to run. Thomas bolted, and the police followed in pursuit. The foot chase lasted for nearly ten minutes. Thomas ran down an alley not far from the corner of Thirteenth Street and Republic. Officer Roach circled around the block and waited for Thomas at the end of the alley with his gun ready to fire. Thomas stopped suddenly and, according to one version of the events later offered by Officer Roach, appeared to reach into the waistband of his oversized pants. Roach fired, hitting Thomas once, killing him. No weapon was found on Thomas's body.

Thomas was the fifteenth African-American male who had been killed by the Cincinnati police, and the fourth in the previous six months. As word spread the next day about Thomas's killing, many residents of Over-the-Rhine and other black neighborhoods throughout the city were overwhelmed with grief and outrage. Spontaneously, people went into the streets, venting their hostility against the symbols of white power and property. Garbage cans were hurled through plate glass windows; fires were started in white-owned businesses along the central business district of the neighborhood; property and goods were looted. Cincinnati Mayor Charlie Luken responded by declaring a "state of emergency" and imposing an 11:00 P.M. curfew until the rebellion stopped. Police were outfitted in riot gear and armed with tear gas and bean bags filled with metal shot. As the rioting continued on April 10 and 11, businesses closed and the city buses in inner-city neighborhoods stopped running. Thousands of urban residents who relied on public transportation were unable to go to work. After four days of unrest, the police tactics succeeded in suppressing most of the urban unrest. Cops traveled in pairs or teams, never alone, and arrested black women, men, and even children, frequently without cause. As peace was restored, 837 people had been arrested and dozens injured.

The vast majority of black Cincinnati residents had not participated in the street disturbances, and a number of black elected officials, religious leaders, and community activists publicly urged African Americans to show restraint and not to violate the police curfew. On April 14, the funeral service for Timothy Thomas was held at the New Prospect Baptist Church. Attended by hundreds of people, the service attracted many who wanted to make a political statement against the epidemic of police brutality present in Cincinnati and throughout the United States. The new Black Panther Party, an eccentric group of black nationalists who bear little resemblance to the original group of African-American community activists, served as pallbearers. As the family and a small number of friends buried Thomas in a private service, more than 2,000 protesters marched quietly through the Over-the-Rhine district. A series of national civil-rights leaders attended the protest march or came to speak in the city within weeks after the civil unrest, including NAACP President Kweisi Mfume, the Reverend Al Sharpton, Martin Luther King III, and the Reverend Fred Shuttlesworth. Much of the attention on local leadership focused on a charismatic black minister, the Reverend Damon Lynch, an Over-the-Rhine activist whose constructive work with youth had earned him much respect.

On May 7, 2001, one month after Thomas's death, a Cincinnati grand jury indicted Officer Roach on only two misdemeanor counts, negligent homicide and "obstruction of official business," which together were punishable by less than one year in prison. Roach was tried in criminal court, and on September 26, 2001, he was found not guilty. About a hundred social-justice activists stood outside the courtroom awaiting the decision. When it was announced, they were stunned. The police anticipated a strong reaction to the decision and were prepared to use force if necessary to quell any spontaneous demonstrations. When some protesters attempted to organize a march outside the courthouse, they were quickly dispersed. Mayor Luken, taking no chances, imposed a curfew for several days.

The social unrest and public violence precipitated by the Thomas killing was the culmination of decades of structural racism and official indifference. In 1967, Cincinnati experienced a racial uprising in its ghetto areas that had resulted in hundreds of arrests and the destruction of several million dollars' worth of private property. Police relationships with the city's African-American population became tense again in the late 1970s, when four white officers and four black civilians were killed in a series of armed confrontations. The police demanded and were given the authority to carry .357 magnums with powerful exploding bullets, began to wear bulletproof vests, and acquired state-of-the-art weapons for crowd control and assault.

In the 1970s and 1980s, tens of thousands of middle- and upper-class whites moved out of the city. Over-the-Rhine, which for many years had been racially and ethnically diverse, became predominantly African American, and overwhelmingly poor. According to Cincinnati's City Planning Department, the total population of the city declined by 6 percent, or 21,417 people, from 1980 to 1990. Fourteen percent of all households were on public assistance, 18 percent were headed by females, and 24 percent fell below the federal poverty line. The median household income citywide in 1990 stood at $21,006, the ninth lowest out of the seventy-five largest U.S. cities. The rate of home ownership, at only 35 percent of all households, was also the ninth lowest of that group.

The statistics for Cincinnati's Empowerment Zones, impoverished urban districts targeted for development under federal legislation, were even more disturbing. About three out of four of the 50,000 residents living in these zones were African Americans. Their 1989 median income was $10,877; more than one-fourth survived on public assistance, 45 percent were defined by federal poverty criteria as poor, and six out of ten children were living in poverty. Nearly one-half of the adults over the age of twenty-five did not have a high-school diploma. Fewer than one-fifth of all households owned their own homes, and 44 percent of all adults were not in the paid labor force.

The political and corporate establishment's approach to addressing these expanding pockets of poverty and despair only made matters worse. The city spent millions of tax dollars to subsidize the construction of downtown sports stadiums and to advertise Cincinnati as a Midwestern mecca for tourism and convention gatherings. Relatively little was spent to enhance the quality and availability of housing for low-to median-income families, to upgrade public schools, or to assist in the development of community-based, black-owned businesses. Major highway construction and downtown developments disrupted and divided neighborhoods and displaced the homeless and the poor. Yet the plight of Cincinnati's racialized urban poor was little different from the situation confronting black, brown, and oppressed populations elsewhere in the decaying cores of America's depopulated urban landscapes. And it was these socioeconomic conditions, the normal inequalities of daily life, that had fostered and perpetuated the volatile climate of black alienation, white anxiety, and excessive police force that caused Thomas's death.

There was a new determination in Cincinnati's black community not to allow the tragedy to go unanswered. On Tuesday, April 24, 2001, African-American leaders throughout the city met to devise a concrete plan of action. Notes from this remarkable discussion of "African American Grassroots Leadership" provided by black community leader Reginald Boyd indicate the profound soul searching in the black community in the aftermath of the urban uprising. The general discussion focused on generating practical strategies to foster community empowerment. Relatively few comments centered on the immediate issues of police brutality and the lack of governmental accountability, because a clear consensus about these issues was readily apparent to nearly everyone at the meeting. "What happened in Cincinnati was not a RIOT," one participant said, "it was a REBELLION and in SELF DEFENSE." The "police are out of control inside and outside the City of Cincinnati." Another participant suggested changing "the policy that pays suspended officers," because "if they are not paid then there will be fewer problems because suspension will stop their income." Others encouraged the group to "look carefully at the homicide investigations into the death of African-American children" and to contribute to a "legal defense fund to assist those who were arrested." Participants in the conference were clear that public safety was necessary for people to live and work in the neighborhoods, and that responsible law enforcement was necessary in the preservation of civil order. One black police officer expressed these sentiments by observing, "We want and need policing in our community, but we want GOOD POLICING."

The African American Grassroots Leadership conference focused on several practical steps to enhance the political clout of Cincinnati's black community. Suggestions included putting "our own candidates on the ballot for mayor, prosecutor, [and] judges"; beginning an African-American Political Action Committee; launching major voter-registration drives while helping to "introduce new voters to the process and procedures of voting"; getting "absentee ballots to our nursing homes, hospitals, and colleges so our people can vote"; and urging blacks to attend City Council and committee meetings. There were some differences of opinion about the role of local as well as national black elected officials and established civil-rights leaders in pursuing the grassroots leadership's goals. Suggestions ranged from creating a strong African-American political base to keep leaders accountable, along the lines of the Congressional Black Caucus but on a smaller scale, to increasing "the number of young men receiving training and instruction from the Nation of Islam." One participant recommended extending an invitation to Jesse Jackson "to lead and organize peaceful demonstrations [and] sit ins. . . . With the spirit of God's help we can all utilize the same path for greater change but it has to be on-going." Others had serious reservations about top-down leadership, and especially the role of middle-class African-American leaders. "Rich blacks who have move(d) away should come back to help our community in our struggle!" one participant declared. Another emphasized that both black and white leaders must be made "accountable."

Economic strategies received as much attention as political ones. Some participants favored the tradition of Booker T. Washington and Louis Farrakhan, which advocated black entrepreneurship, home ownership, self-reliance, and patriarchal family values. Suggestions in this line of argument also included: "pooling dollars within our community"; starting "black banks"; urging businesspeople to "mentor youth and teach them how to move forward"; and getting "foreign storeowners who do not share our values out of our community." Some participants believed that the Internet and digital knowledge were the keys toward the future development of the black ghetto. "Build a world class computer center in our community with Internet access for the use of the whole community," advised one woman, adding that the group should also "train our young people to read the stock page."

Others thought that economic development efforts should focus specifically on young women and men who had become victims of the prison industrial complex. Several people present were members of a prisoners' rights group; one pointed out that "prisons are not rehabilitating anyone." The need for job programs "for reformed felons" came up, and one participant called for a program to "rehabilitate drug dealers," observing: "I've stopped selling drugs but I can't get a job. Brothers are willing to come in and stop selling, but we need jobs. Advertise the jobs so people will know where they are." One economic strategy for grassroots reparations suggested that "economic inclusion for the African-American community" should be "written into the City Charter," with a designated percentage of the "total city budget" allocated directly to black areas.

Others focused on change not at the political or economic level but at a more personal, spiritual level. Some believed that black children must be taught "personal responsibility to avoid self-destructive behavior." A member of the Evanston Youth Association suggested holding a "church retreat for young black males," featuring "rights of passage" rituals.

At times, the discussion about political tactics and strategies for grass-roots resistance and reform fragmented into differences of opinion. Some felt African Americans had no reliable allies within the white community or even among other racialized minorities in the struggle for freedom. One participant stressed the need to "remove outsiders from our community" in order to "solve our own problems." Black unity was essential "to fight the system; we have to help ourselves." Others vigorously dissented. "Blacks and whites have to work together," another participant insisted. Another participant urged the inclusion of "other ethnic groups in our cause," such as Arab immigrants. And radical activists suggested that compromise measures were ineffective. "We must go to the streets," one participant declared. Another proposed the comprehensive boycotting of all downtown businesses: "Then business owners will start screaming, the police [will] stop abusing and killing minorities. This and voting seems to be the only way to stop injustice and blatant racism. We have to unite on this."

The Cincinnati City Council used the racial crisis to push through a series of repressive measures aimed at the poor and working poor, who are of course predominantly blacks and other racialized minorities. Panhandling was outlawed "during the night hours, at bus stops, on private property, and within twenty feet of a bank or at an ATM." Those immediately hurt by the new law were the street vendors of the local newspaper *Streetvibes*, printed by the Cincinnati Coalition for the Homeless. *Streetvibes* vendors were often homeless people who purchase the newspapers for 20 cents and subsequently sell them for one dollar. Mayor Luken, however, denounced them as "beggars armed with newspapers."

In October 2001, the City Council passed the "Housing Impaction Ordinance," which was designed, according to researchers Jonathan Diskin and Thomas A. Dutton, to deny "funding for the network of non-profit housing corporations that work in poor neighborhoods to develop affordable housing." City Council members had been persuaded by "the

popular but misguided view that the concentration of low-income housing is the root of most problems in Over-the-Rhine and other 'impacted'
neighborhoods." Completely ignored were "the more fundamental
causes for neighborhood decline: the disappearance of good jobs for
low-skilled workers, declining wages, poor education, persistent patterns of racial discrimination, [and] government rollbacks in social services (including 'welfare reform')." Kathy J. Wilson, a regular columnist
for the *Cincinnati City Beat*, observed that the Cincinnati Metropolitan
Housing Authority's (CMHA) basic urban redevelopment plan was "to
replace some of its subsidized housing with more of the same and to
mix that with market-rate housing ranging in price from $150,000 to
$240,000." The Housing Authority's objective was "to keep residents sep-
arate but unequal; the CMHA housing units will not be near the market
housing." Wilson concluded, "So although folks of disparate income levels will be living together, they won't *really* be living together."

In early 2002, the Cincinnati Black United Front, led by the Reverend
Damon Lynch, came together with two other progressive groups,
Stonewall Cincinnati and the Coalition for a Just Cincinnati, to initiate a
nationwide boycott against the city's economic elite. The boycott campaign urged celebrities, business and social groups, and others planning
conferences or events in downtown Cincinnati to cancel their engagements. The coalition announced that the boycott would be terminated
only when city leaders met its "demands for neighborhood economic
development, police accountability, support and enforcement of civil
rights, and government and election reform." At first, the politicians and
the media largely ignored the boycott effort, stating that it would be ineffective. But within weeks, a host of prominent performers canceled their
local engagements, including Wynton Marsalis, Bill Cosby, Whoopi
Goldberg, Smokey Robinson, and the Temptations. Many civic and fraternal organizations pulled out. The city government responded by
launching an ad campaign touting the area's incredibly rich "diversity"
and pushing the banal slogan, "Cincinnati Can: You Can Too!"

In early February 2002, when I visited the Cincinnati area, I walked
through the Over-the-Rhine community and spoke before the Black
United Front. Local television stations were filled with stories about

black workers who had been dismissed from their jobs at downtown restaurants and shops due to the boycott. Mayor Charlie Luken and several prominent blacks with ties to Cincinnati's largest corporate employer, Proctor and Gamble, charged that the economic campaign was destroying the city's reputation and damaging any hope for improving the material conditions of poor black people.

These and other shrill attacks against the Black United Front were largely ineffective. Not unlike the 1980s campaign to promote divestment of U.S. corporations from engaging in business in South Africa, the Cincinnati boycott created the necessary political pressure to force the city's corporate and political establishment to reach a settlement with their critics. Almost one year after Thomas's slaying and the urban uprising, Mayor Luken admitted to the press that Cosby's decision was a crucial blow: "Cosby gave it legs. . . . It had a negative effect on our image." A tentative agreement was soon reached between city government officials and representatives of the Black United Front and other African-American constituencies, the police union, and the American Civil Liberties Union. New guidelines were established, according to the *New York Times*, "to deal with decades of racial profiling complaints by African Americans." Luken "promised to get behind the new agreement with fresh job, education and housing opportunities for needier neighborhoods." Luken informed the media, "We want to be the model that other cities will look to and say, hey they put all their problems out on Front Street and they're dealing with them the right way." In the most stunning move, Luken appointed Valerie A. Lemmie, an African-American woman and the respected city manager of Dayton, Ohio, to become Cincinnati's city manager. As the city's highest-ranking official, Lemmie promised black residents, "There'll be no smoke and mirrors in getting this done. . . . This is all about respect for other human beings."

Despite these positive changes, many in the boycott coalition favored continuing the pressure on the local political and corporate elite to ensure that promises made would be kept. As Diskin and Dutton observed, "the coalition of non-profit community-based organizations and other groups that are supporting the boycott have called for economic inclusion, a greater political voice, police accountability, housing rights, and job production. This renewed and broad-based participation must translate into policies and practices that help build local communities."

II

An important lesson can be drawn from the events in Cincinnati following the death of Timothy Dewayne Thomas: To challenge the effects of neoliberalism and revive those suffering from civil death, a black political project must be grounded in grassroots struggles around practical questions of daily life. Such struggles bring into the public arena diverse and sometimes contradictory ideological and social forces. In the Cincinnati grassroots resistance movement, a wealth of new ideas were brought out in public brainstorming sessions, especially in the areas of public-policy issues and economic development. It is at this grassroots level that blacks might begin the difficult task of constructing new social theory and political strategies, extrapolating from their collective experiences and practices of neighborhood and community-based activism. This approach to politics starts with the micro-battles of neighborhood empowerment to bring about change in the macro-contexts of national and international processes impacting African Americans.

There is unfortunately a widespread belief that the Black Freedom Movement has been extinguished. Nothing could be further from the truth. At the national level, no new organizational forms have yet emerged in the activist traditions of the early NAACP, the National Negro Congress of the Great Depression years, the Southern Christian Leadership Conference of the 1950s, or the Student Nonviolent Coordinating Committee and the League of Revolutionary Black Workers from the 1960s. Yet virtually unnoticed at the local level, in hundreds of black communities across the nation, successful models of resistance are flourishing. Many different protests strategies and new organizational forms are constantly emerging from the shifting sites of contestation inside communities.

During the period of Jim Crow segregation, any references to the "Negro community" could be immediately understood on both sides of the color line. "The black community" was a territorial, geographical, and sociopolitical site occupied by blacks. Its existence was simultaneously a product of coercion and voluntary activity. With the processes of desegregation, class stratification, and to some degree middle-class outmigration from the inner cities, the meaning of "community" for African Americans is less clear-cut. All communities are sites of collective imagination, social processes rather than mere locations for living and work. Within the concept of the black community, there is a social geography of blackness—a set of political, social, and economic experiences and relations with whites as a dominant group that to a large extent define and construct our collective understandings of daily life. Where we work, whether we obtain home mortgages, the quality of medical treatment we receive, and the encounters our sons may have with the police all contribute to a sense of membership and kinship to an "imagined" black community. In this larger sense, it is possible to talk about a black community's rituals, folklore, discourses, and contested forms of cultural construction that are independent of a territorial space.

Many community-based protest organizations have focused on the issue of jobs. In Chicago, a series of job-site protests have been initiated by the Chicago Black United Communities (CBUC). Founded in 1980, the CBUC is a coalition of diverse activists whose stated goals are "to change the personal and community lives of Black people in terms of oppressive politicians and limited services, and to conduct programs that provide as much information, knowledge and clarity about the systems and processes which affect and impact our lives." When the administration of Mayor Richard Daley was slow to enforce affirmative-action mandates in the construction industry, the CBUC began, in June 1994, to picket one dozen construction sites, demanding the employment of skilled African-American workers. In several instances, CBUC protesters climbed the scaffolding at construction sites with workers' equipment and tools, sometimes provoking physical confrontations that halted all work. Eddie Read, the president of the CBUC, was arrested on several occasions. As the protests mounted, members of Operation PUSH, a civil-rights group led by Jesse Jackson, joined the picket lines. The white press was nearly unanimous in its condemnation of these protests, describing the efforts to forcibly shut down construction sites as "extortion." Nevertheless, after a spirited campaign lasting one year, the CBUC was responsible for the placement of almost 100 skilled black workers into appropriate jobs.

Other grassroots organizations in Chicago have also employed confrontational tactics. In July 1991, members of the New Mt. Sinai Baptist Church and other activists picketed a construction project in the Englewood community. A white construction firm had been awarded a $26 million redevelopment contract over black competitors. Protesters denounced the company's failure to hire black workers at the site. In September 1994, 1,000 demonstrators protested the celebration activities at the newly opened United Center, which would serve as the site for the 1996 Democratic National Convention. Demonstrators demanded "more convention-related contracts and jobs for blacks and other minorities."

Similar black community-based labor struggles are occurring across the South. In Greensboro, North Carolina, hundreds of mostly black workers at a Kmart distribution center began a series of boycotts and peaceful demonstrations in 1994, when the giant retailer refused to negotiate in good faith with their union, the Union of Needle Trades, Industrial and Textile Employees (UNITE). By 1996, demonstrations against Kmart had spread to Atlanta, Memphis, Norfolk, Houston, and cities outside the region. Most of these involved several thousand union members and community activists. In March 1996, Kmart granted a 50-cent across-the-board wage increase at the Greensboro site, which still left workers earning up to $4 per hour less than Kmart workers at other distribution centers. As the Greensboro protests continued, other community groups began to participate. Eighty Greensboro churches belonging to an interfaith group called the Pulpit Forum endorsed the demonstrations. Protesters pointed to the generous $1 million tax break that Kmart had received for building the Greensboro redistribution center in 1992. Reverend William Wright, president of the Pulpit Forum, described the Greensboro struggle as representing "a trend that is sweeping the nation. Corporate entities recognize huge profits, but those who help them achieve it are being pushed through the cracks of poverty."

Black working-class women have been in the forefront of these grass-roots movements for change in local communities. In several North Carolina cities and towns, for example, they have established "housekeepers associations" to challenge local housekeeping employers. In 1996, the University of North Carolina Housekeepers Association pressured university management to grant it recognition as a union and agree to "meet and confer" with it on all pertinent issues. At nearby East Carolina University, housekeepers also formed an association and led several protest marches, demonstrating even on the front lawn of the university chancellor's residence. In all these protests, union struggles have been expanded in scope to incorporate activists from churches, civic associations, and political organizations involved in antiracist struggles. For example, when Ku Klux Klansmen burned two black churches in Claredon County, South Carolina, UNITE contributed $7,500 to each church to assist in rebuilding.

Following the 1992 Los Angeles civil unrest after the Rodney King incident, California's leading black charity, the Brotherhood Crusade, initiated protests at various construction sites where black and Latino workers were underrepresented. In September 1992, a broad coalition of former gang members, ministers, trade unionists, and representatives from community-based groups, such as the Watts branch of the NAACP, joined with the Brotherhood Crusade to demonstrate at the Gardena Shopping Center construction site. Protesters carried signs reading, "If we don't work, nobody works," and "No Jobs, No Peace!" Finally, through the intervention of the Justice Department, the general contractor at the Gardena Shopping Center agreed to employ thirty additional black construction workers. The agreement confirmed that black workers would be given "maximum opportunity to participate in construction projects." The Brotherhood Crusade also led demonstrations at another Los Angeles construction site managed by the Nage Construction Company. After negotiations, the company agreed to hire black carpenters onsite and to work with black subcontractors. However, the Brotherhood Crusade's controversial president, Danny Bakewell, has more than his share of critics. Possessing a divisive, confrontational style, Bakewell's involvement in economic redevelopment projects, according to author Mike Davis, "has leveraged fabulous profits from city land discounts and direct subsidies" in the impoverished Compton community. Bakewell has also "been prominent in sensationalized fights with Latino and Korean communities."

There are probably several thousand black community-based organizations focusing on the special problems of young people. Most of them are of course nonprofit corporations and social-service groups, and many were initiated by African-American churches, civil-rights, and fraternal organizations. One example in New York City is the Manhattan Valley Youth Program. Founded in 1979 by community advocate John H. Bess, "the Valley" provides educational and social-welfare programs to more than 10,000 mostly Latino and black city youth. In 1995, the Valley cosponsored a "Crisis of Black Youth Conference" hosted by the Institute of Research in African American Studies at Columbia University, bringing together representatives from more than seventy-five groups from Harlem and other black communities in the city. There is also the Rheedlen Centers for Children and Families, a nonprofit organization focusing on the needs of urban and racial minority youth. The Rheedlen Centers is headed by activist Geoffrey Canada, who has become a powerful, progressive voice of children's rights nationally. Both Bess and Canada are actively involved in broader political struggles affecting black New Yorkers as well. Canada has argued that black politics lost its direction when black leaders were "pulled further and further away from their communities."

In Boston, a united front of some forty religious institutions established the 10 Point Coalition, which, among other projects, sponsors "the Brotherhood" group that reaches out to counsel young black males. Black activists at Atlanta's Holistic Stress Control Institute have established SIMBA—the Saturday Institute for Manhood Brotherhood Actualization program. SIMBA conducts regular visitations to more than 120 young men in local juvenile corrections centers, sponsoring counseling and conflict-resolution sessions. In San Francisco, black activists in the Omega Boys Club offer a counseling program to hundreds of young men each year and serve as advocates during court proceedings involving juvenile defendants. Omega has also initiated a popular radio program, "Street Soldiers," promoting violence-prevention and related community issues.

Few of these organizations would be described as being "political," much less radical. Yet for hundreds of thousands of young African Americans, they make a critical difference in their quality of life, and they help to make community activism possible. The black freedom struggle a generation ago learned to tap into these self-help, community-uplift groups for both resources and personnel necessary to successfully engage in local campaigns.

Undoubtedly the most dynamic community-based groups to emerge in the past decade among African Americans are those designed to address the problems of police brutality and racism within the criminal-justice system. The vast majority of local coalitions or neighborhood associations focusing on relations between police and the black community are initiated or led by African-American and Latina women whose husbands, brothers, or sons have been victims of police violence. Many of these groups are temporary coalitions of religious and civil-rights organizations that come together briefly to hold one or a series of public protests. Sometimes, such ad-hoc coalitions solidify into permanent organizations, serving as "watchdog" groups publicizing new incidents of police brutality and uses of excessive force. Literally hundreds of examples of these public marches, civil disobedience protests, and anti-police violence coalitions have been documented in the national African-American press.

The most prominent mass mobilizations against police brutality in recent years that generated national and international media attention both occurred in New York City, with the brutal torture of Haitian immigrant Abner Louima by members of the New York Police Department, and the subsequent shooting of West African immigrant Amadou Diallo on February 4, 1999, by the department's notorious Street Crimes Unit. Although the Louima and Diallo cases became national cause célèbres, there were a series of local anti-police brutality mass mobilizations that had led up to these better known human-rights violations.

For example, in New York City on June 28, 1996, 10,000 people marched down Fifth Avenue from 59th Street to the United Nations to protest "the burning of Black churches and police brutality." Singing "We Shall Overcome" and "Ain't Gonna Let Nobody Turn Us Around," the marchers represented a range of religious, labor, and civil-rights organizations. In the Bronx, protesters outraged at the shootings of two Hispanic young men by the police staged a "boisterous sit-in" in October 1995 outside of the Bronx district attorney's office. On June 13, 1996, in Brooklyn, Aswan Keshawn Watson, an unarmed twenty-one-year-old black male, was killed by two white plainclothes officers who fired eighteen bullets into him. Activists in central Brooklyn held a mass forum on August 5, 1996, charging that Watson's death was "evidence of blatant police contempt." On May 2, 1997, a Brooklyn grand jury found that the officers "were justified in believing themselves to be in danger" when they mistakenly judged a steering-wheel lock for a gun.

In Paterson, New Jersey, in February 1995, teenagers led a demonstration outside that city's police headquarters to protest the killing of a sixteen-year-old boy by a rookie police officer. In Staten Island on May 1, 1994, hundreds of schoolchildren, parents, and working people marched in the Clifton section of the borough to protest the death of Ernest Savon, who allegedly was fatally beaten by police. To publicize the scores of police shootings of black and Latino young men in metropolitan New York, since 1993 several mothers' groups and community activists have organized an annual protest called "Racial Justice Day." The April 1997 rally brought 300 protesters to City Hall Park. As the demonstration moved uptown toward Washington Square Park, chanting "The people united will never be defeated," hundreds of onlookers joined the march, bringing the estimated number of protesters to 1,000.

In other major American cities, the same situation exists. In Chicago, on July 30, 1995, Joseph Gould, an unarmed homeless black man, was killed by an off-duty white police officer. The policeman was first charged only with "official misconduct," but after a series of public demonstrations the Illinois state attorney increased the charge to "armed violence." On October 3, 1995, Honduran immigrant Jorge Guillen died in police custody from suffocation. The state attorney refused to prosecute, claiming "lack of evidence of any criminal conduct." These and other incidents prompted some Chicago activists to organize a demonstration marking a "National Day of Protest Against Police Brutality, Repression and Criminalization of a Generation" on October 22, 1996.

The list of such protests extends to city after city. In San Francisco in June 1995, militant protesters packed a meeting of the city's police commission to denounce the killing of a black man by officers. In July 1994, a crowd of demonstrators protested at a police district station in Baltimore, denouncing the death of a black man, Jesse Chapman, while in police custody. In nearby Prince George's County that same year, Archie Elliott III, a black man, was shot fourteen times by two county police officers. Dorothy Copp Elliott, the deceased's mother, began speaking out at community events and neighborhood churches "to protest her son's death." And in Seattle, a black mother, Harriet Walden, was outraged when her teenage sons, Tunde and Omari, were harassed and arrested by local police. In 1990, Walden funded "Mothers Against Police Harassment," which within several years had become a sixty-member, multiracial organization.

In the South, incidents of police misconduct have also sparked unrest. In 1993 in Jeanerette, Louisiana, a black man, Eddie Lewis, was shot and killed by a local police officer as a suspect to an armed robbery. Lewis's death prompted black activists to picket and boycott white-owned stores in the town. Local authorities called on state troopers to "handle any protests." On October 17, 1996, in Leland, Mississippi, a black small business owner named Aaron White was killed by a white police officer. As reported by journalist Salim Muwakkil: "Initially, police say the 29-year-old White was trying to escape the scene of a traffic accident and fired first on Officer Jackie Blaylock, who successfully returned fire. The police later revised their story, saying White accidentally killed himself in the escape attempt." In St. Petersburg, Florida, on October 24, 1996, a white policeman shot and killed an unarmed, eighteen-year-old black man, Tyrone Lewis. Black community residents who witnessed the killing were so enraged that a riot spontaneously broke out. The unrest covered an area of twenty square blocks; twenty-nine buildings were burned and eleven people injured. Three weeks later, more unrest occurred when a local grand jury decided not to indict the police officer who had shot Lewis.

One of the most prominent community struggles over police brutality in recent years occurred in Pittsburgh on October 12, 1995, when thirty-one-year-old black businessman Jonny E. Gammage died of suffocation while in the custody of five white police officers. Gammage had been unarmed and had no criminal record. His death became publicized only because his cousin and business partner, Ray Seals, was a defensive end on the Pittsburgh Steelers. The coroner's jury called for all five officers to be charged with criminal homicide. The district attorney, however, dropped all charges against two of the officers and reduced the charges for the remaining three officers to involuntary manslaughter.

This decision outraged the African-American community and sparked a series of demonstrations beginning in November 1995. Churches, community groups, and the local branch of the NAACP became actively involved. They argued that Gammage's killing was only one example of a general pattern of excessive police force against minorities in the area. Of 400 complaints of harassment in Pittsburgh in 1994, only twenty-three were sustained, and only one officer was suspended for one day. When an all-white jury acquitted one of the officers in the Gammage case in November 1996, nearly 4,000 high-school and middle-school students walked out of their classrooms in protest. In May 1997, another round of marches and demonstrations broke out when a judge barred the district attorney's office from attempting to retry the remaining officers.

Although black solidarity and struggles against racism are behind most community-initiated protests, they are not the only driving force behind black grassroots mobilizations. Black activism is frequently found in protest campaigns initiated by whites, or in multiracial coalitions where African Americans are only one of many different groups. In Milwaukee in the late 1990s, a struggle to improve local public transportation by building a light rail system in low-income neighborhoods has brought together groups reflecting divergent class and ethnic backgrounds. The Central City Transit Task Force, the primary force that pushed for low-cost public transportation, reached out to religious, community, trade union, and business organizations. Some groups that supported the campaign included Repairers of the Breach, a Catholic-sponsored homeless advocacy organization, environmental groups like

Communities for a Better Environment, and members of the African American Chamber of Commerce and the Ujamaa Project, an economic-development cooperative.

When the first wave of drastic cuts from Clinton's welfare bill began on March 1, 1997, as single adults were scheduled to lose food-stamp benefits, a spontaneous wave of multiracial, multiclass demonstrations and civil disobedience actions occurred across the country. In Oakland, California, for example, 2,000 protesters organized by the People for Bread, Work and Justice coalition marched through the downtown district. The demonstration was endorsed by more than 100 welfare-rights, community, religious, labor union, and political organizations. In Raleigh, North Carolina, 300 protesters turned out, organized by the newly formed North Carolina Coalition for Economic Justice and a Living Wage; this demonstration, too, was endorsed by different religious, labor, and community groups. In Cleveland, a "speak-out" demonstration against welfare cuts was supported by groups such as the Northeast Ohio Coalition for the Homeless, the YMCA, the Labor Party, and Women for Racial and Economic Equality.

In several cities, successful coalition campaigns have created the basis for more permanent united fronts. One excellent example was the Progressive Alliance of Alameda County in the Bay Area. At its founding convention in June 1996, a twenty-seven member leadership council was elected. Within six months, the multiracial coalition had 400 dues-paying members. The Progressive Alliance sponsored a series of successful public programs and activities: membership teach-ins on campaign finance reform, health care, tenants rights, and proportional representation; weekend voter-registration drives; and a "United Progressive Proposition Campaign" that included preelection canvassing and door-to-door leaflet distribution.

III

To begin anew a counter-hegemonic black political project, African-American progressive activists and intellectuals must learn from the experiences, successes, and failures of these community-based coalitions, mobilizations, spontaneous protests, and even voluntary, self-help groups. Our task should not be to impose a set of theoretical prescriptions on these local formations that constantly emerge, disintegrate, then unexpectedly reemerge into new organizational forms. Rather, it is to construct new strategies and theory based on critical observations and descriptions of the struggles from daily life as they actually develop on the ground. In other words, we can learn from the experiences of hundreds of black neighborhoods as well as of multiethnic and multiracial communities of working-class and poor people. In this process, we must challenge the liberal integrationists' traditional emphasis and reliance on electoral politics, and focus on struggles emerging directly from trade unions and from community-based coalitions and associations. We must also give much greater weight in our practice and theory to issues of gender, recognizing the powerful roles black women activists play as the central organizers of many of these community-based groups.

We need new organizational forms to accomplish our goals: not a party based on a vanguard, cadre-type organization, which unfortunately characterized much of the Left in the 1960s and 1970s, but a national network of black radical activists who are directly involved in community organizing, feminist, labor, lesbian/gay, and progressive black nationalist causes. New theory can emerge only when the actual struggles and campaigns now being waged within black communities can be analyzed and critically discussed by other activists. Young people just now joining local formations need to learn the history of the Black Freedom Movement, acquiring organizing skills and technical expertise. The development of summer schools or educational forums bringing young black activists from throughout the country would accelerate this process. The veterans of the civil-rights, Black Power, African liberation solidarity and black feminist organizations from the 1960s and 1970s, most of whom are now over fifty years old, must assume a pivotal, but not leadership, role in the construction of this new grassroots movement.

It is helpful to consider black political theorist Adolph Reed's warnings about the pitfalls of black community-based politics. In a perceptive

1996 article, Reed argued, "The main internal obstacle to generating a popularly based progressive black political movement is the very concept of 'black community,' and the rhetoric of authenticity that comes with it." For Reed, "the ideal of community is a mystification, however, and an antidemocratic one at that." For decades, black activists provided critical support to a series of community-based "leaders" who in turn manipulated race to practice brokerage politics. "I suspect that black activists' continuing romance with political hustlers and demagogues ('Up with hope, down with dope!') stems from their seductive promise of connection to a real, mobilizable constituency," Reed suggested. "There are no significant forces on the ground in black politics attempting to generate any sort of popular, issue-based civic discourse, and the language of community is largely the reason."

Much of what Reed says I absolutely agree with. Community-based politics always reflect the many contradictions existing in all communities—homophobia, sexism, class elitism and privilege, anti-immigrant bias, and so forth. Conservative black nationalists like Farrakhan have historically manipulated the language of community for their own purposes. Liberal integrationist politicians may espouse the goal of black cultural and political advancement into the mainstream, but they also utilize the concept of community to mask their own class interests and support for the political establishment. That is exactly why a class-based, progressive intervention around community-based organizing is so urgently necessary.

Many community-based protests, as I have illustrated, are simultaneously class-based struggles around clear-cut economic justice issues. Community-based coalitions struggling for affordable public transportation, health care, decent schools, or an end to police brutality in their neighborhoods may all eventually contribute to black and multiracial progressive movements for democratic change. Even more important, community organizations are frequently the sites where many working-class and low-income black, Asian, and Latina women become actively engaged in day-to-day resistance. These neighborhood struggles led by women greatly enrich our understanding of the possibilities for change within the entire society and we should support them and learn from them. At the same time, we must consciously oppose the racial essentialism and antidemocratic trends that Reed correctly cited as inherent in many community-based formations and struggles.

One great difficulty in building black community-based capacity from below is the contradictory impact of racism on the oppressed. "Race" is constantly and continuously constructed from without and within the sites of human activity and experience. That is to say, "race" is not real, but "racism" is manufactured constantly by the formal institutional barriers that reproduce inequality, which in turn shape the texture and contours of the lives of the people living under such a regime. The sites of racialized existence become spaces for fighting back, for noncooperation, for hope and courage when the objective realities of one's situation appear to negate all possibilities for change. It is through the veil of race that the oppressed comprehend and interpret the social forces that impact their families, friends, and communities. But the strengths of racialized radicalism also produce cultural, social, and even psychological barriers to building movements across racial boundaries. As in the intense public debate recorded at the African American Grassroots Leadership conference in Cincinnati, there are real schisms within many black communities about how to relate to other racialized ethnic groups and immigrant populations that do not share our own history. Petty differences drawn from language, cultural traditions and mores, and codes of public conduct and courtesy can be misinterpreted in antagonistic ways, dividing communities who share in most respects common material and political interests.

The Over-the-Rhine neighborhood is more than 80 percent black—but about one in six community residents are white, Latino, or Muslim. There are several working-class neighborhoods in Cincinnati where white household median income falls below the national average and where chronically high rates of unemployment exist. The debate over the Cincinnati boycott, as it was projected in the national media, was presented solely in black versus white terms, which grossly misrepresented the real political dynamics in that city's struggle. There were prominent African Americans, including one NAACP local leader, who publicly opposed the boycott, and there were liberal, religious, and community activist whites who supported it. The same media distortions about the multiracial character of community-based coalition politics exist nationally.

If you watched commercial television twenty-four hours a day for an entire year, you'd never guess that poor whites existed in the United States. Poor white people are never depicted in television commercials, and only rarely are they mentioned in the electronic media. The great American national narrative, the story everybody learns, is that this country resolved the problems of disadvantaged whites sometime between the Great Depression and the Great Society. Exposés illustrating the impact of workfare requirements seldom profile white single mothers and their children.

In reality, there are several million white people who are trapped within what ideologically conservative sociologists call the "underclass," neighborhoods in which 40 percent or more of the residents live below the government's poverty line. These urban pockets of white poverty exhibit the same kinds of devastating socioeconomic statistics that Daniel Patrick Moynihan nearly forty years ago mistakenly attributed to the cultural and social pathology of black female-headed households—high percentages of school dropouts, teenage pregnancies, single-parent families, unemployment, and mass incarceration.

Using an extremely narrow definition of white underclass poverty— two contiguous census tracks in which at least 50 percent of the residents were non-Hispanic whites, at least 40 percent lived below the poverty line, and more than 300 were headed by single white females— U.S. News and World Report in 1994 identified fifteen areas that by any standard fell into William Julius Wilson's category of the "truly disadvantaged." In the eastside communities of La Grange–Central and Vestula in Toledo, Ohio, an area with 13,000 residents, nearly 600 households consist of white female-headed families with children, and 46 percent of all people exist below the federal government's poverty line. In the economically depressed area near the westside of Syracuse, a

neighborhood of 11,800 residents, 49 percent are poor. In Flint, Michigan, the home of thousands of unemployed white autoworkers, 56 percent of all households in the mostly white areas of the central city on
the south and east sides are below the poverty line. In the depressed
Whittier and Phillips neighborhoods in Minneapolis, which have a combined population of 22,000, two-thirds of all families live in poverty. And
in the southern tip of South Boston, which is virtually all white, there
were 453 white female-headed families with children, and the poverty
rate was a staggeringly high 73 percent.

In 1994, Ronald Mincy of the Ford Foundation and researchers at the
Urban Institute found that black and white ghettoes are similar in several
important respects: "Both white and black underclass areas are filled
with men who abandoned the work force and residents who dropped
out of high school." In these so-called "white underclass" census tracts,
an average of 42 percent of all adults had failed to complete secondary
school, 55 percent of all adult males were not in the paid labor force, and
53 percent of all households were single-parent, female-headed families.
For many social liberals, these statistics seemed to validate the color-
blind thesis that poverty, not race, was the principal factor in perpetuat-
ing the underclass.

As attractive as this thesis might be to neoliberals and class-based reformers, it fails to hold up for several reasons. First, in terms of the concrete realities and practical experiences of daily life, poor whites and
poor blacks living side by side both know that blacks have it worse.
African Americans consistently have higher rates of single-parent families, chronic unemployment and underemployment, secondary school
dropouts, and substandard housing. Whites also have an important material asset that allows many of them to escape the greatest liabilities and
disadvantages of poverty—their whiteness. White Americans who are
homeless, unemployed, and/or uneducated for the most part still believe in the great American master narrative of opportunity and upward
mobility. If they scrape together enough money to buy a new suit, they
will find it relatively easy to obtain employment, albeit at subsistence
wages. They know that with the same set of skills and level of educa-

tional attainment as the black householders across the street, they stand a superior chance of being hired. Whiteness creates a comfortable social and psychological safety net for the white poor: Everyday may not be a lucky day, but nobody has to sing the blues for too long.

A different situation exists for the Latino urban poor. With the significant exception of the white Cuban community, Latinos suffer from the same socioeconomic factors that make social mobility and neighborhood development so difficult for blacks. For example, the poverty rate for Latinos as an ethnic group rose significantly, from 19.8 percent in 1973 to 26.5 percent in 1991, a rate more than three times that of white households. One out of every four Mexican-American families and 40 percent of all Puerto Rican families lived in poverty. Millions of undocumented workers from Central America and the Hispanic Caribbean are trapped in low-wage jobs without benefits. Many Latinos who are gainfully employed encounter many of the same problems African Americans routinely experience, from their inability to obtain home mortgages or loans from banks and lending institutions, to being harassed and insulted by police in their own neighborhoods.

Inner-city neighborhoods like Harlem and south central Los Angeles, which have historically and culturally been identified as black, are becoming predominantly Latino. On the eve of the 1992 Los Angeles urban uprising over the Rodney King beating, 45 percent of the south central area was Hispanic. Although about 80 percent of Los Angeles's population was Mexican American, by 1990 there were also 200,000 Guatemalans and 600,000 Salvadorans living in the barrios of the "City of Angels." These neighborhoods were, and still are, plagued by high rates of poverty and unemployment. Thus, it should not have been surprising that the depths of alienation and resistance displayed by Southern California's black community after the verdict was announced were also present among several million Latinos living in the same depressed neighborhoods. For example, in the week immediately following the King verdict, 7,100 rioters were arrested in the City of Los Angeles on charges such as assault, looting, and violating curfew. About 850 of those arrested were white, more than 3,500 were Hispanic, and 2,600 were

African American. Nineteen Latinos were killed during the 1992 Los Angeles uprising, only three less than the total number of blacks who died. About one in ten of the rioters who were arrested were undocumented immigrants. Hispanic grievances and bitterness against the Los Angeles Police Department ran as deep as those within the black community.

The example provided by Los Angeles in this context has been repeated in other major American cities. In 1991, for example, in the Mount Pleasant neighborhood of Washington, D.C., Salvadorans rioted and destroyed property after a Salvadoran man was killed by a police officer. In Miami's impoverished Wynwood section in 1990, hundreds of Puerto Ricans rioted in the streets following the acquittal of police officers who had beaten a Puerto Rican to death.

What do these major demographic shifts in the racialized ethnic composition of American cities mean for black Americans? The language of black resistance to police brutality, to poverty, and to hyper-unemployment must be expressed in Spanish as well as in English. It will even require the extremely difficult task of educating and liberating low-income whites from the bondage and blindness of their whiteness.

The old models of liberal integrationism and black separatist nationalism are unable to accomplish these tasks. A radical alternative, anchored in civil society and based on capacity-building and extensive networking between multiracial, multi-class constituencies, is now necessary to revive the Black Freedom Movement. A key first step in building this alternative is to popularize the essential idea that the masses, not charismatic leaders, are the fundamental force with the capacity to challenge American governmental and corporate power. As historian Clayborne Carson has reflected: "Waiting for the messiah is a human weakness unlikely to be rewarded more than once in a millennium. Careful study of the modern black freedom struggle offers support for the more optimistic belief that participants in a mass movement can develop their untapped capacities and collectively improve their lives."

The classical model of class-based organizing historically focused on issues located at the workplace: struggles over employment access, increases in wages and fringe benefits, and improved working conditions.

In the postindustrial cities of America, however, the decisive battleground has shifted from the workplace to the living space. A significant
number of the working poor, unemployed, and marginally employed
people express their political activism through civil society rather than in
trade unions or formal electoral political parties. These small-scale, ad
hoc, grassroots organizations represent a "great well of democracy," an
underutilized resource that has the potential to redefine our democratic
institutions.

Chapter 9

Forty Acres and a Mule

The Case for Black Reparations

For more than two centuries our forebears labored in this country without wages; they made cotton king; they built the homes of their masters while suffering gross injustice and shameful humiliation—and yet out of a bottomless vitality they continued to thrive and develop. If the inexpressible cruelties of slavery could not stop us, the opposition we now face will surely fail.

—Martin Luther King, Jr.
"Letter from Birmingham Jail," April 16, 1963

I

Malcolm X frequently asserted that every revolution ultimately was about land and the basic resources required to produce society. Although enslaved African Americans could never have anticipated Malcolm's analysis, they certainly acted in harmony with his politics. In December 1860, several months before the outbreak of the Civil War, a widespread conspiracy, involving hundreds of African Americans and, remarkably, several poor southern whites, was uncovered by Alabama law-enforcement authorities. The conspirators had called for the general redistribution of "the land, mules, and money." The *Montgomery Advertiser* outlined the rebels' plans: "We have found out a deep laid plan among the negroes of our neighborhood, and from what we can find out from our negroes, it is general all over the country. . . . They have gone far enough in the plot to divide our estates, mules, and household furniture." Authorities were frustrated that only a relatively small number of the plotters were arrested, or very probably coerced into confessions. In the end, about twenty-five African Americans and four poor whites were executed. This aborted pre–Civil War uprising, planned and nearly carried out in the Alabama Black Belt only miles from what would be the first capital of the Confederate States of America, indicates the depths of black unrest throughout every level of southern society. But it also speaks to Malcolm's dictum, that the first order of business for newly freed blacks would be compensation, or reparations, a fair share of "the land, mules, and money."

Historian Thomas Holt, reviewing the struggles of ex-slaves in South Carolina in the 1860s, observed that they held one objective above all others, "the acquisition of the land they had tilled and developed and learned to think of as their own." By 1863, even before the Union army had liberated their areas, thousands of slaves began to demand compensation in wages for their labor. In Arkansas, federal authorities declared that African Americans had become free under President Lincoln's Emancipation Proclamation of January 1, 1863, and therefore were owed back wages from their former slaveholders. My great-grandfather, Morris Marable, shared the same aspirations of millions of other slaves, the yearning for freedom. When his master, a Confederate army officer, was seriously wounded in battle, Morris dutifully transported him back from the battlefront to his home in Black Belt, Alabama. But soon after, late at night, Morris carefully collected all of his personal items on the plantation—plus forty dollars in gold hidden in the master's house—and made his escape. To Morris, forty dollars was only partial compensation for years of unpaid exploitation.

Even before it became certain that the South would lose the war, rumors had widely circulated about a general land redistribution to the former slaves. Abolitionists like Frederick Douglass pressured the Lincoln administration to follow up the Emancipation Proclamation with provisions for black land tenure and educational opportunities. In early January 1865, African-American leaders met with General William T. Sherman and Secretary of War Edwin Stanton to develop a broad approach to the issue of black landownership. General Sherman subsequently issued Field Order 15, which granted African Americans the rights to any confiscated properties along the Georgia and South Carolina coast. Horses and mules in the army's possession that were no longer needed were provided to freedmen. In less than six months, about 40,000 African-American farmers had received more than 400,000 acres of land. On March 3, 1865, Congress approved an "Act to Establish a Bureau for the Relief of Freedmen and Refugees," which created the Freedmen's Bureau. The new law, signed by President Lincoln, stipulated that the commissioner of the Freedmen's Bureau, under the president's direction:

> shall have authority to set apart, for the use of loyal refugees and freedmen, such tracts of land within the insurrectionary states as shall have been abandoned, or to which the United States shall have acquired title by confiscation or sale, or otherwise, and to every male citizen, whether refugee or freedmen, as aforesaid, there shall be assigned not more than forty acres of such land, and the person to whom it was so assigned shall be protected in the use and enjoyment of the land for the term of three years at an annual rent not exceeding six per centum upon the value of such

land, as it was appraised by the state authorities in the year eighteen hundred and sixty, for the purpose of taxation, and in case no
such appraisal can be found, then the rental shall be based upon
the estimated value of the land in said year, to be ascertained in
such manner as the commissioner may by regulation prescribe. At
the end of said term, or at any time during said term, the occu-
pants of any parcels so assigned may purchase the land and receive
such title thereto as the United States can convey, upon paying
therefore the value of the land, as ascertained and fixed for the
purpose of determining the annual rent aforesaid.

Historians rarely ponder the question of "what if?," because that is not
the objective of our profession. Historians live in the realm of the dead,
where all of history's battles and debates have already been won or lost.
But briefly, let us suppose that the general redistribution of abandoned
and confiscated plantations had been carried out. We could even specu-
late that if Frederick Douglass had been appointed land commissioner, by
edict he might have expropriated the properties of all Confederate officers, elected and appointed officials, and members of the state judiciaries.
There were approximately 350 million acres of land and 1 million black
families living in the South in 1865. Forty acres allotted to each African-
American family would have been only 40 million acres. This reform
could have been accompanied by the general redistribution of lands to
poor whites, nearly all of whom had owned no slaves. Had comprehensive land reform occurred in the South in 1865–1866, and had the ex-slave
population been armed to protect its newfound property, the history of
black America would have been fundamentally different. Jim Crow segregation would not have been imposed on southern society, and there
would have been no need for the Civil Rights Movement a century later.
   Lincoln's assassination, Andrew Johnson's succession to the presidency, and the new chief executive's Proclamation Pardon of May 1865,
which pardoned nearly all the Confederates and restored their property
rights, began the process of shutting history's door to justice for African
Americans. Radical Republican Congressman Thaddeus Stevens's proposal to confiscate the property of all former slaveholders who had

owned more than 200 slaves, and subdivide the land into forty-acre plots, was rejected by Johnson as extremist. The Johnson administration also turned down the proposal of the American Missionary Association to give homestead properties in the west to black families. The only minor concessions made at the federal level to address the black demand for land were the provisions of the 1866 Homestead Act, which set the price of undeveloped federally owned land at five dollars per acre. Most African Americans, still penniless, simply could not afford it, and only about 1,000 freedmen finally obtained land under the act.

Across the South, the ex-Confederates were initiating new legislative measures of their own, called "Black Codes," which severely restricted African Americans' rights. South Carolina, for instance, passed a law stating that African Americans would have to obtain a court license in order to be employed as an artisan, mechanic, or shopkeeper anywhere in the state. In some states, blacks were still forbidden to testify in court against whites, were not allowed to own weapons, and were forced into signing labor contracts with former slaveholders. Johnson's impeachment, the imposition of congressional Reconstruction, and the deployment of federal troops throughout the South in 1867 voided most of these Black Codes.

But only ten years later, after the Compromise of 1877, when the federal government abandoned its promises to the newly freed black community, the Black Codes would return under the informal name of Jim Crow. The occupying Union army had done little to redistribute the land from the former masters to their former slaves. With great difficulty and tremendous sacrifices, blacks were able to buy hundreds of thousands of acres of land in Alabama, Mississippi, Louisiana, and other states in the deep South, but the great majority of African-American families were forced into sharecropping or tenant farming. By the end of Reconstruction, the upper 5 percent of all white southern farmers owned more than 40 percent of the region's productive farmland. In virtually every southern state, the upper 10 percent of white farming households owned 50 to 70 percent of each state's total farmland.

Against overwhelming odds, the first two generations of African Americans following emancipation successfully struggled to become their own masters—and they knew that the key was the ownership of private property. They soon learned that racial segregation laws had the effect of creating business opportunities for blacks in segregated consumer markets. By pooling their meager resources, poor black farmers, mechanics, and artisans started their own businesses and small banks. By 1913, African Americans owned 550,000 homes and had accumulated $700 million in personal wealth. As of 1915, blacks collectively owned 15.7 million acres of land in the United States—the largest amount of land that they would ever own again. Two hundred thousand black farmers in 1915 owned their own land, including Morris Marable. My great-grandfather's expropriation of forty dollars in gold had become the down payment for more than 100 acres of farmland near Wedowee, Alabama. By the 1890s, Morris Marable had purchased a cotton gin and had gone into competition with local white-owned ginneries and cotton merchants who routinely cheated black tenants and small farmers.

Tragically, a series of calamities—including the region-wide infestation of the boll weevil, the increased mechanization of southern agriculture, the massive disfranchisement of black male voters, widespread lynching across the region, and the collapse of European markets for cotton export sales during World War I—crippled the development of a black capitalist strategy for empowerment based on land tenure in the South. By the one hundredth anniversary of the Emancipation Proclamation, blacks owned only 6 million acres of land nationwide.

The concept of black reparations—some kind of financial restitution or redistribution of wealth, in part due for generations of chattel enslavement—continued to resurface in various guises. The Universal Negro Improvement Association's "Declaration of Rights of the Negro Peoples of the World," issued in August 1920, affirmed, "That we believe in the supreme authority of our race in all things racial; that all things are created and given to man as a common possession; that there should be an equitable distribution and apportionment of all such things, and in consideration of the fact that as a race we are now deprived of those things that are morally and legally ours, we believe it right that all such things should be acquired and held by whatsoever means possible." The Nation of Islam, under the leadership of Elijah Muhammad, demanded that "a

separate state or territory" be established inside the continental United
States in recognition of "our people in America whose parents or grandparents were descendants from slaves." In 1915, the U.S. Treasury Department was sued for $68 million in reparations based on unpaid labor under
slavery. The case was summarily dismissed on the grounds of sovereign
immunity—the inability to sue the government without its consent.

Such efforts made little headway. One of the obstacles to progress in
the reparations movement was the statute of limitations. The individuals who had personally experienced chattel slavery were rapidly disap-
pearing by the first decades of the twentieth century. Who would be the
plaintiffs, and who would be liable for damages? Yet the black reparations concept refused to disappear. In 1955, black activist Queen Mother
Moore initiated the Reparations Committee of Descendants of United
States Slaves, which kept the modest campaign alive for several decades.
In 1969, former Student Nonviolent Coordinating Committee activist
James Forman presented a controversial "Black Manifesto" in New
York's Riverside Church, calling for faith-based institutions to donate
half a billion dollars to the black community for reparations.

Forman was not the only one to raise the issue of black reparations in
the 1960s. In fact, interest in black reparations had been revived by the
militant struggles against southern segregation and northern ghettoization. During the height of the desegregation campaign, Dr. Martin
Luther King, Jr., declared that the African American, who had experienced over two centuries of brutal enslavement, "was during all of those
years robbed of wages of his toil. No amount of gold," King declared,
"could provide compensation for the exploitation and humiliation of the
Negro in America down through the centuries. Yet a price can be placed
on the unpaid wages." King recommended that "the payment should be
in the form of a massive program, by the government, of special com-
pensatory measures which could be regarded as a settlement in accor-
dance with accepted practices of common law." Although millions of
white Americans might reject this comprehensive approach to close the
country's racial divide, King believed that the time had come to act decisively, because "the moral justification for special measures for Negroes
is rooted in the robberies inherent in the institution of slavery."

Although the issue of black reparations was raised numerous times and in various ways during the late nineteenth century and throughout the twentieth, it never got the attention that it deserved, even from most blacks, and at times seemed to go underground. I believe that there are two main reasons for this. First, the demand had for years been identified with race-based, black nationalists, who had long written off the possibility of white America redeeming or reforming itself. Most black nationalists, from Garvey to Elijah Muhammad, Malcolm X, and Louis Farrakhan, perceived black America as quite literally a "nation within a nation." As such, the black population had a democratic right to renegotiate its relationship with the U.S. government, redefining the boundaries of civil society and citizenship. Imari Obadele and other leaders of the Republic of New Afrika carried this interpretation of black history to its logical conclusion by calling for a United Nations–supervised plebiscite across the remnants of the South's Black Belt. Arguments along these race-based lines made absolutely no sense to most middle-class African Americans. Nor did black leaders committed to racial integration and state-based liberal reforms take up the theme. How could we work in partnership with the federal government, the integrationists asked, if we were suing that same government over a quixotic demand? Second, most black radicals on the Left in Communist and socialist circles also disliked the reparations issue, because they feared it would lead to racial divisiveness between black and white workers, who of course faced a common enemy, the capitalist ruling class.

In retrospect, the state-based reformers grossly underestimated the destructive long-term consequences of slavery in undermining any collective efforts of an oppressed people to build institutional capacity for themselves. Lincoln didn't "free" the slaves; the Emancipation Proclamation was a wartime executive order, carried out primarily to deprive the South of its essential labor force. In the aftermath of slavery and Reconstruction, African Americans were largely an illiterate, landless peasantry. In Du Bois's words: "For the first time he sought to analyze the burden he bore upon his back, that deadweight of social degradation partially masked behind a half-named Negro problem. He felt his poverty, without a cent, without a home, without land, tools, or savings; he had entered into competition with rich, landed, skilled neighbors. To be a poor man is hard, but to be a poor race in a land of dollars is the very bottom of hardship."

II

It was in the aftermath of World War II that the global discourse about the legal and political concept of "reparations" changed fundamentally. The horrific mass crimes against humanity committed by Nazi Germany were almost impossible to comprehend. The systematic extermination of six million European Jews in the Holocaust, and the deaths of millions of others, forced the entire world community to confront the evil that fascism embodied. In 1951, about two dozen Jewish organizations came together to establish the Conference on Jewish Material Claims Against Germany. The following year, the new government in West Germany reached a settlement with the Claims Conference that included the transfer of 450 million deutsche marks to Holocaust survivors and a pledge to carry out laws that would provide restitution to all victims who had suffered under the Nazi regime.

Jewish organizations and the Israeli government continued to examine the records of corporations, financial institutions, and governments that in any way profited directly from Holocaust crimes. In 1962, after pressure from these groups, the Swiss Bankers Association finally required the country's banks to investigate their accounts to ascertain if they held assets belonging to Holocaust victims. Swiss banks ultimately remitted nearly 10 million Swiss francs to Holocaust survivors and heirs—which would years later prove to be only a small share of the enormous wealth that had been stolen from the Jewish people. It was subsequently discovered that the Paris branch of Chase Manhattan Bank had collaborated with the Germans under the Nazi occupation, had seized bank accounts and safe deposit boxes from French Jews, and had failed to return or provide any account of these assets.

In the early 1990s, a coalition of Jewish groups initiated the World Jewish Restitution Organization, which was designed to locate and demand the retrieval of all wealth taken from European Jews during the Holocaust. During the international events organized to commemorate the end of World War II, B'nai B'rith International and other Jewish groups mobilized support around the issues of reparations and restitution for the Holocaust. Multimillionaire Edgar Bronfman and other prominent Jewish leaders lobbied the Clinton administration and Congress to address Holocaust reparations. Clinton responded in May 1996 by establishing the Volker Commission to investigate Swiss bank accounts. In the U.S. Senate, New York Senator Al D'Amato held hearings on Jewish assets held in Swiss banking establishments before the Senate Committee on Banking, Housing, and Urban Affairs. In October 1996, Gizella Weisshaus, a survivor of the Holocaust, filed the first class-action suit in the United States against Swiss banks, demanding a full accounting of what happened to Jewish assets.

Pressure mounted against the Swiss banks as American politicians began actively supporting the reparations campaign. For example, New York State Comptroller Carl McCall, an African American, barred the use of Swiss banks for overnight investments and threatened other economic sanctions. Finally, beginning in July 1997, the Swiss Bankers Association began to release the list of Swiss and non-Swiss dormant accounts and all remaining assets. In August 1998, U.S. District Court issued a judgment approving a settlement with the Swiss banks and other Swiss institutions for the amount of $1.25 billion. Subsequently, on November 22, 2000, a plan to allocate and distribute settlement proceeds was approved. The plan included the transfer of $100 million to elderly, low-income Jewish victims and payments to Jews who had been forced to perform slave labor.

Throughout most of our history, African Americans have usually maintained a special kinship and political connection with the Jewish community. The majority of black leaders, including Du Bois, Garvey, and King, were sympathetic toward Jewish Zionist efforts to establish the state of Israel, at least up to the 1967 Yom Kippur War. Blacks widely acknowledged the great inhumanity of the Holocaust as well, placing this horrific event in the context of their own historical experiences in the United States. Nazi pseudoscientific theories about racial purity, the segregationist Nuremberg Laws, the slave labor camps in World War II—all have striking parallels within the African-American experience.

This shared history of oppression is not always acknowledged by others, however, forming a point of contention for the black and Jewish communities. As historian Robert G. Weisbord has observed, "All too often Jews have spoken of the Jewish experience in the 1930s and '40s as an unparalleled human calamity which dwarfs in its inhumanity all other cases of genocide." African Americans for years have been troubled by the fact that a permanent memorial and museum exist in Washington, D.C., to commemorate the millions of victims of the Holocaust, yet no memorial exists honoring the millions of victims who perished in the transatlantic and domestic U.S. slave trade and under Jim Crow segregation. Some of these underlying tensions about the "hierarchy of victimization" were apparent during the 1979 controversy generated by Jesse Jackson's trip to Israel. Israelis and many American Jews were deeply offended when Jackson, while touring Israel's Holocaust memorial, described the historic calamity as "tragic but not necessarily unique." As many historians have noted, the Holocaust was distinct as an apocalyptic event because the explicit goal of Nazi state power was the complete physical elimination of the Jewish people. Yet the sufferings of Jews in Nazi slave camps were not significantly unlike the cruel ordeals of my great-grandparents. As Weisbord commented:

> It is noteworthy that compensation, though inadequate, has now been paid by German companies to at least some of their erstwhile slave laborers. In addition, the West German government paid some reparations to Holocaust survivors for their mistreatment by the Third Reich. In contrast, the United States, its egalitarian rhetoric about liberty and justice for all notwithstanding, refused to give former Black bondsmen even the 40 acres and a mule which was proposed in 1865. They were never compensated at all

for their slave labor. In fact, neither slaves nor their descendants have received a formal apology from the American government or the American people.

The Holocaust lawsuits and international settlements for restitution established a new model for international groups that had been victimized by governments and had experienced enslavement, genocide, and other "crimes against humanity" as the term was technically defined under international law. Asian Americans were the first racialized minority in the United States to employ similar demands to win restitution. During World War II, the U.S. government had interned by force 120,000 Japanese Americans, or Nisei. In the years immediately after the war, Congress voted to provide limited restitution to more than 25,000 claimants constituting less than 10 percent of their estimated property losses. Japanese-American groups continued to publicize the historic grievances of the Nisei. Growing public awareness of the case pressured President Gerald Ford to issue Proclamation 4417 in 1976, in which the U.S. government acknowledged that Japanese internment constituted a "national mistake." Under President Jimmy Carter, Congress authorized a bipartisan Commission on Wartime Relocation and Internment of Civilians to review actions of the government against the Nisei. In 1981, the Wartime Relocation Commission took testimonies from hundreds of Japanese-American victims of internment, which generated tremendous sympathy for this group. In 1988, President Ronald Reagan signed the Civil Liberties Act, recognizing that Japanese-American internment was wrong and inspired by racism. Each surviving internee finally received a tax-exempt payment of $20,000, and an education fund of $1.25 million was initiated.

Along parallel lines, the historic grievances of American Indians began to receive new attention. Prior to 1972, American Indians had received an estimated $800 million in restitution from the U.S. government to settle various treaty disputes and land seizure claims. In 1980, the Supreme Court declared that the U.S. government owed the Sioux nation $122 million for its illegal seizure of the Black Hills territory in what is now South Dakota. That same year, the Blue Lake region of New Mexico was returned to the Taos Pueblo tribe. In 1988, Indian reservations were granted the authority to establish gambling entertainment facilities, subject to the approval of state and tribal officials. It was not until 2000, however, that the Bureau of Indian Affairs formally apologized for the federal agency's long history of racism and discriminatory policies.

The striking successes of the American Indian decades-long campaign for reparations had a profound effect on African-American leaders, who quickly saw the possibility for using similar arguments on behalf of black Americans. Any direct analogies between American Indian grievances and those of African Americans, however, would prove to be difficult to make in courts. Unlike black people, the American Indian population was indigenous to the North American continent. Native American scholars, such as Vine Deloria, have resisted the description of Indians as an "ethnic group," pointing out that hundreds of treaty violations constituted the legal framework for Indian restitution litigation.

By the 1990s, the cumulative successes of these different reparations campaigns, internationally and nationally, inspired other groups with specific grievances to seek legal compensation. One of the many examples of these recent legal and political initiatives is the case of U.S. prisoners of war in Japanese slave labor camps. During World War II, more than 25,000 Americans became prisoners of war under the Japanese, and many were forced into slave labor camps under extraordinarily brutal conditions. In 1951, the United States and its Allies reached an agreement with the new Japanese government prohibiting direct restitution for claims by former prisoners of war against Japan. In 1999, however, California passed a law granting state courts the authority to hear claims brought by former prisoners of war and their heirs against the Japanese government until 2010. Within less than one year, several dozen suits were filed naming the Japanese government as well as major Japanese corporations, including Mitsubishi and Nippon Steel. In September 2000, a U.S. District Court judge in San Francisco rejected these lawsuits on the grounds that they were prohibited by the 1951 international treaty with Japan. Setting a new international precedent, in November 2000, the United Kingdom agreed to give approximately 6,000 former British prisoners of war and 4,000 widows of survivors 10,000 British pounds each.

The U.S. Congress unanimously passed a resolution requesting the State Department to pursue discussions to resolve any outstanding claims for compensation by former American prisoners of war held by the Japanese government and exploited as slave laborers by Japanese corporations.

These reparations campaigns illustrate that there are indeed effective avenues for getting around the issues of sovereign immunity and statute-of-limitations restrictions. There are many international conventions or legal covenants to which the U.S. government is a signatory that define fundamental violations of human rights, including the Universal Declaration of Human Rights and the International Covenant on Civil and Political Rights. The Genocide Convention outlaws all policies and practices that would exterminate any people on the basis of their racial identity. The Geneva conventions after World War II also established legal criteria for what constituted "crimes against humanity." There is no international statute of limitations for mass murder and genocide. It became clear to many African-American activists by the 1980s, however, that the reparations issue was not simply a demand for compensation for slavery, but for restitution from the government and corporations for ongoing practices and deliberate policies of racial oppression.

III

In 1987, a number of black activist organizations in the United States established the National Coalition of Blacks for Reparations in America (N'COBRA). The organization's central purpose was "asking for the trillions of dollars due [people of African descent in the United States] for the labor of [their] ancestors who worked for hundreds of years without pay." Led by attorney-activist Adjoa A. Aiyetoro, N'COBRA was a membership organization that soon developed chapters across the country. It mobilized supporters to "petition the United States for immediate, emergency reparations payments which may include government owned property along with funds to meaningfully address the crisis of incarceration." It sought the establishment of a reparations fund that would allow U.S. taxpayers "to designate, voluntarily, a portion of their taxes to be held in trust to begin the long overdue payment of reparations while having a minimal effect on the United States budget." N'COBRA demanded that Congress initiate a national commission to hold a series of public hearings on the need for black reparations, "which would prove to be educational while producing a public record."

On November 20, 1989, Congressman John Conyers introduced a bill calling for a commission to study the long-term effects of slavery in American society and the subsequent disadvantages and inequities that blacks experience as a consequence of their enslavement. The bill died in the House Judiciary Committee, but Conyers's symbolic act did generate new interest and awareness about the concept throughout the country. On April 10, 1991, when Conyers reintroduced his bill (H.R. 1684, 102 Cong., 1st Session), the measure had been endorsed by the Southern Christian Leadership Council, the city councils of Detroit, Washington, D.C., and Inglewood, California, and the Detroit chapter of the NAACP. Although this bill, too, died in the House Judiciary Committee, it inspired legislative initiatives in several states. In Massachusetts in 1991, State Senator William Owens introduced a reparations bill calling for compensation to all people of African descent for centuries of racial oppression. In 1993, Conyers's reparations bill was reintroduced again in the House with twenty-eight cosponsors, eighteen of whom were black.

Conyers's persistence and N'COBRA's grassroots activism within black nationalist–oriented communities gave new legitimacy to the concept of reparations. Prominent black journalists, such as Salim Muwakkil, and scholars, including Robert Allen, Richard America, Rhonda V. Magee, and Vincene Verdun, published articles on the issue. Many publications and magazines in the early and mid-1990s, such as the *Christian Century, Commonweal, The Review of Black Political Economy, In These Times,* and several law review journals, examined the reparations concept and how it could be implemented through federal legislation.

The renaissance of the U.S. reparations movement also coincided with the development of similar movements in the United Kingdom and Africa. In 1990, an international conference was held in Lagos, Nigeria, on the feasibility of pursuing reparations for people of African descent transnationally. The following year, Bernie Grant, a member of Parliament in the U.K., was instrumental in establishing an Organization of African Unity–sponsored "Group of Eminent Persons" who would add credibility and attract media attention to the African reparations effort. Members of this group included South African artist Miriam Makeba, Graça Machel of Mozambique, African scholar Ali Mazrui, and Dudley Thompson, Jamaica's foreign minister under Prime Minister Michael Manley. In April 1993, a major reparations conference was held in Abuju, Nigeria. This historic gathering produced the "Abuju Declaration," which outlined in considerable detail the practical steps African states should take to realize the objective of reparations. These initiatives included demands for the immediate return of all artifacts that had been taken from the continent and the cancellation of all debt to U.S. and European financial institutions and the World Bank; in addition, they pledged to "use all lawful means to obtain Reparations for the enslavement and colonization of African people in Africa and in the African Diaspora"; "to educate and inform African youth, on the continent and in the Diaspora, about the great African cultures, languages and civilizations"; and "to seek an apology from western governments for the enslavement and colonization of African people." In the United Kingdom, the reparations activists, led by Grant, established the African Reparations Movement, a nonprofit organization that coordinated British educational and political initiatives. And in August 1999, African leaders for reparations established an African World Reparations and Repatriation Truth Commission, which began developing a strategy to file claims for restitution against international agencies and organizations, including trade-union federations, corporations, and banks, in various legal venues, such as the International Court of Justice in the Hague, Netherlands.

In the 1980s, the issue of black reparations received its first national publicity in the United States since the late 1960s debate over James Forman's Black Manifesto. The publicity was generated by disturbing new revelations about a racial massacre in Rosewood, Florida, years before. On New Year's Day in 1923, a rampaging white mob had attacked the all-black community of Rosewood based on false accusations by a white woman who claimed she had been raped by a black man. The white mob burned nearly every black-owned home and butchered as many as

200 African-American residents of the town. White police and politicians did nothing to halt the violence and made no attempts to apprehend the perpetrators. Black survivors of the massacre fled the area; many left the state, and local whites illegally seized black-owned properties.

The Rosewood tragedy was largely forgotten until a St. Petersburg journalist, Gary Moore, investigated the story in 1982. His account of the massacre attracted the interest of the national television program *Sixty Minutes*, which aired a segment on Rosewood in 1983. Several years later, film producer Michael O'McCarthy, who was interested in making a film on the event, tracked down a list of survivors of the massacre. With considerable difficulty, O'McCarthy finally convinced several survivors to present their terrible story to a national audience. In 1993, O'McCarthy and two of the surviving victims, Minnie Lee Langley and Lee Ruth Davis, appeared on the nationally syndicated television program *The Maury Povich Show*. Tampa television station WFLA-TV aired a detailed investigative report on Rosewood, documenting, in its words, "this dark, shameful incident from Florida's past." The television program effectively used archival photographs and recent interviews with the survivors and descendants of former residents to piece together the actual events.

The media attention about Rosewood was largely responsible for Florida House Speaker Bolley L. Johnson's initiative to establish a study determining the state's responsibility for these crimes and exploring possible reparations for the victims and their descendants. The completed study concluded that local and state officials had been grossly negligent in their failure to protect the civil rights and property rights of Rosewood residents. The reparations bill submitted to the Florida legislature was largely modeled on federal legislation that awarded reparations to Japanese Americans who had been interned during World War II.

As a Rosewood compensation bill was introduced, white conservatives warned that such legislation would force the state of Florida into bankruptcy. Despite shrill opposition, the measure carried both state houses by wide margins in April 1994. The law provided $150,000 for emotional trauma for each of four survivors. Half a million dollars was allocated to descendants of individuals or families whose property had been destroyed or stolen by whites. The state of Florida created a Rosewood college scholarship for the victims' descendants and allocated $100,000 to Florida A&M University to continue historical scholarship on the 1923 massacre.

Just as the Rosewood atrocities of 1923 were receiving national coverage, a similar racial tragedy that occurred during the same historical period came to public attention. On May 31, 1921, in Tulsa, Oklahoma, a large mob of whites threatened to lynch a black man named Dick Rowland who had been accused of attempting to rape a white woman and was being held under police custody. A group of African Americans tried to protect Rowland from being taken from custody, and white rioters became uncontrollable. Local, county, and state officials did nothing to quell the white violence as black-owned businesses and homes were looted and burned. Many of Tulsa's "special deputies" led the mob, participating in murder, assault, and robbery against African-American victims. The white mob targeted its rage on the city's black middle-class neighborhood of Greenwood, which African Americans commonly referred to as the "Black Wall Street." An estimated 10,000 whites ransacked Greenwood, destroying its hospital, library, and virtually every school, church, and business. Perhaps as many as 300 people, nearly all African Americans, were killed. Although property damage at that time was estimated at $2 million, and more than 1,200 homes had been destroyed, local prosecutors and law-enforcement officers failed to arrest or indict a single white rioter. Local officials changed Tulsa building-code regulations to make it difficult for the black survivors of the riot to rebuild their homes and businesses in the Greenwood neighborhood.

For the next seventy years, state and local leaders successfully suppressed any inquiry into these racial atrocities. Finally, in 1997, State Representative Don Ross successfully sponsored a bill creating a state commission to investigate the Tulsa race riot. There were several factors that contributed to the success of the commission's subsequent investigations. Foremost was the fact that about 100 African-American survivors of the riot were still alive and effectively testified about the events of May 31–June 1, 1921. Unlike slavery, the tragedy was close enough to our time for most whites to feel connected with and in some cases even responsible for the breakdown of civil authority resulting in mass murder. In February 2001, the Oklahoma state commission recommended that reparations be paid to the survivors and called for scholarships and the construction of a state memorial to mark the tragedy. Republican Governor Frank Keating formally apologized, describing the Tulsa riot as "an unforgivable, unexplainable part of our history."

For African Americans in the 1990s, the reparations successes in Rosewood and Tulsa offered hope in an otherwise dismal environment for change. Despite some advances—the absolute size of the African-American middle class had increased more than 400 percent between the assassination of Dr. Martin Luther King, Jr., on April 4, 1968, and the Million Man March on October 16, 1995, and the annual gross receipts of African American–owned businesses in those same years had increased at least by five times—the political atmosphere was not promising. Congress was controlled by extreme Republican conservatives, and blacks felt betrayed by the Clinton administration. Moreover, the trial of O. J. Simpson seemed to be a symbolic representation of the legal lynchings that blacks had faced all too often in American courts. Throughout this same period, affirmative-action programs were being shut down and eliminated. As a result, the center of black America shifted away from state-based, traditional liberal integrationist remedies for addressing racial discrimination toward new, bolder initiatives. Gradually, many intellectuals, public leaders, and organizers in the black community concluded that the only way racial justice was going to be achieved in the twenty-first century was around the paradigm of racial reparations and class-action lawsuits. Rosewood and Tulsa had shown that seeking reparations could be the most effective model for making a political case against American structural racism in a post–Civil Rights era.

As the discourse of black reparations became more widespread, other historically oppressed sectors of the African-American community stepped forward to register their grievances against structural racism. In 1997, more than 600 African-American farmers filed a $2.5 billion lawsuit in federal court against the U.S. Department of Agriculture (USDA), charging it with massive violations of civil-rights laws and unequal employment opportunity guidelines and procedures. The legal brief noted that back in 1983, the U.S. Commission on Civil Rights had criticized the USDA's racially discriminatory practices and policies toward African-American farmers. The USDA's loan programs were funneled for decades to huge corporate agribusinesses, while being largely denied to small, struggling black farms. As a direct consequence of federal neglect and administrative racism, the total number of African-American farmers plummeted from 33,250 in 1982 to 18,816 ten years later. In 1999, the USDA and about one-fourth of the black farmers who were claimants in the lawsuit accepted reparations of $50,000 each, and any outstanding or unpaid government farm loans they held were forgiven.

The black farmers' successful lawsuit illustrated the components of an effective campaign to win reparations. The farmers group was politically astute, building a bipartisan political constituency, effectively presenting its case in the national media, and building coalitions with traditional civil-rights organizations such as the NAACP. The class-action lawsuit of the farmers was designed to win the case in the court of public opinion, not within the narrow confines of established law. The facts of systematic discrimination by the USDA were so egregious that Congress took the unusual step of waiving the statute of limitations, allowing the lawsuit to be heard.

The Rosewood settlement had set the stage for a series of other successful initiatives targeting both corporate and governmental racist practices. In 1996, Texaco was sued for $175 million in a racial discrimination case in which one Texaco executive described African-American employees as "black jelly beans." Texaco ultimately negotiated a settlement. In 1997, Liberty Mutual insurance company was pressured by the federal government to settle racial discrimination "redlining" allegations. Eventually, Liberty Mutual agreed to pay a fair housing coalition $3.25 million. The following year, lawsuits against Nissan Motors Acceptance Corporation and General Motors Acceptance Corporation provided convincing statistical evidence that black buyers were consistently charged higher financing rates than white consumers. In 2000, a racial-discrimination case against Home Depot was settled for $106 million. When legal researcher Deadria Farmer-Paellmann contacted Aetna Insurance Company in February 2000, with specific information that the company had written and profited from life-insurance policies on African-American slaves, Aetna representatives reportedly at first agreed to publicly apologize and to provide restitution in the form of black college and university scholarships. According to Farmer-Paellmann, however, several days later, perhaps after consulting with its attorneys, Aetna retreated from its commitments, claiming it had no "legal liability."

Meanwhile, in April 2000, Chicago became the first major U.S. city to hold public hearings on the issue of the damaging legacy of slavery on the African-American community. Congressman Bobby Rush and historian Lerone Bennett, among others, testified before the City Council's special session, calling for that body to endorse Conyers's bill to create a national commission on black reparations. By an overwhelming margin of 46 to 1, the resolution passed. Weeks later, the Washington, D.C., City Council approved almost the identical reparations resolution. Other major cities adopting measures encouraging Congress to initiate an inquiry into the black reparations issue included Dallas and Atlanta. In June 2000, Congressman Tony P. Hall proposed a congressional resolution that called upon the U.S. government to offer an apology to African Americans for its support of the enslavement of their ancestors. Hall, Congressman John Lewis of Georgia, and others also called for a national museum and a memorial to honor the millions of victims of the transatlantic slave trade and American slavery.

When Jesse Jackson announced at the 2000 Rainbow/PUSH convention that pressure should be placed on corporate insurers to compensate the descendants on slaves, the issue began to attract national media attention. In January 2001, California implemented a law that obligated U.S. insurance firms doing business in the state to cooperate fully with any investigations of their corporate archives and records to discover whether these firms issued policies that slaveholders took out on their slaves. In February 2001, more than 600 African-American elected officials, educators, community activists, and others attended the first "National Reparations Convention for African-American Descendants of African Slaves" in Chicago.

The African-American leader most responsible for generating the current interest in black reparations was Randall Robinson, founder and president of Transafrica, the organization that for a quarter-century had been a major influence on U.S. policies in Africa and the Caribbean. In the 1980s, Robinson and other civil-rights activists built a massive anti-apartheid movement that successfully ended the Reagan administration's policy of "constructive engagement" with the white minority regime in South Africa. In the 1990s, Robinson played a central role in the restoration of democracy in Haiti. In 2000, with the publication of his deeply moving and eloquent book *The Debt: What America Owes to Blacks,* the modern reparations movement found its manifesto.

The Debt was a profoundly personal yet scholarly examination of how African Americans as a people have been systematically exploited by the U.S. political and economic system and had never received just compensation for their material contributions to society. It presented powerful arguments favoring reparations as being in the national interest of all Americans, regardless of race. To many whites, *The Debt,* which became a national bestseller, represented a warning: If African Americans are "not compensated for the massive wrongs and social injuries inflicted upon them by their government, during and after slavery, then there is *no* chance that America will solve its racial problems," Robinson said. He observed that the economic gap established by slavery "has now ossified. It is structural. Its framing beams are disguised only by the counterfeit manners of a hypocritical governing class."

In an ironic accident of history, the black American reparations debate was thrust into international mass media attention in early 2001 by conservative gadfly David Horowitz. Horowitz had drafted a controversial polemic, "Ten Reasons Why Reparations for Blacks Is a Bad Idea—and Racist, Too," and astutely sent it to more than fifty college newspapers as a paid advertisement. The statement, which solicited donations of up to $1,000, was filled with gross distortions and racist insults deliberately designed to outrage African Americans. But when newspapers rejected the advertisement, Horowitz charged that his first-amendment rights to freedom of speech had been violated by "politically correct fascists." Horowitz calculated correctly that the corporate media would seize primarily on the issue of "free speech" and would pillory blacks for refusing to grant his statement fair and free access in the marketplace of ideas. In debating Horowitz on CNN, I observed that his ploy was plainly a public-relations stunt, because no first-amendment issues had been at risk. The law has recognized for years the critical difference between "commercial speech" (advertising) and "public speech." Newspapers have absolutely no legal obligation to publish all paid advertisements.

The Horowitz statement was historically inaccurate and racially offensive, as noted in historian John Hope Franklin's eloquent rebuttal. Dr. Franklin observed that all white Americans, even those who had not owned slaves, benefited materially and psychologically from

> having a group beneath them. . . . Most living Americans do have a connection with slavery. They have inherited the preferential advantage, if they are white, or the loathsome disadvantage, if they are black; and those positions are virtually as alive today as they were in the 19th century. The pattern of housing, the discrimination in employment, the resistance to equal opportunity in education, the racial profiling, the inequalities in the administration of justice, the low expectation of blacks in the discharge of duties assigned to them, the widespread belief that blacks have physical prowess but little intellectual capacities and the widespread opposition to affirmative action, as if that had not been enjoyed by whites for three centuries, all indicate that the vestiges of slavery are still with us.

The majority of college newspapers refused to carry the Horowitz advertisement, but many did, claiming that free-speech considerations were more important than blacks' offended sensibilities. Students at several campuses staged mass demonstrations, linking the publication of Horowitz's anti-reparations statement with campus administrative policies that failed to foster multicultural diversity and affirmative action in student, faculty, and staff recruitment. Hundreds of students at Duke University seized partial control of an administrative building, explaining to the media that their civil disobedience was in the "tradition" of Black Power protest takeovers at Duke thirty years before. At Brown University, student activists seized and destroyed several thousand copies of the campus newspaper in which the Horowitz statement was printed. The acting president of Brown immediately labeled these students' actions as irresponsible, without engaging them in a constructive dialogue. The director of the African-American Studies Program, who publicly defended the Brown students, received scores of hate messages and racist letters, even threatening his wife. Yet by the end of the spring semester of 2001, hundreds of thousands of students at college campuses throughout the United States were debating the issue of black reparations. In many respects, the issue was acquiring the character of a mass democratic protest movement in its preliminary stages of development, as more young people began to identify it as their own cause.

IV

By the beginning of 2002, the reparations debate had become widely known, and it continued to attract increased national and international attention. In February 2002, CNN and *USA Today* commissioned the Gallup organization to conduct a national poll to assess public opinion on the issue. The results seemed to directly mirror the nation's parallel racial universes that are reproduced by structural racism. When asked whether "corporations that made profits from slavery should apologize to black Americans who are descendants of slaves," 68 percent of African Americans responded affirmatively, with 23 percent opposed, while 62 percent of all whites rejected the call for an apology, with only 34 percent supporting it. On the question of financial compensation, however, whites closed ranks around their racial privileges. When asked whether corporations benefiting from slave exploitation should "make cash payments to black Americans who are the descendants of slaves," 84 percent of all whites responded negatively, with only 11 percent supporting payments. A clear majority of African Americans polled, by contrast, endorsed corporate restitution payments, by a 57 to 35 percent margin, with 8 percent expressing no opinion. When asked if the government should grant "cash payments" to blacks, nine out of ten white

Americans rejected the proposal, while a strong majority of blacks favored it, by 55 to 37 percent.

Inspired by Robinson's The Debt, a stellar group of trial lawyers, led by Johnnie Cochran, the lead attorney in the O. J. Simpson criminal trial, and Harvard University law professor Charles Ogletree, began to meet regularly to map legal strategy. Other attorneys with extensive experience in winning litigation around victim compensation claims became involved, including Richard Scruggs, who won a $368.5 billion settlement from the tobacco industry, and Alexander Pires, who won more than $1 billion to compensate black farmers for the decades of racially discriminatory policies by the U.S. Department of Agriculture.

It was inevitable that as the demand for reparations achieved majority support among African Americans, black conservatives would be trotted out to defend the preservation of white power and privilege. The premier black apologist for the worst policies of the Reagan administration in the black community, economist Thomas Sowell, declared that "the first thing to understand about the issue of reparations is that no money is going to be paid." Sowell argued that the reparations cause was nothing more than an elaborate plot by black "demagogues," because "they are demanding something they know they are not going to get. . . . But if we start operating on the principle that people alive today are responsible for what their ancestors did in centuries past, we will be adopting a principle that can tear any society apart, especially a multiethnic society like the United States." Conservative economist Walter Williams seconded Sowell's objections, observing that "the problem, of course, is both slaves as well as their owners are all dead. . . . What moral principle justifies forcing a white of today to pay a black of today for what a white of yesteryear did to a black of yesteryear?"

Economist Glen Loury, noted for his recent public evolution from extreme conservatism toward more liberal views, also questioned the wisdom of the reparations effort. "This will isolate black Americans from our natural allies among working-class whites and immigrants," Loury warned. "We need allies to press for more expansive social policy that can get aid to those at the bottom." Younger black neoconservatives such as John McWhorter pointed out that even if the reparations movement succeeded in its efforts to create a national "slavery fund" to provide new resources to impoverished black communities, it would only reproduce the unequal structures of black dependency. "The reparation crowd's move from individual checks to a general fund will allow community-wide assistance," McWhorter admitted, "but this model has done nothing for forty years now. Who would get the money? For what purpose?"

The "race traitors'" criticisms and complaints can easily be addressed. First, there is a crucial difference between "guilt" and "responsibility." White Americans who are alive today are not guilty of enslaving anyone, in the legal definition of the term. Most white Americans below the age of fifty played no role in directly supporting Jim Crow segregation and are not guilty of overt acts to block the integration of public accommodations and schools. But white Americans, as a group, continue to be the direct beneficiaries of the legal apparatuses of white supremacy, carried out by the full weight of America's legal, political, and economic institutions. The consequences of state-sponsored racial inequality created a mountain of historically constructed, accumulated disadvantage for African Americans as a group.

The living legacy of that racialized, accumulated disadvantage can easily be measured by looking at the gross racial deficits that segment Americans by race, in their life expectancies and in their unequal access to home ownership, business development, and quality education. The U.S. government, for nearly two centuries, established the legal parameters for corporations to carry out blatantly discriminatory policies and practices. Consequently, it is insufficient for us to simply say that once the Jim Crow laws were changed, the state's responsibility to redress those victimized by discriminatory public policies ended. The U.S. government and the various state governments that created and perpetuated legal racial disparities are "responsible" for compensating the victims and their descendants. As citizens of this country, whites must bear the financial burden of the crimes against humanity that were carried out by their own government.

Another way of thinking about this is to point to the fiscal mismanagement and repressive social policies of the Reagan administration two decades ago. Billions of dollars of tax money paid by blacks and whites alike were allocated to the military industrial complex to finance global military interventions and a nuclear arms race. The vast majority of African Americans strongly opposed these reactionary policies. We were not "guilty" of participating in the decisions to carry out such policies. Yet, as citizens, we are "responsible" for paying to finance Reagan's military Keynesianism, which left the country deeply in debt. We have an obligation under law to pay taxes. Thus, all citizens of the United States have the same "responsibility" to compensate members of their own society that were deliberately stigmatized by legal racism. Individual "guilt" or "innocence" is therefore irrelevant. America's version of legal apartheid created the conditions of white privilege and black subordination that we see all around us every day.

One of the advantages of the reparations discourse is to promote a national discussion about the "unfinished" character of the struggle for civil rights in the United States. How do we, as Americans, combat the forces of "civil death" that actively destroy the capacity of individuals stigmatized by the effects of structural racism to play meaningful roles in civic life? "Civic reparations" could include: ex-felon re-enfranchisement, the restoration of full voting rights for all former prisoners who have been disfranchised by repressive state laws; ex-felon amnesty, the elimination of felony conviction records for individuals who have been previously incarcerated, who have successfully fulfilled the requirements of parole, and who have not committed a crime two years after parole has been completed; and the reinstatement of Pell Grants to permit prisoners to enroll in college-level courses while incarcerated. The idea behind civic reparations would be to promote the capacity of every citizen to participate fully in public life and to eliminate the barriers that restrict individuals from becoming civic stakeholders in democratic society.

"Economic reparations" could take a variety of forms, any of which could be practically implemented. I favor the establishment of a reparations social fund that would channel federal, state, and/or corporate funds for investment in nonprofit, community-based organizations, economic empowerment zones in areas with high rates of unemployment, and grants or interest-free loans for blacks to purchase homes or to start businesses in economically depressed neighborhoods. However, there are other approaches to the reconstruction of black economic opportunity. Sociologist Dalton Conley has suggested the processing of "individual checks via the tax system, like a refundable slavery tax credit." Major corporations and banks that were "unjustly enriched" by either slave labor or by Jim Crow–era discriminatory policies against African Americans could set aside a portion of future profits in a trust fund to financially compensate their victims and their descendants. Universities whose endowments were based on the slave trade or on slave labor and/or companies that were unjustly enriched by racial segregation laws could create scholarship funds to give greater access to African-American students.

I believe, however, that the greatest and most lasting benefit of the national reparations debate will be to foster an honest discussion about the historical consequences and moral challenges presented by structural racism. The reparations debate reflects the central conflict over the nature of U.S. democracy and the possibilities of transformation for a deep racialized and class-stratified society. From the vantage point of those favoring black reparations, racial peace can come about only as a product of social justice—coming to terms with the meaning of American, and even Western, civilization, as they have structured the unequal realities of life for millions of people of African descent. As historian and Garvey scholar Robert Hill observed in a conversation about the issue, the campaign for black reparations is "the final chapter in the five hundred year struggle to suppress the transatlantic slave trade, slavery, and the consequences of its effects."

Perhaps the most difficult challenge in winning the public-relations debate over black reparations inside the United States is that of persuading African Americans to believe that reparations *can be won.* A clear majority now exists among African Americans that favors reparations, but at present, most do not believe that the demand can overcome white opposition. Black people in a racist society must constantly struggle to free themselves from cultural domination and psychological dependency in order to believe in their own capacity to create social change. The quest for power begins first in one's mind. You cannot become free unless you begin to *think* like a free woman or man.

Indeed, this was Malcolm X's greatest insight and gift to future generations of African-American people: He changed the way black people thought about themselves. Malcolm attempted to move African Americans from being the footnotes in someone else's history to becoming the key actors in the making of their own new history. Instead of singing someone else's song, they discovered the beauty of their own voices. Reparations thus becomes a way for black people to challenge and subvert the master narrative of white capitalist America and to testify to the truth of their own history.

During colonialism, slavery, and segregation, people of African descent were diverted forcibly into the history of another people. To reclaim their birthright, they must emotionally and historically return to the sites of the original crimes and begin to speak on behalf of the victims who perished so long ago. Oppressed people empower themselves by bearing witness on their own behalf, to "speak truth to power," to tell their untold stories embedded in fractured, fragmented memories long past. History is more than a simple record of the past; it is the prologue to the future. When oppressed people return to the source of their own history, they may unlock new doors to finding their own identity. They can begin to imagine themselves in new and exciting ways, as architects and builders of a new history, the tellers of stories not yet written, of great accomplishments and discoveries still distant from their view. I believe Malcolm X really understood this. This partially explains the fierce loyalty and intense identification that so many African Americans feel about Malcolm. One of my students several years ago explained the critical difference between how many black folk perceive Martin and Malcolm in this way: "Dr. Martin Luther King, Jr., belongs to the entire world, but Malcolm X belongs to us."

Black reparations "belong to us" in a similar way. "Reparations" means "to repair," "to make whole again." The "double consciousness" of Americans of African descent first described by W.E.B. Du Bois, the age-old chasm between our identification with this country and our cultural affinity toward the black diaspora and Africa, cannot be bridged until there is a final rendezvous with our own history. This is why, ultimately, the demand for black reparations is *not* fundamentally about the money. The rape victim does not press charges and go to court simply to receive financial compensation. The rape victim desires and demands that the truth should be told about the crime. The Jewish survivors and their descendants of the Holocaust in Europe during World War II, and the Armenian people who experienced mass genocide under the Turkish Ottoman Empire in World War I, are not motivated primarily by financial restitution. Victims want the public record to reflect what actually happened.

Oppressed people live their lives in a kind of state-imposed traumatic existence in which the criminality and violence hurled against us are rarely acknowledged. They are presented to the world by their racist oppressors as being a people outside of history, devoid of a past of any consequence. To heal the effects of trauma, their stories must be told and retold. The oppressed thus perceive themselves in a new and liberating way. They can now, at long last, become actors and exercise agency at the vanguard of a new history. The divided double consciousness becomes a greater, critical, truer consciousness, creating the capacity to speak with clarity and confidence about oneself and the totality of society.

At the August–September 2001 United Nations World Conference Against Racism in Durban, South Africa, I witnessed these same points being made, in different ways, by many representatives from the Third World. The brilliant international attorney and former foreign minister of Jamaica, the Honorable Dudley Thompson, explained to hundreds attending the reparations plenary session: "Reparations is *not* about asking for money. You can't pay me for your raping my grandmother. You cannot compensate me for lynching my father. What we demand is the restitution of our human dignity, the restoration of full equality, politically, socially and economically, between the oppressors and the oppressed." Harvard University law professor Charles Ogletree, a key theorist and organizer in the United States on behalf of black reparations, also made clear the linkage between the past and the present at the Durban conference. He reminded delegates that there are "millions of

Africans today languishing in unmarked graves at the bottom of the Atlantic Ocean, . . . for whom reparations is a final vindication." Ogletree also predicted: "This is a movement that cannot be stopped. There are no plaintiffs that will not be considered. I promise that we will see reparations in our lifetime."

At the United Nations conference, the official U.S. position was that the enslavement of millions of African people was *not* "a crime against humanity." Around the same time as the conference, National Security Adviser Condoleezza Rice defended the Bush administration's refusal to negotiate with much of the black and brown world about the lasting effects of the slave trade, slavery, and colonialism. "Slavery is more than 150 years in the past and of course there is a continuing stain," Rice stated. "We have to turn now to the present and to the future." Rice was emphatically opposed to black reparations as well: "I think reparations, given the fact that there is plenty of blame to go around for slavery, plenty of blame to go around among African and Arab states and plenty of blame to go around among Western states, we are better to look forward and not point fingers backward." Rice is essentially saying that for us to get along in American society, black people will have to learn to forget.

Yet Rice herself grew up in Birmingham, Alabama, site of church bombings and police brutality against nonviolent black protesters. Denise McNair, the youngest victim of the Sixteenth Street Baptist Church bombing, was Rice's classmate and friend. Rice did not participate in or become involved in the great moral and political desegregation struggles in her city—and has recently suggested that integration could have been achieved without nonviolent protests. Rice may forget that history; black America cannot afford to. The divided racial history of the past must finally be confronted if it is to be overcome. It is time for the wages of slavery and segregation finally to be paid.

Chapter 10

The Hip-Hop Revolution

I know this is going to sound corny, but [hip-hop music is] about black love and esteem. . . . [It's] about the resilience of the spirit to move forward. I'm proud to be who I am—my history and heritage are rich. My ancestors were incredibly formidable people who survived things in history that killed others. . . . It's because of them that we can be here saying things like "blacker than the nighttime sky/of Bed-Stuy in July."

—Mos Def, 1998

I

At first impression, it appeared to be an unlikely alliance: hundreds of public school teachers, mostly white, middle class, and many Jewish; tens of thousands of African-American, Caribbean, and Latino teenagers; representatives of black nationalist and radical political organizations, from the Nation of Islam to the Communist Party USA; celebrities from the entertainment industry, such as Cynthia Nixon, costar of the popular television show *Sex and the City*; and many of hip-hop music's elite performance artists. In May 2002, New York City's newly elected Republican mayor, Michael Bloomberg, announced that due to the economic devastation in the city in the aftermath of the September 11 attacks, as much as $1 billion had to be cut from the city's public-school budget. Responding to the crisis of public-school funding, hip-hop impresario Russell Simmons took the lead to put together an ad-hoc coalition for staging a nonviolent protest at City Hall. Representatives from the United Federation of Teachers and the Alliance for Quality Education met with Simmons and agreed to cosponsor the rally. The protest demonstration, which was named "Mobilization for Education," was planned and coordinated by Simmons's chief political adviser and key figure in the year-old Hip-Hop Summit Action Network, Minister Benjamin Muhammad, formerly Benjamin Chavis.

Organized over a period of only several weeks, the Mobilization for Education reached out across racial, ethnic, and class boundaries. Simmons gave a series of interviews and issued press releases to the media explaining the broad purposes of the rally: "Education is a vital issue for Hip-Hop. I visit schools all the time and I'm tired of hearing about kids sharing books and having no desks of their own. I'm tired of the debate of 'Who will manage the schools?' when the real issue is 'Who will prioritize the funding of our children's education?'" Using Simmons's prestige in the hip-hop community, Chavis secured the endorsements of some of its best-known and most popular artists, including Jay Z, Fat Joe, Nas, Ja Rule, Mos Def, Wu-Tang Clan, The Lox, Ashanti, dead prez, Charlie Baltimore, Lady May, Megahertz, Rah Digga, Reverend Run, Chuck D, and Vita. Black Entertainment Television VJs A. J. Calloway,

Free, and Big Tigger gave their support. To build enthusiasm and a strong turnout among hip hop's core constituents, Simmons appeared on many public-service announcements in the media, joined frequently by other hip-hop celebrities. Simmons's message was to encourage people to congregate "in a peaceful act of civil disobedience. We urge parents, teachers and students to shut the city down and let them know we won't tolerate them stealing from our kids anymore! You can find money for jails, you can find money for schools."

On a hot and humid Tuesday afternoon, June 4, more than 50,000 people, the vast majority of whom were children, teenagers, and young adults, rallied in front of City Hall to send a message to the mayor. The massive turnout in defense of public education stunned observers, who'd never witnessed anything like it. "I think many of us have been asleep for too long and I feel this march was a wake-up for some," Simmons announced to the cheering crowd. It was clear that for most of the demonstrators under the age of eighteen, the real attraction of the demonstration was the hip-hop stars. Teresa Wiltz of the *Washington Post* described the somewhat chaotic scene: "Things get crazy very early on. Kids cram the streets, tens of thousands crowding every inch of pavement for blocks. . . . There are gaggles of girls, drunk on heat and hormones and the prospect of seeing a favorite rap star: Jay-Z, P. Diddy, Cool J. Common, Noreaga, RZA from Wu-Tang Clan. And so they shove and push, and heave and squeeze, until the barricades come crashing down. Sure, they're here to protest school budget cuts, but on this first Tuesday in June, at least, the vibe is more rap concert than City Hall demonstration." Wiltz concluded that "hip-hop, approaching its 30th year," looks like it has come "of age politically."

The New York demonstration to support public education was the culmination of the political evolution of both Simmons and hip-hop culture over a period of several years. In 1996, rap star LL Cool J was behind the development of Rock the Vote's "Hip-Hop Coalition," which endeavored to reach out to African-American and Latino youth to register and to turn out on election day. The Hip-Hop Coalition attracted the enthusiastic support of several prominent hip-hop stars, including Queen Latifah and Chuck D, and registered about 70,000 voters in the hip-hop generation. Chuck D and Hip-Hop Coalition coordinator Donna Frisby subsequently created Rappers Educating All Curricula through Hip-Hop (REACH), which was designed to bring hip-hop artists into direct contact with young people to promote education and civic engagement. In 1998, former Nation of Islam Minister Conrad Muhammad established the Conscious Hip Hop Activism Necessary for Global Empowerment (CHHANGE), which promotes voter education, registration, and community organizing. Along similar lines, the late Lisa Sullivan, who believed that hip-hop culture could become the framework for fostering youth leaders, established the Local Initiative, Support, Training and Education Network (LISTEN) in Washington, D.C. In San Francisco, local activist Van Jones established the Ella Baker Center for Human Righters, mobilizing hundreds of young people to become involved in progressive, social-justice causes.

The development of these grassroots political trends probably prompted Simmons to take a more assertive role in shaping the political agenda of the hip-hop generation. As the founder and chairman of Rush Communications, a multimedia empire that includes Def Jam recordings, Russell Simmons Television, Def Pictures, Rush Arts Management, online magazines Oneworld and 360hiphop, and the clothing company Phat Farm, Simmons was in a position to leverage his clout among corporate executives in the entertainment industry to help finance his political and philanthropic projects. Beginning in 2000, he made plans to create an unprecedented coalition of rap artists, music executives, and leaders from politics, civil-rights organizations, and universities to be called the Hip-Hop Summit Action Network. Partial funding for the Network was contributed by board members Sean "P. Diddy" Combs, *The Source* publisher David Mays, and Hilary Rosen, the president of the Recording Industry Association of America. A political action committee of the Network was also planned, called NuAmerica. Simmons recruited veteran black organizer and leader Benjamin Muhammad to put together the forces to create a new movement.

On June 11–12, 2001, the first Hip-Hop Summit was held in midtown Manhattan's Hilton Hotel, garnering national and international media coverage. Virtually every prominent hip-hop artist from the past quarter-century was present at some point at the gathering, from hip-hop "Old School" legends such as Afrika Bambaataa, Grandmaster Flash, Kool Herc, Crazy Legs, Fab Five Freddy, and D.J. Red Alert to the contemporary artists. Even more impressive, perhaps, to media observers was the presence and active involvement of a segment of black America's political elite, including NAACP leader Kweisi Mfume, Martin Luther King III, Congresswoman Cynthia McKinney, and Nation of Islam leader Louis Farrakhan. Since the event was orchestrated by Muhammad (Chavis), there was for me a sense of political déjà vu. Seven years earlier, as head of the NAACP, Chavis had produced a similar high-profile conference, the 1994 African American Leadership Summit. Back in 1994 at the Baltimore gathering, hip hop's representatives were not at the table. By 2001, hip hop was largely driving the political agenda, and it was the established black leaders who had to come calling.

The establishment of the summit fostered numerous follow-up events, both in New York City and nationally. On Dr. Martin Luther King, Jr.'s, holiday in 2002, the first hip-hop youth summit was held at York College in Queens. Featuring prominent hip-hop artists such as Nas, Reverend Run of the legendary group Run-DMC, Wu-Tang Clan, rap activist Sister Souljah, and Fat Joe, the conference focused on building youth memberships and chapters across the country. Programs discussed included the "Read to Succeed Project," which is designed to bring hip-hop artists into the public schools to emphasize literacy, and the antidrug "Game Over" public-service campaign. In February 2002, Simmons and Muhammad hosted the first Hip-Hop Summit in Los Angeles. As in the New York event, hundreds of influential performance artists, music executives, grassroots activists, public leaders, and others gathered to address key issues and to establish a progressive political agenda. Prominent participants included rapper Kurupt, DJ Quik, the Outlawz, Mack 120, Boo-Yaa Tribe, and radio personality and comedian Steve Harvey. Significantly, the keynote address was delivered by Nation of Islam leader Louis Farrakhan, who spoke for nearly three hours to a standing-room-only audience.

There has always been a fundamental struggle for the "soul" of hip-hop culture, represented by the deep tension between politically conscious and "positivity" rap artists and the powerful and reactionary impulses toward misogyny, homophobia, corporate greed, and crude commodification. This struggle for hip hop's "soul" was vividly expressed at the 2002 West Coast Hip-Hop Summit. Respected rappers, such as anti-gang leader Mike Concepcion and the D.O.C., and Simmons, emphasized the need to mobilize artists around progressive goals, such as supporting voter-education and registration campaigns. Solidarity was expressed for progressive feminist poet/artist Sarah Jones, who was suing the Federal Communication Commission for violating her freedom of speech because it imposed a fine against an Oregon radio station for playing of her song, "Your Revolution." Farrakhan urged the hip-hop community to renounce lyrics promoting violence and social divisiveness. "From the suffering of our people came rap," Farrakhan observed. "That should make you a servant of those that produced you."

However, the forces of "negativity" were also present, reflected in the controversial remarks of the founder of Death Row Records Marion "Suge" Knight. Launching into an attack against artists such as Dr. Dre, Master P, and Janet Jackson, Knight criticized sisters in attendance for "wanting to be men." When Knight then argued that women "were not strong enough to be leaders," observers were stunned. Muhammad later placed Knight's remarks into context: "A summit is where diverse forces come together. . . . You saw the compassion side and the raw side of hip-hop. You saw the focus on economics and the side that focuses on social transformation."

On January 28, 2002, Simmons and I engaged in a "public dialogue" hosted by the Institute for Research in African-American Studies at Columbia University before several hundred people. Since my participation in the 2001 national Hip-Hop Summit, I had been meeting privately with both Simmons and Muhammad to develop a "hip-hop initiative," which might include a summer youth leadership training institute and ongoing public conversations between rap artists and political leaders around social-justice issues such as the prison industrial complex, discrimination in the juvenile justice system, voter education, and music censorship. Although our public conversation lasted over ninety minutes and covered a wide range of concerns, Simmons clearly laid out several political observations that appeared to form the basis of his critique of contemporary politics. The hip-hop generation, Simmons contended, has no confidence in the current African-American political establishment. Part of Muhammad's role was to reach out to black elected officials and middle-aged civil-rights leaders, whom Simmons characterized as "old folks who don't realize the value of young people because they don't like their language or their attitude. They say to Ben, 'As a minister, you should be offended by all this language and the content of hip hop music,' He says, 'I'm offended by poverty and the conditions that these people are in. I'm not offended by any language.'" Simmons emphasized that the older generation is largely in a state of "denial" about the politics behind the music:

They just don't get it. They don't see these statements and this music as a kind of road map for change and success in the future. A lot of rappers are saying important things today and just nobody's listening except young people.

Rappers have very generous souls—just about everybody's got a foundation, but they lack finance and infrastructure. Then we got these big old civil rights organizations with all this money. And infrastructure and don't do s—t with the people. Young people don't know what the f—k they are or what they do. The people who work at the board of directors at the NAACP and the Urban League sit there and say, "Why don't the young people come to our convention and help us?"

Why the chasm between the "We Shall Overcome Generation" and the "Hip-Hop Generation"? According to Simmons, part of the problem is found in the contradictory politics of liberal integrationism. "Integration took a hell of a toll on our communities, from the black doctor to the black lawyer to the black plumber. They were integrated so they were pulled away from the community." This is part of the reason why Simmons, a multimillionaire with a summer home in the Hamptons, feels most at home in the ghettoes and barrios of America's central cities, or working closely with the Nation of Islam to eliminate drug trafficking in black neighborhoods, or reaching out to African-American prisoners. "Minister Farrakhan is really the conscience of the black community today," Simmons stated. Growing up in Queens, New York, he recalled: "If you were nodding from being high and the Muslims came by, you'd stand up straight. So the Muslims were always a positive influence, and it was obvious to me and anybody my age that they reformed a lot of lives. I always had an appreciation for the work that Minister [Farrakhan] did in the community."

Simmons's intimate relationship with the Nation of Islam and his respect for Farrakhan is a tribute to the strong Islamic orientation of many hip-hop artists. One of today's best and most "conscious" hip-hop artists, Mos Def, opened his 1999 album *Black on Both Sides* with a Muslim prayer. Rap artists in the NOI include Ice Cube, K-Solo, and Mc Ren. Even more hip-hop artists have been influenced by the NOI offshoot, the Five Percent Nation—such as Wu-Tang Clan, Busta Rhymes, and Poor Righteous Teachers. What also seems clear is that most of the liberal integrationist, middle-class black establishment has largely refused for two decades to engage in a constructive political dialogue with the hip-hop nation. Since the Nation of Islam's reorganization and reemergence under Farrakhan in the early 1980s, it has understood that black culture is directly related to black politics. To transform an oppressed community's political behavior, one must first begin with the reconstruction of both cultural and civic imagination. Malcolm X's greatest strength as a black leader was his ability to change how black people thought about themselves as "racial subjects." Revolutionary culture does the same thing. Through music and the power of art, we can imagine ourselves in exciting new ways, as makers of new history. The reluctance of the black bourgeoisie to come to terms with the music its own children listen to compromises its ability to advance a meaningful political agenda reflecting what the masses of our people see and feel in their daily lives. It speaks volumes about the cultural divisions and political stratification within the African-American community, as Simmons noted in our interview, that Run-DMC was on the covers of *Rolling Stone* and *Vanity Fair* before it was on *Emerge* or *Ebony*, the leading African-American publications.

Hip-hop culture's early evolution was closely linked with the development of a series of political struggles and events that fundamentally shaped the harsh realities of black urban life. For example, hip-hop historians sometimes place the true origins of rap as an art form in the 1970 release of the self-titled album, *The Last Poets*, based on the spoken word. *The Last Poets* was recorded and released during an intense period of rebellion closely coinciding with the 1970 murder of two African-American students and the wounding of twelve others by police at Jackson State University in Mississippi, the mass wave of ghetto rebellions during the summer of 1970, and the FBI's nationwide campaign to arrest and imprison prominent black activist Angela Davis. In New York City in 1973–1974, Afrika Bambaataa (Kevin Donovan) established the Zulu Nation, a collective of DJs, graffiti artists, and breakers, with the stated political purpose of urban survival through cultural empowerment and peaceful social change. Hip hop's first DJ, Kool Herc (Clive Campbell), developed rap as a cultural mode of aesthetic expression.

At about the same time, graffiti art exploded everywhere across the city—on subway cars, buses, and buildings—and soon became recognized as an original and creative art form. What helped to shape these cultural forms, which later would become known as hip hop, was the economic and political turmoil occurring in New York City during these years. The city government was lurching toward bankruptcy as urban unemployment rates rose during the most severe economic recession since the end of World War II. These years also marked the beginnings of more extreme forms of deadly violence among African-American and Hispanic young people. In 1977, even DJ Kool Herc was stabbed three times at his own party, reflecting in part escalating competition between rival crews, as well as the growth of violence to resolve disputes. Yet the sites of greatest oppression frequently can produce the strongest forces of resistance. The culture that the world one day would know as hip hop was born in that context of racial and class struggle.

II

In his autobiography, *Life and Def*, Russell Simmons defined hip hop as "modern, mainstream young urban American culture." Although hip hop "is primarily a musical form," it is "more expansive in the ways it manifests itself and as a result, its impact is wider." Simmons's definition may be accurate by twenty-first-century standards, but it doesn't tell us how this "young urban culture" captured the imaginations of millions of young people throughout the world. In the 1970s, the four core elements of hip hop were developed—break-dancing, graffiti art, emceeing, and dejaying. All were creative expressions of an underground, rebellious culture that was directly and fundamentally at odds with the "mainstream." In the beginning, as Nelson George astutely observed, "hip hop was not a mass market concept" or a "career move." The original DJs, such as Grandmaster Flash, Bambaataa, and Herc, never "expected anything from the music but local fame, respect in the neighborhood, and the modest fees from the parties given at uptown clubs. . . . They may have pocketed a couple hundred bucks here or there but none thought these gigs would make them millionaires." More than anything else, it was "the spirit of openhearted innocence that created hip hop culture." Thus, many Old School rappers ended up being brutally exploited by unscrupulous business practices by both white and black managers and music-industry executives, many of whom recognized the profit-making potential of this insurgent, bold art form before the artists themselves did. One early example of this occurred in 1979, when Grandmaster Caz received neither credit nor financial compensation for the use of rhymes he had created when Big Bank Hank used them in the early hit, "Rapper's Delight."

From the early years of hip hop, there was a current of "socially conscious rap," a progressive political orientation about how young people understood the oppressed conditions of their communities and how they interacted within them. As Nelson George put it, hip hop was certainly "rebellious," but it was never "a political movement in the usual sense. . . . It doesn't present a systematic (or even original) critique of white world supremacy. Nor has it produced a manifesto for collective political agitation." Nevertheless, the artists observed the same social contractions that political activists in their neighborhoods did, and it was inevitable that explicitly political messages would find their way into the music. The first breakthrough to socially conscious hip hop was Grandmaster Flash and the Furious Five's single, "The Message," which would later inspire a new generation of political activists and artists alike:

> Broken glass everywhere
> People pissin' on the stairs, you know they just don't care
> I can't take the smell, can't take the noise
> Got no money to move out, I guess I got no choice
> Rats in the front room, roaches in the back
> Junkies in the alley with a baseball bat
> I tried to get away but I couldn't get far
> 'Cuz a man with a tow truck repossessed my car
> Don't push me 'cuz I'm close to the edge
> I'm trying not to lose my head
> Uh huh ha ha ha
> It's like a jungle sometimes
> It makes me wonder how I keep from goin' under.

"The Message" went gold in three weeks and platinum in six, and the song reached number eight on the British charts. The following year, Keith Leblanc of Tommy Boy Records released "No Sell-out," incorporating the powerful voice of Malcolm X into the rap single. This marked the beginning of the incorporation of Malcolm's uncompromising words and political message, which would be sampled in hundreds of hip-hop songs, especially in the late 1980s and early 1990s. Also in 1983, Grandmaster Flash and Melle Mel released their anti-cocaine anthem "White Lines (Don't Do It)," which was designed to promote greater antidrug social awareness within black and Latino communities. Nearly a decade later, as hip hop migrated to the West Coast, seminal rap group NWA recorded the song "Dope Man," which, upon close examination, reveals an emphatic antidrug message, despite its explicit lyrics.

Social critics like Kevin Powell have described the period between 1987 and 1992 as the "golden age" of hip-hop music, a time of enormous creativity and artistic originality. More than any other group at that time, Public Enemy (PE) set the standard for progressive, socially conscious rap. The group's three principal members, Chuck D (Charles Ridenhour), DJ Terminator (Norman Rogers), and Flavor Flav (William Drayton), were dubbed "prophets of rage" in the media, but all they did was to tell the truth about police brutality and the political dimensions of structural racism. As PE declared in their song, "Fight the Power":

> To revolutionize make a change nothin's strange
> People, people are the same
> No we're not the same
> Cause we don't know the game
> What we need is awareness, we can't get careless
> You say what is this?
> My beloved, let's get down to business
> Mental self defensive fitness
> (Yo) bum rush the show
> You gotta go for what you know
> Make everybody see, in order to fight the powers that be
> Lemee hear you say
> Fight the Power
> . . . Cause I'm Black and proud
> I'm ready and hyped plus I'm amped
> Most of my heroes don't appear on no stamps
> Sample a look back you look and find
> Nothing but rednecks for 400 years if you check . . .
> Right on, c'mon
> What we got to say
> Power to the people no delay
> To make everybody see
> In order to fight the powers that be
> Fight the Power . . .

Though not as commercially successful as PE, KRS-One and his group Boogie Down Productions also changed the content of rap albums, beginning with the 1987 album *Criminal Minded*. Other similar examples include the 1989 release of "Daddy's Little Girl" by MC Nikki D (Nichelle Strong), who was the first female rapper to rhyme about abortion from a young woman's perspective; the brilliant (and under-appreciated) rapper Paris, the self-proclaimed "black panther of hip hop," who called for radical social change and incorporated images of Malcolm X and the Black Panther Party into his videos; the 1989 release of the debut record by A. Tribe called *Quest,* preaching Afrocentric awareness, collective love, and peace; KRS-One's 1989 "Stop the Violence Movement" and the Boogie Down Productions release of "Self Destruction" to promote awareness of black-on-black violence, featuring legendary artists such as Public Enemy, MC Lyte, and Kool Moe Dee; Salt-n-Peppa's 1991 remake of the song "Let's Talk About Sex" into "Let's Talk About AIDS," a public-service announcement that promoted HIV/AIDS awareness and sex education, with all the proceeds from the sale of both the single and the video donated by the group to the National Minority AIDS Council and the TJ Martell Foundation for AIDS Research; and the collective protest response to the brutal police beating of Rodney King in March 1991 by progressive rap artists such as Chuck D, Ice Cube, Tupac Shakur, and Sister Souljah.

The most progressive black "womanist" artist in hip hop's golden age was Queen Latifah. Although Latifah did not describe herself as a feminist, her video "Ladies First" depicted powerful images of freedom fighters Angela Y. Davis, Winnie Mandela, and Sojourner Truth. Her strong support for the struggle to overthrow the apartheid regime of South Africa and her criticisms of corporate power at that time opened new avenues for the development of other women hip-hop artists.

While art and politics are indeed connected, it is not the case that cultural workers, musicians, and even entertainment entrepreneurs like Simmons coming out of hip-hop culture represent a new political leadership. Yvonne Bynoe, one of hip-hop culture's most insightful observers, paraphrased Chuck D by saying that "we do not need hip-hop doctors or hip-hop politicians. The leadership that will come from the post–civil rights generation must be able to do more than rhyme about problems; they have got to be able to build organizations as well as harness the necessary monetary resources and political power to do something about them." Bynoe's argument makes absolute sense, because the most politically committed artists throughout history, such as Paul Robeson, Pete Seeger, and Bernice Reagon, understood that although art is always political, artists usually shouldn't be politicians. As Bynoe noted: "A rap artist who aspires to be a community leader cannot lead a dual life. . . . The electorate for instance would not be expected to call their representative, Congressman Ol' Dirty Bastard. . . . Political activism is a full-time, contact sport, necessitating players who are fully dedicated to learning the rules of the game, then playing to win."

It must be emphasized, however, that hip-hop artists can lend their legitimacy (or in the hip-hop vernacular, their "juice") to many different political causes or public figures. Their very presence or words can act as lightning rods of attention for the masses of youth who identify with hip hop. When Public Enemy's Chuck D rhymed "Farrakhan's a prophet that I think you ought to listen to," many listeners were attracted to the Nation of Islam's message of black nationalism. As a result, rappers such as PE and Ice Cube in his prime helped NOI to reach a whole new generation of disaffected youth. Political leaders have often sought the aid of influential musical artists, and in the realm of black liberation and struggle, hip-hop culture has provided an undeniable galvanizing platform. The "politics of art" is essentially about the politics of collective imagination, the transformative politics of freeing one's mind. In a recent interview, KRS-One observed that hip hop "is the only place where Dr. Martin Luther King's 'I have a dream' speech is visible. . . . Today, with the help of hip hop, they're all hip-hoppers out there. . . . I mean, black, white, Asian, Latino, Chicano, everybody. Hip-Hop has formed a platform for all people, religions, and occupations to meet on something." KRS-One added, "That, to me, is beyond music."

There is no longer any question about the significance and power of hip-hop music and culture as a transnational commercial force. One recent example of this was the 2001 release of Tupac Shakur's *Until the End of Time,* which debuted at number one on Billboard's top 200 albums chart, selling more than 425,000 copies in the first week. Since his murder on September 8, 1996, Tupac's albums have sold at a rate three times higher than during his lifetime. Rap music's consumer market in the United States is approximately 80 percent white. This brings into sharp focus the central political contradiction that socially conscious hip-hop cultural workers must address: how to anchor their art into the life-and-death (and "def") struggles of African-American and Latino communities, which largely consist of poor people and the working poor, the unemployed, and those millions who are warehoused in prisons and jails. Even "a nation of millions" cannot "hold us back," if we utilize the power embedded in hip-hop art as a matrix for constructing new movements and institutions for capacity and black empowerment. Hip hop's passion and power, when expressed in progressive political terms, is potentially a force that can combat the civil death and social marginalization of contemporary urban life.

Chapter 11

When the Spirit Moves

The Politics of Black Faith

The judgment of God is upon the church as never before. If today's church does not recapture the sacrificial spirit of the early church, it will lose its authenticity, forfeit the loyalty of millions, and be dismissed as an irrelevant social club with no meaning for the twentieth century.

—Martin Luther King, Jr.
"Letter from Birmingham Jail," April 16, 1963

Where there is no vision, the people perish.

—**Proverbs 29:18**

I

It was one of Macon County's smaller churches, perched halfway up a pine-covered hill along a narrow, red clay dirt road. But on that particular Sunday morning in midsummer, the tiny house of the Lord somehow accommodated at least two hundred perspiring worshipers. Young black girls in perfectly ironed dresses sat in neat rows of metal folding chairs. A young man, wearing an oversized, starched white shirt and white gloves, stood ready at the entrance, opening the door for late arrivals. Several heavy, older women busily cooled themselves with colorfully designed cardboard fans, provided by a local undertaker. Most of the fans featured portraits of Dr. Martin Luther King, Jr., or Jesus, standing in the middle of a multiracial group of children. All eyes were directed toward a large, frayed, and slightly soiled red plush chair with a high back and armrests, where the pastor sat comfortably above his congregation. After the opening hymn, all was quiet.

The short, potbellied man, wearing an ill-fitting black suit, stood slowly, facing the congregation. He closed his eyes tightly, raised his sweating palms toward the rafters, and prayed aloud in a deep, resounding baritone: "Blessed Jesus, we thank you for life, the greatest blessing of the world, life. We thank you, for the blood that circulates through our bodies. We thank you, for the blood and the air so we can stand on our feet. We thank you, for the loving hand of mercy bestowed upon us; that Thou art in our midst. Prepared us for our souls' journey through this unfriendly world, and when our life on this earth has ended, receive us into Thy home which art in heaven."

Moans and exclamations resounded from all corners of the small sanctuary: "Lord have mercy, Lord have mercy, Amen." The choir, joined by the entire congregation, began to sing softly, "We'll Understand It Better By and By."

I had witnessed this ritual, or others like it, hundreds of times during my summer visits to my father's home in Alabama. Our family reunions and Sunday suppers were always organized around such services. Throughout my entire life, as far back as memory can take me, I have loved the majesty and full beauty of African-American religious music.

On those Sunday mornings, I would sometimes close my eyes and feel the incredible passion embedded within the soulful expression of black spirituality in human motion, sweeping wave after wave of emotional energy all over us. In some respects, perhaps I was nothing more than a participant observer, or a prodigal son. I had been born and raised up north as an Episcopalian. Nowhere in my formal religious experience there had I witnessed such outpourings of devout fervor. I had been trained as a child to consider matters of faith as the successful mastery of the catechism, a sequence of logical and coherent sacred words. But here, in my father's rural church, the textual logic of faith was swept aside by a sea of black compassion and pain.

Finding faith meant to these rural black folk transcending the temporal boundaries of place and time. Du Bois, a century earlier, observing similar scenes in rural Tennessee, reflected that the "frenzy" expressed in the African-American religion was that moment "when the spirit of the Lord" passes by. "Without this visible manifestation of God there could be no true communion with the Invisible."

My first real teaching job began more than a quarter of a century ago, when I accepted a faculty appointment at Tuskegee Institute, a position that also included the chairmanship of the Political Science Department. At the time I was completing my Ph.D. dissertation at the University of Maryland and working as a lecturer in African-American Studies at Smith College. When my cosmopolitan and radically hip friends, black and white, learned that I had deliberately chosen to teach at Tuskegee over Smith, they unanimously questioned the wisdom of my decision. There were the standard academic arguments against going to an institution with heavy instructional responsibilities and limited research funds. Historically, black colleges were notoriously conservative, and as I soon learned, administrators at most levels were expected to wear suits and ties as regular attire. But beneath these criticisms was a veiled reservation about the religious evangelicalism and socially conservative character of African-American rural life and culture. There were unspoken assumptions about the cultural backwardness of such an existence. To be "political," to be truly modern, was to embrace a secular existence. God was dead, even if most black southerners didn't know it.

In recent years, however, there has been a significant shift in how most Americans talk about religion in the context of politics and public policy. Philosopher Michael Novak has observed, "There was a convention until 20 years ago, in academic circles and journalism, that you didn't raise religious convictions. Now there is more freedom and people go out of their way to talk about religion." Other scholars have noted the change from pure secularism to a marked increase in scholarship drawing upon insights and ideas from faith-based traditions. As public affairs scholar Hugh Hecio, coeditor of *Religion Returns to the Public Square,* noted: "It's not the old values debate of the culture wars, but 'What do we think are the grounds for deciding if something is right or wrong?' It's inescapable if you're representing a democracy in which people believe in God." Conversely, the vast majority of scholars oppose what is widely described as the intrusion of religion into science.

Stephen Carter also examined this problem in *The Culture of Disbelief.* In his view, there is a deeply secularist bias that permeates many sectors of U.S. society, including the media, the court system, academic institutions, and to a lesser degree, political institutions. Public actors who are largely motivated by their personal beliefs are frequently marginalized and even trivialized. Carter argued that this reinforces the view that religion has no important role to play in the world of politics. Although I have differences with much of Carter's thesis, I agree that religious values and the struggle for the freedom to express one's faith against the sanctions and restrictions of state authority have always shaped the evolution and content of U.S. politics, since the beginning of European colonization and the coerced migration of African people to this continent. There was always a legal separation between church and state, but strict secularism in government did not really develop until the beginning of the twentieth century.

As a young man, I was searching to mediate my own ideas about faith and spirituality within the context of defining my life's work and intellectual mission. All my years of training in higher education had oriented me away from the beauty and simplicity of what I had known as a boy spending summers in the Black Belt South. To better understand my own people, it was necessary for me to return to my father's home mentally and physically, at least for a time. And to really know any people, one must comprehend and feel what they most deeply believe and cherish. This prodigal son had to make this necessary sojourn, to rediscover the spiritual dimensions of the "souls of black folk."

But what, after all, is the meaning of "soul"? From the interior of our own being, it is an ethical foundation for the choices we make in our lives and the sense of responsibility we feel in how we relate to other people. "Soul" also implies the possibility of transcendence—the shared capacity of human beings to realize something beyond the elements of our material existence, traveling toward a richer, deeper knowledge of the meaning of existence. Certainly, from the terrain of African-American culture and history, "soul" also implies memory, agency, and hope in the face of despair. The souls of black folk have encountered terrible exploitation and inhumane conditions, a degraded and desperate physical reality that would force most reasonable people to conclude that God, or whatever else one might call universal truth, had abandoned and forsaken them. But to maintain faith under these horrific circumstances, to have the confidence and inner strength to endure, potentially can give agency to oppressed people. And in the construction of African-American culture—as reflected richly in our music, both sacred and secular, in our folklore, rituals, symbols, and language—to have "soul" is to be truly at home with oneself and with the people. "Soul" helps us to navigate the hostile currents of an unequal and unfair world, a world stratified by color and class, where all too frequently there seems to be no justice. "Soul" reminds us that we are a people who possess history and memory, and that we have the capacity to discover and know our own truths.

In his brilliant study of African-American religion in the early nineteenth century, Eddie S. Glaude, Jr., provided a historical explanation for the construction of "soul" as a site of existential meaning. "To live under the threat of violence, to be subjected daily to various forms of humiliation, and to know that only those who look like you, regardless of class, experience this kind of humiliation and suffer this form of brutality create feelings of terror and uncertainty that necessitate forms of solidarity," Glaude observed. This commitment to cultural solidarity permitted the development of "a sense of self-respect repeatedly denied in antebel-

lum America." From self-respect came a recognition of collective obligation, the understanding that the individual's welfare and existence did
not lie outside of the fate of the larger group. Thus, it was through both
suffering and struggle that black America's "moral and national identity"
was forged, "the sense of being a person and community of a particular
kind, who lives and exists by some values rather than others."

Thus, the meaning of faith to African Americans who profess to be
Christians is not simply a black "version" of the Christian religion as
practiced by Euro-Americans. For white Americans, "freedom of religion" is generally interpreted to mean the separation of church and
state, the personal liberty to worship without governmental interfer-
ence. For black Americans, Glaude explained, black faith was inextricably linked to what he termed "Exodus politics." The biblical narrative
that outlined the struggles of an ancient, oppressed people was a "story,
by direct or indirect reference, [that] gave expression to what can be
call[ed] the soul of the nation. . . . Moreover, the story told of black
America's sojourn and directed consciousness of the group back to significant points in its common history, enabling, as it were, a constant renewal of community through collective memory." Thus, the Hebrew
covenant with the Lord was directly connected with the struggle for human emancipation and freedom. The Bible, more than any other single
book, was essential in the construction of African-American national
consciousness and identity as a people.

Faith can permit black people to stand outside of the dialectics of the
master-slave relationship, which is still deeply embedded in America's
master narrative and even in the original words of the Constitution.
Through faith, it becomes possible to reject the status of "nothingness"
that white supremacy offered us. "God," for the black oppressed, becomes a catalyst for achieving a higher consciousness, the moral courage
required not to surrender to the power of racism.

I began reading about the meaning of faith in black southern culture
and soon encountered the writings of sociologist Charles S. Johnson.
Forty years earlier, Johnson had studied black life in Tuskegee and the
surrounding rural environment of Macon County. Through careful ob-

servation, he gradually acquired an understanding of the deep emotional and spiritual core at the center of everyday lives of rural African Americans. In *Growing Up in the Black Belt,* Johnson observed that "among rural Negroes the church is still the only institution which provides an effective organization of the group, an approved and tolerated place for social activities, a forum for expression on many issues, and an outlet for emotional repressions." Black faith reproduced the central structures of the rural black population's conservative conceptions of life, work, and human development. Class distinctions within the African-American community were also strikingly expressed in faith-based terms. The members of Tuskegee's black professional middle class generally were Episcopalians, Presbyterians, and sometimes Catholic, while the rural poor and working class overwhelmingly belonged to Baptist, Pentecostal, and Holiness churches.

As I began teaching at Tuskegee, I learned that the institute had waged a long-standing religious crusade to "uplift" the cultural and intellectual level of the black working class and peasantry. For decades, Tuskegee chaplains had participated in local black pastors' conferences. The Tuskegee Women's Club, an organization of middle-class women who either taught at the institute or were faculty spouses, had organized "open-air Sunday schools" in poor neighborhoods to provide a more refined alternative to local itinerant preachers. The more "respectable" local ministers from the poorer neighborhoods might be invited to deliver sermons at the institute's chapel on Sunday mornings or called upon to give the invocation at special events on the campus.

Such attempts to "upgrade" the level of spiritual discourse among the black rural poor were never entirely successful. As observers from Ralph Ellison to Zora Neale Hurston have long observed, faith is absolutely central to black folk culture because it is expressed as an integral part of daily life, with all of its many contradictions and inconsistencies. Biblical analogies were a normal part of daily conversation, but so, too, were ribald expressions of love, sexuality, and humor. At one family dinner after Sunday's church service, for instance, I was surprised to hear this informal prayer:

Oh Lord,
Send down your Thunderbolt
To kill all the white folks
And let the niggers stay
So we can eat lean meat
And "heavendust"
Three times a day.
Amen.

It was only years later that I fully comprehended that I should *not* have been surprised. The basic expression and objective of black American political life, the freedom to dismantle structural racism, is inextricably linked to how most African Americans experience their faith and spirituality. In other words, for most black people, there was no firm or absolute boundary between the black secular and the sacred, between the black public and the private. Black religiosity was embedded everywhere—from the naming of our children to the civic organizations we created to enhance the quality of our schools under the oppressive regime of de jure segregation. It was faith that gave folks hope and courage to organize against the Ku Klux Klan and racist vigilantes who tried to suppress the struggle for equality. Black faith has also expressed what Michael Eric Dyson correctly characterized as "a healthy skepticism about the white church, which lent theological credence to slavery and Jim Crow." This was one major reason why "the gospel of freedom," as Dyson said, "influenced many religious blacks who were leaders and foot soldiers in the NAACP, CORE and SNCC."

II

Didn't my Lord deliver Daniel,
Deliver Daniel, deliver Daniel?
Didn't my Lord deliver Daniel?
An' why not everyman?
He delivered Daniel from de lion's den,

Jonah from de belly of de whale.
And de Hebrew children from de fiery furnace,
An' why not everyman?

The most important concepts and values that are at the heart of African-American faith and spirituality did not begin with slavery. "On their own soil," Melva W. Costen observed, "Africans created innumerable religious beliefs, customs, languages, and symbols which gave them unique and separate identities." Therefore, when Africans arrived in the Americas, they constructed their own rituals based in part on their previous cosmology. "Armed with their African belief systems," Costen wrote, "thoroughly aware of an omnipotent, omniscient God, African Americans set about the awesome task of honing and shaping liturgical and musical styles commensurate with their abiding faith in God."

Although attempts to promote Christianity among enslaved Africans in British North America were initiated by the London-based Society for the Propagation of the Gospel in the early eighteenth century, it was only in the 1740s and 1750s, with the "Great Awakening" of religious fervor, that hundreds of thousands of blacks identified themselves as Christians. As historian Kenneth Morgan noted, "These evangelical stirrings of the soul were associated largely with the Presbyterians, Methodists and Baptists, who favoured itinerancy, extempore preaching, minimizing doctrinal differences, conversion as a result of God's saving grace, open-air gatherings, fervent hymn singing, and the prospect for all who joined the Christian faith and maintained their faith to live in the hope of everlasting peace in the life hereafter." Thousands of blacks converted, generating real fears among the planter elite that "baptism of slaves and the evangelical message might steer African Americans towards the legitimization of freedom." By the outbreak of the American Revolution, approximately one-third of Virginia's Baptists were African Americans. Although the vast majority of white Christians perceived no contradiction between their faith and the brutal reality of human bondage, there were important exceptions, which blacks quickly recognized. Quakers were among the first Euro-Americans to denounce slavery. Prominent Methodist leaders such as John Wesley attacked "the immorality of

slaveholding." As Morgan noted, the more evangelical wing of the An-
glican Church "opposed black bondage by emphasizing the Christian
duty to behave benevolently, to accept the bounty for God's providence,
and to fulfill the goal of progressive revelation." Skin color, in short,
should not be a barrier in receiving God's grace.

When Richard Allen, Absalom Jones, and other African Americans
walked out of St. George's Methodist Episcopal Church in Philadelphia
to denounce the church's racially segregated seating arrangements in
November 1787, a new stage in the development of a uniquely black
Christianity occurred. By 1794, there were two black congregations in
Philadelphia, both owning their own buildings. The African Methodist
Episcopal Church and other black denominations soon created their
own sacred traditions, fighting to build their own communities in the
face of white supremacy. Before the Civil War, tens of thousands of free
blacks in the North had formed their own Baptist, Methodist, and Presbyterian associations and conventions. Will B. Gravely observed that
black Protestants soon sought to remove "themselves from white supervision and connections." The black religious experience "was to affirm,
audaciously to many whites, an elemental core within each denomina-
tional tradition, and behind that, within Christianity itself, which was
not created or controlled by white Christians."

The religious worldview of enslaved African Americans was best reflected in their sacred music, the spirituals. Costen and other scholars of
black religion have interpreted this unique musical form as "the heart
and soul of American music." These songs were indeed "rooted in West
African traditions," but they also "depict the worldview of those in
bondage." Within the institutional constraints imposed by enslavement,
blacks creatively used the narratives from their masters' religion to fashion their own language, to express their pain and suffering. "Freedom to
use the language and concepts of the Bible to retell their story was a
birthright of African people," Costen noted. Scholars have long been
aware of the powerful political themes embedded within black spirituals. "Steal away to Jesus," for example, refers to the possibility of flight
from the slave South, as well as a song of devotion to Christ. Slaves constantly made references to their desire for freedom:

O Freedom! O Freedom!
O Freedom! I love thee,
And before I'll be a slave
I'll be buried in my grave
And go home to my Lord and be free.

After the hopeful turmoil of war and Reconstruction, the long night of Jim Crow segregation was imposed upon the black community, and the church was the most important institution that could provide the necessary resources to allow blacks to survive. The church service was one of the few gatherings where black people had constructed free social space to find their own voices and to be fully themselves. Where the political conditions were more liberal, the churches sought to encourage members to register to vote and to become active participants in local public affairs. They initiated countless community renewal efforts around issues like neighborhood crime, homelessness, hunger, and unemployment. The more progressive black clergy asserted that the divine is expressed by practical engagement on behalf of the oppressed, challenging the institutional evils we see around us every day. The black church fostered a public theology of resistance and renewal and a practical politics informed by morality.

The black preacher was largely "created" by the black community's marginalization from the mainstream. He was the only interlocutor between the segregated worlds of white and black. His salary depended on his fidelity to the concerns of black poor and working people, but his effectiveness rested on his ability to understand "the art of the deal" with whites in power. This faith-based elite continued to dominate black politics after Reconstruction for several generations. The mass migration of millions of African Americans to urban areas beginning in the early twentieth century did not reduce the social and political influence of the black clergy as a social group, but it did contribute to the splintering of black mainstream denominations and the proliferation of new, more evangelical churches. The period between 1915 to 1950 witnessed the explosion of new, dynamic faith-based institutions: the Moorish Science Temple, Pentecostals, Holiness Nation of Islam, African Orthodox

Church, the Black Jews, and Father Divine's movement. Most of these new faith-based groups recruited many of their members from first-generation southern black migrants who had just arrived in the cities. This new religious leadership was less engaged in practical politics and influence brokering than the better established, more middle-class Methodist, Baptist, and Presbyterian black churches that had practiced effectively for decades.

The first serious challenge to the leadership hegemony and political authority of the black clergy developed with the emergence of the "Talented Tenth"—the small yet rapidly growing black professional, managerial, and entrepreneurial class in the early 1900s. Over a period of nearly a century, there was a gradual decline in the social weight and political influence of the black clergy, especially in urban areas, compared to this emerging black professional elite. Part of this decline can be observed from U.S. Census statistics alone. In 1890, there were 12,199 African-American ministers in the United States, representing 1.62 per 1,000 blacks—a remarkably high percentage of the total black population. That same year, there were only 909 doctors, 431 attorneys, and 14,100 schoolteachers who were African American. But as the black middle class grew, the percentage of the black clergy as part of that class shrank. By 1940, there was a total of 17,102 black ministers in the United States, compared to 3,524 doctors, 1,052 attorneys, and 63,697 educators. By 1970, the per capita number of black clergy in the general African-American population had dropped to 0.53 per 1,000, compared to 1.18 per 1,000 for whites. In 1970, only 6 percent of the nation's full-time clergy were African Americans. Although millions of African Americans continued to go to church every Sunday, a growing percentage of younger blacks became disaffected from the restrictive social environment of faith-based institutions. The growth of older, mainstream black churches began to level off and even decline as the Pentecostal and Holiness churches found new converts.

Since the Civil Rights Movement, it has become a standard myth that the black church was the central institution in the struggle to desegregate the South, providing essential resources and leadership. While it is certainly true that African-American clergy—including Dr. Martin

Luther King, Jr., C. T. Vivian, James Lawson, Andrew Young, Hosea
Williams, Ralph David Abernathy, Wyatt T. Walker, Fred Shuttlesworth,
and many more—were major figures in the struggle for civil rights, the
black church as an institution was deeply divided over the protest strategies and tactics of the desegregation campaigns. The Reverend Joseph
H. Jackson, the president of the National Baptist Convention, the largest
African-American denomination, urged his ministers not to join King's
new civil-rights group, the Southern Christian Leadership Conference,
in 1957. In 1961, King and 800 activist ministers were in effect forced out
of Jackson's Baptist organization; they created the more liberal Progressive Baptist Convention. And although many black ministers permitted
their churches to be used as "freedom schools," sites for political organizing and voter-registration training, other churches stood on the political sidelines. Many ministers who for years had been on the private pay-
roll of white political and business elites had a financial interest in
maintaining the Jim Crow status quo. These clergy had become clients
or buffers between white institutions and the masses of working-class
and poor blacks who gave them donations every Sunday.

The legislative and legal triumphs of liberal integrationism, represented by the passage of the 1964 Civil Rights Act and the 1965 Voting
Rights Act, as well as the implementation of affirmative action, set the
stage for a new African-American leadership elite, the black elected officials, or BEOs. As a rule, they were somewhat better educated and more
affluent than the black clergy. Their power, like that of the black church
leaders, was a by-product of racially segregated residential patterns. It
was no accident that the first African American elected to Congress after
Reconstruction, Oscar DePriest, represented America's most racially
segregated city, Chicago. But unlike their faith-based brethren, the politicians aggressively sought to leverage the state from within. As their
numbers grew, the relative power of the African-American clergy continued to decline in significance.

The potential for the black church to play once again a major role in
African-American politics only became apparent with the Reverend Jesse
Jackson's 1983–1984 Rainbow Coalition presidential campaign. It is
largely forgotten today that when Jackson announced his decision to run

for the presidency, the vast majority of African-American elected officials and civil-rights leaders opposed his campaign. The NAACP and the
National Urban League "unofficially" supported the candidacy of former Vice President Walter Mondale. The Coalition of Black Trade
Unionists and the majority of black Democratic officials were also
pledged to Mondale. Jackson astutely decided to appeal directly to the
black church, rhetorically linking the active role of black ministers in the
desegregation campaigns of the 1960s with the necessity to struggle
against Reaganism in the 1980s. Benjamin Chavis, who at the time was
the deputy director of the United Church of Christ's Commission for
Racial Justice, described Jackson's presidential candidacy announcement
as "more of a sermon, in the tradition of great Baptist preachers, than a
speech by an aspiring politician." Chavis defined Jackson's political theology as "a theology of liberation, informed by the Black Church religious
experience and in dialogue with the religious and political experiences of
the world community, particularly the Third World."

An estimated 90 percent of all African-American ministers endorsed
Jackson's campaign in 1984. The first major group to back Jackson was
one of the most politically moderate, the National Baptist Convention,
with 6.5 million members. The Pentecostal Church of God in Christ,
with 3.7 million members, quickly followed. Jackson's national campaign
director, Arnold Pinkney, equated the near-unanimous support Jackson
had received from the black church with the support of labor for whites,
saying it was as significant as "the endorsement of the AFL-CIO" to
other Democratic Party candidates. The enthusiastic backing of the
black church "brings masses of people, financial resources and a fantastic credibility to the candidacy."

The 1984 Jackson campaign illustrated that the black church could effectively mobilize its members to circumvent the African-American political establishment. In the 1988 Jackson campaign, black elected officials, learning from their mistakes four years earlier, quickly embraced
the black insurgent presidential candidate. Consequently, the impact of
the African-American church on the 1988 electoral mobilization, while
substantial, was not as crucial as it had been in 1984. What could no
longer be questioned, however, was the potential strength of African-

American faith-based institutions as a pressure group in national politics and public-policy debates.

III

Precious Lord, take my hand
Lead me on, let me stand,
I am tired, I am weak, I am worn.
Through the storm, through the night
Lead me on to the light,
Take my hand, precious Lord,
Lead me home.

As the economic crises of America's central cities grew, and as public-sector institutions atrophied, the black church was increasingly called upon to perform much of the African-American community's "heavy lifting." As of the late 1990s, the eight major historically black Christian denominations—the African Methodist Episcopal Church, the African Methodist Episcopal Zion Church, the Christian Methodist Episcopal Church, the Church of God in Christ, the National Baptist Convention of America, the National Baptist Convention, USA, the National Missionary Baptist Convention, and the Progressive National Baptist Convention—had a combined membership of 20 million and owned 65,000 churches. A 1998 study published by the Urban Institute examined "faith-based service providers" in the Washington, D.C., area and found that 95 percent of these churches provided outreach services, including everything from financial counseling to giving away food and clothing to the disadvantaged.

Large urban churches, such as the First African Methodist Episcopal Church in Los Angeles, led by the Reverend Cecil Murray, were extensively involved in the renovation of abandoned apartments and office buildings located in south central Los Angeles, also providing employment services and loans. In West Los Angeles, the Church of God in Christ started a community development corporation in 1995; five years later it had completed 44 low-income housing units and had 112 units under construction. At the December 2000 conference of the Congress of National Black Churches held in Kansas City, church leaders outlined an aggressive economic development strategy for inner cities that included "consumer and investment seminars, economic development funds, food co-ops and summits to deal with education and politics." By the late 1990s, elements in the black church had also belatedly confronted the AIDS/HIV epidemic that was ravaging black communities across the country. In San Diego, the Concerned African American Clergy and Laity challenged the homophobia and social conservatism within many local black churches and initiated in 2001 a city-wide AIDS awareness and education campaign. In March 2001, more than 10,000 faith-based institutions, led by black churches, participated in a "National Week of Prayer for the Healing of AIDS" with the goal of using "the power of the black pulpit to educate their communities about HIV/AIDS."

The African-American church's extensive involvement in social-service activities did not escape the attention of conservative white evangelical and fundamentalist Christians, a major constituency within the Republican Party. For decades, the Republicans had tried a number of unsuccessful strategies to win over a critical mass of black voters. During the national debate in 1995–1996 over the termination of Aid to Families with Dependent Children, many white conservatives began to push the concept of what became known as "charitable choice." Then-Senator John Ashcroft of Missouri pushed to include a provision in the Personal Responsibility and Work Reconciliation Act of 1996 that permitted government funding of faith-based social-service programs under a new set of unprecedented guidelines. Similar provisions were also included in the Community Services Block Grant in 1998 and a child health bill in 2000. The charitable-choice provisions allowed faith-based institutions to obtain federal funding for social-service programs for the first time without creating their own separate nonprofit organizations. Traditional restrictions on the overtly religious character of programs sponsored by religious institutions were largely waived. Christian conservatives and "right-wing ideologues find charitable choice attractive," researcher Bill Berkowitz noted, "because it not only reduces government involvement in service-delivery but also injects their religious and 'moral framework' into the welfare debate. Welfare is no longer a question of poverty or the economic inequities in our society; the debate is framed within such time-honored right-wing moral premises as an epidemic of out-of-wedlock births and the lack of personal responsibility— behaviors that conservatives believe contribute to the general moral breakdown of our society."

White religious conservatives also proposed other initiatives to attract black support. In 1997, the Christian Coalition announced plans to donate as much as $10 million in direct grants to black churches under a program called the "Samaritan Project." That same year, former Watergate felon Charles Colson initiated the Prison Reconciliation Fellowship Project, a charitable-choice program financed with government funding. By early 2001, Colson's program had expanded to three states, with the central purpose of accomplishing "rehabilitation through Christian redemption." Technically, prisoners selected for the program "do not have to profess Christianity," but they were obligated to regularly attend Christian services while still incarcerated, and going to church was stipulated as one of their requirements of parole.

With the election of George W. Bush and his appointment of Ashcroft as the new attorney general, charitable-choice proposals received yet another boost. On January 29, 2001, surrounded by Jewish, Muslim, and Christian leaders, President Bush signed an executive order creating the White House Office of Faith-Based and Community Initiatives. Black ministers were prominently projected in the media as charitable choice's strongest supporters. Widely cited also at the time was a 1998 survey of 1,200 religious congregations, conducted by sociologist Mark Chaves, indicating that "64 percent of predominantly black congregations were willing to apply for government funds, compared with 28 percent of predominantly white congregations." Even Rosa Parks publicly endorsed Bush's faith-based initiative, calling it "a good beginning."

Most observers who followed the media debate over faith-based initiatives have come away with the impression that the overwhelming majority of the African-American clergy support charitable choice. This is simply wrong. The most prominent representatives of black faith-based organizations have consistently opposed charitable choice for a number of reasons. First and foremost, it takes the pressure off of the government to provide necessary services for its citizens and channels state resources into private institutions. Charitable choice erodes the historic constitutional barriers between church and state, possibly leading to the deliberate advancement of certain religious beliefs at the expense of others. Charitable-choice funding could ultimately limit the autonomy and independence of religious organizations, especially if they become heavily dependent on governmental grants.

Research on faith-based social-service providers also shows that they have, at best, a mixed record. Public-policy researcher David Reingold, who is conducting a comprehensive comparison of the effectiveness of faith-based versus secular social-service providers for welfare recipients, stated that there is absolutely no research out there that systematically demonstrates that "faith-based organizations are more effective." Researchers Jim Castelli and John McCarthy of Pennsylvania State University have also determined that there is "no infrastructure at the national, state or local levels" for faith-based organizations "to administer programs and large amounts of [government] funding." Any major "expansion would require faith communities to wholly change funding priorities in order to build their capacity." The majority of black churches are relatively small, with fewer than 250 members, so they lack the organizational resources and personnel to step into a social service–provider role. Even the majority of larger black churches currently do not receive government funds through their nonprofit-affiliated organizations.

Given these contradictions, "charitable choice" as it has been generally advocated by the Republicans and conservative Democrats does not advance the larger interests of the African-American community. In saying this, however, I do not mean to imply that faith-based institutions should play no role in social services. I favor a much greater degree of nonfinancial cooperation between religious organizations and governmental agencies in a wide variety of contexts. A number of religious groups that engaged in a two-year dialogue about faith-based social services produced a critical study in 2001, "In Good Faith," which outlines possible areas for government and religious organizations to cooperate more effectively with each other. Such support could include:

> providing information to the public and to persons in need about the availability of programs offered by religious and other community organizations; providing access to education and training opportunities for program staff and volunteers of religious and other community organizations; inviting faith community representatives to join community-wide program task forces; advising social service beneficiaries of mentoring support, and advocacy resources available from community organizations, including religious non-profit agencies or houses of worship; listing houses of worship and religious non-profit agencies among the organizations that may provide community service placements to welfare recipients; making information about the community, such as census tract data, directories of service providers, or needs assessments available to help community service providers, including religious organizations, do planning, networking, and grassroots organizing; [and] encouraging charitable contributions through appropriate tax relief.

Within strict guidelines, greater government funding should also be allocated to religious affiliated institutions that perform secular work, but beneficiaries must have the right not to participate in religious activities. Governmental funding to religious providers of social programs should in no way discriminate between beneficiaries who are eligible to receive support based on their faith affiliation. And antidiscrimination laws relating to the employment of personnel working at such facilities should be enforced. Within such parameters, African-American faith-based organizations could play an even more effective role in the construction of a more civil and democratic society.

Moreover, there can and should be greater cooperation between organized labor and faith-based institutions around issues of economic justice. During the 2000 transit strike in Los Angeles, for example, union activists met regularly at the Holman United Methodist Church to discuss and plan organizing strategies. In 2001, the AFL-CIO and the National Interfaith Committee for Worker Justice launched a "Labor in the Pulpit" program, organizing parishioners to support issues concerning working-class families, such as living-wage ordinances and workers rights.

The black church should also be challenged to become much more involved in criminal-justice issues, pushing for the outlawing of mandatory minimum-sentencing laws and racial disparities in sentencing by judges. One recent example of effective political mobilization along these lines was the role of New Jersey's Black Ministers Council in that state's 2001 gubernatorial race. The 600 African-American churches of the Black Ministers Council warned both major-party candidates for governor to support effective measures outlawing racial profiling by New Jersey's state troopers. The Reverend Reginald T. Jackson, executive director of the council, warned both candidates that "it is not enough to come to our churches, attend our events, parade in our communities and smile in our faces."

Black faith-based institutions are uniquely situated in the struggle to overcome civil death in the black community. Religious organizations and educational programs that are affiliated with theology schools have the greatest access to inmates inside of prisons. Masjids and churches can foster programs for families on the outside to maintain contact with incarcerated family members. Faith-based institutions have frequently taken the lead in developing alternatives to the juvenile justice system to reduce neighborhood crime among young people. Ministers also have the power of moral authority, as well as potential political constituencies represented by the members of their congregations, to challenge structural racism wherever it exists.

IV

On Sunday morning, September 15, 1963, about 400 people gathered at the Sixteenth Street Baptist Church in Birmingham, Alabama, to attend religious services. Suddenly a bomb exploded at the rear of the church.

Four little black girls were murdered: Denise McNair, Cynthia Wesley, Addie Mae Collins, and Carole Robertson. One child had been decapitated. The explosion destroyed part of one wall of the church, and people covered with shards of glass and splattered with blood stumbled into the street. Several people looked up and noticed that the bomb had destroyed Christ's face depicted on the church's beautiful, stained-glass window. Several days later, Dr. Martin Luther King, Jr., gave the eulogy at a joint funeral for three of the four children. King attempted to comfort the mourners with the assertion that "they did not die in vain. God still has a way of wringing good out of evil." He observed: "History has proved again and again that unearned suffering is redemptive. The innocent blood of these little girls may well serve as the redemptive force that will bring new light to this dark city."

This murderous assault deeply affected me at the time, and its bitter memory is still quite vivid for millions of black Americans. It was not that the white racists would strike out against us. Being black in America had long since taught us that violence against black folk was "as normal as cherry pie," to paraphrase H. Rap Brown. It was not simply that our little children had been targeted for assassination. We remembered the children's march in Birmingham earlier that same year, in 1963, when police chief Bull Connor unleashed vicious dogs and used clubs against black children engaged in peaceful, civil disobedience. What was most striking, perhaps, was the symbolic meaning of the racists' actions. The African-American church has been, since slavery, the central social institution of the black community. It has been the spiritual heart of the black experience, through our long sojourn through this nation. To destroy the black church is to cut out the heart of the black community.

This act of brutality did not occur in a political vacuum. The Birmingham church bombing occurred when white segregationists in Congress were attempting to block the passage of the Civil Rights Act, which would desegregate public accommodations throughout the country. White Citizens Councils were trying to stop voter-registration drives among southern blacks. Alabama Governor George Wallace was calling for "segregation forever" and blocked the doors at the University of Alabama in an unsuccessful attempt to maintain white supremacy in higher education. The bombing of Sixteenth Street Baptist Church was only one aspect of a long racist assault against black people as a whole.

A generation after the Birmingham bombing, an epidemic of terrorism and violence against black faith-based institutions once again occurred. Between 1995 and 1998, an estimated 670 religious institutions were either destroyed by fire, firebombed, or desecrated. Several hundred of these houses of worship were African-American churches, with the great majority located in the South. Although subsequent investigations showed that there was no organized "national conspiracy" to destroy black churches, the growing number of firebombings prompted the Clinton administration's Justice Department to respond to this terrible assault on religious freedom. In June 1996, Clinton established the National Church Arson Task Force to coordinate local, state, and federal agencies to investigate the burnings and to prosecute those responsible for this wave of violence. For several years, thousands of volunteers of all racial backgrounds went to the South to help rebuild African-American churches. Several of my own graduate and undergraduate students at Columbia University took time off from their studies to volunteer their labor to reconstruct several black houses of prayer.

C. Eric Lincoln observed at the time of the 1990s church fires that "the bombing . . . is a malevolent, well-orchestrated conspiracy to get at the spiritual and cultural heartbeat of black America." The defenders of racial inequality understand the potential power of the black church and actively seek to either subvert it or destroy it. It is for these reasons that those who are dedicated to a democratic and more socially just society must place greater emphasis on building extensive networks and cooperation with black faith-based institutions. The black church, more than any other institution, is the central repository of national identity of the African-American people. The struggle to rebuild the Black Freedom Movement, and to reconstruct the democratic project called America, must of necessity be anchored here. Faith, when linked with a passion for human equality and social justice, can help us to imagine a world without permanent barriers or borders, moving us more closely toward the ideal of King's "beloved community."

Chapter 12

9/11

Racism in the Time of Terror

Over the past few years I have consistently preached that nonviolence demands that the means we use must be as pure as the ends we seek. I have tried to make clear that it is wrong to use immoral means to attain moral ends. But now I must affirm that it is just as wrong, or perhaps even more so, to use moral means to preserve immoral ends. . . . As T. S. Eliot has said, "The last temptation is the greatest treason: To do the right deed for the wrong reason."

—Martin Luther King, Jr.
"Letter from Birmingham Jail," April 16, 1963

I

It is still mourning time here in New York City. No matter how much time passes, the tragedy of the terrorist attack against the World Trade Center towers will remain brutally fresh and terribly vivid to millions of residents in this overcrowded metropolis. The horrific specter of nearly 3,000 human beings incinerated in less than 100 minutes, of screaming people free-falling more than 1,000 feet to their deaths, cannot be comprehended or even explained. For those of us who live and work here, or for any American who loves New York City, the grief was almost overwhelming.

As I first witnessed the smoke billowing across the city's skyline, I knew that the criminals who had obliterated the World Trade Center and part of the Pentagon were attempting to make a symbolic political statement about the links between transnational capitalism and U.S. militarism. But by initiating acts of mass murder, those who plotted and carried out these crimes totally destroyed any shred of political credibility they might have had. There can be no justification, excuse, or rationale for the deliberate use of deadly force and unprovoked violence against any civilian population. This was not essentially an act of war, but a criminal act, a crime against not only the American people, but all of humanity. I immediately felt that all of those who planned, financed, and assisted in carrying out these crimes had to be apprehended and brought to justice—but under the aegis of international law and the United Nations. I feared that unilateral military action by the United States might provoke new terrorist assaults against American cities and civilians.

In the days following the unprecedented terrorist attacks, some elements of the sectarian U.S. Left, including a few black activists, took the bizarre position that those who carried out these crimes were somehow "freedom fighters." These "leftist" critics implied that these vicious, indiscriminate actions must be interpreted within the political context of the oppression that gave rise to those actions. In short, the brutal reality of U.S. imperialism, including America's frequent military occupation of Third World countries, they said, somehow justified the use of political terrorism as a legitimate avenue for expressing resistance. It is certainly true that the American Left was correct to vigorously challenge the Bush administration's militaristic response to this crisis, because the unleashing of massive armed retaliation would have inevitably escalated the cycle of terror. Progressives, however, should have also affirmed their support for justice—first and foremost, by expressing our deepest sympathies and heartfelt solidarity with the thousands of families who lost loved ones in this tragedy. How can a Left that claims to defend workers' rights ignore the fact that in the World Trade Center attack an estimated 1,000 labor union members were killed; approximately 1,500 children lost a parent; and hundreds of undocumented immigrants may have also perished, but their families were unable to step forward to governmental authorities because of their illegal residence in the United States?

Political condemnation of the members of the Al Qaeda group should not, however, support their demonization, their description as "evildoers," as in the denunciations of President George W. Bush. We must denounce their actions as criminal while also resisting the Bush administration's and media's racist characterizations of their political beliefs as "pathological" and "insane." Bush's rhetoric only fed racist attacks against Middle-Eastern peoples and Muslims here in the United States. Perhaps one of the most effective criticisms would be to highlight the important differences between the sectarianism of Islamic fundamentalism and the rich humanism that is central to the Islamic faith. In the eloquent words of the late Muslim intellectual Eqbal Ahmad, Islamic fundamentalism promulgates "an Islamic order reduced to a penal code, stripped of its humanism, aesthetics, intellectual quests, and spiritual devotion. It manipulates the politics of resentment and fear, rather than sharing and alleviating the oppression of the masses in the Third World."

Once again, as in my earlier discussion concerning black reparations, we must make a clear distinction between "guilt" and "responsibility." The Al Qaeda terrorist group was indeed guilty of committing mass murder. But the U.S. government was, and is, largely responsible for creating the conditions for reactionary Islamic fundamentalism to flourish. During Reagan's administration, the Central Intelligence Agency (CIA) provided more than $3 billion to finance the mujahadeen's guerrilla war against the Soviet Union's military presence in Afghanistan. The CIA used Pakistan's Inter-Services Intelligence, or secret police, to equip and train tens of thousands of Islamic fundamentalists in the tactics of guerrilla warfare.

According to one 1997 study, the CIA's financing was directly responsible for an explosion of the heroin trade in both mujahadeen-controlled Afghanistan and Pakistan. By 1985, the region had become, according to researcher Alfred McCoy, "the world's top heroin producer," supplying 60 percent of U.S. demand. The number of heroin addicts in Pakistan subsequently rose "from near zero in 1979 . . . to 1.2 million by 1985." Our Pakistani "allies" operated hundreds of heroin laboratories. The Taliban regime consolidated its authoritarian rule in the mid-1990s in close partnership with Pakistan's secret police and ruling political dictatorship. And the Clinton administration was virtually silent when the draconian suppression of women's rights, public executions, and mass terror became commonplace across Afghanistan. As *The Nation* columnist Katha Pollitt observed, under the Taliban dictatorship, women could not work or attend school, had "virtually no healthcare," and could not "leave their houses without a male escort." The Bush administration's current allies in Afghanistan, the so-called Northern Alliance, are no better. As Pollitt noted, both fundamentalist groups were equally "violent, lawless, misogynistic [and] anti-democratic."

One fairly standard definition of "terrorism" is the use of extremist, extralegal violence and coercion against a civilian, or noncombatant, population. Terrorist acts may be employed to instill fear and mass intimidation or to achieve a political objective. By any criteria, Al Qaeda is a terrorist organization. Most Americans have never experienced terrorism, but we have unleashed terrorism against others throughout our history. The mass lynchings, public executions, and burnings at the stake of thousands of African Americans in the early twentieth century were homegrown, domestic acts of terrorism.

The genocide of millions of American Indians was objectively a calculated plan of mass terrorism. The dropping of the atomic bomb on Japanese cities during World War II, resulting in the fiery incineration of

several hundred thousand civilians, was certainly a crime against humanity. The U.S.-sponsored coup against the democratically elected government of Chile in 1973, culminating in the mass tortures, rapes, and executions of thousands of people, was nothing less than state-financed
terrorism. There is a common political immorality linking former
Chilean dictator Augusto Pinochet, Osama bin Laden, and former U.S.
Secretary of State Henry Kissinger: They all believed that their political
ends justified their means.

II

This global tragedy has been most profoundly felt by the 8 million residents of New York City. It is difficult, if not impossible, to explain the
deep emotional loss people felt and in many ways continue to feel here,
the emptiness of spirit, as if one's soul has been taken. The sense of personal insecurity and civic uncertainty has permeated all things for more
than a year. The sheer enormity of the crime and the media's moving
presentations of the many individuals who perished and of their grief-
stricken families created the image of a city united, both in its pain and
its determination.

Rudolph Giuliani, who for nearly eight years had played a profoundly
polarizing role as the city's aggressive, confrontational mayor, assumed
overnight the image of compassionate, heroic leadership. Journalists and
novelists tried to put into words the qualities that gave all New Yorkers
the capacity to endure. As Roger Rosenblatt observed in the *New York
Times*, "What makes the city different is a civilized wildness born of com-
pression. Deep in their hearts, New Yorkers live comfortably with a
thrilling irrationality, perhaps because the city itself is so hard to believe."

The post–September 11 image of a unified city transcending boundaries of class and color became widely and quickly popularized. Adding
to the public perception of a unified city were the media's images of the
faces of the 9/11 victims. Based on the countless photos reproduced in
the city's newspapers and on the local all-news cable channel, it appears
that the majority of those who died were either workers, people of

color, and/or recent immigrants. As labor historian Joshua Freeman observed: "The September 11 attack and the response to it have once again
made working class New Yorkers visible and appreciated. Not only were
the rescuers working class, but so were most of the victims. . . . Killed
that day, along with fire, police and emergency medical workers, were
accountants, clerks, secretaries, restaurant employees, janitors, security
guards and electricians." Writers and intellectuals celebrated both the
city's resilience and its pluralistic, multicultural character. Peruvian nov-
elist Maria Vargas Llosa, for example, praised New York City as "a fairy-
tale cosmopolis." Vargas poetically observed: "New York is of no man
and every man: of the Afghan taxi driver who barely speaks English, the
turbaned Sikh, the wok-wielding cook in Chinatown and the singer of
Neapolitan songs in the restaurants of Little Italy. It is of the Domini-
cans and Puerto Ricans who fill streets with plena, salsa and merengue;
and the Russians, Ukrainians, Kosovars, Andalusians, Greeks, Nigerians,
Irish, Pakistanis, and Ethiopians who, as soon as they arrive, are turned
into New Yorkers by the absorbent magic of the city."

Yet Vargas's eloquent description of the "city that never sleeps" is an
illusion. Despite the newfound civic hype, the harsh reality is that this remains a bitterly divided city. American apartheid is strikingly and visu-
ally apparent in almost every neighborhood of New York City, and the
events of September 11 have only made the racial and class stratification
worse. According to the New York–based journal *City Limits*, the 2000
Census indicates that "in New York City, the ostensible capital of diversity, the segregation of Asians, Latinos and black residents from white
households is at virtually the same level today as it was in 1960."

Out of 331 metropolitan areas surveyed in the United States, New
York City now ranks first in both Asian-white segregation and Latino-
white segregation. New York's black-white residential segregation also
worsened during the Giuliani years, moving from seventh overall in the
1990 Census to third place, just below Detroit and Milwaukee. New York
City's Latino population doubled in the 1990s, yet the vast majority of
new immigrants were concentrated in Spanish-speaking enclaves like
Washington Heights and Sunset Park. As the white population became a
minority group within a city that was predominantly defined by people

of color, many middle- and upper-class whites retreated from any meaningful, direct interaction with segregated black communities. As *City
Limits* observed, New York's children, like other children throughout the
country, increasingly live their lives "in segregated neighborhoods,
schools, clubs, sports teams and friendship networks."

The city's hypersegregated neighborhoods not only perpetuate dis-
trust and social isolation behind color-coded barriers, but also obscure
from public attention other major social problems reflected in the statistics of poverty and unemployment. In the immediate aftermath of 9/11,
an estimated 80,000 people in the city's metropolitan area lost their jobs.
About 60 percent of the jobs lost, however, paid under $23,000 per year.
The largest single group of workers who became unemployed after September 11 were waiters and waitresses, numbering more than 4,200. The
Fiscal Policy Institute of New York calculated that the average hourly
salary of these waiters and waitresses was $7.08. The second occupation
group most devastated by the World Trade Center's collapse comprised
nearly 3,400 cleaning and maintenance workers who took home an average of $14.90 per hour. The next five occupations most affected were re-
tail sales clerks (2,843 unemployed, averaging $9.15 per hour), food prepa-
ration workers (2,284 unemployed, averaging $8.90 per hour), cashiers
(2,282 unemployed, averaging $7.36 per hour), housekeeping workers
(1,840 unemployed, averaging $13.42 per hour), and food preparation and
fast-food servers (1,718 unemployed, averaging $7.09 per hour).

Most of these individuals were employed at hotels, bars, restaurants,
and private transportation companies. Only 4 percent were employed at
Wall Street brokerage firms. Over four-fifths of the affected workers
probably could not afford to live in Manhattan. About half lived in
Brooklyn and Queens, with another 12 percent residing in the Bronx.
Many of the jobs destroyed in Manhattan, in fact, were in Chinatown.
The Fiscal Policy Institute's survey found that about 20 of that neighborhood's 200 sewing sweatshops went under financially. More than 1,000
members of Unite, the city garment workers union, had been fired by
early November.

The vast majority of these jobless low-income workers did not benefit from the hundreds of millions of dollars donated to charities for the

World Trade Center's victims. Only one-third of the jobless workers were covered by unemployment insurance, partially because in most instances, self-employed and part-time workers cannot qualify for it. As of the end of 2001, a second federal aid program, Disaster Unemployment Assistance, had extended benefits to only 2,350 jobless workers. As autumn turned into winter, New York's mostly volunteer-staffed food pantries and soup kitchens were reaching the limits of their capacity. As of November 2001, Food for Survival was supplying food for 275,000 meals a day, and City Harvest was providing another 20,000 meals—yet Joel Berg, director of the New York City Coalition Against Hunger, estimated that 30 percent of all pantries would soon have to "turn people away because they ran out of food."

Federal bureaucratic disorganization and poor planning compounded the problems of tens of thousands of families in New York City affected by 9/11. For example, the Federal Emergency Management Agency (FEMA) was charged by Congress to provide resources to needy families to cover the costs of rent or mortgages. In the first nine months of FEMA's efforts in New York City, an estimated 79,000 people contacted the agency for assistance. Less than one half, 33,000 people, were judged to be potentially eligible for rent or mortgage assistance. Of that number, only 3,585 families received FEMA money between September 2001 and June 2002, amounting to $20.6 million, and with an average monthly payment of $1,140. Most of FEMA's case evaluators were temporary workers hired from other states who had no knowledge of the city's neighborhoods or workforce. FEMA's applications were only available in English for nine months. Not surprisingly, the rejection rate for applicants was a staggeringly high 70 percent, far higher than the rejection rates by FEMA at other disaster areas.

Politically, the net effect of 9/11 in New York City was tremendous fragmentation within the city's liberal political establishment. Throughout Giuliani's controversial administration, literally hundreds of civil-rights, labor, women's, and community-based organizations have marched, picketed, and protested. Everyone assumed that the city's public advocate, Mark Green, a well-known Upper West Side liberal, would be elected the new mayor with little difficulty. But the severe impact of

9/11 diverted the attention of community-oriented coalitions and progressive groups toward addressing more immediate political issues. Some organizations focused attention on efforts to raise public awareness about the dangers involved in the U.S. war effort in Afghanistan; others emphasized the threat to American civil liberties and constitutional rights represented by new federal antiterrorism legislation. Civil-rights organizations highlighted problems of anti-Muslim hate crimes and ethnic profiling by law-enforcement officers. Grassroots activists who worked primarily on the issues of low-income people found themselves soon overwhelmed by the crises of widespread joblessness and food shortages. Individual donors and some foundations redirected funds largely to relief efforts and away from community-oriented and antiracist organizing. Very few groups dedicated to progressive change had the infrastructural capacity to engage in emergency activities while at the same time maintaining their commitments to long-term objectives.

The result, in many ways, was a sense of diffused energies, the performance of good and humanitarian activities lacking the broad, strategic vision essential for restructuring the city's power structure. At the general election in November, less than 30 percent of the city's registered voters bothered to go to the polls. In a city where registered Democrats outnumber Republicans by a margin of five to one, a novice candidate, Republican billionaire Michael Bloomberg, narrowly defeated the veteran Democratic politician Mark Green. Power remained firmly in the hands of those who owned the city, while its black and brown population slid farther into economic recession and political marginalization.

III

Did "everything fundamentally change" in the aftermath of the 9/11 attacks? Yes, there was an upsurge of public patriotism and national chauvinism, an understandable desire to "avenge" the innocent victims of the Al Qaeda network's terrorism. Perhaps these terrible events marking the real "beginning" of the twenty-first century are, however, not a radical departure into some new, uncharted political territory, but rather the culmination of deeper political and economic forces set into motion decades before.

The core ideology of "Reaganism"—free markets, unregulated corporations, the vast buildup of nuclear and conventional weapons, aggressive militarism abroad, the suppression of civil liberties and civil rights at home, and demagogical campaigns against both "terrorism" and Soviet communism—has become central to the Bush administration's current policy initiatives today. Former President Ronald Reagan attempted to establish a national security state where the legitimate functions of government were narrowly restricted to matters of national defense, public safety, and tax subsidies to the wealthy. Reagan pursued a policy of what many economists have termed "military Keynesianism," the deficit spending of hundreds of billions of dollars on military hardware and speculative weapons schemes such as "Star Wars."

This massive deficit federal spending was largely responsible for the U.S. economic expansion of the 1980s. Simultaneously, the Soviet Union was pressured into an expensive arms race that it could not afford. The fall of Soviet communism transformed the global political economy into a unipolar world characterized by U.S. hegemony, both economically and militarily. The result was a deeply authoritarian version of American state power, with increasing restrictions on democratic rights of all kinds, from the orchestrated dismantling of trade unions to the mass incarceration of racialized minorities and the poor. By the end of the 1990s, 2 million Americans were behind bars and over 4 million former prisoners had lost the right to vote, for life. "Welfare as we know it," in the words of former President Clinton, was radically restructured, with hundreds of thousands of women householders and their children pushed down into poverty.

Behind much of this vicious conservative offensive was the ugly politics of race. The political assault against affirmative action and minority economic set-asides was transformed by the Right into a moral crusade against "racial preferences" and "reverse discrimination." Black and Latino young people across the country were routinely "racially profiled" by law-enforcement officers. DWB, "Driving While Black," became a familiar euphemism for such police practices. As the liberal welfare state of the 1960s mutated into the prison industrial complex of the 1990s, the white public was given the unambiguous message that the goal of racial justice had to be sacrificed for the general security and public safety of all. It was, in short, a permanent war against the black, the brown, and the poor.

The fall of communism transformed a bipolar political conflict into a unipolar, hegemonic New World Order, as the first President Bush termed it. The chief institutions for regulating the flow of capital investment and labor across international boundaries were no longer governments. The International Monetary Fund, the World Trade Organization, and transnational treaties such as the North American Free Trade Agreement (NAFTA) took on these roles, exercising significantly greater influence over the lives of workers in most countries than their own governments. By the year 2000, 51 of the world's 100 wealthiest and largest economies were actually corporations, and only 49 were countries. The political philosophy of globalization, termed "neoliberalism," emphasized privatizing government services and programs, eliminating unions, and applying the aggressive rules of capitalist markets to public institutions such as schools, hospitals, and even postal services. The social contract between U.S. citizens and the liberal democratic state was being redefined to exclude the concepts of social welfare and social responsibility to the truly disadvantaged.

A new, more openly authoritarian philosophy of governance was required to explain to citizens why their long-standing democratic freedoms were being taken away from them. A leading apologist for neo-authoritarian politics was former New York mayor Rudolph Giuliani. In 1994, soon after his initial election as mayor, Giuliani declared in a speech: "Freedom is about authority. Freedom is about the willingness of every single human being to cede to lawful authority a great deal of indiscretion about what you do and how you do it." As we all know, the Giuliani administration won national praise for reducing New York City's murder rate from 2,000 to 650 a year. The rate of other violent crimes also plummeted. But the social cost to New York's black, brown, and poor communities was far more destructive than anything they had known previously. The American Civil Liberties Union has estimated that between 50,000 and 100,000 New Yorkers were subjected annually to "stop-and-frisk" harassment by the police under Giuliani. The city's notorious Street Crimes Unit terrorized black and Latino neighborhoods.

Many white liberals in New York City passively capitulated to this new state authoritarianism. It is even more chilling that in the wake of the September 11 attacks, *New York Times* journalist Clyde Haberman immediately drew connections between "the emotional rubble of the World Trade Center nightmare" and Amadou Diallo, the unarmed West African immigrant gunned down in 1999 by forty-one shots fired by four Street Crimes Unit police officers. "It is quite possible that America will have to decide, and fairly soon, how much license it wants to give law enforcement agencies to stop ordinary people at airports and border crossings, to question them at length about where they have been, where they are heading, and what they intend to do once they get where they're going," Haberman predicted. "It would probably surprise no one if ethnic profiling enters the equation, to some degree." Haberman reluctantly acknowledged that Giuliani may be "at heart an authoritarian." But he added that, "as a wounded New York mourns its unburied dead, and turns to its mayor for solace," public concerns about civil-rights and civil-liberties violations would recede. Haberman seemed to be implying that the rights of individuals like Amadou Diallo are less important than the personal safety of white Americans.

As the national media enthusiastically picked up the Bush administration's mantra about the "War on Terrorism," a series of repressive federal and state laws were swiftly passed. New York State's legislature, in the span of one week, created a new crime—"terrorism"—with a maximum penalty of life in prison. Anyone convicted of giving more than $1,000 to any organization defined by state authorities as "terrorist" would face up to fifteen years in a state prison. When one reflects that, not too many years ago, the United States considered the African National Congress a "terrorist organization," it becomes apparent that the danger of being severely penalized for supporting any Third World social-justice movement has now become very real. This policy suppresses legitimate activities by U.S. citizens.

At all levels of government, any expression of restraint or caution about the dangerous erosion of our civil liberties is equated with treason. The antiterrorism bills in the New York State Assembly were passed, with no debate, by a margin of 135 to 5. The U.S. Senate, on October 12, 2001, passed the Bush administration's antiterrorism legislation by 96 to 1. The militarism and political intolerance displayed in the Bush administration's response to the September 11 attacks created a natural breeding ground for bigotry and racial harassment. For the Reverend Jerry Falwell, the recent tragedy was God's condemnation of a secularist, atheistic America. He attributed the attacks to "the pagans and the abortionists and the feminists and the lesbians" and to "the ACLU [and] People for the American Way." After a firestorm of criticisms, Falwell was forced to apologize. Less well-publicized were the hate-filled commentaries of journalist Ann Coulter, who declared: "We should invade their countries, kill their leaders, and convert them to Christianity." Similar voices of racist intolerance are also being heard in Europe. For example, Italian Prime Minister Silvio Berlusconi stated that "Western civilization" was clearly "superior to Islamic culture." Berlusconi warmly praised "imperialism," predicting that "the West will continue to conquer peoples, just as it has Communism." Falwell, Berlusconi, and others illustrate the direct linkage between racism and war, between militarism and political reaction.

Even on college campuses, there have been numerous instances of the suppression of free speech and democratic dissent. When City University of New York faculty held an academic panel that presented a variety of viewpoints about the historical and political issues leading up to the terrorist attacks, the university's chief administrator publicly denounced some of the participants. "Let there be no doubt whatsoever," warned CUNY Chancellor Matthew Goldstein, "I have no sympathy for the voices of those who make lame excuses for the attacks on the World Trade Center and the Pentagon based on ideological or historical circumstances." Conservative trustees of CUNY sought to censure or even fire the faculty involved. According to the *Chronicle of Higher Education*, hundreds of Middle-Eastern college students were forced to return home from the United States as a result of widespread ethnic and religious harassment. At UCLA, Library Assistant Jonnie Hargis was suspended without pay from his job when he sent an e-mail on the university's computers that criticized U.S. support for Israel. When University of South Florida professor Sami Al-Arian appeared on television talking about his relationships to two suspected terrorists, he was placed on indefinite paid leave and ordered to leave the campus "for his [own] safety," university officials later explained. The First Amendment right of free speech, the constitutional right of any citizen to criticize policies of our government, is now at risk.

Perhaps the most dangerous element of the Bush administration's current campaign against democratic rights has been the deliberate manipulation of mass public hysteria. Millions of Americans who witnessed the destruction of the World Trade Center are still experiencing Post-Traumatic Stress Disorder anxiety and depression. According to the *Wall Street Journal,* during the last two weeks of September, pharmacies filled 1.9 million new prescriptions for Zoloft, Prozac, and other antidepressants, a 16 percent increase over the same period in 2000. Prescriptions for sleeping pills and short-term anxiety drugs such as Xanax and Valium also rose 7 percent. The American public has been bombarded daily by a series of media-orchestrated threats focusing on everything from the potential of crop-dusting airplanes being used for bioterrorism, to anthrax-contaminated packages delivered through the U.S. postal service. People are constantly warned to carefully watch their mail, their neighbors, and one another. Intense levels of police security at sports stadiums and armed National Guard troops at airports have begun to be accepted as "necessary" for the welfare of society.

By the beginning of 2002, we began to witness "dissident profiling": the proliferation of electronic surveillance, roving wiretapping and harassment at the workplace, the infiltration and disruption of antiwar groups, and the stigmatization of any critics of U.S. militarism as disloyal and subversive. As historian Eric Foner has noted, "Let us recall the F.B.I.'s persistent harassment of individuals like Martin Luther King, Jr., and its efforts to disrupt the civil rights and anti-war movements, and the C.I.A.'s history of cooperation with some of the world's most egregious violators of human rights. The principle that no group of Americans should be stigmatized as disloyal or criminal because of race or national origin is too recent and too fragile an achievement to be abandoned now." I believe that one cannot preserve democracy by restricting and eliminating the democratic rights of any group or individual. To publicly oppose a government's policies that one believes to be morally and politically wrong, as Dr. Martin Luther King, Jr., asserted, is to express the strongest belief in the principles of democracy.

Those of us who oppose our government's course of action must clearly explain to the American people that the missile strikes and indiscriminate carpet bombings we unleashed against Afghanistan's peasants did *not* make us safer. The policies of the Bush administration actually placed our lives in greater danger, because the use of government-sponsored terror will not halt brutal retaliations by the terrorists. The national-security state apparatus we are constructing today is being designed primarily to suppress domestic dissent and racially profiled minorities, rather than to halt foreign-born terrorists at our borders. In 2000 alone, there were 489 million persons who passed through our border inspection systems. More than 120 million cars are driven across U.S. borders every year, and it is impossible to thoroughly check even a small fraction of them. Restricting civil liberties, hiring thousands more police and security guards, and incarcerating more than 1,000 Muslims and individuals of Arab descent without due process only foster the false illusion of security. The "War on Terrorism" is being used as an excuse to eliminate civil liberties and democratic rights here at home.

This "war at home" also has a profoundly racial dimension. Because U.S. democracy was constructed on institutional racism, the government has always found it difficult to present a clear, democratic argument to advance its interests in the pursuit of warfare. Instead, it relies on and manipulates the latent racism and xenophobia at all levels of society. Usually, racism is used to target external enemies, such as "Japs" during World War II. But in general, whenever the United States mobilizes militarily and goes to war, white racism goes with it hand in hand.

The extreme degree of racial segregation in New York City provides part of the explanation for the rash of hate crimes committed here after September 11. For example, in the days immediately following the attack, according to the Asian American Legal Defense and Education Fund, a Sikh man in Richmond Hill, Queens, "was assaulted with a baseball bat and shot at with a BB gun," and a "Huntington, Long Island, man tried to run down an Asian woman with his car." Arab and Muslim street vendors and store owners throughout the city experienced verbal and physical harassment and were threatened with economic boycotts. Such incidents, of course, were not confined to New York City. The New York–based South Asian American Leaders of Tomorrow (SAALT) issued a report based on more than 400 media sources documenting 645 separate incidents of hate-inspired violence against Arabs, Asians, and Muslims in the United States during the first week after September 11. These included 3 murders, 49 assaults, and 92 incidents of arson and property damage.

Those who are coded or classified by appearance, dress, language, or name, as those of Muslim or of Arab background are, have been rudely escorted off airplanes and Amtrak trains, and many have been detained without formal charges or access to attorneys. Anecdotal evidence suggests that a significant number, perhaps even the majority, of the people of color singled out for harassment as potential "terrorists" have not been Muslims or Arabs at all. In Seattle and other West Coast cities, dozens of Hawaiians, Central Americans, South Asians, and even American Indians have been subjected to verbal insults and harassment because they "appear" to be vaguely "non-American." On the East Coast, many Sikhs and Hindus have been victimized, along with non-English-speaking and non-European undocumented immigrants. Most white middle-class Americans in the so-called heartland of the country, the Midwestern states, lack both the cultural capacity and geopolitical awareness to make fine distinctions between "Muslims" and racialized others who happen to be non-Muslims.

The great exceptions to this phenomenon of new racialization in the time of terror, curiously, were African Americans. People of African descent, having lived on the American continent since 1619, occupy a unique position in the construction of white American identity and national consciousness. State power was deliberately constructed to exclude black participation; but black labor power was absolutely essential in the economic development of the nation. Black culture, moreover, contributed the most creative and original elements defining American national culture and various forms of representation.

Thus, the African American is unquestionably a recognized member of the American national household—but has never been a member of the American family. We are the Other that everybody knows. Yet there is a necessary kind of dialectical connection here, linking the false superiority of whiteness as a political and social category in the United States to the continued and "normal" subordination of blackness. Without "blacks," whiteness ceases to exist as we know it. White supremacy has difficulty imagining a world without black people, but has no reservations about the indiscriminate mass bombing of Afghan peasants, or about supporting an embargo against Iraq, which is responsible for the deaths of hundreds of thousands of Muslim children, according to international human-rights observers.

The great sociologist Oliver C. Cox understood this contradiction, the subtle distinctions between white racism, social intolerance, and xenophobia. As Cox put it: "The dominant group is intolerant of those whom it can define as anti-social, while it holds race prejudice against those whom it can define as subsocial. In other words, the dominant group or ruling class does not like the Jew at all, but it likes the Negro in his place." In a time of political terror, the "terrorist" becomes the most dangerous Other and is recognized by certain "subhuman" qualities and vague characteristics—language, strange religious rituals, unusual clothing, and so forth. The "terrorist Other" thus is presented to the white public as an uncivilized savage who has richly merited our hatred and must be destroyed to assure our safety and the preservation of the American Way of Life.

The fundamental contradiction that has always confronted black Americans during these periods of racist wars is whether or not to take advantage of this situation in order to advance up the racial and political hierarchy. I began noticing the large number of American flags, for example, displayed on the fronts of black homes and businesses. On New York City subways immediately following the attacks, I saw more blacks and Latinos wearing red, white, and blue buttons, caps, and other patriotic paraphernalia than at any other time in my memory.

Even before the devastating economic impact of 9/11, black Americans and Latinos were experiencing an economic downturn coinciding with the inauguration of the Bush administration. Between September 2000 and June 2001, African-American unemployment nationwide had increased from 7.2 percent to 8.4 percent. Latino jobless rates during the same period also rose, from 5 percent to 6.6 percent. Thousands of minority and low-income heads of household who owned homes through the Federal Housing Administration's government-insured program became delinquent in their mortgage payments. After the terrorist attacks, black jobless rates soared: 9.7 percent as of October 2002 and 10.1 percent by November 2002. Urban job-counseling centers experienced significant increases in African Americans searching for employment. In the Urban League's Job Centers in the Los Angeles area, there was a 25 percent jump in clients in 2001 "attributed mainly to Sept. 11–related job loss." A number of black-owned businesses, both in New York City and nationally, were seriously affected by the terrorist attacks. Most prominent on this list were Rice Financial Products, *Black Enterprise*'s tenth-ranked investment bank, with total issues of $10 billion, which was located on the fifty-second floor of the World Trade Center's north tower; and another black investment bank, M. R. Beal and Company, ranked fourth in *Black Enterprise*, with $46.5 billion in total issues, located several blocks from the towers.

Like most Americans, African Americans were generally outraged by the terrorist attacks, and during this moment of national crisis they gave unprecedented levels of support for the Bush administration. The most widely publicized post-9/11 poll, conducted by the Gallup organization, found that 70 percent of blacks "approved of the way Mr. Bush was handling his job." Probably more accurate was the survey of the Pew Research Center, which found that 49 percent of African Americans generally supported the president, up from 32 percent prior to the attacks.

But the majority of blacks were also troubled by the exuberant hyper-patriotism of whites and the possible linkages between racism, national chauvinism, and the suppression of democratic rights. Bishop Cecil Bishop, a leader of the Congress of National Black Churches, reminded the press that "African-American people themselves have been terrorized . . . [by] the killings, lynchings, hangings years back," as well as the more recent examples, such as the killing of Amadou Diallo by New York policemen. The Reverend James A. Forbes, Jr., pastor of New York's Riverside Church, called for blacks to espouse a critical "prophetic patriotism. . . . You will hold America to the values of freedom, justice, compassion, equality, respect for all, patience and care for the needy, a world where everyone counts." National Urban League director Hugh Price asserted that "black America's mission, as it has always been, is to fight against the forces of hatred and injustice." Price condemned the "morally repugnant notion that the need for increased security justifies racial profiling. . . . There is no excuse for singling out and stopping some Americans for no reason other than the color of their skin or their ethnic background or the way they dress."

The African Americans who were made to feel most vulnerable in the aftermath of the attacks were Muslims. In the early 1970s, there were only about half a million adherents to Islam in the United States, including roughly 100,000 members of the Nation of Islam. By September 2001, the American Muslim community numbered nearly 7 million, which is larger than the U.S. Jewish population. About one-third of all Muslims, more than 2 million, are African Americans. The most influential Muslim leader, Imam W. Deen Muhammad, is the son of the NOI's late patriarch, Elijah Muhammad. As the head of the orthodox Muslim American Society, W. Deen Muhammad has been described as "fiercely patriotic." For years, the Muslim American Society's national newspaper, the *Muslim Journal*, has featured on its cover page an American flag at the upper left corner.

Virtually all prominent Muslim religious leaders and civic representatives of the Arab-American community unconditionally condemned the attacks. Even Farrakhan denounced the criminals behind the assault as

"depraved wild beasts," while at the same time urging the U.S. government to reevaluate its Middle East policies. Muslims overwhelmingly opposed U.S. military intervention in Afghanistan and favored some type of
United Nations resolution to the crisis. They justly feared that the non-
Muslim, white majority would aim its desire for retaliation indiscrimi-
nately, classifying all Muslims, recent immigrants and native-born citizens alike, as potential terrorists.

By the spring of 2002, many prominent African-American leaders and
organizations had voiced criticisms of Bush's "War on Terrorism" and
expressed concerns about the permanent deployment of U.S. troops in
Afghanistan. Numbers of African-American and Latino activists participated in antiwar demonstrations and teach-ins, many led by working-
class and poor people of color, that were largely ignored or unreported
in the media. In San Francisco, for example, the People Organizing to
Win Employment Rights (POWER) led a May Day 2002 rally and march
calling for "Land, Work, and Peace." The broad range of participating
organizations included the Chinese Progressive Association, the Homeless Pre-Natal Program, Hogares Sin Barreras (Housing Not Borders),
and Mujeres Unidas y Activas (United and Active Women). On April 20,
2002, an estimated 80,000 people attended a Washington, D.C. protest
demonstration against the Bush administration's "Permanent War on
Terrorism." Significantly, at least one-third of those participating in the
demonstration were Arab Americans and/or Muslims.

But the national media's attention focused exclusively on stories
about the "new American patriotism," and people of color were frequently featured center stage. Blacks were reminded constantly that
Colin Powell, after all, is President Bush's secretary of state, and Condoleezza Rice is his national security adviser. I also suspect that the new
xenophobia was being viewed by a significant sector of African Americans as not entirely a bad thing, if jobs that had previously gone to
non-English-speaking immigrants would now go to blacks. There is considerable hostility in cities such as Detroit and Houston between impoverished and working-class black urban neighborhoods and Arab shop-
keepers. Blacks in 2000 voted overwhelmingly for the Gore-Lieberman
ticket, while at least 40 percent of Arab Americans supported Bush-

Cheney, based in part on their political and religious hostility toward Lieberman.

Part of the frustration the African-American community feels is rooted in our complicated love-hate relationship with our own country. That U.S. democracy was crudely constructed on the mountain of black bodies destroyed by centuries of enslavement, segregation, and exploitation is abundantly clear to us. Yet there is also that knowledge, gleaned from our centuries-old struggle for freedom, that the finest ideals of American democracy are best represented by our own examples of sacrifice. This was undoubtedly behind W.E.B. Du Bois's controversial editorial, "Close Ranks," which endorsed African-American participation in the U.S. war effort during World War I. It is important to remember, however, that immediately after World War I ended, the "Red Summer" of 1919, during which hundreds of African Americans were lynched, beaten, and even burned at the stake, erupted. Most African Americans understood, however, that we cannot overturn the structural racism against us if we accommodate or compromise with war and racism against others.

IV

The bombing campaign against the people of Afghanistan may be described in future history books as "The United States Against the Third World." The launching of high-tech military strikes against a feudal peasant society did little to suppress global terrorism and only eroded American credibility in Muslim nations around the world. The question, repeatedly asked in the U.S. press in the days after 9/11, "Why do they hate us?" can only be answered from the vantage point of the Third World's widespread poverty, hunger, and economic exploitation.

The U.S. government cannot engage in effective multilateral actions to suppress terrorism because its behavior illustrates its thinly veiled contempt for international cooperation. The United States owed $582 million in back dues to the United Nations, and it paid up only when the 9/11 attacks jeopardized its national security. Republican conservatives demanded that the United States be exempt from the jurisdiction of an International Criminal Court, a permanent tribunal established at The Hague, Netherlands. For the 2001 United Nations–sponsored World Conference Against Racism in South Africa, the U.S. government authorized the allocation of a paltry $250,000, compared to more than $10 million provided to conference organizers by the Ford Foundation. For three decades, the United States refused to ratify the 1965 United Nations Convention on the Elimination of Racism. Is it any wonder that much of the Third World questions our motives? The carpet bombing of the Taliban seems to Third World observers to have less to do with the suppression of terrorism than with securing future petroleum-production rights in Central Asia.

The U.S. media and opinion makers repeatedly went out of their way to twist facts and to distort the political realities of the Middle East by insisting that the Osama bin Laden group's murderous assaults had nothing to do with Israel's policies toward the Palestinians. Nobody else in the world, with the possible exception of the Israelis, really believes that. Even Britain, Bush's staunchest ally, cited Israel's intransigence toward negotiations and its human-rights violations as having contributed to the environment for Arab terrorist retaliation. In late September 2001, during his visit to Jerusalem, British Foreign Secretary Jack Straw stated that frustration over the Israeli-Palestinian conflict might create an excuse for terrorism. Straw explained: "There is never any excuse for terrorism. At the same time, there is an obvious need to understand the environment in which terrorism breeds." Millions of moderate and progressive Muslims who sincerely denounced terrorism were nevertheless frustrated by the extensive clientage relationship the United States has with Israel, financed by more than $3 billion in annual subsidies. They want to know why the United States has allowed the Israelis to relocate more than 200,000 Jewish settlers—half of them after the signing of the 1993 peace agreement—to occupied Palestine.

How did terrorist Osama bin Laden gain loyal followers transnationally, from northern Nigeria to Indonesia? Perhaps it has something to do with America's massive presence—in fact, its military-industrial occupation—of Saudi Arabia. In the past two decades, U.S. construction companies and arms suppliers have made over $50 billion in Saudi Arabia. As of late 2001, more than 30,000 U.S. citizens were employed by Saudi corporations or by joint Saudi-U.S. corporate partnerships. ExxonMobil, the world's largest corporation, signed a 2001 agreement with the Saudi government to develop gas projects worth between $20 billion and $26 billion. Can Americans who are not orthodox Muslims truly appreciate how spiritually offensive the presence of 5,000 U.S. troops in Saudi Arabia is for them?

There is a clear link between 9/11 and the shameful political maneuvering committed by the United States at the United Nations World Conference Against Racism held in Durban, South Africa, only days before the terrorist attacks. There, the U.S. government opposed the definition of slavery as "a crime against humanity." It refused to acknowledge the historic and contemporary effects of colonialism and racial segregation on the underdevelopment and oppression of the non-European world. The majority of dark humanity is saying to the United States that racism and militarism are not the solutions to the world's major problems.

If the fundamental challenge of U.S. democracy in the twenty-first century is that of "structural racism," then at an international level, the central problem of the twenty-first century is the growth of "global apartheid." The wealth and resources of all humanity are unequally divided, and warfare and systemic forms of violence are employed to preserve that gross inequality. According to a United Nations Human Development Report in 1998, the world's 225 wealthiest individuals had a combined net wealth of $1 trillion, which was equal to the combined income of the planet's most impoverished 2.5 billion people. One-half of the people currently living on earth, slightly more than 3 billion individuals, exist on the equivalent of $2 or less per day. About 1.3 billion people survive on less than $1 each day. The overwhelming majority of those 3 billion people live in Africa, Asia, and Latin America. For them, globalization is nothing less than a new phase of racialization on a global scale.

Terrorism is frequently the tool of the weak. A global superpower that possesses overwhelming material resources and armaments can afford the luxury of buying off its Third World opponents, or overthrowing unfriendly governments, through covert action and the collusion of local elites. A classical mixture of fraud and force is preferable because it maintains the facade of democratic procedures and processes. But for extremist fundamentalists in the Third World, terror is a cheap, low-tech alternative for striking back. The American people must understand what the black and brown world already knows: The threat of terrorism will not end until a new global dialogue is established that constructively works toward the elimination of the routine violence of poverty, the violence of disease, the violence of hunger. Global apartheid is essentially only a form of violence.

To stop the extraordinary violence of terrorism, we must stop the daily violence of class inequality and poverty. To engage in the struggle for justice—to find new paths toward reconciliation across the boundaries of religion, culture, and color—is the only way to protect our cities, our country, and ourselves from the terrible violence of terrorism. Without justice, there can be no peace.

A year after 9/11, Afghanistan remained occupied territory, as will be the case into the foreseeable future. The Western donor nations pledged $4.5 billion in economic aid to the devastated nation, but only one-third of the promised aid had been delivered after one year. More than half the country's population of 27 million had directly benefited from humanitarian aid such as food shipments or housing resettlement. Hundreds of local schools, hospitals, and health clinics had been rebuilt or newly constructed. Yet an unknown number of Afghani citizens, perhaps thousands, were killed or maimed by the "friendly fire" of U.S. forces. More than 1.5 million refugees had reentered the country from Pakistan in 2002, most of whom were living in intolerable conditions.

What I have also learned from the experience of being near Ground Zero on 9/11 is the simple truth that sometimes, even for intensely political people, "politics" is not enough. No political ideology, no crusade, no belief in a virtuous cause, can justify the moral bankruptcy of terror. Yet, because of the military actions of our own government, any claims to moral superiority have now disintegrated, in the minds of much of the black and brown world. The American bombings have indeed destroyed the ruthless Taliban regime, but in the process the lives of innocent civilians were also lost. Martin Luther King, Jr., possibly, would have admonished us for using "moral means to preserve immoral ends." We were, and are, politically and morally right to oppose the violence of terrorism. But by employing the tools of violence and repression, we blur the brutal boundaries between the killers and the victims. We must share history's terrible judgment of common responsibility, making sinners of us all. As T. S. Eliot observed seven decades ago:

Because these wings are no longer wings to fly
But merely vans to beat the air
The air which is now thoroughly small and dry
Smaller and dryer than the will
Teach us to care and not to care
Teach us to sit still.
Pray for us sinners now and at the hour of our death
Pray for us now and at the hour of our death.
                         —T. S. Eliot, "Ash Wednesday," 1930

Chapter 13

Epilogue

The Souls of White Folk

*In 1960, when students all over the South started sitting-in at lunch counters, . . .
they were really standing up for the best in the American dream, and taking the
whole nation back to those great wells of democracy which were dug deep by the
founding fathers in the Declaration of Independence and the Constitution. . . .
We've got some difficult days ahead. But it really doesn't matter with me now, because I've been to the mountaintop.*

                                        —Martin Luther King, April 3, 1968

At the conclusion of his "Letter from Birmingham Jail," Martin Luther King, Jr., expressed the "hope that the dark clouds of racial prejudice will soon pass away and the deep fog of misunderstanding will be lifted from our fear-drenched communities." Each element of this final passage is important toward an analysis of the problem of American white identity.

Most white Americans still live their entire lives in "a deep fog of misunderstanding" about the character, construction, and reproduction of white racism as a social system. For many, there are permanent "clouds of racial prejudice" that have become a normal part of everyday life. Racial hierarchies are seen as "natural" and are unquestioned; incidents of police brutality and "racial profiling" are "unfortunate" but "probably unavoidable"; school busing to promote racial integration is harmful to "neighborhood schools" and "quality education"; affirmative-action programs are "racial quotas" that give "special preferences" to unqualified applicants for jobs and college admissions; economic set-aside programs unfairly favor minority-owned businesses and deny government contracts to more competitive, cost-effective firms; and "no blacks or Hispanics" regularly attend our church because for some strange reason, "none live in our neighborhood." One of the luxuries of being white in a racist society is that you never have to talk about *being white*. When something is viewed as normal, then there's nothing unusual about it, so there's nothing to talk about.

The media does its best to keep white Americans in a permanent fog by refusing to call the American dilemma by its real name: *racism*. Media critic William E. Alberts recently observed that during former President Clinton's so-called "Race Initiative," the major newspapers deliberately employed code words in their editorials, headlines, and news stories that would "make the *ism* disappear from 'race.'" For example, the *Washington Post* repeatedly used phrases such as "the country's racial picture," "the overall racial climate," "relations between Americans of different races and ethnic backgrounds," "racial matters," "the race theme," "an incendiary topic," and (my favorite) "this most delicate and politically dangerous of subjects." In the *New York Times,* the aversion to the word "racism" was just as strong. The *Times* frequently used phrases such as "the state of race relations," "the racial front," "the racial climate," and "black-white relations." Imbedded in the news coverage of Clinton's Race Initiative was an implied "solution" to the nation's racial problems, which was the challenge "to change the hearts and minds" of Americans about race. This was expressed in a nearly endless series of platitudes: "toward racial harmony"; "to prod Americans to talk to one another and get beyond skin color and ethnicity"; "inspiring Americans to appreciate its racial diversity"; fostering "racial healing"; "color-blindness"; and learning "how the races can get along on a day-to-day basis." Nearly all of the media coverage presumed that racial categories are fixed and that racial differences could be negotiated by changing attitudes rather than by reallocating resources and power.

The main pillars of structural racism throughout American history have been prejudice, power, and privilege. By "prejudice," I mean a deep and unquestioned belief in the natural superiority of white people over nonwhites. In his 1920 essay "The Souls of White Folk," W.E.B. Du Bois described white supremacy as the belief "that every great soul the world ever saw was a white man's soul; that every great deed the world ever did was a white man's deed; that every great dream the world ever sang was a white man's dream." A belief in the purity of whiteness demands—and is dependent on—the degradation of blackness. As Du Bois put it: "Darker peoples are dark in mind as well as in body; of dark, uncertain, and imperfect descent; of frailer, cheaper stuff; . . . they have no feelings, aspirations, and loves. . . . They are not simply dark white men. They are not 'men' in the sense that Europeans are men."

Du Bois's language may seem, by twenty-first-century standards, too extreme and anachronistic; legal racial discrimination disappeared forty years ago in the United States, and even apartheid has been dismantled in South Africa. Yet the essence of what Du Bois wrote in 1920 still in many respects holds true today. A major reason that millions of white Americans remain detached from the terrible reality of 1 million black people who are currently incarcerated in this nation's prisons is the unspoken assumption that they belong there. The lower life expectancies, high infant-mortality rates, higher rates for hypertension, diabetes, and most other diseases, are largely caused, it is assumed, by poor health habits and a "culture of poverty." The fact that black unemployment rates remain twice as high as those of whites in good times as well as bad is attributed to the absence of a work ethic and to welfare dependency. If we are less than human, then our pain is not the equal of white pain; our hunger is not as severe; our imprisonment is not as cruel; our denial of voting rights not a violation of democratic procedures. As Du Bois reminded us of the legal basis for this ideology of white supremacy: "A white man is always right and a black man has no rights which a white man is bound to respect."

One of the great paradoxes of being black in a racist society is that we must become preoccupied with understanding, as thoroughly and completely as possible, the very thing that we are determined to destroy: racism. In our daily lives, racism presents itself as a virtually endless series of "racialized moments," in which part of our humanity is stolen or denied. Du Bois, in his classical interpretation of the meaning of race in American life, *Darkwater: Voices from Within the Veil*, framed the problem of everyday racism as a sequence of terrible events in which "you are losing your own soul." Such events do happen, but "not all each day." Du Bois observed: "But now and then—now seldom, now sudden; now after a week, now in a chain of awful minutes; not everywhere, but anywhere—in Boston, in Atlanta. That's the hell of it. Imagine spending your life looking for insults or for hiding places from them—shrinking (instinctively and despite desperate bolsterings of courage) from blows that are always but ever; not each day, but each week, each month, each year."

Du Bois's vivid description of "racialization," written more than eighty years ago, still strikes home for me: the denial of a home mortgage or a car loan, and wondering whether race played a factor in the decision; the whites who refuse to sit next to a black person on a crowded bus or subway car, even when the seat is vacant; the taxicabs that speed past my outstretched arms, but cruise to a halt half a block later to pick up whites; the state highway patrol officer on the New Jersey Turnpike who pulls me over to do a "routine check" of my license and registration, even though I am driving under the speed limit; the restaurant delivery dispatcher who curtly informs me that take-out service in Manhattan is unavailable above 120th Street. For black working class and poor people, the consequences of racism are, of course, far more destructive: higher rates of infant mortality, unemployment and poverty, police brutality and mass incarceration, social exclusion and civil death.

This book has been an attempt to present an alternative interpretation or narrative on the meaning of race in American life, particularly as it has been constructed around the black-white social axis. I have argued throughout the text that structural racism, the elaborate institutions informed by white prejudice, power, and privilege, predated the establishment of the U.S. democratic state. Consequently, most of America's political institutions and parties have been or are currently now compromised by white racism. Today's ideological conservatives pursue, in the words of sociologist Howard Winant, a "white, conservative racial project" that "seeks to preserve white advantages through the denial of racial difference"—a clever appeal to American traditional values of individualism and universalism while at the same time rationalizing gross disparities between racial groups as inevitable and normal. The neoliberal racial project, according to Winant, "actively promotes a pragmatic vision of greater substantive equality, linking class and race, and arguing for the necessity of transracial coalition politics." Yet it also fails as a strategy to deconstruct the racist state, because it "does not challenge whites on their willingness to receive a 'psychological wage,' which amounts to a tangible benefit acquired at the expense of nonwhites. . . . Indeed, the neoliberal project does not challenge whites to abjure the real wage subsidies, the artificially low unemployment rates, or the host of other material benefits they receive by virtue of their whiteness."

Since the three-fifths compromise in 1787, the U.S. state has been largely designed to perpetuate undemocratic, unequal power for white elites at the expense of nonwhites and the majority of the white population as well. The U.S. Senate provides an excellent example of the undemocratic structure of political power. A total of 60 senators out of that legislative body's 100 members, represent from their thirty states only about 25 percent of the nation's total population. Most of these states are overwhelmingly white. Since the founding of this nation, only four African Americans have served in the U.S. Senate—Hiram Revels and

Blanche K. Bruce, representing Mississippi during and immediately after Reconstruction, Edward Brooke of Massachusetts, and Carol Mosely Braun of Illinois. Only two blacks have served on the Supreme Court— Thurgood Marshall and Clarence Thomas. The paucity of black representation has been no accident.

In this book I have also attempted to examine counter-hegemonic, oppositional forces to structural racism and the racial state. The middle classes of racialized minority groups, particularly the black bourgeoisie, have long histories of democratic resistance to injustice. Yet with the increased class polarization within black and brown communities since the 1960s, the growth of suburbanization, and the dismantling of legal segregation, the middle class has largely lost its capacity to play a decisive role in transforming power relations around issues of race and class. The trade union movement, another potential source of opposition, has steadily declined in power. In the 1950s, nearly 35 percent of the entire U.S. labor force was unionized, a figure that plummeted to 13.9 percent by 1998, with less than 10 percent of all workers in the private workforce unionized. About 30 percent of the American labor force today, economic researchers Chuck Collins and Felice Yeskel have noted, "work independently, including freelancers, independent contractors, temps, part-timers, contingent workers, and people who work from the home." Given the weakness of unions, antiracist social movements anchored to class-based politics will be difficult to sustain. Similarly, simplistic race-based politics, in the post–civil rights era, with its class stratification within the black community, cannot work.

What can succeed, however, is the creative construction of new centers of antiracist democratic power: community-based groups and non-governmental organizations, faith-based progressive groups, youth organizations, coalitions of the working class, women's groups, poor people fighting for a livable wage, and people directly affected by mass incarceration and the civil death created by the prison industrial complex. Despite their organizational limitations and internal contradictions around issues such as gender, sexuality, race, and immigrant status, there exists the potential to build new definitions of democracy from the most disadvantaged elements of American society. These new resistance movements will not be based primarily on electoral politics, although demands for creating a more democratic, accessible political process must be made.

The demand for black reparations, while at first appearing to be racially divisive, is absolutely essential to the process of constructing a new democratic discourse on the historical origins and meaning of race in our society. Both conservatives and neoliberals, for very different reasons, want to take "race" off the political table. We can't allow them to do it. To deconstruct and to uproot the structures of white privilege, they must be identified by name; we cannot reach a nonracist future unless we talk frankly about our common racist past. At the grassroots level, in thousands of faith-based institutions, neighborhood centers, union halls, and community networks and coalitions, a new discourse about overcoming the living legacy of structural racism must begin.

The reparations discussion is also helpful in giving white Americans a better understanding of the different ways that white privilege is reproduced. In "The Souls of White Folk," Du Bois remarked that "always, somehow, some way, silently but clearly, I am given to understand that whiteness is the ownership of the earth forever and ever, Amen!" Every day, white Americans receive the message that they are entitled to better treatment and a better quality of life than everybody else on the planet—and especially people of African descent. The higher rates of home ownership, longer life expectancies, significant advantages in annual incomes and personal net wealth, favorable treatment by police and in the courts, and so on, are all woven into the fabric of whites' daily lives. What whites also need to understand is that white privilege is best exercised when *nobody talks about it*. Traditional liberals, for example, studied and measured the dynamics of black inequality and oppression; conservatives deny both exist. Yet what unites both is their focus on the "black problem," as if we are the ones with the problem. If the real problem is structural racism, then the challenge before us is reconstructing and reconfiguring white American identity. That will require a massive reeducation campaign that would enable whites to study their own history from the Other's point of view. The reparations discussion will generate healthy tensions but also a broader, more universal understanding of where we've been as a nation.

Why should middle-class white folks engage in this new democratic conversation with the most marginalized and disadvantaged members of their society? From the long view of history, white supremacy is not a sustainable idea. As Du Bois and other scholars of race have frequently observed, "whiteness" is a relatively new concept. "The discovery of personal whiteness among the world's peoples is a very modern thing,—a nineteenth and twentieth century matter, indeed," Du Bois reflected in "The Souls of White Folk." "The ancient world would have laughed at such a distinction." Intellectually and in terms of scientific thought, there is no biological justification for the defense of white superiority. In terms of labor force projections in the United States, the work force has become and is still becoming increasingly brown and black. As the median age of the white population grows older, whites will become increasingly dependent on the material contributions of nonwhites to the running of the economy and society.

White racism impedes whites from understanding the vast economic changes that are occurring in our country and throughout the world, driven by globalization and neoliberalism. Yet it has become increasingly difficult for white solidarity to mask these growing economic contradictions. The American myth that anyone who works hard will get ahead, and that wealth accumulation is a product of individual effort and merit, is no longer sustainable. About 10 percent of the U.S. population owns 90 percent of all business equity and over 85 percent of all stock. These are the people who largely control our political system. According to Collins and Yeskel, "less than one percent of the population contributes more than eighty percent of all money in federal elections in the amounts of $200 or more." The authors also noted the racial dimensions of political financing: "95 percent of contributors to Congressional campaigns that give $200 or more are white and 81 percent have incomes of $100,000, with the top 20 percent in the $500,000-or-more category."

The institutional entitlements of whiteness in countries like South Africa and the United States are being reconfigured, due in part to the pressures of globalization and the growth of transnational capital. The older legal structures of white supremacy—apartheid and Jim Crow segregation—began to be viewed as inefficient and anachronistic by transnational capital. With its reliance on multinational labor forces and management teams, global capital's requirements will be increasingly at odds with ethnic and racialized hierarchies based in local settings. Global competition under neoliberal governmental policies means fewer entitlements and social guarantees for all workers, including most whites. This is not to suggest that Eurocentrism will disappear—far from it. It is to suggest that "whiteness" is being restructured to include new minority elites who have previously been defined in racialized groups: affluent Asians, Latinos, and yes, even sections of the black professional and managerial middle class. Under apartheid South Africa, Japanese were classified as "honorary whites"; in Brazil, a common saying about race translates as "Money lightens the skin." A similar process is now occurring in the United States. A select elite among African Americans may still encounter personal discrimination, but their class status and economic affluence provide the space to create "white lives." Conversely, as race, class, and ethnicity are reconstructed in new ways in the context of the global economy, many of the old truisms about white privilege that white Americans for generations have taken for granted will no longer hold.

The great danger, of course, is that white Americans, becoming acutely conscious of what white privilege is, will fight desperately to keep it. Much of the reactionary populism, national chauvinism, and anti-immigrant bashing by politicians like Patrick Buchanan is motivated by the desire to maintain the entitlements of being "free, white and twenty-one." But there is another alternative: a multicultural democratic society.

Through education, white Americans can come to appreciate a new history, one in which they have frequently been marginal in the construction of democratic traditions. Can we imagine an American society with a national commitment to eliminating the major racialized deficits that separate blacks and whites into their respective racial universes: in life expectancy, health-care access, college enrollments, quality public education, and home ownership? Could we dream of a time when racial epithets, racial profiling, and the discriminatory redlining practices of banks and lending institutions decline in significance, if not disappear? Racial peace will not and cannot be sustained without justice; but with justice, a new relationship and a democratic renewal of American society can occur. As Langston Hughes observed in "Theme for English B":

> You are white—
> yet a part of me, as I am a part of you.
> That's American.
> Sometimes perhaps you don't want to be a part of me.
> Nor do I often want to be a part of you.
> But we are, that's true!

We can negotiate a new understanding of democracy, but only if all of us are stakeholders in a common civic project. We will find the courage "to get along," in the words of Rodney King, only when there is mutual trust and civility based on the principle of human equality. When the "great wells of democracy" are renewed and expanded to include those once outside of America's social contract, a new history can begin.

Notes

Preface

vii *"Embodied in our echoing demands":* Martin Luther King, Jr., "Letter from Birmingham Jail," in *Why We Can't Wait* (New York: Harper & Row, 1964).

xi *"A world of brutality and war":* Benjamin Mays, quoted in Stephen B. Oates, *Let the Trumpet Sound: The Life of Martin Luther King, Jr.* (New York: Harper and Row, 1982), p. 497.

xi *"Like a mighty stream":* Martin Luther King, Jr., "I Have a Dream," reprinted in Manning Marable and Leith Mullings, eds., *Let Nobody Turn Us Around: Voices of Resistance, Reform and Renewal: An African American Anthology* (Lanham, Md.: Rowman and Littlefield, 2000), pp. 403–406.

Chapter 1
Introduction: What We Talk About When We Talk About Race

1 *"Groups tend to be more immoral than individuals":* Martin Luther King, Jr., "Letter from Birmingham Jail," in *Why We Can't Wait* (New York: Harper & Row, 1964).

4 *Under a system most of us call "democracy":* See "The State of the Estate Tax," *Washington Post,* June 6, 2002.

7 *"Doctors, lawyers and Cadillac dealers":* Kevin Phillips, "Dynasties! How Their Wealth and Power Threaten Democracy," *The Nation,* July 8, 2002, pp. 11–14.

7 *"Greater than any comparable period during the 19th century":* Kevin Phillips, "The New Face of Another Gilded Age," *Washington Post,* May 26, 2002.

7 *Inequality that is structured across the entire American social order:* See Matt Moore, "Wal-Mart Passes Exxon to Top Fortune 500 List," *Washington Post,* April 1, 2002.

10 *Classified as nonwhite after 1923:* See Gary Okihiro, "Cheap Talk, er, Dialogue," *Souls,* vol. 1, no. 3 (Summer 1999), pp. 52–58; and Ronald Takaki, *A Different Mirror: A History of Multicultural America* (Boston: Little, Brown, 1993).

Chapter 2
Structural Racism: A Short History

21 *"Before the pilgrims landed . . . we were here":* Martin Luther King, Jr., "Letter from Birmingham Jail," in *Why We Can't Wait* (New York: Harper & Row, 1964).

22 *"And the islands of the sea":* W.E.B. Du Bois, *The Souls of Black Folk,* originally published in 1903 (New York: Dover Publications, 1994), p. 9.

23 *Racism . . . as "an American Dilemma"*: See Gunnar Myrdal, *An American Dilemma: The Negro Problem and Modern Democracy* (New York: Pantheon, 1944).

24 *"Or of any other part of the world"*: W.E.B. Du Bois, *Color and Democracy: Colonies and Peace* (New York: Harcourt, Brace, 1945), p. 128. Reprinted in 1975 by the Kraus-Thomas Organization Limited.

24 *"Or any other field of public life"*: Ion Diacou, "The Definitions of Racial Discrimination," Paper prepared for the fifty-fifth session of the Commission on Human Rights, United Nations, February 26, 1999.

25 *Such as those represented by Islam*: Ibid.

26 *"The nation must cleave"*: Etienne Balibar, "Paradoxes of University," in David Theo Goldberg, ed., *Anatomy of Racism* (Minneapolis: University of Minnesota Press, 1990), p. 284.

26 *"Designated stigmata of exteriority and impurity"*: Ibid.

27 *"Inseparable from the individuals"*: Ibid., p. 286.

27 *"The destiny of societies and peoples"*: Ibid., p. 287.

28 *Having now overthrown communism, have become "white"*: Cited in Manning Marable, "The Future of the Cold War," in Leon Wofsy, ed., *Before the Point of No Return* (New York: Monthly Review Press, 1986), pp. 120–125.

28 *"Urban slums and rural backwaters across the nation"*: Randall Kennedy, *Race, Crime, and the Law* (New York: Pantheon Books, 1997), pp. 7, 14.

29 *"May stand on a racial foundation"*: Robert C. Lieberman, *Shifting the Color Line: Race and the American Welfare State* (Cambridge, Mass.: Harvard University Press, 1988), p. 231.

30 *Transporting . . . West Africans to the Caribbean and North America*: See Jay Coughtry, *The Notorious Triangle: Rhode Island and the African Slave Trade, 1700–1807* (Philadelphia: Temple University Press, 1981).

31 *Receive the sum of $600 from Aetna*: See "The Children of Slavery," *The Economist*, December 23, 2000.

31 *Policies that would protect slave owners from loss*: John Friedman, "Chase's Historical Ledger," *The Nation*, October 9, 2000.

31 *Yale University*: See Antony Dugdale, J. J. Fueser, and J. Celso de Castro Alves, *Yale, Slavery and Abolition* (New Haven, Conn.: The Amistad Committee, Inc., 2001).

31 *"To his son . . . and his partner in Jamaica"*: Cynthia A. Kierner, *Traders and Gentlefolk: The Livingstons of New York, 1675–1790* (Ithaca, N.Y.: Cornell University Press, 1992), pp. 65–72. Also see Roberta Singer, "The Livingstons as Slaveholders: The Peculiar Institution on Livingston Manor and Clermont," in Richard T. Wiles, ed., *The Livingston Legacy: Three Centuries of American History* (Annandale, N.Y.: Bard College Office of Publications, 1987), pp. 67–97.

33 *"Compounded the health problems among Black Africans"*: W. Michael Byrd and Linda A. Clayton, cited in National Colloquium on African American Health, ed., *Racism in Medicine and Health Parity for African Americans: "The Slave Health Deficit"* (Washington, D.C.: National Medical Association, March 2001), pp. 12–13. Also see W. Michael Byrd and Linda A. Clayton, eds., *An American Health Dilemma*, vol. 1, *A Medical History of African Americans and the Problem of Race: Beginnings to 1900* (New York: Routledge, 2001).

33 *Extremely high fetal, infant, and childhood death rates*: See Robert W. Fogel, *Without Consent or Contract: The Rise and Fall of American Slavery* (New York: W. W. Norton, 1989).

34 *"Without any attempt at analysis"*: Roger Wilkins, *Jefferson's Pillow: The Founding Fathers and the Dilemma of Black Patriotism* (Boston: Beacon Press, 2001), pp. 61, 100–101.

35 *"No rights which the white man was bound to respect"*: Roger B. Taney, excerpt from *"Obiter Dictum* on *Dred Scott v. Sanford,"* 1857, reprinted in Manning Marable and Leith Mullings, eds., *Let Nobody Turn Us Around: Voices of Resistance, Reform and Renewal, An African American Anthology* (Lanham, Md.: Rowman and Littlefield, 2000), pp. 92–95.

35 *"Open for white fantasies to become truth"*: Wilkins, *Jefferson's Pillow,* p. 101.

36 *Property and literacy qualifications*: Manning Marable, *Black Leadership* (New York: Penguin Books, 1999), p. 10.

37 *"And call us, who are free men . . . their property!!!!"*: Excerpt from David Walker, "David Walker's Appeal," reprinted in Marable and Mullings, eds., *Let Nobody Turn Us Around,* pp. 23–35.

38 *"Inclusion," or integration, versus "autonomy," or black nationalism*: See Manning Marable and Leith Mullings, "The Divided Mind of Black America: Race, Ideology and Politics in the Post–Civil Rights Era," *Race and Class,* vol. 36, no. 1 (1994), pp. 61–72.

41 *About 95 percent of whom were in the South*: Manning Marable, *How Capitalism Underdeveloped Black America: Problems in Race, Political Economy, and Society,* updated ed. (Cambridge, Mass.: South End Press, 2000), p. 118.

42 *"To the white man's virtue and social order"*: Gunnar Myrdal, *An American Dilemma,* vol. 2 (New York: Pantheon, 1944), pp. 98, 100.

42 *"The law is white"*: Allison Davis, Burleigh B. Gardner, and Mary R. Gardner, *Deep South: A Social Anthropological Study of Caste and Class* (Chicago: University of Chicago Press, 1941), pp. 297–301.

43 *"The same standards of living as white people"*: Paul Gaston, "My University Under Attack: The Anti-Affirmative Action Brigade Comes to Virginia," *Southern Changes,* vol. 21, no. 2 (Summer 1999), p. 10.

43 *"Sexually threatening, through their men, to white women"*: Ibid., pp. 10–11.

44 *Employed in domestic services*: See "Representation Ratios for Broad Occupational Categories, 1940," quoted in William A. Sundstrom, "The Color Line: Racial Norms and Discrimination in Urban Labor Markets, 1910–1950," *Journal of Economic History,* vol. 54, no. 2 (June 1944), pp. 382–396.

44 *Proportion of African Americans living in urban areas rose*: Anthony W. Marx, *Making Race and Nation: A Comparison of South Africa, the United States and Brazil* (Cambridge: Cambridge University Press, 1998), p. 153.

45 *Virtually all-black neighborhoods*: Douglas S. Massey and Nancy A. Denton, *American Apartheid: Segregation and the Making of the Underclass* (Cambridge, Mass.: Harvard University Press, 1993), pp. 45–47. Massey and Denton argued that residential segregation plays a "special role . . . in enabling all other forms of racial oppression. Residential segregation is the institutional apparatus that supports other racially discriminatory processes and binds them together into a coherent and uniquely effective form of racial subordination" (p. 8).

46 *"The passive acceptance, if not the active support, of most whites in the United States"*: Ibid., pp. 14–15.

47 *"Human savagery of which the world is and ought to be thoroughly ashamed"*: "The Niagara

Movement Declaration of Principles," 1905, reprinted in Marable and Mullings, eds., *Let Nobody Turn Us Around*, pp. 227–230.

48 *"Into a beautiful symphony of brotherhood":* Martin Luther King, Jr., "I Have a Dream" speech delivered at the March on Washington, August 28, 1963, in Marable and Mullings, eds., *Let Nobody Turn Us Around*, pp. 403–406.

49 *Designed to maintain that city's pattern of residential segregation:* Stephen Grant Meyer, *As Long As They Don't Move Next Door: Segregation and Racial Conflict in American Neighborhoods* (Lanham, Md.: Rowman and Littlefield, 2000), pp. 178–181.

49 *"Even in Selma":* Ibid., p. 186.

49 *"Impervious to socioeconomic influences":* Massey and Denton, *American Apartheid*, p. 88.

50 *"The outcasts of a standard social system":* Marcus Garvey, "An Appeal to the Conscience of the Black Race to See Itself," 1925, reprinted in Massey and Denton, *American Apartheid*, pp. 264–268.

51 *"I see an American nightmare":* Malcolm X, "The Ballot or the Bullet," delivered in Cleveland, Ohio, April 3, 1964, reprinted in Massey and Denton, *American Apartheid*, pp. 427–436.

52 *"The relation which they sustain to labor can no longer be delayed":* T. Thomas Fortune, "Speech delivered on April 20, 1886, Brooklyn Literary Union, first published in the *New York Freeman*, May 1, 1886, reprinted in Massey and Denton, *American Apartheid*, pp. 143–146.

54 *"The content of their character":* Martin Luther King, Jr., "I Have a Dream" speech, in Marable and Mullings, eds., *Let Nobody Turn Us Around*, pp. 403–406.

55 *"When first he see light above":* W.E.B. Du Bois, "The Social Significance of These Three Cases," lecture delivered at Yale University Law School, January 11, 1951, reprinted in Herbert Aptheker, ed., *Against Racism: Unpublished Essays, Papers, Addresses, 1887–1961, by W.E.B. Du Bois* (Amherst: University Massachusetts Press, 1985), pp. 276–283.

56 *"A wide gulf . . . remains":* Lawrence D. Bobo, "Mapping Racial Attitudes at the Century's End: Has the Color Line Vanished or Merely Reconfigured?" Unpublished paper prepared for the Aspen Institute, November 12, 1988, p. 42.

58 *"More reluctant to hire blacks than any other group":* Michael A. Fletcher, "Race Board's Focus Turns to Economic Gap: Range of Explanations Offered for Disparity," *Washington Post*, January 15, 1998.

58 *"Harsh, often dehumanizing, low-wage work settings":* See William Julius Wilson, *The Truly Disadvantaged: The Inner City, the Underclass, and Public Policy* (Chicago: University of Chicago Press, 1987); and Wilson, *When Work Disappears: The World of the New Urban Poor* (New York: Alfred A. Knopf, 1996).

59 *Accumulated wealth of the average white family:* Henry S. Terrell, "Wealth Accumulation of Black and White Families: The Empirical Evidence," *Journal of Finance*, vol. 26, no. 2 (May 1971), pp. 363–377.

59 *Discrimination in access to credit and capital:* Cindy Loose, "Racial Disparity Found in Credit Rating," *Washington Post*, September 21, 1999.

60 *They supply 55 percent of all home loans:* Editorial, "Foreclosures Rise As Lenders Take Advantage of Poor," *USA Today*, March 29, 2000.

61 *Laissez-faire racism at work:* See Rochelle Sharpe, "In Last Recession, Only Blacks Suffered Net Employment Loss," *Wall Street Journal*, September 14, 1993.

62 "More healthful diets . . . and health education to reverse mounting black mortality": See W.
    Michael Byrd and Linda A. Clayton, eds., An American Health Dilemma, vol. 2, Race, Medi-
    cine, and Health Care in the United States: From 1900 to the Dawn of the New Millennium (New
    York: Routledge, 2001).

63 "Blacks and Latinos with broken bones or post-operative pain": Denise Grady, "Discrimination
    Is Painful: It Can Also Be Agonizing," New York Times, April 9, 2000.

63 "Poor and underserved patients": National Colloquium on African American Health, ed.,
    Racism in Medicine, p. 6.

63 "Physical examinations, histories, and laboratory tests": Ibid., pp. 5–6.

63 "A minor or nonexistent problem": Ibid., p. 6.

Chapter 3
The Politics of Race and the Limits of Electoral Reform

67 "Not the servant or master of either": Quotation in Stephen B. Oates, Let the Trumpet Sound:
    The Life of Martin Luther King, Jr. (New York: Harper and Row, 1982), p. 159.

70 Los Angeles Convention in 1960: David A. Bositis, Blacks and the 2000 Democratic National Con-
    vention (Washington, D.C.: Joint Center for Political and Economic Studies, 2000), pp. 9, 17.

70 The black vote in 1960: Ibid., p. 9.

71 The number of black adults who were registered to vote: Vincent Harding, Robin D.G. Kelley,
    and Earl Lewis, "We Changed the World: 1945–1970," pp. 445–542, in Robin D.G. Kelley
    and Earl Lewis, eds., To Make Our World Anew: A History of African Americans (New York:
    Oxford University Press, 2000).

71 Appointed in the federal bureaucracy: John Hope Franklin and Alfred A. Moss, Jr., From Slav-
    ery to Freedom: A History of African Americans, 7th ed. (New York: McGraw-Hill, 1994), p.
    525; and Manning Marable, Race, Reform and Rebellion: The Second Reconstruction in Black
    America, 1945–1990 (Jackson: University Press of Mississippi, 1991), p. 145.

73 Or even by white leaders of the Democratic Party: Marable, Race, Reform and Rebellion, p. 221.

73 "Interpret white identity in positive political terms": Howard Winant, "Behind Blue Eyes:
    Whiteness and Contemporary U.S. Racial Politics," in Michele Fine, Lois Weis, Linda C.
    Powell and L. Mun Wong, eds., Off White: Readings on Race, Power and Society (New York:
    Routledge, 1997), p. 44.

75 Represented employment opportunities for African Americans: Franklin and Moss, From Slavery
    to Freedom, pp. 537–539.

76 That mainstream Republicanism once represented: Marable, Race, Reform and Rebellion, pp.
    202–205.

76 Dukakis was easily defeated: Franklin and Moss, From Slavery to Freedom, p. 526; and
    Marable, Race, Reform and Rebellion, p. 216.

77 Being held hostage by "special interests": Marable, Race, Reform and Rebellion, p. 216.

77 "Tools they need to prosper in the New Economy": Jon F. Hale, "The Making of the New De-
    mocrats," Political Science Quarterly, vol. 110 (Summer 1995), pp. 207–232.

79 "Why not kill a white person?": Thomas B. Edsall, "Clinton Stuns Rainbow Coalition: Can-
    didate Criticizes Rap Singer's Message," Washington Post, June 14, 1992.

80 *"I just disagree with that":* Joan Didion, *Political Fictions* (New York: Alfred A. Knopf, 2001), p. 143.

82 *"An inability to serve the larger public interest":* William Jefferson Clinton, *Between Hope and History: Meeting America's Challenges for the 21st Century* (New York: Times Books, 1996).

84 *"Below half the poverty line in many states":* Peter Edelman, "Reforming Welfare—Take Two," *The Nation,* February 4, 2000), pp. 16–18, 22, 24.

Chapter 4
Losing the Initiative on Race

93 *"And now call this nation to repentance":* Transcript from Minister Louis Farrakhan's remarks at the Million Man March, October 16, 1995, www.cgi.com/US/9510/megamarch/10-16/transcript.

94 *"Rights of property," which "is the first object of government":* James Madison, cited in Herbert Aptheker, *Early Years of the Republic* (New York: International Publishers, 1976), pp. 59–60.

94 *"Incremental nature of our system usually mitigates the loss of the losers":* Lucius J. Barker, "Limits of Political Strategy: A Systemic View of the African American Experience," vol. 88, no. 1 (March 1994), pp. 6–7.

95 *"To deal forthrightly with matters of race":* Ibid., p. 7. Also see Dianne M. Pinderhughes, *Race and Ethnicity in Chicago Politics: A Reexamination of Pluralist Theory* (Urbana: University of Illinois Press, 1987); Rodney E. Hero, *Latinos and the U.S. Political System: Two-Tiered Pluralism* (Philadelphia: Temple University Press, 1992); and Michael C. Dawson, *Behind the Mule: Race and Class in African-American Politics* (Princeton: Princeton University Press, 1994).

95 *Vote for Jackson dropped off to 13 percent:* Manning Marable, *The Crisis of Color and Democracy: Essays on Race, Class and Power* (Monroe, Maine: Common Courage Press, 1992), p. 160.

96 *"On urban political activism that points to social change":* James Jennings, *The Politics of Black Empowerment: The Transformation of Black Activism in Urban America* (Detroit: Wayne State University Press, 1992), pp. 27, 57.

96 *"Control of the contents of a black public agenda":* Ibid., p. 161.

96 *"By the content of their character":* Martin Luther King, Jr., "I Have a Dream," delivered August 28, 1963, at the 1963 March on Washington, D.C., reprinted in Manning Marable and Leith Mullings, eds., *Let Nobody Turn Us Around: Voices of Resistance, Reform, and Renewal: An African American Anthology* (Lanham, Md.: Rowman and Littlefield, 2000), pp. 403–406.

97 *"Strategies were fixed, and the African American caused advanced":* Marable, *The Crisis of Color and Democracy,* pp. 190–191.

98 *"We must seek common ground":* Ibid., p. 192.

98 *"Social mainstream processes within American society":* Jennings, *The Politics of Black Empowerment,* pp. 165–166.

99 *Black males between the ages of twenty and twenty-nine:* Marable, *The Crisis of Color and Democracy,* pp. 26–27, 177–179.

100 *"Hope to hold back the nihilistic threat to black America":* Cornel West, *Race Matters* (Boston: Beacon Press, 1992).

101 *"The society as a whole that lay at the core of civil unrest"*: Robert Garcia, "Riots and Rebellion: Civil Rights, Police Reform and the Rodney King beating," at www.ldfla.org/introduction.html; and Clark Staten, "L.A. Insurrection Surpasses 1965 Watts Riots, 38 Dead, More Than 1,200 Injured," May 1, 1992, at www.emergency.com/la-riots.htm.

102 *"Two who were long-time appointed government officials"*: Clarence Lusane, "Unity and Struggle: The Political Behavior of African American Members of Congress," *Black Scholar*, vol. 24, no. 4 (Fall 1994), pp. 16–27.

103 *Voted in favor of NAFTA:* Ibid., p. 21.

103 *Accountability or responsibility to them as blacks:* Ibid., pp. 22–23; and Andrew Hacker, *Two Nations: Black and White, Separate, Hostile and Unequal* (New York: Scribners, 1992), p. 209.

103 *"They avoided replacing old dependencies with new ones"*: Clayborne Carson, "African American Leadership and Mass Mobilization," *Black Scholar*, vol. 24, no. 4 (Fall 1994), pp. 2–7. Carson continues: "The black freedom struggle's largely decentralized structure made it responsive to local needs and encouraged leaders to emerge from groups of gender, poverty, background, educational deficiencies, and age" (p. 6).

105 *"And that's exactly what we did"*: "Conversation: Minister Benjamin Muhammad," *Souls*, vol. 3, no. 1 (Winter 2001), pp. 61–76.

107 *"Atone for the abuse we have heaped on our women"*: See Leith Mullings, *On Our Own Terms: Race, Class, and Gender in the Lives of African American Women* (New York: Routledge, 1997), p. 146.

107 *"He will never regain the respect of the larger society"*: Ibid., p. 147.

110 *Farrakhan's keynote address at Million Man March:* Transcript at www.cgi.com/US/9510/megamarch/10-16/transcript.

111 *Increased by one-fifth in the years between 1992 and 1997:* John Simons, "Even Amid Boom Times, Some Insecurities Die Hard: Black Middle Class Gains Ground, But Still Finds Its Situation Shaky," *Wall Street Journal*, December 10, 1998.

111 *Not a primary constituency on the Mall that day:* See "Marchers Express Support for Farrakhan, but Most Came for Black Men, Survey Says," *Washington Post*, October 17, 1995; and "Rally Is Part Politics, Part Religion and Part Farrakhan," *Chicago Tribune*, October 17, 1995.

113 *"Group-centered leaders" rather than "leader-centered groups"*: Carson, "African American Leaders and Mass Mobilization," p. 6.

115 *"The world's first truly multiracial democracy?"*: "Excerpts From Clinton's Speech on Race in America," *New York Times*, June 15, 1997; and "Opening a Conversation on Race," Editorial, *New York Times*, June 16, 1997.

115 *"Let the conversation proceed"*: "Opening a Conversation on Race," Editorial, *New York Times*, June 16, 1997.

115 *His own peculiar notions about blacks:* Steven A. Holms, "Gingrich Outlines Plan on Race Relations," *New York Times*, June 19, 1997.

116 *"Offers only his words, not his soul"*: "Race from the Pulpit," Editorial, *The Nation*, June 30, 1997, p. 3.

116 *"On whom one can hold back"*: David R. Roediger, *The Wages of Whiteness: Race and the Making of the American Working Class* (New York: Verso, 1991), p. 13. Winant criticizes Roediger and other so-called "new abolitionist racial theorists" for failing to recognize that whiteness is also "an overdetermined political and cultural identity nevertheless, hav-

ing to do with socioeconomic status, religious affiliation, ideologies of individualism, opportunity, and citizenship, nationalism, etc." See Winant, "Behind Blue Eyes: Whiteness and Contemporary U.S. Racial Politics," in Michele Fine, Lois Weis, Linda C. Powell, and L. Mun Wong, eds., *Off White: Readings on Race, Power and Society* (New York: Routledge, 1997)," pp. 47–48.

116 *Whiteness above the realization of racial justice:* One short but excellent definition of "whiteness" is provided by Ruth Frankenberg: "Whiteness refers to a set of locations that are historically, socially, politically, and culturally produced and moreover are intrinsically linked to unfolding relations of domination. Naming 'whiteness' displaces it from the unmarked, unnamed status that is itself an effect of its dominance. Among the effects on white people both of race privilege and of the dominance of whiteness are their seeming normativity, their structured invisibility." See Ruth Frankenberg, *White Women, Race Matters: The Social Construction of Whiteness* (Minneapolis: University of Minnesota Press, 1993), p. 6.

117 *And while on public transportation, 6 percent:* "Changing Race Relations in the USA," *USA Today*, June 11, 1997. The Gallup telephone poll of 1,680 whites and 1,269 blacks was conducted January 4, 1997–February 28, 1997.

118 *To push the country's racial discourse forward:* John Hope Franklin and Alfred A. Moss, Jr., *From Slavery to Freedom: A History of African Americans*, 7th ed. (New York: McGraw-Hill, 1994), p. 462.

118 *"Federal policy of hands off in matters involving civil rights":* Ibid., p. 494.

119 *Two societies, one black, one white—separate and unequal:* Quoted in W. Augustus Low and Virgil A. Cliff, eds., *Encyclopedia of Black America* (New York: Da Capo Press, 1981), p. 239.

119 *At least, that's what the plan was:* Bositis, *Blacks and the 2000 Democratic National Convention* (Washington, D.C.: Joint Center for Political and Economic Studies, 2000), p. 6.

120 *Committed to addressing this great American tragedy:* "A Conversation with John Hope Franklin," *Souls*, vol. 1, no. 3 (Summer 1999), pp. 73–91.

121 *Despite a fifteen-month process:* Patricia Williams, "What Happened to the National Race Dialogue? An Interview with Angela Oh," *Color Lines*, vol. 2, no. 1 (Spring 1999), pp. 24–26.

122 *"Just today's version of a Buffalo Soldier":* Ward Churchill and Glenn T. Morris, "Clinton's Initiative on Race: The Latest Chapter in America's Indian Wars," *Souls*, vol. 1, no. 3 (Summer 1999), pp. 59–67.

123 *"And collective bargaining rights for all":* Howard Winant, "The President's Race Initiative: Race-Conscious Judo Meets the Still-Funky Reality," *Souls*, vol. 1, no. 3 (Summer 1999), pp. 68–72.

123 *"And thereby appreciation through dialogue":* Gary Okihiro, "Cheap Talk, er, Dialogue," *Souls*, vol. 1, no. 3 (Summer 1999), pp. 52–58.

124 *Since black people have had "their turn":* Mary Frances Berry, "Color Codes," *Emerge*, vol. 10, no. 3 (December/January 1999), pp. 55–60.

Chapter 5

Race and Educational Inequality

125 *"When our race will gain full equality":* David J. Garrow, *Bearing the Cross: Martin Luther King, Jr., and the Southern Christian Leadership Conference* (New York: Vintage, 1986), p. 83.

130 *Complaining that it failed to "serve the poor"*: See "Who Gets to Choose, and Who Has to Pay?" *Saint Mary's College Update*, vol. 22, no. 2 (Winter 2001), p. 16.

130 *About 1,000 charter schools nationwide*: Robert S. Peterkin and Janice E. Jackson, "Public School Choice: Implications for African American Students," *Journal of Negro Education*, vol. 63, no. 1 (Winter 1994), pp. 126–138.

131 *The majority were Latino*: Ibid., pp. 126–138.

131 *"Limited-English-proficient students often are discouraged from applying"*: Gary R. George and Walter C. Farrell, Jr., "School Choice and African American Students: A Legislative View," *Journal of Negro Education*, vol. 59, no. 4 (Autumn 1990), pp. 521–525.

132 *"Points of view other than their own"*: See "The Educational Value of Diversity: Research from Louisville High School," in *Diversity Digest*, vol. 5, no. 2 (Winter 2001), pp. 10–11.

132 *"Students have to attend school somewhere"*: Alexander W. Astin, "Educational 'Choice': Its Appeal May Be Illusory," *Sociology of Education*, vol. 65, no. 4 (October 1992), pp. 255–260.

133 *"Potential well-being of their communities"*: Faustine C. Jones-Wilson, "Race, Realities, and American Education: Two Sides of the Coin," *Journal of Negro Education*, vol. 59, no. 2 (Spring 1990), pp. 119–128.

133 *"The external purpose is to build community"*: See J. A. Gray, "California's Education Reform: Will It Bear Fruit?" *Saint Mary's College Update*, vol. 22, no. 2 (Winter 2001), pp. 14–15.

135 *"The prospects of minorities and the poor"*: Mark Nathan Cohen, *Culture of Intolerance: Chauvinism, Class and Racism in the United States* (New Haven: Yale University Press, 1998), p. 264; and Sheila Slaughter and Gary Rhoades, "The Neoliberal University," *New Labor Forum*, no. 6 (Spring/Summer 2000), p. 5.

136 *What the price of a four-year college degree should be*: Colin Woodard, "Worldwide Tuition Increase Sends Students into the Streets," *Chronicle of Higher Education*, vol. 46, no. 35 (May 5, 2000), pp. A54–A56.

136 *The impact . . . is profoundly racial*: Joni Finney and Kristin Conklin, "Enough of Trickle Down: It's Time for a Flood of Aid for Needy Students," *Chronicle of Higher Education*, vol. 46, no. 35 (May 2000), p. A68; and Sara Hebel, "Pending: A Snapshot of a New Bill Facing Higher Education," *Chronicle of Higher Education*, vol. 46, no. 34 (April 28, 2000), p. A39.

137 *Only 20 percent for Hispanics*: Robert J. Samuelson, "Rule by the Rich? No," *Washington Post National Weekly Edition*, April 24, 2000; and Finney and Conklin, "Enough of Trickle Down."

138 *Limited academic credentials*: Kit Lively, "Giving to Higher Education Breaks Another Record," *Chronicle of Higher Education*, vol. 46, no. 35 (May 5, 2000), pp. A41–A42; and Jodi Wilgoren, "A Man of Big Achievement but Very Little Fanfare," *New York Times*, May 27, 2000.

138 *A goal of $400 million*: "Give and Take," *Chronicle of Higher Education*, vol. 46, no. 34 (April 28, 2000), p. A40.

138 *Estimated to be worth several billion dollars*: Slaughter and Rhoades, "The Neoliberal University," p. 73.

139 *"High-risk private equity, including venture capital"*: Kimberly Quinn Johnson and Joseph Entin, "Graduate Employee Organizing and the Corporate University," *New Labor Forum*, no. 6 (Spring/Summer 2000), pp. 100–101.

139 *"They run educational institutions on the side"*: Henry Hansmann, quoted in Johnson and Entin, "Graduate Employee Organizing," p. 101.

139 *"More . . . dependent on management than are faculty"*: Slaughter and Rhoades, "The Neo-liberal University," pp. 73–74.

140 *Increasingly shifted to academic management*: See *1993 National Study of Postsecondary Faculty* (Washington, D.C.: National Center for Education Statistics, 1993); and Gary Zabel, "A New Campus Rebellion," *New Labor Forum*, no. 6 (Spring/Summer 2000), pp. 90–91.

140 *"Adjust course syllabi to include such issues"*: Peter Schmidt, "Faculty Members Say They Prize Diversity," *Chronicle of Higher Education*, vol. 46, no. 38 (May 26, 2000), p. A38.

141 *"If it meant denying admission to other students"*: Ben Gose, "Most Students Oppose Racial Preferences in Admissions, Survey Finds," *Chronicle of Higher Education*, vol. 46, no. 35 (May 5, 2000), p. A52.

144 *University policies toward the working poor?* See graph, "Voluntary Support of Higher Edu-cation, 1998–99," *Chronicle of Higher Education*, vol. 46, no. 35 (May 5, 2000); John Nichols, "Unfair Harvard," *The Nation*, vol. 270, no. 22 (June 5, 2000), p. 9; and Jess Walsh, "Living Wage Campaigns Storm the Ivory Tower: Low Wage Workers on Campus," *New Labor Forum*, no. 6 (Spring/Summer 2000), pp. 80–89.

144 *"Could not compete on equal footing for a job"*: Cohen, *Culture of Intolerance*, p. 265.

Chapter 6
Facing the Demon Head On: Race and the Prison Industrial Complex

147 *"Freedom . . . must be demanded by the oppressed"*: Martin Luther King, Jr., "Letter from Birmingham Jail," in *Why We Can't Wait* (New York: Harper & Row, 1964).

149 *"The parole board is not going to let them out"*: Joel Stashenko, "Prisoner Complaints Are Not New," Associated Press Newswires, December 27, 1999.

150 *"But you have to put it out of your mind"*: Ted Conover, *Newjack: Guarding Sing Sing* (New York: Random House, 2000), p. 135.

150 *"The correctional system would come tumbling down"*: Ibid., p. 135.

153 *More than 71,000 in New York State correctional facilities*: "Following the Dollars: Where New York State Spends Its Prison Moneys," a policy paper prepared by the City Project, New York, March 2000.

153 *Unemployed at the time of their arrests*: Manning Marable, *Race, Reform and Rebellion: The Second Reconstruction in Black America, 1945–1990* (Jackson: University Press of Mississippi, 1991), p. 193.

153 *Under the apartheid regime of South Africa*: Ibid., p. 196.

154 *Will be arrested at some point in their lifetime*: See *Conference Summary and Action Plan—Money, Education, and Prisons: Standing at the Crossroads*, produced by the Milwaukee Money, Education and Prisons Project, sponsored by the Benedict Center, University of Wisconsin at Milwaukee, December 1999.

155 *With undergraduate, masters, and doctoral degrees—combined*. See *New York State of Mind? Higher Education Funding vs. Prison Funding in the Empire State, 1988–1998*, study produced by the Correctional Association of New York and the Justice Policy Institute, Washing-ton, D.C., October 1998; and Stan Choe, "The Fund-A-Mentality Difference Between Prisons and Schools," *Black Issues in Higher Education*, vol. 15, no. 23 (January 7, 1999), pp. 12–13.

156 *Solitary confinement . . . is becoming increasingly the norm:* See the series of articles on New York State prisons published in the *Albany Times Union,* March 26, 2000, including Paul Grendahl, "Sensible Control or Senseless Cruelty?"; Graph, "In the Box: Special Housing Unit or Supermax Prison Beds Across the U.S."; "A Violation of Human Rights"; and "Walls and Rules Define Life in The Box."

157 *Tuition benefits program for state prisoners:* Robert Bruce Slater, "Locked In but Locked Out: Death Sentence for the Higher Education of Black Prison Inmates?" *Journal of Blacks in Higher Education,* vol. 1, no. 6 (Winter 1994–1995), pp. 101–103.

158 *"Associated with blacks are those . . . involving violence":* Andrew Hacker, *Two Nations: Black and White, Separate, Hostile, and Unequal* (New York: Ballantine, 1995), p. 188.

158 *Latino youths are incarcerated 305 days:* See "Juvenile Justice Called Unequal in a Report," *New York Times,* April 25, 2000.

159 *Recorded by SWAT teams from 1995 to 1998:* Christian Parenti, "SWAT Nation," *The Nation,* May 17, 1999, pp. 16, 18, 20–21.

160 *The Sentencing Project:* Jamie Fellner and Marc Mauer, *Losing the Vote: The Impact of Felony Disenfranchisement Laws in the United States,* report by Human Rights Watch and the Sentencing Project, October 1998. Also see Patricia Allard and Marc Mauer, *Regaining the Vote: An Assessment of Activity Relating to Felon Disenfranchisement Laws,* the Sentencing Project, January 2000.

161 *"The resentment and bitterness . . . [is] deep and pervasive":* Alvin J. Bronstein, "Offender Rights Litigation: Historical and Future Developments," in Ira P. Robbins, ed., *Prisoners' Rights Sourcebook,* vol. 2 (New York: Clark Boardman Company, 1980), pp. 5–28.

162 *"Are prison memoirs, in whole or in part":* Ibid., p. 9.

163 *Arbeit Macht Frei ("Work Makes Us Free"):* From "Arbeit Macht Frei—Work Liberates," at www.cympm.com/arbeit.html; and the Auschwitz Alphabet, at www.spectacle.org/695/arbeit.html.

Chapter 7
The Death of the Talented Tenth

165 *"Give a damn about being Negro anymore":* In Stephen B. Oates, *Let the Trumpet Sound: The Life of Martin Luther King, Jr.* (New York: Harper and Row, 1982), p. 441.

166 *"Incalculable good for the Negro race":* W.E.B. Du Bois, "Careers Open to College-Bred Negroes," 1898, in Philip S. Foner, *W.E.B. Du Bois Speaks: Speeches and Addresses, 1890–1919* (New York: Pathfinder Press, 1970), pp. 86–101.

167 *"The Training of Negroes for Social Power":* Ibid., pp. 130–141.

167 *A total of 10,000 black college graduates were produced:* W.E.B. Du Bois, *Dusk of Dawn: An Essay Toward an Autobiography of a Race Concept* (New York: Schocken, 1968), p. 209.

168 *"Outside of black communities, including myself":* bell hooks, "Simple Living: An Antidote to Hedonistic Materialism," in Walter Mosely, Manthia Diawara, Clyde Taylor, and Regina Austin, eds., *Black Genius: African American Solutions to African American Problems* (New York: W. W. Norton, 1999), p. 137.

168 *"Farther and farther away from the community":* Julianne Malveaux, "Wall Street, Main Street, and the Side Street," in Mosely et al., *Black Genius,* p. 163.

171 *"The social poverty of the black world"*: Harold Cruse, *The Crisis of the Negro Intellectual: from Its Origins to the Present* (New York: William Morrow, 1967), p. 454.

171 *"Intellectuals within both worlds"*: Ibid., p. 455.

173 *"It's long past time blacks opted out of blackness"*: See Debra Dickerson, *An American Story* (New York: Pantheon, 2000).

173 *"The reign of the Afro"*: Ibid.

174 *"Tiger Woods," "jazz or gospel," and "no me"*: Ibid.

174 *"Who was not African American"*: See John H. McWhorter, *Losing the Race: Self-Sabotage in Black America* (New York: Free Press, 2000).

174 *"Trapped by their defeatist thought patterns"*: Ibid.

176 *"Mr. Non-Negro Politics"*: Chuck Stone, *Black Political Power in America,* rev. ed. (New York: Delta, 1970), pp. 174–175.

177 *Affirmative action which strives for . . . "'equality of result'"*: Michael Omi and Howard Winant, *Racial Formation in the United States: From the 1960s to the 1980s* (New York: Routledge and Kegan Paul, 1986), pp. 27–28.

179 *"Cowardice, or well-intentioned self-deception"*: Clarence Thomas, "Be Not Afraid," *Wall Street Journal,* February 16, 2001; and Bruce Shapiro, "Thomas Speaks!" *The Nation,* March 12, 2001, pp. 6–7.

179 *"I break God's law"*: Tony Mauro, "Can a Deeply Religious Person Be Attorney General?" *USA Today,* January 16, 2001.

179 *"Unable to make the grade"*: Jacques Steinberg, "Houston Schools Chief Used Innovative Methods to Reform Education," *New York Times,* December 30, 2000.

180 *"The lines are shorter"*: Jennifer Frey, "Rod Paige's Life Lessons," *Washington Post* (Weekly Edition), vol. 18, no. 22 (March 26–April 1, 2001).

180 *"Will not apply affirmative action (in university appointments)"*: Elaine Sciolino, "Women in the News: Condoleezza Rice," *New York Times,* December 18, 2000.

182 *"Widespread alienation of black voters"*: Armstrong Williams, "Republicans and the Black Vote," commentary dated November 2000, available at http://images.mychurches images.com/3660/pdf/Republicans_and_the_Black_Vote.pdf; also David Wagner, "Black Out: Despite the Awakening of Black Conservatism, Many Republicans Still Write Off the Black Vote," *Insight,* vol. 12, no. 33 (September 1996), p. 15.

182 *"More symbolic . . . than substantial and meaningful"*: Hanes Walton, Jr., *Black Politics: A Theoretical and Structural Analysis* (Philadelphia: J. B. Lippincott, 1972), p. 83.

184 *Pushed the NAACP aggressively back into national politics in the 2000 elections*: See Lori Rodriguez, "93rd Annual NAACP Convention," *Houston Chronicle,* July 7, 2002.

184 *The Black Freedom Movement historically*: See Michael Snyder and Andrew Guy, Jr., "93rd Annual NAACP Convention," *Houston Chronicle,* July 8, 2002; and Kim Cobb, "93rd Annual NAACP Convention: NAACP's Focus Shifts to Education Disparities," *Houston Chronicle,* July 6, 2002.

185 *"Dealing with them individually"*: Lori Rodriguez, "93rd Annual NAACP Convention: LULUA Leader's Speech at Convention First Ever," *Houston Chronicle,* July 11, 2002.

186 *Honoring the most outstanding college chapters*: See Andrew Guy, Jr., "93rd Annual NAACP Convention/Celebrating a Good Rap/Hip Hop Mogul Lauds Youths' NAACP Work," *Houston Chronicle,* July 10, 2002; Andrew Guy, Jr., "NAACP Convention/Organizers Using

Stars to Meet Goal of Reaching Youth," *Houston Chronicle*, July 11, 2002; and Deborah Kong, "NAACP Convention," Associated Press Newswires, July 11, 2002.

186 *"Operating out of the United States Department of Justice"*: "NAACP's Chairman Denounces Bush on Civil Rights Record," *The (Madison, Wis.) Capital Times*, July 8, 2002.

187 *"As patriots, not as partisans"*: DeWayne Wickham, "NAACP's Bond Not Afraid to Criticize White House," Gannett News Service, July 9, 2002.

187 *"The epitome of insensitivity"*: "NAACP: Getting a Rise Out of Bush," National Journal Group, Inc., July 9, 2002; Editorial, "NAACP Scare Tactics," *Wall Street Journal*, July 12, 2002.

187 *"Racial profiling has gained a false legitimacy"*: Julian Bond, open letter to "Freedom Under Fire," 2002 NAACP Convention Program Book.

187 *"Knowing that freedom will prevail"*: Kweisi Mfume, open letter to "Freedom Under Fire," 2002 NAACP Convention Program Book.

188 *The "far, far right"*: "NAACP: Getting a Rise Out of Bush," National Journal Group, Inc., July 9, 2002.

188 *Contractors that normally control convention business*: Lauren Bayne Anderson, "NAACP Convention Planners Try to Help Minority Business," *Houston Chronicle*, July 9, 2002.

189 *"Future that leaves no one behind"*: ExxonMobil advertisement, "Freedom Under Fire," 2002 NAACP Convention Program Book.

189 *More than $1.5 million to assist the NAACP*: "Microsoft Donates $670,000 to NAACP," PR Newswire, July 10, 2002.

189 *"Closely aligned with that of the NAACP's"*: "BellSouth and NAACP Continue Tradition with Live Internet Broadcast of NAACP Convention," Business Wire, July 3, 2002.

190 *"A long, long way from where we were"*: Anthony Breznican, "National Security Advisor Condoleezza Rice Chosen for Special NAACP Image Award," Associated Press Newswire, February 23, 2002.

Chapter 8
Building Democracy from Below: Community Empowerment

196 *"Protect the robbed and punish the robber"*: Martin Luther King, Jr., "Letter from Birmingham Jail," in *Why We Can't Wait* (New York: Harper & Row, 1964).

196 *No weapon was found on Thomas's body*: See J. White, "Misdemeanor Charges for Cincinnati Cop Who Killed Unarmed Black Teenager," www.wsws.org/articles/2001/may2001/cinc-mo8.shtml; Terry Kinney, "Cincinnati Lifts Curfew: 'An Opportunity for a New Cincinnati,'" Associated Press, Cincinnati bureau, April 16, 2001; and Zein El-Amine, "The Cincinnati Rebellion," *Left Turn*, vol. 1, no. 1 (2001), pp. 20–22.

197 *837 people had been arrested, and dozens injured*: El-Amine, "The Cincinnati Rebellion," p. 20.

198 *Work with youth had earned him much respect*: See J. Prendergast, "Mourners Hear Call for New Cincinnati," *Cincinnati Enquirer*, April 15, 2001; and B. Grey, "2000 Demonstrate Against Police Violence in Cincinnati," available at www.wsws.org/articles/2001/apr2001/riot-a16.shtml.

198 *Weapons for crowd control and assault*: El-Amine, "The Cincinnati Rebellion."

199 *Not in the paid labor force:* Statistics from "1990 Census of Population and Housing," prepared by the City Planning Department, Cincinnati, Ohio, 1990.

200 *"But we want GOOD POLICING":* "African American Grassroots Leadership Community Input," April 24, 2001, Urban League of Greater Cincinnati, facilitated by Eric Ellis.

203 *"Government rollbacks in social services (including 'welfare reform')":* Jonathan Diskin and Thomas A. Dutton, "Cincinnati: A Year Later But No Wiser," *Shelterforce,* vol. 24, no. 3 (May/June 2002), pp. 8–11, 13.

203 *"They won't really be living together":* Kathy Y. Wilson, "So Fresh and So Clean: Dispatches from a Ghetto in My Mind," *Shelterforce,* vol. 24, no. 3 (May/June 2002), p. 12.

203 *"Cincinnati Can: You Can Too!"* Diskin and Dutton, "Cincinnati: A Year Later," p. 13.

204 *"This is all about respect for other human beings":* Francis X. Clines, "New Face and New Hope in Cincinnati," *New York Times,* April 7, 2002.

205 *"Policies and practices that help build local communities":* Diskin and Dutton, "Cincinnati: A Year Later," p. 13.

206 *Independent of a territorial space:* See Michael W. Apple, "'Consuming the Other': Whiteness, Education, and Cheap French Fries," in Michele Fine, Lois Weis, Linda C. Powell and Mun Wong, eds., *Off White: Readings on Race, Power and Society* (New York: Routledge, 1997), pp. 121–128. Apple's discussion of the social geography of "whiteness" is also instructive in thinking about the social construction of "blackness."

207 *The placement of almost 100 skilled black workers into appropriate jobs:* Ronald Walters, "The Imperative of Popular Black Struggle: Three Examples from Miami, Los Angeles and Chicago," *Black Scholar,* vol. 24, no. 4 (Fall 1994), pp. 32–38.

207 *Failure to hire black workers at the site:* Les Lester, "Construction Co. Faces Bias Protests," *Chicago Defender,* July 25, 1991.

207 *"Jobs for blacks and other minorities":* Christi Parsons and Terry Wilson, "Protesters Seek Piece of Pie at United Gala," *Chicago Tribune,* September 19, 1994.

207 *"Being pushed through the cracks of poverty":* Yana Ginburg, "Kmart Boycott Spreads Nationally," *Black Enterprise,* July 1996, p. 17.

208 *To each church to assist in rebuilding:* "ECU Housekeepers Demand Rehiring of Fired Housekeeper," "Workers on the Move!" and "Church Burnings," in *Justice Speaks,* published by the Black Workers for Justice, Raleigh, North Carolina, February 1977. The Black Workers for Justice is a grassroots, community-based organization that is extensively involved in labor struggles in the South. Its stated objective is "to build the African American workers' movement as a central force in the struggle for Black Liberation and Worker Power."

208 *"Maximum opportunity to participate in construction projects":* Jocelyn Y. Stewart, "Black Workers' Campaign of Job-Site Protests Gains Broader Backing," *Los Angeles Times,* September 22, 1992; and Walters, "The Imperative of Popular Black Struggle," pp. 34–35.

209 *"Sensationalized fights with Latino and Korean communities":* Mike Davis, *The Nation,* September 19, 1994, p. 271.

209 *"Further and further away from their communities":* Catherine S. Manegold, "Among Blacks, New Voices Emerge," *New York Times,* May 9, 1993.

210 *Promoting violence-prevention and related community issues:* Darrell Dawsey, "Helping Brother in Need," *Emerge,* October 1995, pp. 59–63.

211 *A range of religious, labor, and civil-rights organizations:* Yusef Sallam, "10,000 Marched

Sunday: Men, Women of Every Hue, Religion and Walk of Life," *Amsterdam News*, August 3, 1996. Groups represented in the march included Al Sharpton's National Action Network, the Nation of Islam, Abyssian Baptist Church of Harlem, and Local 144, Hotel, Hospital, Nursing Home and Allied Services Union.

211 *Outside of the Bronx district attorney's office:* Adam Nossiter, "Families of 2 Killed in Police Incidents Protest," *New York Times*, October 12, 1995.

211 *"Evidence of blatant police contempt":* Charles Baillou, "Brooklyn Community Activists Still Angry About Senseless Cop Brutality," *Amsterdam News*, August 24, 1996.

211 *A steering-wheel lock for a gun:* Peter Noel, "Rough Justice: When Cops Get the Benefit of the Doubt," *Village Voice*, June 17, 1997. Myriam Pierre, a twenty-five-year-old hairdresser's apprentice, witnessed Watson's killing. When she shouted in protest at the police officers, reportedly they replied: "Shut the fuck up, you black bitch!"

211 *A rookie police officer:* "N.J. Youths Protest Killing of Teenager by Rookie Officer," *Boston Globe*, February 26, 1995.

211 *Fatally beaten by police:* Debbie Officer, "Staten Island Youths Rally Against Police Brutality," *Amsterdam News*, vol. 85, no. 19 (May 7, 1994), p. 3.

211 *Bringing the estimated number of protesters to 1,000:* Damaso Reyes, "Racial Justice Day Rally for Family Members Killed by NYPD," *Amsterdam News*, April 12, 1997.

211 *"Lack of evidence of any criminal conduct":* Salim Muwakkil, "Getting Away with Murder," *In These Times*, vol. 21, no. 4 (January 1997), p. 16.

212 *"Criminalization of a Generation":* Karen Shields, "Police Brutality Protested," *Chicago Defender*, October 23, 1996.

212 *Killing of a black man by officers:* Susan Sward and Bill Wallace, "Protest Over Police Custody Death," *San Francisco Chronicle*, June 15, 1995.

212 *The death of a black man, Jesse Chapman, while in police custody:* Ursula V. Battle, "Angry Demonstrators in March Protesting Death," *Afro-American* (Baltimore), July 16, 1994.

212 *"To protest her son's death":* Gwen Gilmore, "Mother Rallies After Son's Death," *Afro-American* (Baltimore), July 16, 1994.

212 *A sixty-member, multiracial organization:* George Howland, Jr., "Mothers Take on the Police," *Progressive* (August 1993), p. 16.

212 *"Handle any protests":* "Police Ready for Protests," *Times-Picayune*, August 14, 1993.

212 *"Accidentally killed himself in the escape attempt":* Salim Muwakkil, "Getting Away with Murder," p. 16.

212 *The police officer who had shot Lewis:* Ibid., p. 16.

213 *Attempting to retry the remaining officers:* "Pittsburgh Blacks to Protest Man's Death," *New York Times*, November 9, 1995; Pierre Thomas, "Reaction to Death in Police Custody Exposes Pittsburgh's Racial Gulf," December 24, 1995; Ron Daniels, "African American Students on the Frontline in Pittsburgh," *(Norfolk, Va.) Journal and Guide*, December 25, 1996; Timothy McNulty and Michael A. Fuoco, "N.A.A.C.P. Aims to Disrupt with Peaceful 4 P.M. March," *Pittsburgh Post-Gazette*, May 15, 1997; and Muwakkil, "Getting Away with Murder," p. 16.

214 *The Ujamaa Project, an economic-development cooperative:* John Anner, "Making Tracks for Justice: The Campaign for Fair Transportation in Milwaukee," *Third Force*, vol. 5, no 3 (July–August 1997), pp. 18–20.

214 *"Speak-out" demonstration against welfare cuts:* "March 1 Actions Assail Welfare Cuts," *Corresponder*, vol. 6, no. 1 (February–March 1997), pp. 1, 5.

214 *Preelection canvassing and door-to-door leaflet distribution:* James E. Vann, "Progressive Alliance of Alameda County," *Independent Politics News*, Issue 1 (February–March 1997), p. 8.

216 *"Language of community is largely the reason":* Adolph Reed, Jr., "The Curse of 'Community,'" *Village Voice*, January 16, 1996.

219 *Poverty rate was a staggeringly high 73 percent:* David Whitman and Dorian Friedman, "The White Underclass," *U.S. News and World Report*, vol. 117, no. 15 (October 17, 1994), pp. 40–53.

220 *Insulted by police in their own neighborhoods:* Robert Aponte, "Hispanic Families in Poverty: Diversity, Context, and Interpretation," *Families in Society: The Journal of Contemporary Human Services* (November 1993), pp. 527–537.

221 *Beaten a Puerto Rican to death:* Mike Tharp and David Whitman, "Hispanics' Tale of Two Cities," *U.S. News and World Report*, vol. 112, no. 20 (May 25, 1992).

221 *"Collectively improve their lives":* Clayborne Carson, "African-American Leadership and Mass Mobilization," *Black Scholar*, vol. 24, no. 4 (Fall 1994), p. 7.

Chapter 9
Forty Acres and a Mule: The Case for Black Reparations

223 *"The opposition we now face will surely fail":* Martin Luther King, Jr., "Letter from Birmingham Jail," in *Why We Can't Wait* (New York: Harper & Row, 1964).

224 *"Estates, mules, and household furniture":* Montgomery *Advertiser*, December 13, 1860.

224 *A fair share of "the land, mules, and money":* Manning Marable, *Black Leadership* (New York: Penguin, 1999), p. 14.

224 *"Land they had . . . learned to think of as their own":* Thomas Holt, *Black over White: Negro Political Leadership in South Carolina During Reconstruction* (Urbana: University of Illinois Press, 1977), p. 68.

225 *Only partial compensation for years of unpaid exploitation:* Marable, *Black Leadership*, p. 16.

226 *"Fixed for the purpose of determining the annual rent aforesaid":* "An Act to Establish a Bureau for the Relief of Freedmen and Refugees," March 3, 1865. See http://www.inform.umd.edu/ARHU/Depts/History/Freedman/fbact.htm

227 *Land under the act:* See Claude F. Oubre, *Forty Acres and a Mule: The Freedmen's Bureau and Black Land Ownership* (Baton Rouge: Louisiana State University Press, 1978), pp. 71–73.

228 *Only 6 million acres of land nationwide:* Marable, *Black Leadership*, pp. 16–18, 33.

228 *"Held by whatsoever means possible":* "Declaration of Rights of the Negro Peoples of the World," issued August 1920, in Manning Marable and Leith Mullings, eds., *Let Nobody Turn Us Around: Voices of Resistance, Reform and Renewal, An African American Anthology* (Lanham, Md.: Rowman and Littlefield, 2000), pp. 259–264.

229 *"Parents or grandparents were descendants from slaves":* "Program and Position" of the Nation of Islam, reprinted in Marable and Mullings, eds., *Let Nobody Turn Us Around*, pp. 425–427.

229 *Half a billion dollars to the black community for reparations:* See "Making the Case for Racial

Reparations: Does America owe a debt to the descendants of its slaves? *Harper's* (November 2000), pp. 37–51.

229 *"Inherent in the institution of slavery"*: Martin Luther King, Jr., *Why We Can't Wait* (New York: Harper and Row, 1963), pp. 150–152. Also see James M. Smylie, "Reparations and 'The Wretched of the Earth': MLK Spoke Some Words That Were Not Heeded," *Presbyterian Outlook*, vol. 151, no. 28 (July 28, 1969), pp. 1–6.

231 *"The very bottom of hardship"*: W.E.B. Du Bois, excerpt from *The Souls of Black Folk*, in Marable and Mullings, eds., *Let Nobody Turn Us Around*, pp. 221–226.

232 *Jews who had been forced to perform slave labor:* See "Swiss Holocaust Checks Going Out in Mail Tomorrow," *New York Daily News*, February 25, 1999.

234 *"A formal apology from the American government or the American people"*: Robert G. Weisbord, "Reciprocal Respect: Blacks, Jews and Holocausts," *Jewish Currents*, vol. 56, no. 1 (January–February 2002), pp. 4–8. Also see Lawrence Bush and Jeffrey Dekro, "Jews and the Black Reparations Campaign," *Tikkun*, vol. 15, no. 4 (July/August 2000), pp. 12–18.

237 *How it could be implemented through federal legislation:* For example, see: John W. De Gruchy, "Crimes and Reparations," *Christian Century*, vol. 111, no. 34 (November 23, 1994), p. 1102; "The Economic Basis for Reparations to Black America," *Review of Black Political Economy*, vol. 21, no. 3 (Winter 1993), pp. 99–110; Mike Mattison, "Past Due: Reparations for Slavery," *The Utne Reader*, no. 61 (January 1994); Rhonda V. Magee, "The Master's Tools, from the Bottom Up: Responses to African-American Reparations Theory in Mainstream and Outsider Remedies Discourse," *Virginia Law Review*, vol. 79, no. 4 (May 1993), p. 863; Vincene Verdun, "If the Shoe Fits, Wear It: An Analysis of Reparations to African Americans," *Tulane Law Review*, vol. 67, no. 3 (February 1993), p. 597; Ignacio Martin-Baro, "Reparations: Attention Must Be Paid," *Commonweal*, vol. 117, no. 6 (March 23, 1990), pp. 184–185; Salim Muwakkil, "Blacks Call for Reparations to Break Shackles of the Past," *In These Times*, vol. 13, no. 38 (October 11–17, 1989), p. 6; and Robert Allen, "Past Due: The African American Quest for Reparations," *Black Scholar*, vol. 28, no. 2 (Summer 1998), p. 2–17.

240 *The 1923 massacre:* There is extensive visual material available over the Internet on the Rosewood massacre, including Florida Public Television's 1994 "Rosewood"; CBS's *Sixty Minutes* 1994 segment, "The Rosewood Massacre," reported by journalist Ed Bradley; "In Search of Rosewood," News Channel 8 WFLA-TV, 1993; "Rosewood Reborn," narrated by James Earl Jones, sound recording produced in 1997 by Reality Works; and "Remember Rosewood: The Scream That Started a Nightmare," produced by Discovery Communications, Inc., and aired nationally February 10, 1998.

241 *"Unforgivable, unexplainable part of our history"*: See "Oklahoma Mulls Pay for '21 Race Attacks," *Daily News*, February 5, 2000; Ross Milloy, "Panel Calls for Reparations in Tulsa Race Riot," *New York Times*, March 1, 2001.

244 *The modern reparations movement found its manifesto"*: Randall Robinson, *The Debt: What America Owes to Blacks* (New York: Plume, 2000).

245 *"The vestiges of slavery are still with us"*: John Hope Franklin, e-mail to author.

247 *Majority of blacks favored it, by 55 to 37 percent:* "Reparations in Black and White," CNN/USA *Today*/Gallup Poll, February 8–10, 2002, cited in Ira J. Hadnot, "Bound and Determined," *Dallas Morning News*, August 18, 2002.

247 *"Especially a multiethnic society like the United States"*: Ira J. Hadnot, "Bound and Determined."

247 *"What a white of yesteryear did to a black of yesteryear?"*: Ibid.

247 *"Get aid to those at the bottom"*: Hakim Hason, "Reparations Anxiety," *City Limits*, vol. 27, no. 7 (July/August 2002), pp. 28–29.

248 *"Who would get the money? For what purpose?"*: Ibid., p. 28.

250 *"The tax system, like a refundable slavery tax credit"*: Ibid. p. 28.

253 *"We have to turn now to the present and to the future"*: "Rice Defends US Decision to Quit Racism Conference," Dow Jones International News, September 9, 2001, at http://ptg. djnr.com/ccroot/asp/publib/story.asp.

253 *"Better to look forward and not point fingers backward"*: "Rice Against Reparations for Slavery," *San Diego Union-Tribune*, September 10, 2001.

253 *Integration could have been achieved without nonviolent protests*: Dale Russokoff, "Lessons of Might and Right: While Others Marched for Civil Rights, Condoleezza Rice's Family Taught Her to Make Her Own Freedom," *Washington Post*, September 9, 2001.

Chapter 10
The Hip-Hop Revolution

255 *"Saying things like . . . 'Bed-Stuy in July.'"*: Oliver Wang, interview with Mos Def, *San Francisco Bay Guardian*, September 16, 1998. Available in *Mired*, www.mired.com/mosdef/.

257 *"You can find money for schools"*: Press release, "United Federation of Teachers, The Alliance for Quality Education and the Hip Hop Summit Action Network Form an Unprecedented Coalition to Protest Bloomberg's Education Budget Cuts," May 31, 2002.

257 *"This march was a wake-up for some"*: Felicia R. Lee, "Hip-Hop Is Enlisted in Social Causes," *New York Times*, June 22, 2002.

257 *"Hip hop" . . . looks like it has come "of age politically"*: Teresa Wiltz, "We the Peeps: After Three Decades Chillin' in the Hood, Hip-Hop Is Finding Its Voice Politically," *Washington Post*, June 25, 2002.

258 *Promotes voter education, registration, and community organizing*: See Angela Ards, "Rhyme and Resist: Organizing the Hip-Hop Generation," July 26, 1999, at http://www.past. thenation.com.

258 *To become involved in progressive, social-justice causes*: Wiltz, "We the Peeps."

258 *Put together the forces to create a new movement*: See L. Alexis McGill, "Get Me That Phat Vote!" *Savoy*, vol. 2, no. 1 (March 2002), pp. 80–83.

260 *"Servant of those that produced you"*: Leon Droun Keith, "Farrakhan Urges Rap Artists to Step Back from Violent Lyrics/War on Terrorism Is Condemned," *San Diego Union-Tribune*, February 17, 2002.

260 *"Not strong enough to be leaders"*: Corey Moss, "Suge Knight Gives Hip-Hop Summit Something to Talk About," http://www.vh11.com/thewire/content/news/1452348.jhtml.

260 *"The side that focuses on social transformation"*: "West Coast Hip-Hop Summit Generates Unprecedented Success," *Business Wire*, February 15, 2002, http://ptg.djnr.com/ccroot/asp/publib/story.asp.

261 *"Why don't the young people come to our convention and help us?"*: Manning Marable, "Def America—Russell Simmons," *Souls*, vol. 4, no. 2, pp. 77–100.

262 *"Appreciation for the work that Minister [Farrakhan] did in the community"*: Ibid.

264 *"Its impact is wider"*: Russell Simmons, *Life and Def: Sex, Drugs, Money and God* (New York: Crown, 2001), p. 4.

264 *"Openhearted innocence that created hip hop culture"*: Nelson George, *Hip Hop America* (New York: Penguin, 1998), pp. 20–21.

264 *"A manifesto for collective political agitation"*: Ibid., p. 155.

265 *"It makes me wonder how I keep from goin' under"*: Grandmaster Flash and the Furious Five (artists Grandmaster Melle Mel and Duke Bootee), "The Message," Sugar Hill Records, 1982.

266 *"In order to fight the powers that be/Fight the Power"*: Lyrics from Public Enemy, "Fight the Power," on *Fear of a Black Planet*, Def Jam Records, 1990.

268 *"Learning the rules of the game, then playing to win"*: L. Yvonne Bynoe, "Hip Hop Politics: Deconstructing the Myth," December 8, 1999, at www.politicallyblack.com. Also see Bynoe's excellent publication, *Doula: The Journal of Rap Music and Hip Hop Culture*, which he cofounded.

268 *"That, to me, is beyond music"*: Ibid.

Chapter 11
When the Spirit Moves: The Politics of Black Faith

271 *"Irrelevant social club with no meaning for the twentieth century"*: Martin Luther King, Jr., "Letter from Birmingham Jail," in *Why We Can't Wait* (New York: Harper & Row, 1964).

272 *The choir . . . begins to sing softly, "We'll Understand It Better By and By"*: The black religious service depicted here draws on my own memories of worship in the South, as well as the richly detailed ethnographic observations of sociologist Charles S. Johnson in his *Shadow of the Plantation* (Chicago: University of Chicago Press, 1934), and *Growing Up in the Black Belt: Negro Youth in the Rural South* (New York: Schocken, 1967).

273 *"No true communion with the Invisible"*: W.E.B. Du Bois, *The Souls of Black Folk*, originally published in 1903 (New York: Dover Publications, 1994), pp. 192–193.

274 *"A democracy in which people believe in God"*: Felicia B. Lee, "The Secular Society Gets Religion," *New York Times*, August 24, 2002.

274 *And to a lesser degree, political institutions*: See Stephen Carter, *The Culture of Disbelief: How American Law and Politics Trivialize Religious Devotion* (New York: Basic Books, 1993).

276 *"Exists by some values rather than others"*: Eddie S. Glaude, Jr., *Exodus! Religion, Race, and Nation in Early Nineteenth Century Black America* (Chicago: University of Chicago Press, 2000), p. 110.

276 *"A constant renewal of community through collective memory"*: Ibid., p. 111.

277 *"An outlet for emotional repressions"*: See Charles S. Johnson, *Growing Up in the Black Belt: Negro Youth in the Rural South* (New York: Schocken Books, 1967).

278 *"Leaders and foot soldiers in the NAACP, CORE and SNCC"*: Michael Eric Dyson, commentary in exchange, "Bully in the Pulpit?" *The Nation*, March 12, 2001.

279 *"An' why not everyman?":* "Didn't My Lord Deliver Daniel?" in Henry Louis Gates, Jr., and Nellie Y. McKay, eds., *Norton Anthology of African-American Literature* (New York and London: W. W. Norton, 1997), p. 10.

279 *"Musical styles commensurate with their abiding faith in God":* Melva W. Costen, "Singing Praise to God in African American Worship Contexts," in Gayraud S. Wilmore, ed., *African American Religious Studies: An Interdisciplinary Anthology* (Durham: Duke University Press, 1989), pp. 392–404.

279 *"The legitimization of freedom":* Kenneth Morgan, *Slavery and Servitude in Colonial North America* (New York: New York University Press, 2001), pp. 83–84.

280 *"To fulfill the goal of progressive revelation":* Ibid., pp. 103–104.

280 *"Not created or controlled by white Christians":* William B. Gravely, "The Rise of African Churches in America (1786–1822): Re-examining the Contexts," in Wilmore, ed., *African American Religious Studies*, pp. 301–317.

280 *"A birthright of African people":* Melva W. Costen, "Singing Praise to God in African American Worship Contexts," in Wilmore, ed., *African American Religious Studies*, pp. 392–404.

281 *"And go home to my Lord and be free":* James Cone, "Black Theology as Liberation Theology," in Wilmore, ed., *African American Religious Studies*, pp. 177–207.

282 *Pentecostal and Holiness churches found new converts:* See Marable, *How Capitalism Underdeveloped Black America: Problems in Race, Political Economy, and Society,* updated ed. (Cambridge, Mass.: South End Press, 2000), pp. 198–199.

283 *Poor blacks who gave them donations every Sunday:* Ibid., pp. 203–204.

284 *"The world community, particularly the Third World":* Manning Marable, *Black American Politics: From the Washington Marches to Jesse Jackson* (London: Verso, 1985), p. 271.

284 *"Brings . . . a fantastic credibility to the candidacy":* Ibid., p. 272.

285 *"Take my hand, precious Lord, Lead me home":* Thomas A. Dorsey, "Take My Hand, Precious Lord," in Gates and McKay, eds., *The Norton Anthology of African-American Literature*, p. 20.

285 *"Food and clothing to the disadvantaged":* See Tobi Jennifer Printz, *Faith-Based Service Providers in the Nation's Capital: Can They Do More?* (Washington, D.C.: The Urban Institute, April 1998).

286 *112 units under construction:* Margaret Ramirez, "Church's Bid to Buy Forum Part of Economic Activist Trend," *Los Angeles Times,* July 12, 2000.

286 *"Summits to deal with education and politics":* Mary Sanchez and Helen Gray, "Black Clergy Stress Fiscal Development," *Kansas City Star,* December 7, 2000.

286 *A city-wide AIDS awareness and education campaign:* Sandi Dolbee, "Black Churches on Mission for AIDS Education; Congregations Must Do More, Group Says," *San Diego Union-Tribune,* November 15, 2001.

286 *"To educate their communities about HIV/AIDS":* E. R. Shipp, "There Is a Balm in the Church for AIDS," *New York Daily News,* March 4, 2001.

287 *"The general moral breakdown of our society":* Bill Berkowitz, *Prospecting Among the Poor: Welfare Privatization* (Oakland, Calif.: Applied Research Center, May 2001), p. 16.

287 *The "Samaritan Project":* Franklin Foer and Ryan Lizza, "Holy War: The Bushies' Faith-Based Brawl," April 4, 2001, at www.thenewrepublic.com.

287 *"Predominantly white congregations"*: Laurie Goodstein, "A Clerical and Racial Gap over Federal Help," *New York Times*, March 24, 2001.

287 *Calling it "a good beginning"*: See Rebecca Carr, "Bush Scores Critics of Faith-Based Initiative," *Atlantic Constitution*, June 26, 2001; and Ken Fireman, "Taking His Case to the Mayors: Bush Urges Funding for Religious Social Services," *Newsday*, June 26, 2001.

287 *The impression that . . . the African-American clergy support charitable choice:* For example, see Mary Leonard, "Black Clergy Back Bush Initiative," *Boston Globe*, March 20, 2001; John Leland, "Some Black Pastors See New Aid Under Bush," *New York Times*, February 2, 2001; and Adelle Banks, "Black Ministers Reach Out to Bush," *Minneapolis Star Tribune*, January 27, 2001.

288 *No research . . . that "faith-based organizations are more effective"*: C. Benjamin Saskis, "Act of Faith: Conservatives Don't Just Think Religious Organizations Do a Better Job Helping the Poor, They Know It," *The New Republic*, February 26, 2001, pp. 20–24.

288 *"In order to build their capacity"*: Berkowitz, *Prospecting Among the Poor*, p. 18.

289 *"Charitable contributions through appropriate tax relief"*: "In Good Faith: A Dialogue on Government Funding of Faith-Based Social Services," February 27, 2001, reprinted in *Blueprint for Social Justice*, vol. 54, no. 7 (March 2001). The study was sponsored by the American Jewish Committee and the Feinstein Center of Temple University.

290 *Living-wage ordinances and workers rights:* Charles Ornstein, "Los Angeles; Labor Says Thank You to Black Churches," *Los Angeles Times*, September 3, 2001.

290 *"Smile in our faces"*: Robert Hanley, "Clergy to Ask Minority Voters to Weigh Stances on Profiling," *New York Times*, July 19, 2001.

292 *Religious institutions . . . destroyed by fire, firebombed, or desecrated:* There were 685 burnings or desecration of houses of worship from 1999 to 2001. An estimated 167 involved African-American congregations. Nine were mosques or Islamic centers, five occurring after September 11, 2001. See "Across South Carolina Coalition Report Shows Church Burnings," *Augusta Chronicle*, August 8, 2002.

292 *Prosecute those responsible for this wave of violence:* See Joe Holley, "Who Was Burning the Black Churches?" *Columbia Journalism Review*, vol. 26, September 19, 1996; and Charles Regan Wilson and Christian T. Coon, "Church Burnings and Christian Community," *Christian Century*, no. 890 (September 25, 1996).

292 *"The spiritual and cultural heartbeat of black America"*: C. Eric Lincoln, quoted in "The Fires This Time: Why White Supremacists Bomb Churches and Not Schools," *Journal of Blacks in Higher Education* Issue 12 (Summer 1996).

Chapter 12
9/11: Racism in the Time of Terror

293 *"As T. S. Eliot has said: . . . 'To do the right deed for the wrong reason'"*: Martin Luther King, Jr., "Letter from Birmingham Jail," in *Why We Can't Wait* (New York: Harper & Row, 1964).

296 *"Violent, lawless, misogynistic and anti-democratic"*: Katha Pollitt, "Put Out No Flags," *The Nation*, October 8, 2001.

297 *"The city itself is so hard to believe":* Roger Rosenblatt, "Just Crazy About the Place," *New York Times,* November 22, 2001.

298 *Racial and class stratification only worse:* Hilary Russ, "Organizers Tweak Priorities After September," *City Limits,* vol. 25, no. 10 (December 2001), pp. 89.

298 *"Today as it was in 1960":* Anna Aguiar, "Darkness at Deepvali," *City Limits,* vol. 25, no. 9 (November 2001), p. 9.

300 *Extended benefits to only 2,350 jobless workers:* Editorial, "An Outpouring of Dollars," *New York Times,* October 1, 2001.

300 *"Because they ran out of food":* Matt Pancenza, "9/11: A Flood in the Soup Kitchen," *City Limits,* vol. 25, no. 9 (November 2001), p. 5; and Bob Herbert, "Hunger in the City," *New York Times,* November 22, 2001.

300 *Rejection rates by FEMA at other disaster areas:* David W. Chen, "More New Yorkers Get U.S. 9/11 Aid, But Rejections Leave Bitterness and Frustration," *New York Times,* August 27, 2002.

301 *Slid farther into economic recession and political marginalization:* Eric Alterman, "Requiem for a Liberal," *The Nation,* November 26, 2001, p. 12.

303 *"Indiscretion about what you do and how you do it":* Rudolf Guiliani, quoted in Clyde Haberman, "Diallo, Terrorism and Safety vs. Liberty," *New York Times,* September 13, 2001.

304 *The personal safety of white Americans:* Ibid.

305 *Legitimate activities by U.S. citizens:* Eric Foner, "The Most Patriotic Act," *The Nation,* October 8, 2001, p. 13.

305 *By a margin of 135 to 5:* James C. McKinley, "Unified State Legislators Pass Tougher Anti-Terrorism Laws," *New York Times,* September 18, 2001.

305 *Falwell was forced to apologize:* Gustav Niebuhr, "Falwell Apologizes for Saying an Angry God Allowed Attacks," *New York Times,* September 18, 2001.

305 *Between militarism and political reaction:* Ibid.

306 *Or even fire the faculty involved:* Anemona Hartcollis, "CUNY Chief Repudiates Forum Remarks," *New York Times,* October 4, 2001.

306 *The First Amendment right . . . is now at risk:* "Outspoken Faculty Members Suspended," *Seattle Post-Intelligencer,* October 13, 2001.

306 *Valium also rose 7 percent:* Tara Parker-Pope, "Anxious Americans Seek Antidepressants to Cope with Terror," *Wall Street Journal,* October 12, 2001.

307 *"An achievement to be abandoned now":* Foner, "The Most Patriotic Act."

307 *Liberties and democratic rights here at home:* Stephen E. Flynn, "Safer Borders," *New York Times,* October 1, 2001.

308 *Incidents of arson and property damage:* American Friends Service Committee Report, "After September 11: Standing on the Brink of a 'Brave New World,'" www.afsc.org/justice-visions.html.

308 *Racialized others who happen to be non-Muslims:* Beth McNurtrie, "Arab Students in U.S. Head Home, Citing Growing Hostility," *Chronicle of Higher Education,* vol. 48, no. 6 (October 5, 2001), pp. A42–A44.

309 *"But it likes the Negro in his place":* See Oliver Cromwell Cox, *Caste, Class, and Race: A Study in Social Dynamics* (New York: Monthly Review Press, 1970).

310 *Became delinquent in their mortgage payments:* Dianne Solis, "Slowdown Hitting Minorities Hardest After Advances of '90s," *Dallas Morning News,* July 25, 2001.

310 *"Attributed mainly to Sept. 11–related job loss":* Lee Romney and Karen Robinson-Jacobs, "Jobless Blacks Face Steepest Challenge," *Los Angeles Times,* November 26, 2001; Carlos Torres, "U.S. Nov. Jobless Rate Rises to 5.7%: 331,000 Jobs Are Lost," *Bloomberg News,* December 7, 2001; and Dianne Solis, "Unemployment Among Minorities Increasing at Alarming Rate," *Dallas Morning News,* December 8, 2001.

310 *Located several blocks from the towers:* Derek T. Dingle and Sakina P. Spruell, "Bouncing Back," *Black Enterprise,* December 2001.

310 *Up from 32 percent prior to the attacks:* Steve Miller, "Blacks' Rating of Bush Soars in Wake of Attacks," *Washington Times,* October 3, 2001.

311 *"A world where everyone counts":* Adelle M. Banks and Jeff Brumley, "Black Clergy Raise Questions About Patriotism, Racism," *Stuart (Fla.) News/Port St. Lucie News,* December 8, 2001.

311 *"Their ethnic background or the way they dress":* Hugh Price, "What the Crisis Means to You: The WTC Crisis," *Ebony* (December 2001).

312 *Classifying all . . . as potential terrorists:* See Tania Fuentez, "Black Muslims Say They Feel Increase in Discrimination, Even from Other Blacks," Associated Press State and Local Wire, October 20, 2001; Jonathan Curiel, "Preaching Peace from a Unique View: Religion, History Lead Black Muslim Imams to Oppose Strikes," *San Francisco Chronicle,* October 10, 2001; and Eric Boehlert, "Who Speaks for African-American Muslims?" *Salon,* October 23, 2001, at www.salon.com.

315 *A new phase of racialization on a global scale:* Chuck Collins and Felice Yeskel, *Economic Apartheid in America: A Primer on Economic Inequality and Insecurity* (New York: The New Press, 1999), p. 60.

316 *Killed or maimed by the "friendly fire" of U.S. forces:* Editorial, "To Rebuild Afghanistan," *New York Times,* August 27, 2002.

317 *"Pray for us now and at the hour of our death":* T. S Eliot, "Ash Wednesday," in *The Complete Poems and Plays, 1909–1950* (New York: Harcourt, Brace and World, 1962), pp. 60–67.

Chapter 13
Epilogue: The Souls of White Folk

319 *"I've been to the mountaintop":* Martin Luther King, Jr.'s, last public address, Memphis, Tenn., April 3, 1968.

320 *"Our fear-drenched communities":* Martin Luther King, Jr., "Letter from Birmingham Jail," in *Why We Can't Wait* (New York: Harper & Row, 1964).

321 *"Get along on a day-to-day basis":* See William E. Alberts, "Taking the *ism* Out of 'Race' in the 21st Century: A Study of the Print Media's Coverage of President Clinton's National 'Dialogue on Race,'" *Sage Race Relations Abstracts,* vol. 27, no. 2 (May 2002), pp. 5–44.

321 *"World ever sang was a white man's dream":* W.E.B. Bu Bois, *Darkwater: Voices from Within the Veil,* reprint ed. (Mineola, N.Y.: Dover Publications, 1999), p. 18.

321 *"Not 'men' in the sense that Europeans are men":* Ibid., p. 24.

322 *"Rights which a white man is bound to respect"*: Ibid., p. 25.

322 Events in which *"you are losing your own soul"*: Ibid., p. 132.

322 *"Not each day, but each week, each month, each year"*: Ibid., p. 131.

323 *Material benefits they receive by virtue of their whiteness"*: Howard Winant, "Behind Blue Eyes: Whiteness and Contemporary U.S. Racial Politics," in Michelle Fine, Lois Weis, Linda C. Powell, and L. Mun Wong, eds., *Off White: Readings on Race, Power, and Society* (New York: Routledge, 1997), pp. 40–53.

324 *"Contingent workers, and people who work from the home"*: Chuck Collins and Felice Yeskel, *Economic Apartheid in America: A Primer on Economic Inequality and Insecurity* (New York: The New Press, 1999), pp. 81–83, 150.

325 *"The ownership of the earth forever and ever, Amen!"*: Du Bois, *Darkwater*, p. 18.

326 *"The ancient world would have laughed at such a distinction"*: Ibid., p. 17.

326 *"With the top 20 percent in the $500,000-or-more category"*: Collins and Yeskel, *Economic Apartheid in America*, p. 70.

328 *"But we are, that's true!"*: Langston Hughes, "Theme for English B," in Jay Parini, ed., *The Columbia Anthology of American Poetry* (New York: Columbia University Press, 1995), pp. 480–481.

Index

About the Author

M anning Marable is one of America's most influential and widely read scholars of the black experience. Since 1993, Marable has been professor of history, political science, and public affairs at Columbia University in New York City, where he also serves as founding director of the Institute for Research in African-American Studies.

Born in 1950, Professor Marable has authored and edited almost twenty books and anthologies, including: coeditor, with Leith Mullings, of *Freedom* (London: Phaidon, 2002); coeditor, with Leith Mullings, of *Let Nobody Turn Us Around: Voices of Resistance, Reform, and Renewal* (Lanham, Md.: Rowman and Littlefield, 2000); editor, *Dispatches from the Ebony Tower* (New York: Columbia University Press, 2000); *Black Leadership* (New York: Columbia University Press, 1998); *Speaking Truth to Power* (Boulder: Westview Press, 1996); *Beyond Black and White* (London: Verso, 1995); *Race, Reform and Rebellion* (Jackson: University Press of Mississippi, 1991); *W.E.B. Du Bois* (Boston: Twayne, 1986); *Black American Politics* (London: Verso, 1985); and *How Capitalism Underdeveloped Black America* (Boston: South End Press, 1983).

Professor Marable is also founding editor of *Souls: A Critical Journal of Black Politics, Culture, and Society*, published by Taylor and Francis. Since 1976, he has written a political commentary series, "Along the Color Line," that appears in more than 400 newspapers worldwide. Marable is currently writing a two-volume biography of Malcolm X and directing the Malcolm X Research Project at Columbia University. He also donates much of his time to fundraising and speaking on behalf of prisoners' rights, labor, civil rights, and faith-based institutions and other social-justice organizations. Marable lectures annually in Sing Sing Prison, Ossining, New York, in a master's degree program for prisoners.